WILD ABOUT Battersea

BETWEEN THE COMMONS

By Andrew Wilson

Sponsored by

RAMPTON BASELEY

I would like to dedicate this book to my two lovely children, Sam and Amy and all my nieces and nephews, particularly Charlotte, who has just recently got married to Ewan.

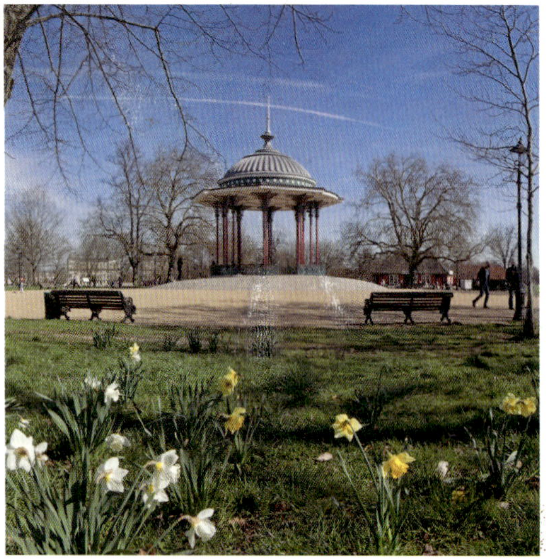
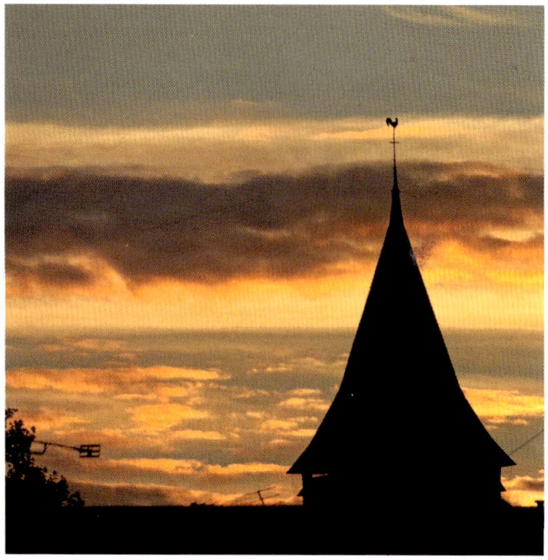
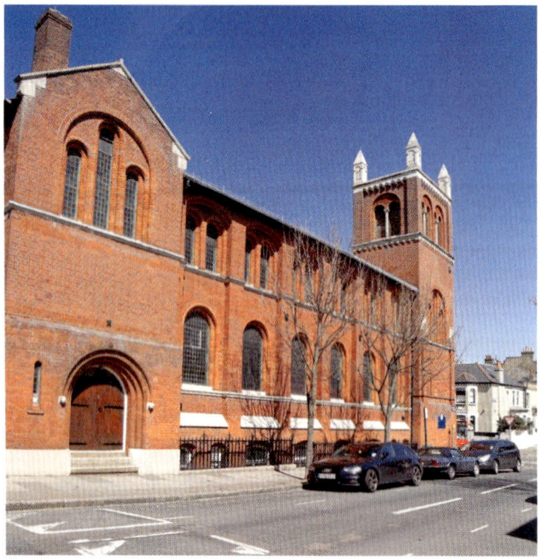
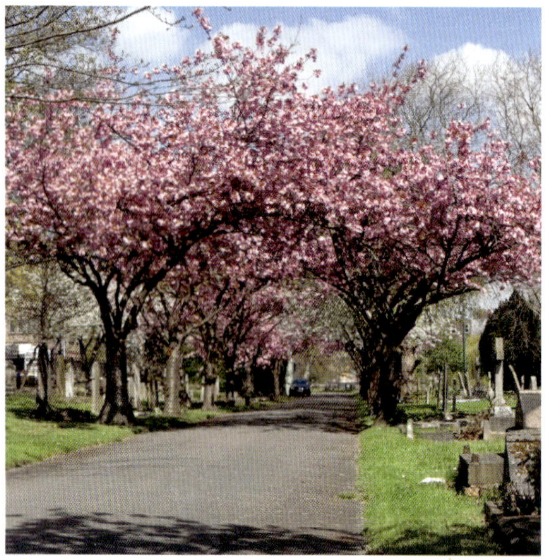

Clockwise from top left: The Bandstand on Clapham Common, St Mark's on Battersea Rise, St Mary's Cemetery off Bolingbroke Grove and Northcote Road Baptist Church.

Opposite: The large lake on Wandsworth Common.

The map on the end papers is taken from John Rocque's famous London Map of 1746.

Contents

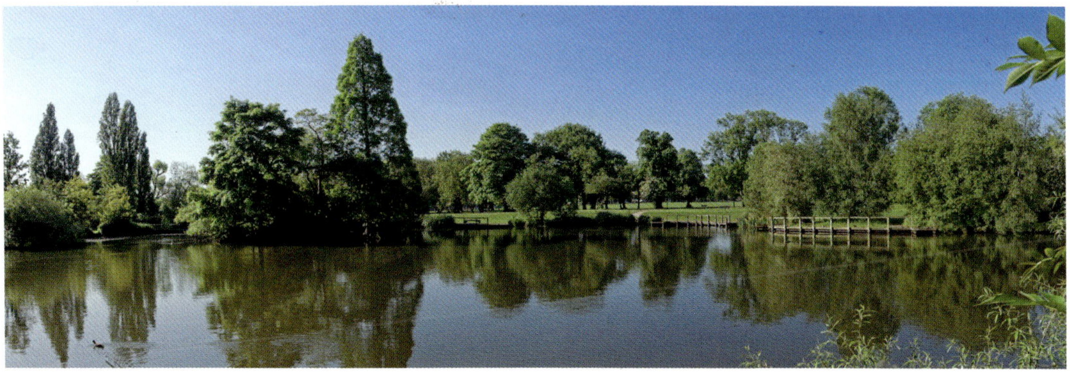

Welcome to Wild About Battersea

Welcome to my latest collection of photographs. I have always been a fan of our London Parks, so I was really pleased to have the excuse over the past year to explore this area, as it has not one but two. South Battersea, as it is known, has at its heart a perfect valley, the Northcote Road, where in years gone by a stream once ran and this natural phenomenon makes for some excellent photographic opportunities. The Northcote Road is a lively please to visit and what an exciting event its annual summer fete is; 100's of stalls and thousands of visitors, what a wonderful day. With so much open space it was also great for my canine companion, who I like to take on as many of my photographic excursions as I can.

My books take some time and effort to produce but this is no one man (and his dog) show and I would like to take this opportunity to thank a few people for helping me. Firstly, Joel Baseley and Patrick Rampton and all the staff at local Estate Agents, Rampton Baseley, who have kindly sponsored my book. Joel and Patrick are rightly proud of their little piece of London and have been very supportive ever since we first met back in January 2013.

I would also like to thank my writer, Philip Beddows, who has over the past seven years led an almost one man campaign to put the name of Battersea back on the map from all those thinking it ought to be called Clapham, with much success I might add. Thank you also to my proof reader Tom Sears, who came in very late and saved me from many a grammatical clanger. Thanks also to Silvina De Vita for her map. Further thanks should go to my designers, Tim and Dan from Ball Design and my great friend and colour printing expert, Paul Sherfield. I may take the pictures but these guys bring them all to life. On the ground, besides Philip, I would also like to acknowledge the help of the Town Centre Manager, Lorinda Freint and to Jenny Sheridan, the editor of The Battersea Society's newsletter, Battersea Matters, who both met with me and passed on invaluable background information.

This book has taken the best part of a year to bring together and I have met many people along the way who have helped or contributed and unfortunately space does not allow me to mention you all, so my apologies if I have missed you off, it isn't personal. I have in many cases made reference to people within the relevant text, so if not here, you may well find yourself in the book itself. There is also only so much space in the book and choices have to be made about what goes in and again, my apologies to some of the places or people that I have missed out. I hope you enjoy my latest book; it was just the best fun.

Andrew Wilson
November 2013

Left: Josie, my springer spaniel and constant companion, outside Hamish Johnstone's cheese shop on the Northcote Road. **Right:** Battersea's local MP, Jane Ellison, and I outside Al Gusto's on the Northcote Road. My thanks to Jane for sparing some of her valuable time to meet with me and apologies for the shorts but it was July. **Opposite:** St Mark's one fabulous evening early October 2013.

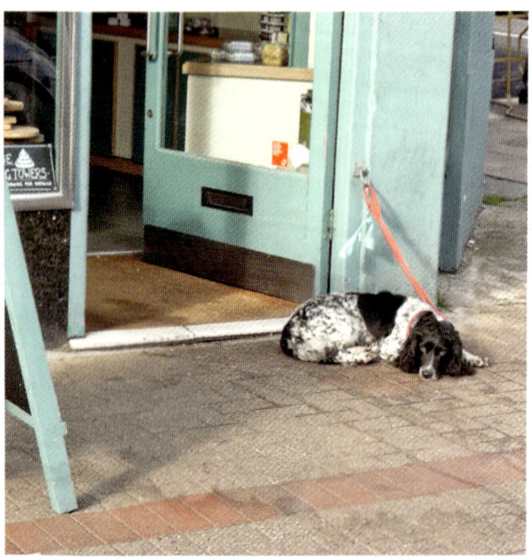

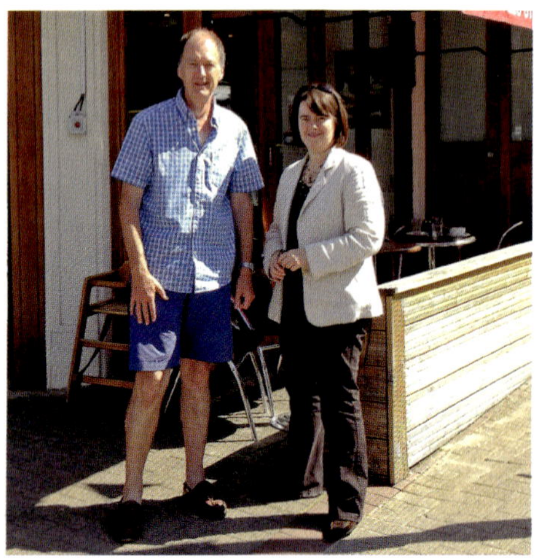

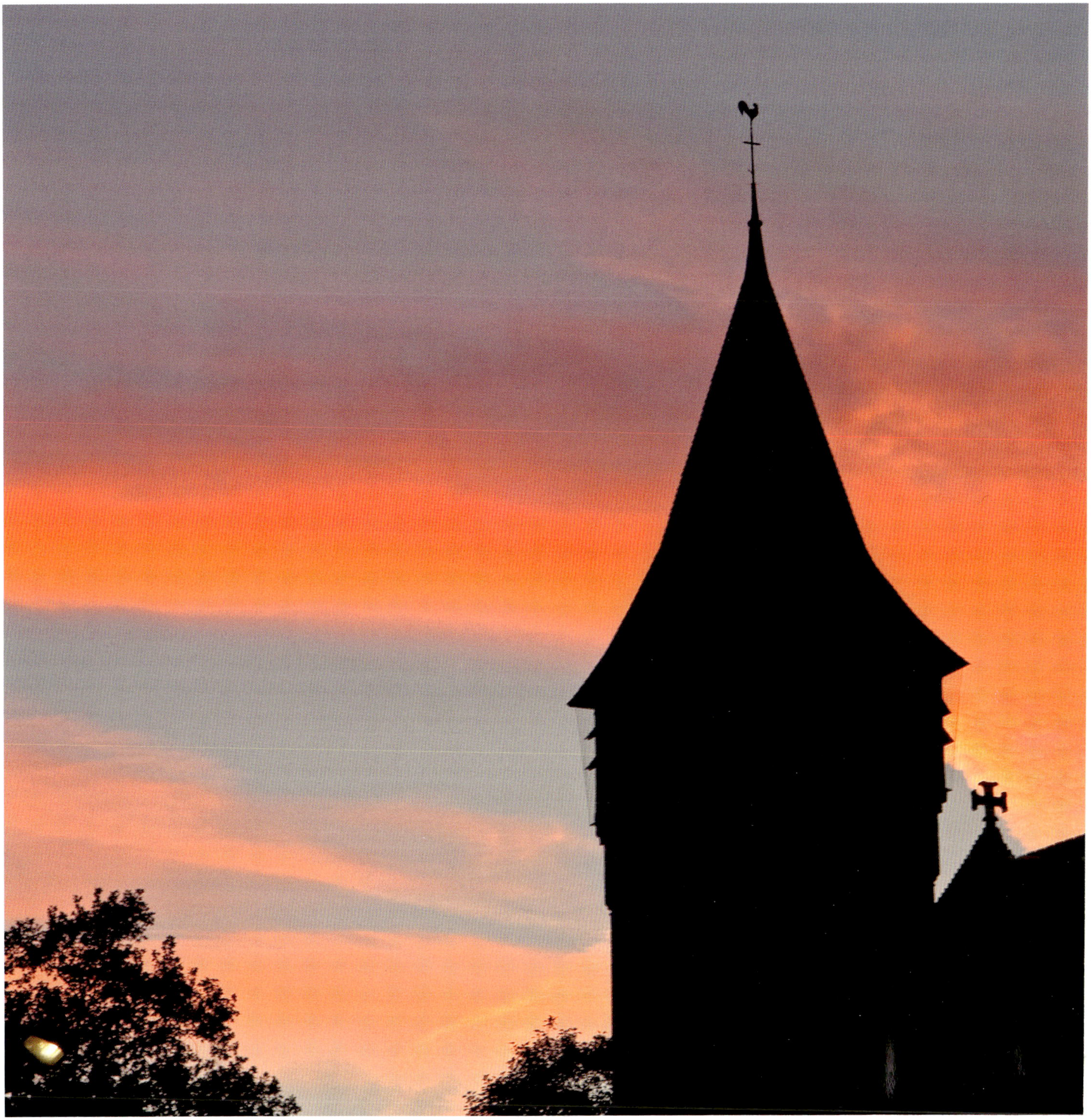

Battersea – Between the Commons

A SHORT HISTORY OF THE AREA
by Philip Beddows

Battersea – the name conjures up images of the riverside, Battersea Park, the beautiful Albert Bridge, Battersea Power Station, and the new developments at Nine Elms. Once a village, Battersea benefited greatly from the trade the Thames brought. Still peacefully existing on the riverbank lies the ancient church of St. Mary's, from whose vestry window Turner painted river scenes.

Battersea first emerges from history in a manuscript dated June 693 AD. The document relates to a grant of land to Westminster Abbey by the Bishop of Dorchester, and refers to *Batrices ege* (meaning 'Badric's Isle') , *Watsingaham*, and finally a portion west of the stream named *Hidaburna*. These names are later found in a 15th Century deed as *Baterseye*, *Wassingham* and *Hideborne*.

Amazingly, despite the gradual disappearance of its farmland, Battersea's medieval boundaries remain. Old cast iron parish boundary posts can still be seen – up Wix's Lane from Lavender Hill, across Clapham Common, down to Clapham South, and along Nightingale Lane to Wandsworth Common behind Trinity Road.

The western boundary of Battersea encompasses almost all of Wandsworth Common, the old Battersea West Heath. The eastern boundary still lies in the middle of Clapham Common, at the edge of what was once Battersea East Heath, remembered in the name of the woodland from The Avenue to the Bandstand – Battersea Woods. The boundary is easy to remember even without the parish marker posts: "B" is for Bandstand, which happily for us lies in Battersea, and "C" is for Café which lies in Clapham! The boundary goes south across the Common, including South Clapham underground station, before dancing westwards along the northern side of Nightingale Lane to Trinity Road. An unexplained 'peninsular' of Battersea jutted southwards including part of the western

The fabulous view you get looking east from the top of the Baptist Church on Northcote Road.

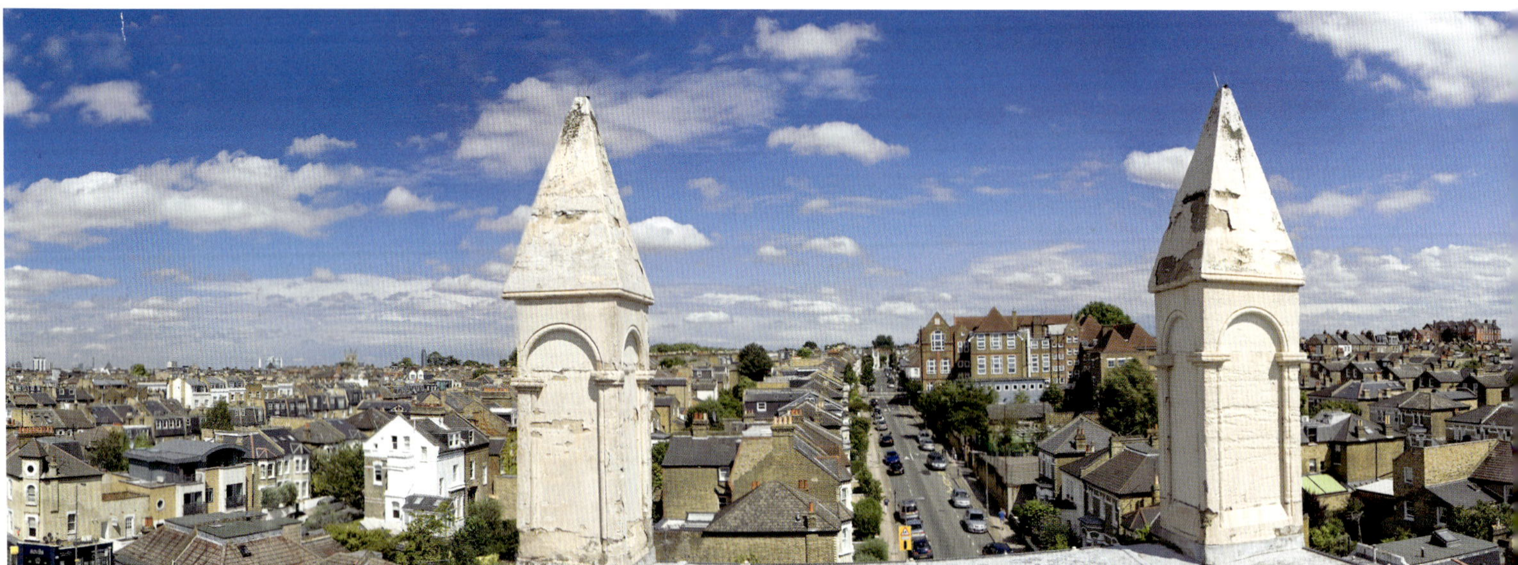

The demographics of the Northcote Road may well have changed over the years but as this photograph shows, with its old equivalent, the buildings have changed less so. The 49 still runs along this route but not on the day I took this picture; I think the road works in St John's Road at the time caused it to be diverted, which was a shame. The picture dates from 1913 and I am grateful to the Battersea Heritage Service from Battersea Library on Lavender Hill (see page 91) for permission to display this image and the other two on the following pages from their archives. Notice even the drain is still there.

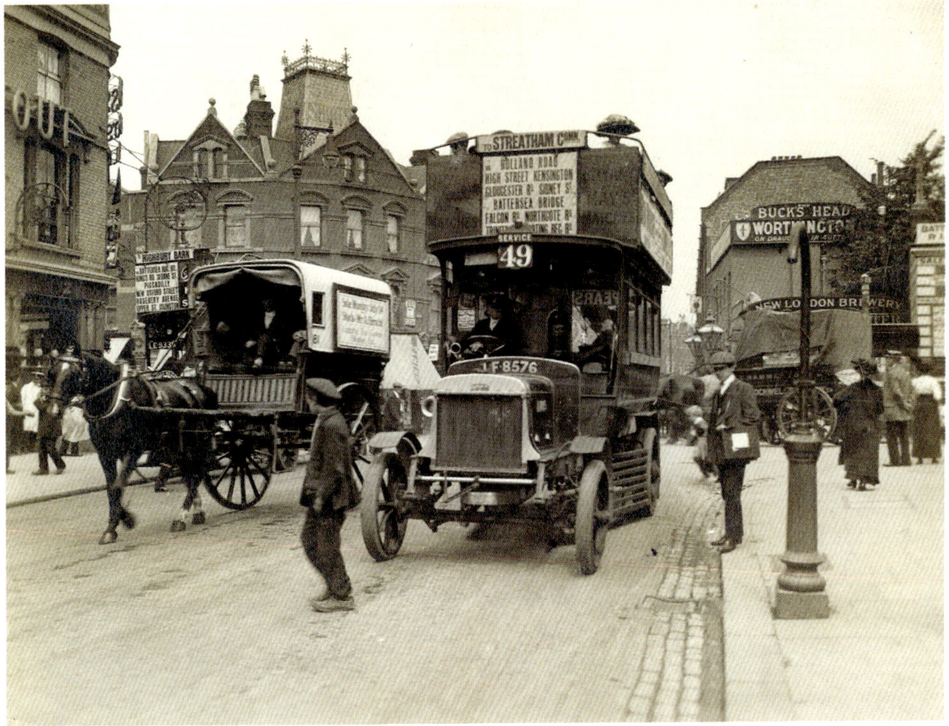

side of Ravenslea Road and the area of today's Wandsworth Common Station, as well as all of Bellevue Road and some nearby streets.

The Georgians and Victorians built elegant homes on the high ground in what was still countryside. The name of the slope that rose up from the valley of the Falcon Brook is remembered today by the road called Battersea Rise. That name used to include the road we now call Clapham Common Westside. On it was found the command centre of the Clapham Sect – Battersea Rise House, the site of which

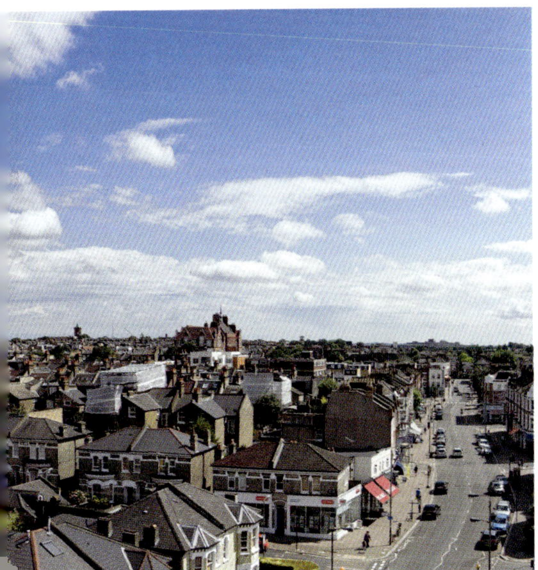

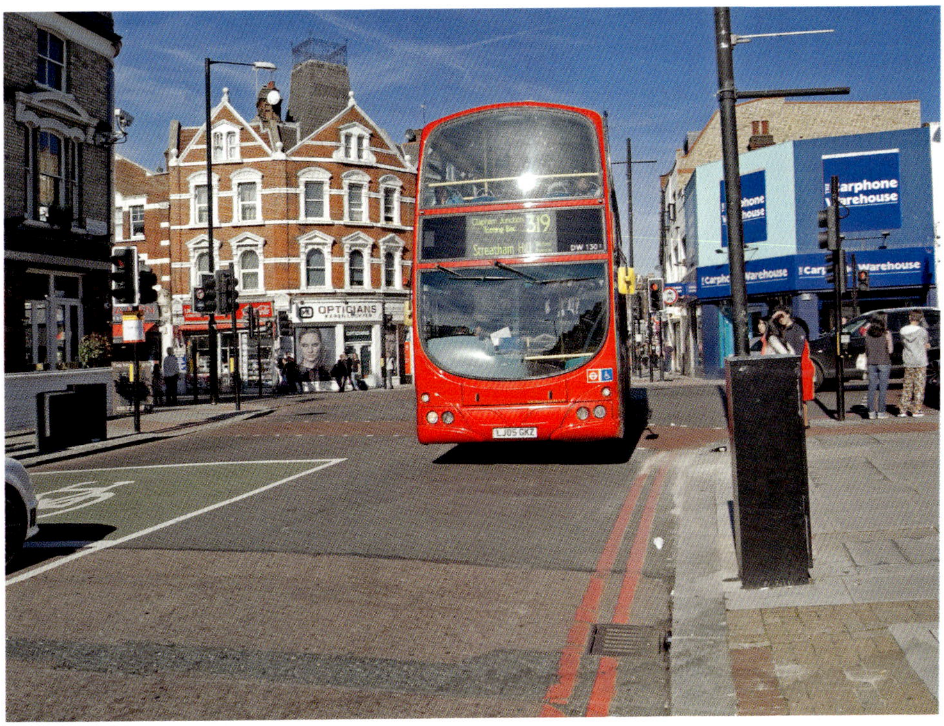

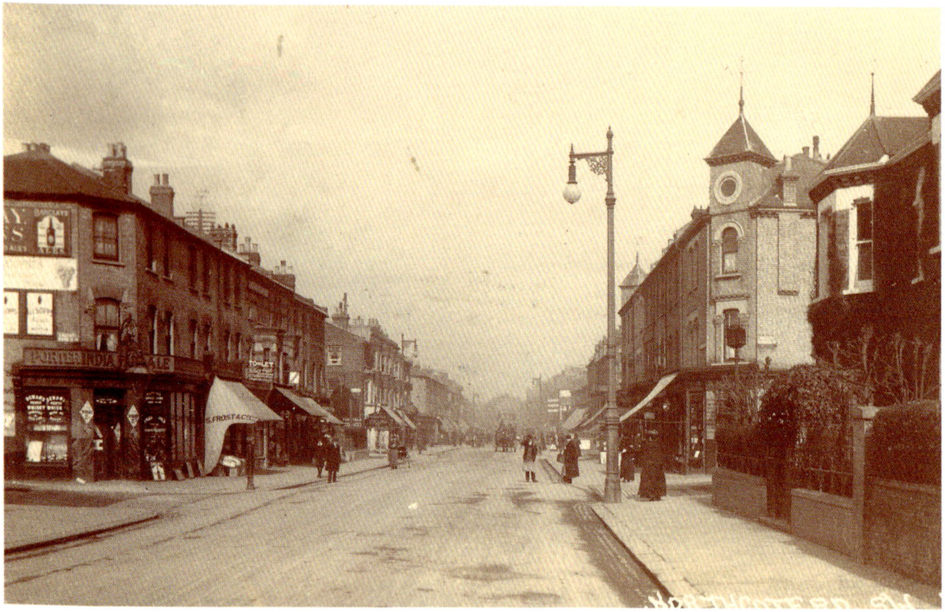

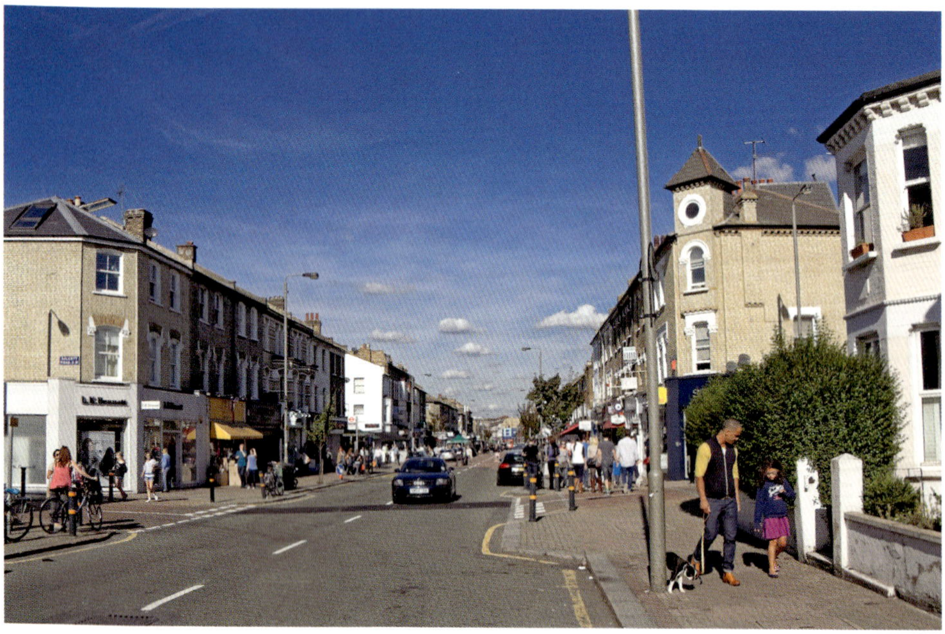

This page: This pair of pictures illustrating how little has actually changed architecturally on the Northcote Road were taken at the junction of Salcott Road looking north. Unfortunately, I am not sure of the year that the old postcard was published but must be around 100 years old.

Opposite: This picture is the view from Bolingbroke Grove looking east towards Clapham Common, with Honeywell School in the middle of the horizon. Thank you to Louise Thurlow and her family for kindly letting me into their home to take this picture from one of their top room windows.

is now hidden under Muncaster Road. There, men and women of Battersea who frequented the nearby Holy Trinity Church on Clapham Common (hence the name 'the Clapham Sect') made history fighting for human dignity and freedom by achieving the abolition of the slave trade.

In the nineteenth century, Battersea's population exploded like the rest of London, and this unleashed an unprecedented flood of building over just a few decades. The commercial heart of Battersea moved south to Lavender Hill. In 1863 a new railway station was built in the centre of Battersea and given the name 'Clapham Junction', which has caused geographic confusion to people ever since, except proud Battersea folk who simply called it 'The Junction'. Battersea Town Hall – now Battersea Arts Centre – and Battersea Public Library were built on Lavender Hill. Arding & Hobbs, an impressive department store, was built across the road from the historic Falcon Pub, which once looked out across the Falcon Brook. St. John's Road became the new High Street. Entertainment arrived on Lavender Hill – The Shakespeare Theatre next to the town hall, and the Pavilion Cinema, which became a bombsite and remains to this day open space as ASDA's car park.

'South Battersea' was developed into the popular residential area that became known as 'Between the Commons'. In the middle is the much loved Northcote Road, built in the valley between the commons on top of the old Hideburna River or Falcon Brook, which still flows underneath in a culvert, and in a 2006 storm flowed as a river once again! The junction of Battersea Rise and Northcote Road is where the old hamlet of Wassingham was located.

With population came necessary sustenance. Shops of all kinds spread along Northcote Road and the 'costermongers' of St. John's Road were moved south to create

Northcote Road's street market.

Spiritual sustenance came next. Canon Erskine Clarke was one of the most significant Vicars of St. Mary's Battersea. Not only did he lead the community fund-raising and building of what became Bolingbroke Hospital – now thankfully saved for community use as the new Bolingbroke Academy – but he led the building of the new churches of south Battersea, to serve the burgeoning population there. St. Barnabas's on Clapham Common, St. Mark's on Battersea Rise, St. Michael's on Bolingbroke Grove – built as a memorial to Rev'd Henry Boutflower Verdon and local benefactor Philip Cazenove; St. Luke's on Ramsden Road, St. John's on St. John's Hill (now the LARA Centre), and many more. The Baptists built their notable church on Northcote Road, the Welsh Presbyterians built one of London's only Welsh Chapels, on Beauchamp Road. The United Reformed Church built St. Andrew's at the top of Battersea Rise on Clapham Common, long since rebuilt on a smaller scale.

In the 1980s another great surge of migration occurred – of young families seeking greater space and more affordable housing than available north of the river in places like Fulham. Also, Wandsworth Council had begun to sell many houses it owned in the area and estate agents became part of the fabric of Northcote Road. All of this spurred the transformation of the area into the place it has become today – 'Between the Commons' – probably the most popular place for young families in London. Its geography lent itself to the now much quoted nickname of 'Nappy Valley'. A few decades ago it housed the greatest concentration of young families in Europe, and is in the midst of yet another baby boom, with the prams to prove it. People simply love to live in this southern part of Battersea. Surveys showed the biggest concentration of broadband accounts in the UK, and it has been said to house more opinion formers than Islington.

This part of Battersea has also become incredibly cosmopolitan. There is a growing French community, leading to the creation of England's first bi-lingual school – École de Wix on Wix's Lane. There are people from Poland, the West Indies, Germany, Scandinavia, Greece, South Africa, Australia (and their 'Aussie Rules' football pitch on Clapham Common), South and North America and from just about everywhere else across the world. The population is younger than the London average. There are writers, artists, musicians, film stars, professionals, mums and kids galore, and city workers. All of these things make it an incredibly energising place to be.

No-one can talk of 'Between the Commons' without mentioning the bars, pubs and coffee houses that have made it such a magnet to the young and old alike. Café culture is well entrenched along Northcote Road. An old market mixes with newer shops and well known brands like Cath Kidston and FatFace, as well as independently owned delights like 'All Good Gifts' and 'Dove & Son' the butchers, now in its 3rd generation of family management. Across the road another family butcher exists – Hennesseys. No high street in London can boast such delicious variety – Hamish Johnston for cheeses, Gail's and The Bread Store for bakery products, The remarkable Hive Honey Shop with its own bee hive. One of the best Thai restaurants in London, 'The Bolingbroke', resurrected the name of the historic Bolingbroke Pub, and Philglas & Swiggot is a wine shop like no other. Tucked off Northcote Road on Chatham Road is a pub the like of which one might expect to find in a characterful Surrey village, 'The Eagle Ale House'. There's no mystery as to why the eagle on its sign looks like Crystal Palace's logo! It also alludes to the falcon crest of the St. John family, Viscounts Bolingbroke, and it has been on Chatham Road before the streets around it were built.

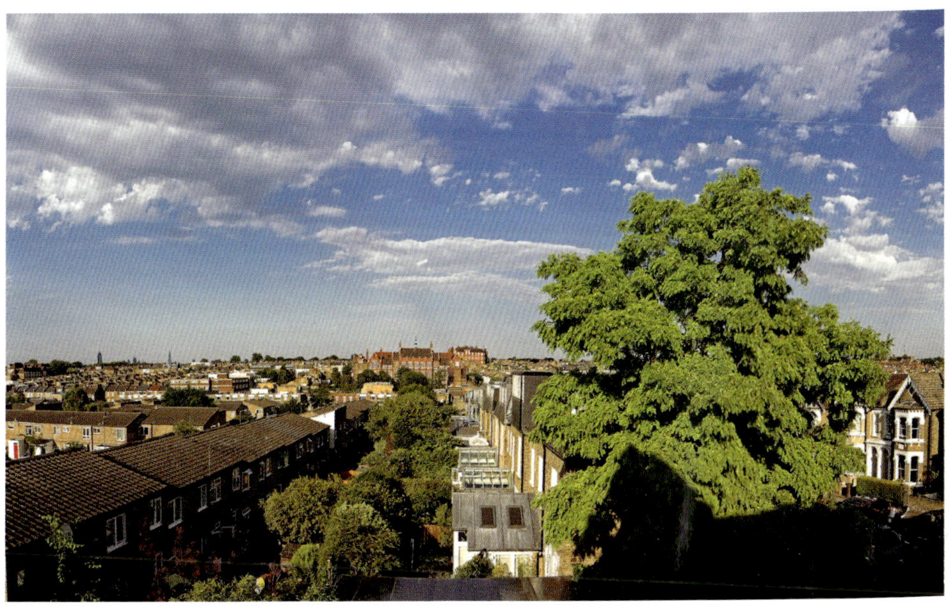

The extensive fields of Lavender that were farmed on Battersea Rise are remembered by the renaming of The Canterbury Road as Lavender Hill. The bees that fed on the nectar of the lavender flowers became another symbol of Battersea, and explains why they appear on the mosaic floor of the old Town Hall, today's 'Battersea Arts Centre'.

Webb's Road above Northcote Road near Clapham Common is one of Battersea's hidden treasures. There is everything from Spanish and French café delis, a diving shop, Oranges & Lemons, one of London's specialist hi-fi shops, osteopaths, vets, a newsagent, hairdressers, a nursery, interior designers, an art gallery, pottery painting heaven, two schools, Amco News and much more.

Next to Clapham South underground, safely within Battersea is Moxons Fishmongers – you can't find more delicious fish in the sea! Moxons is magic.

As for Bellevue Road and its wonderful vista across Wandsworth Common – It's just about one of the most heavenly spots in London, with the character of a countryside village row, which is precisely what it once was.

There's only one Battersea, and it is unique in more ways than just its name.

Andrew's book is a feast for the eyes, the heart and the spirit, and brings alive all that is beautiful and irresistible about Battersea 'Between the Commons'.

Philip Beddows

Follow Philip on Twitter at @*LoveBattersea1* and help put Battersea on the map!

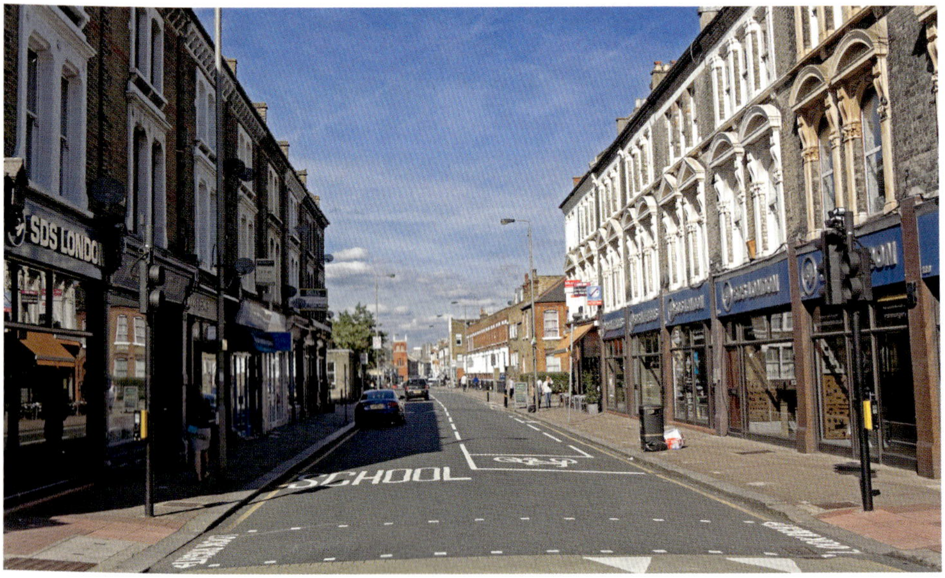

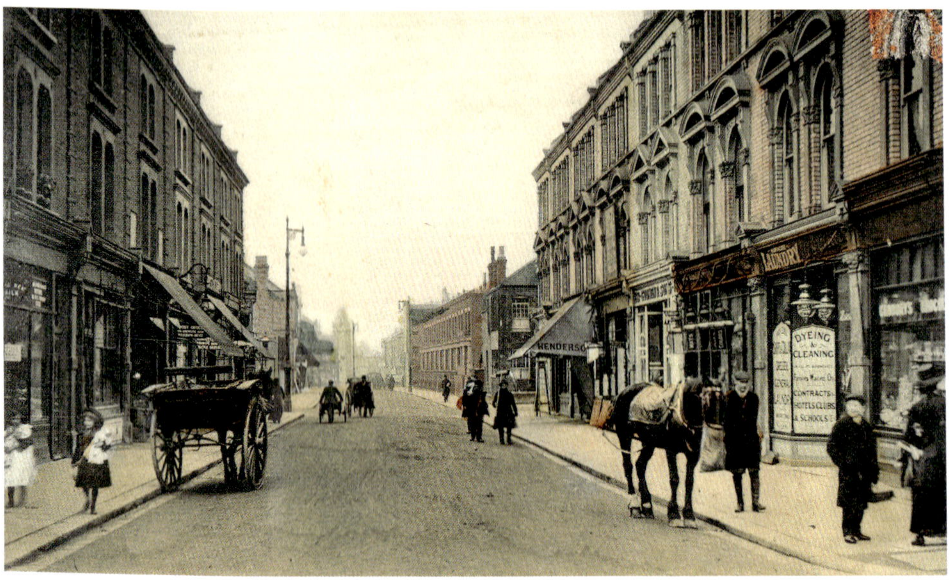

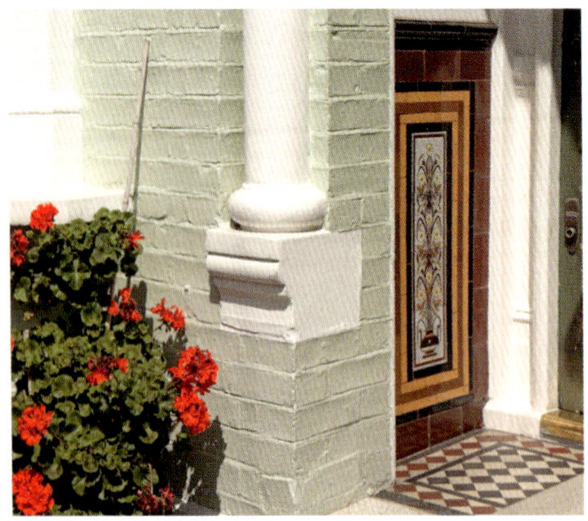

Above: A nice feature of many of the homes between the commons is the original tiles that have been retained by people's front doors – these ones from a home on Wroughton Road.

Left: These two pictures were taken from the junction of Northcote Road and Broomwood Road and looking North. The old picture dates from 1915 and notice that the Baptist Church in the distance on the left still has its tower partially covered at the top.

South Battersea

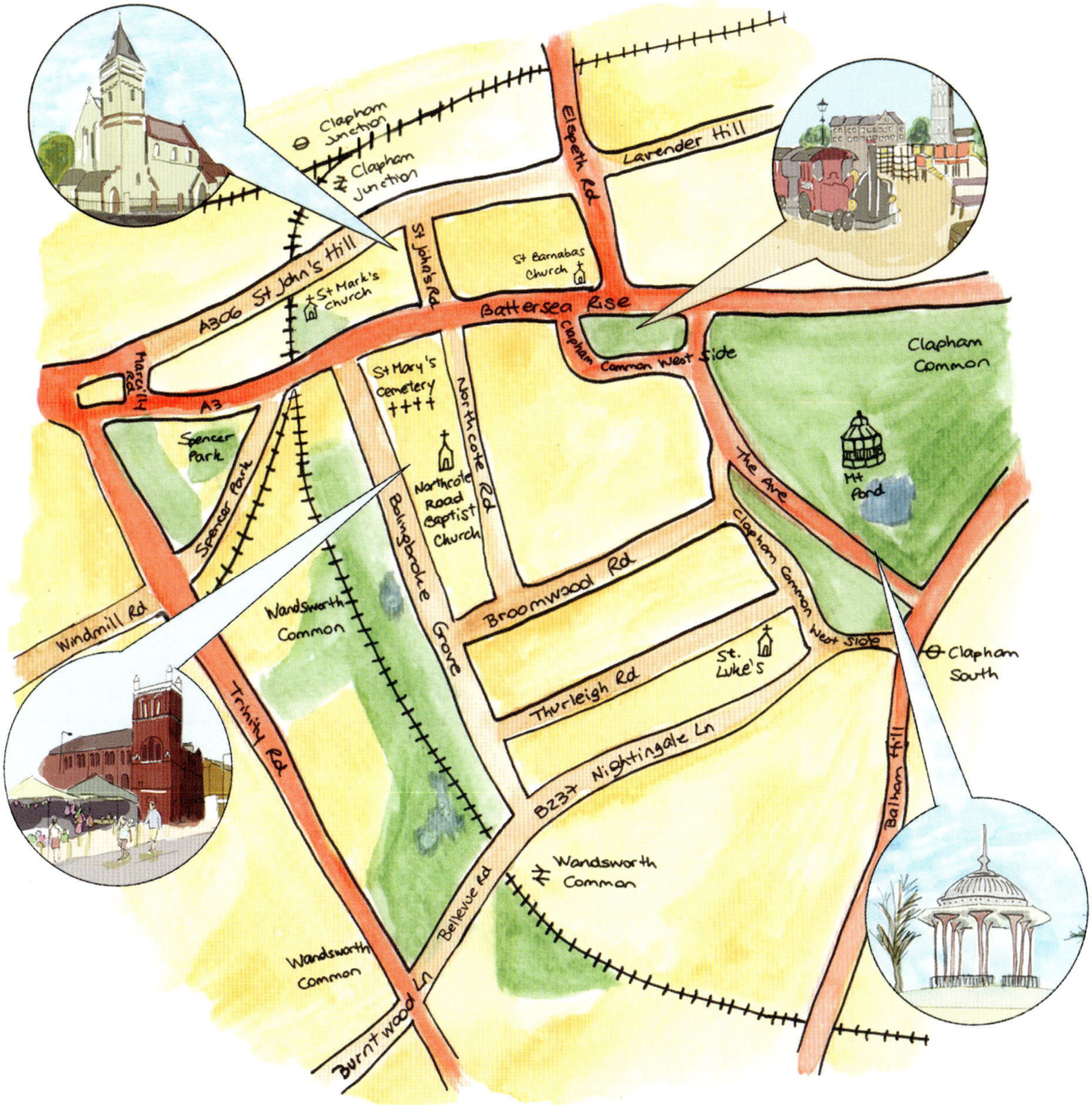

This map was kindly supplied by local artist, Silvina De Vita and is not meant to be absolutely to scale but to give the reader a fun introduction to the area and some of the places covered in this book. Silvina lives and works in Wimbledon and is a graphic designer and artist. She can be contacted via her website *www.silvinadevita.com*

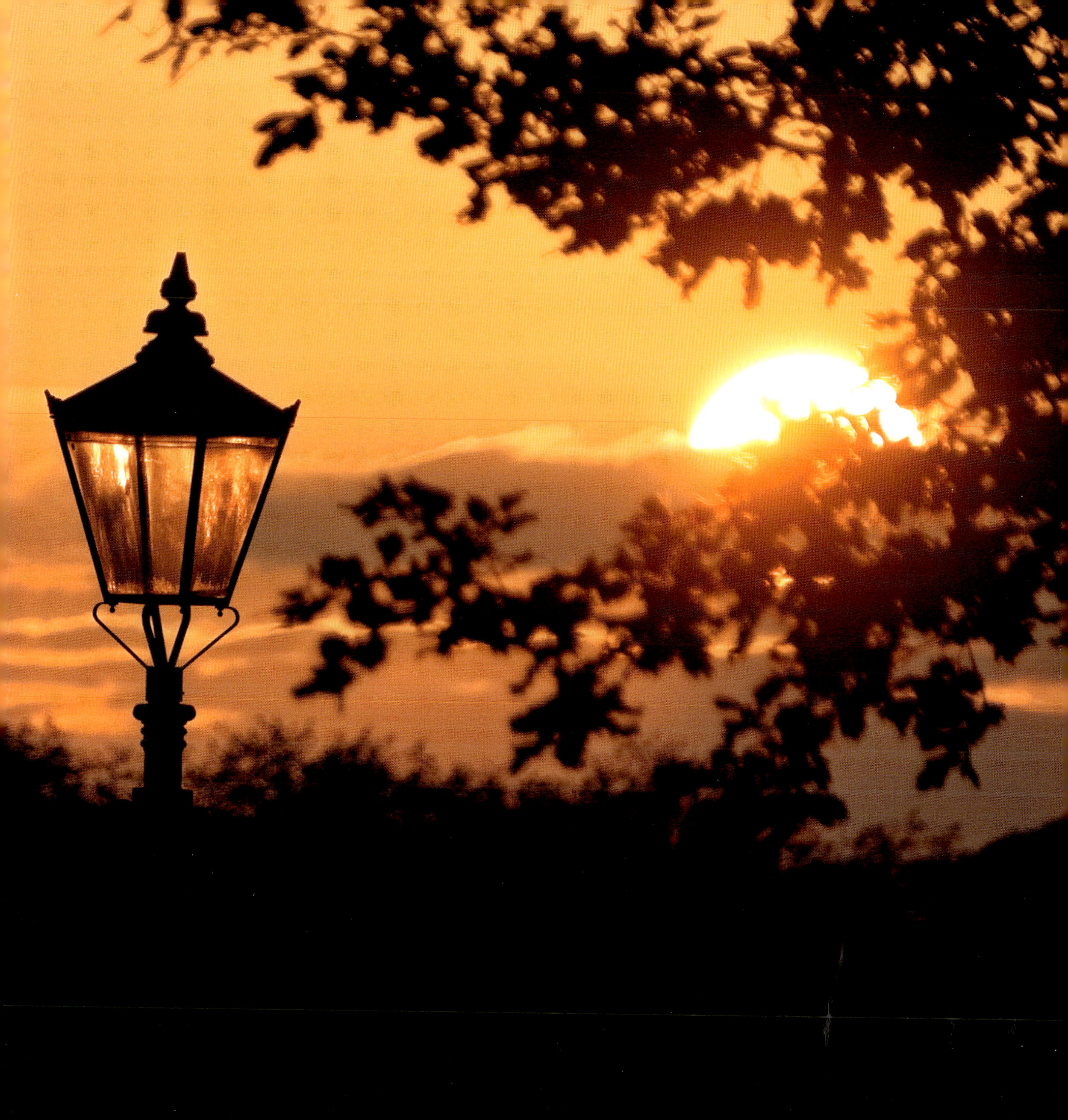

Northcote Road Summer Fête

The Northcote Road Summer Fête can trace its history back almost 50 years, when the then large local Afro-Caribbean community used to hold a carnival here. As time went by and the area changed the event was revived, culminating in what we have today, which started four years ago. Although run by the business community, the Northcote Business Network, they encourage strong links with the local community and always support a local charity. This year (2013) the main beneficiary was Abbie's Army, which was formed in memory of Abbie Misfud, who was only six when she lost her fight against a brain tumour. With over 100 stalls and 5,000 visitors the fête is a hugely successful event and I enjoyed it immensely.

Right: Sliding into the Northcote Fête, next to the Bolingbroke pub, and what a view looking directly north

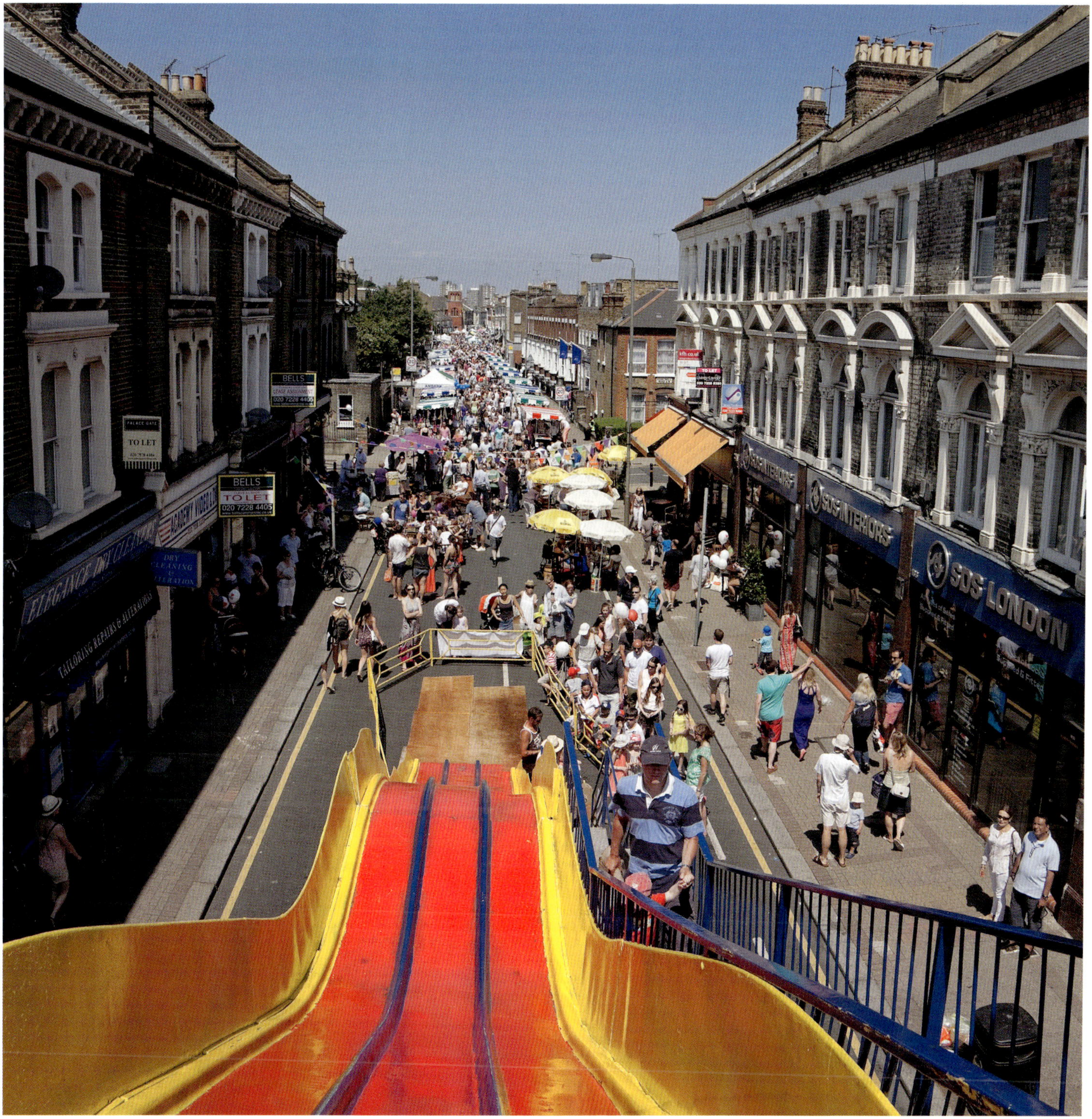
BELLS
TO LET
020 7228 4405
SDS INTERIORS
SDS LONDON
TAILORING REPAIRS & ALTERATIONS

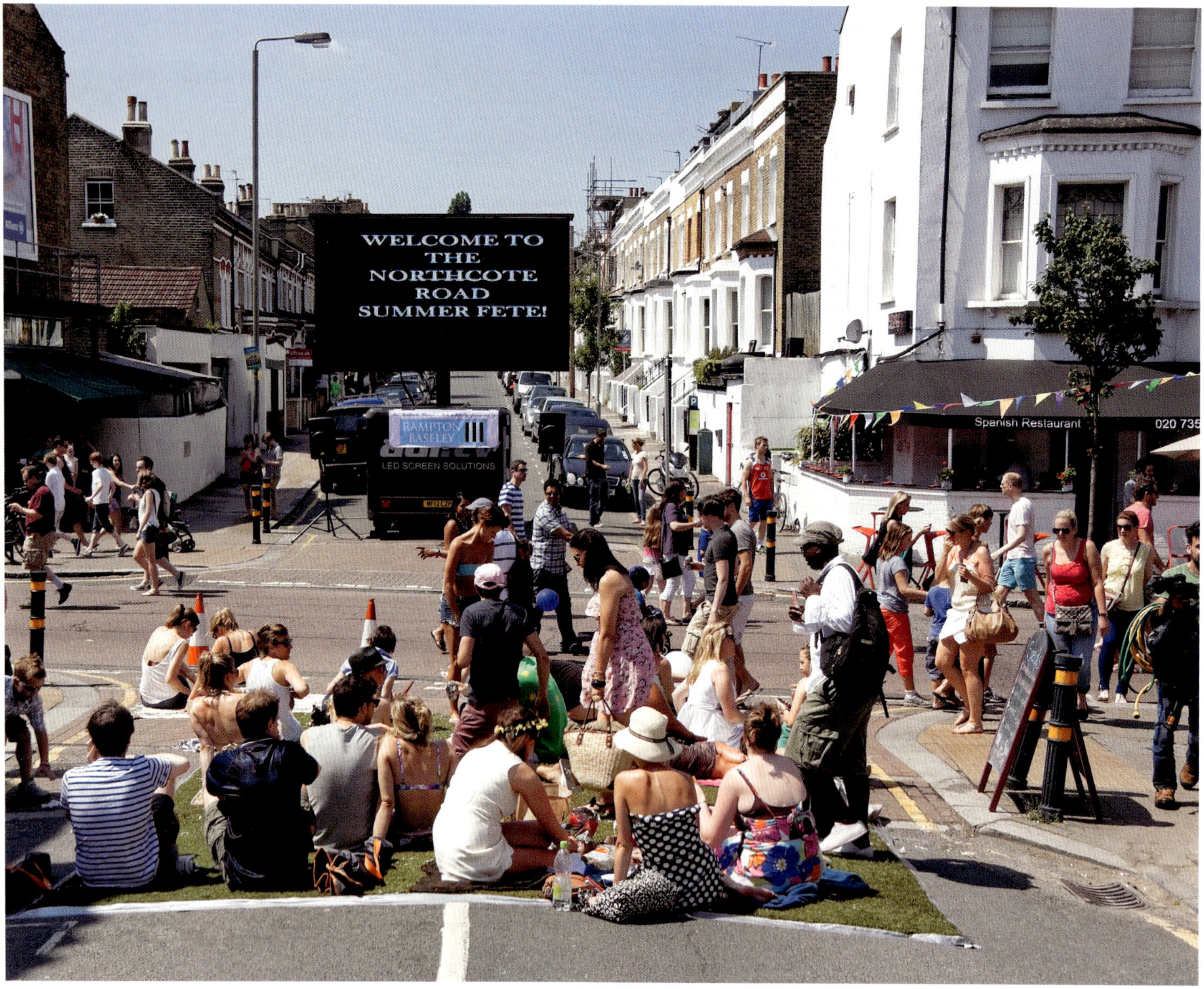

This spread and overleaf: The Northcote Road Summer Fête this year was on what turned out to be not only one of the hottest days of the year but also a very special one for all tennis fans as Andy Murray finally won Wimbledon. The organisers very sensibly put up a big screen and as the day went on, the crowds grew bigger and bigger, and with each point scored it dawned on everyone that this was going to be a history in the making.

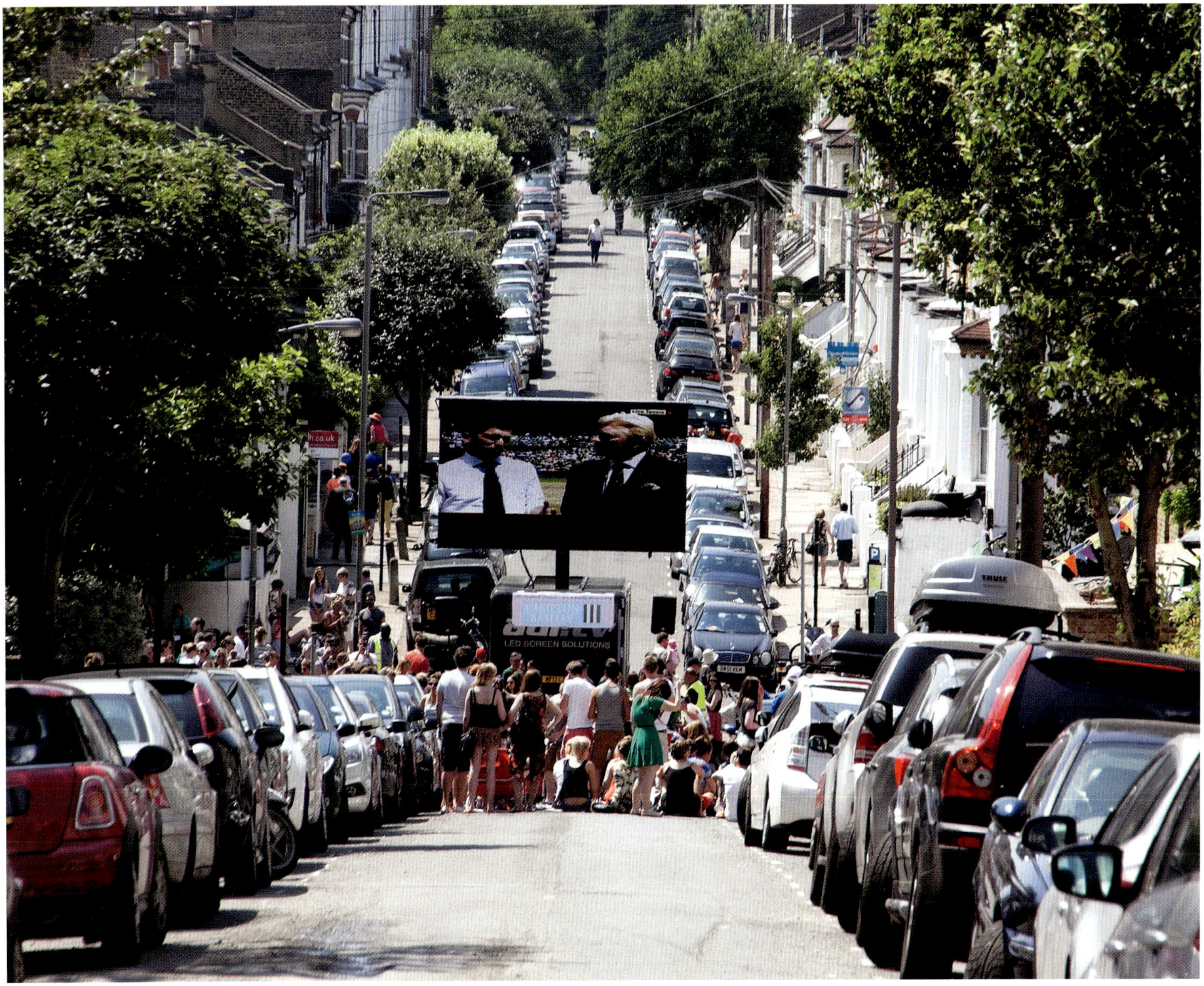
LED SCREEN SOLUTIONS

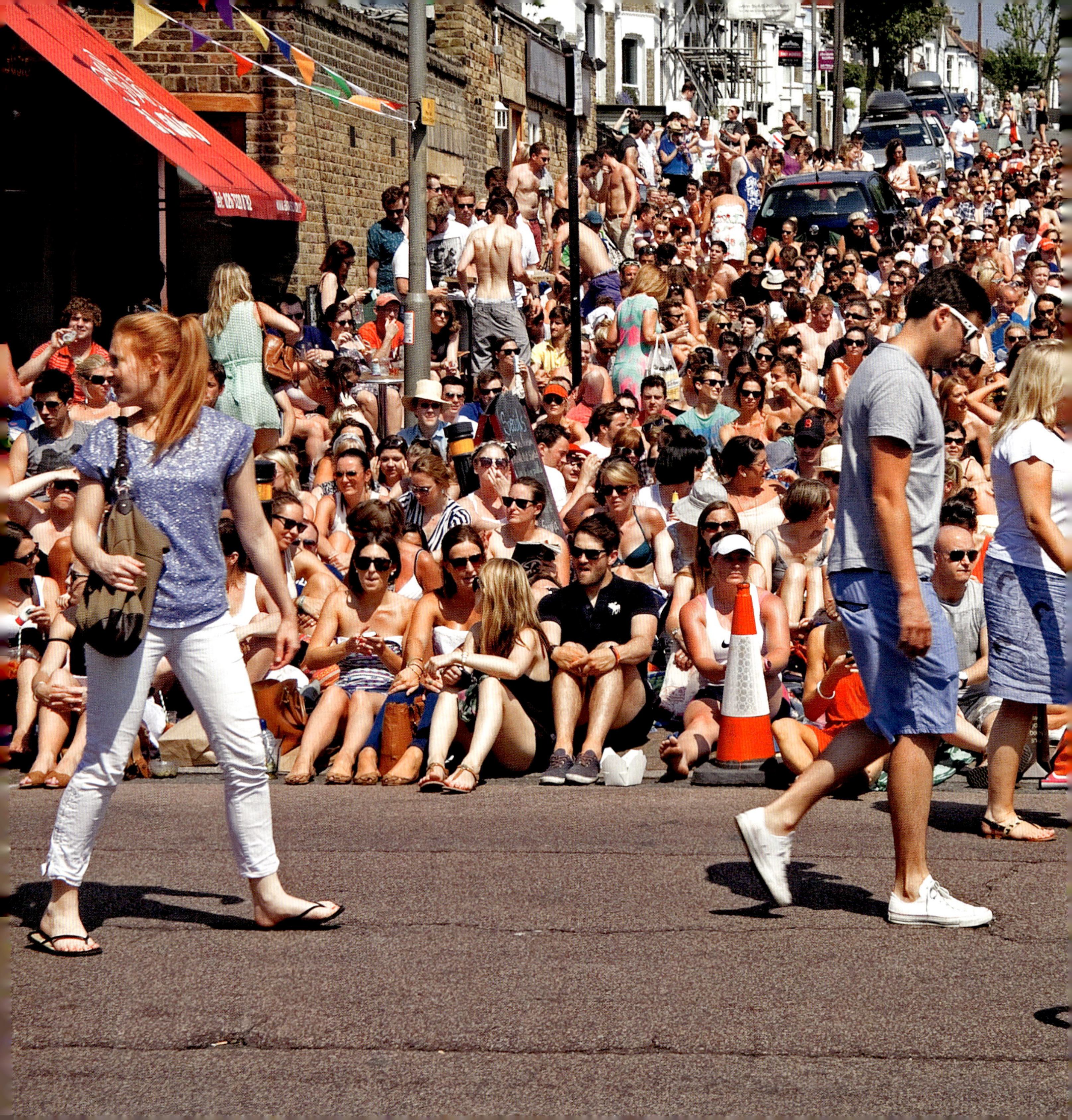

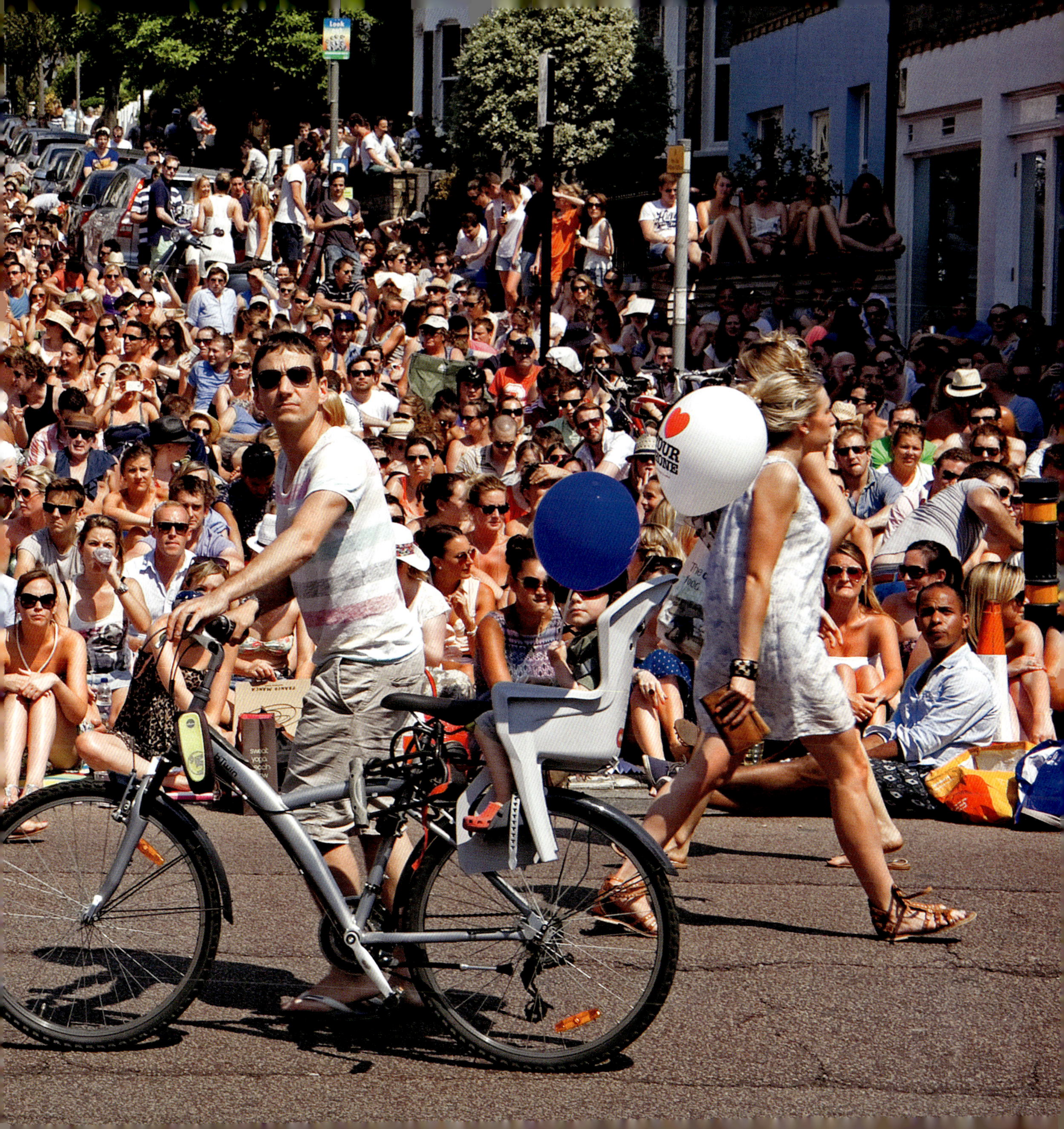

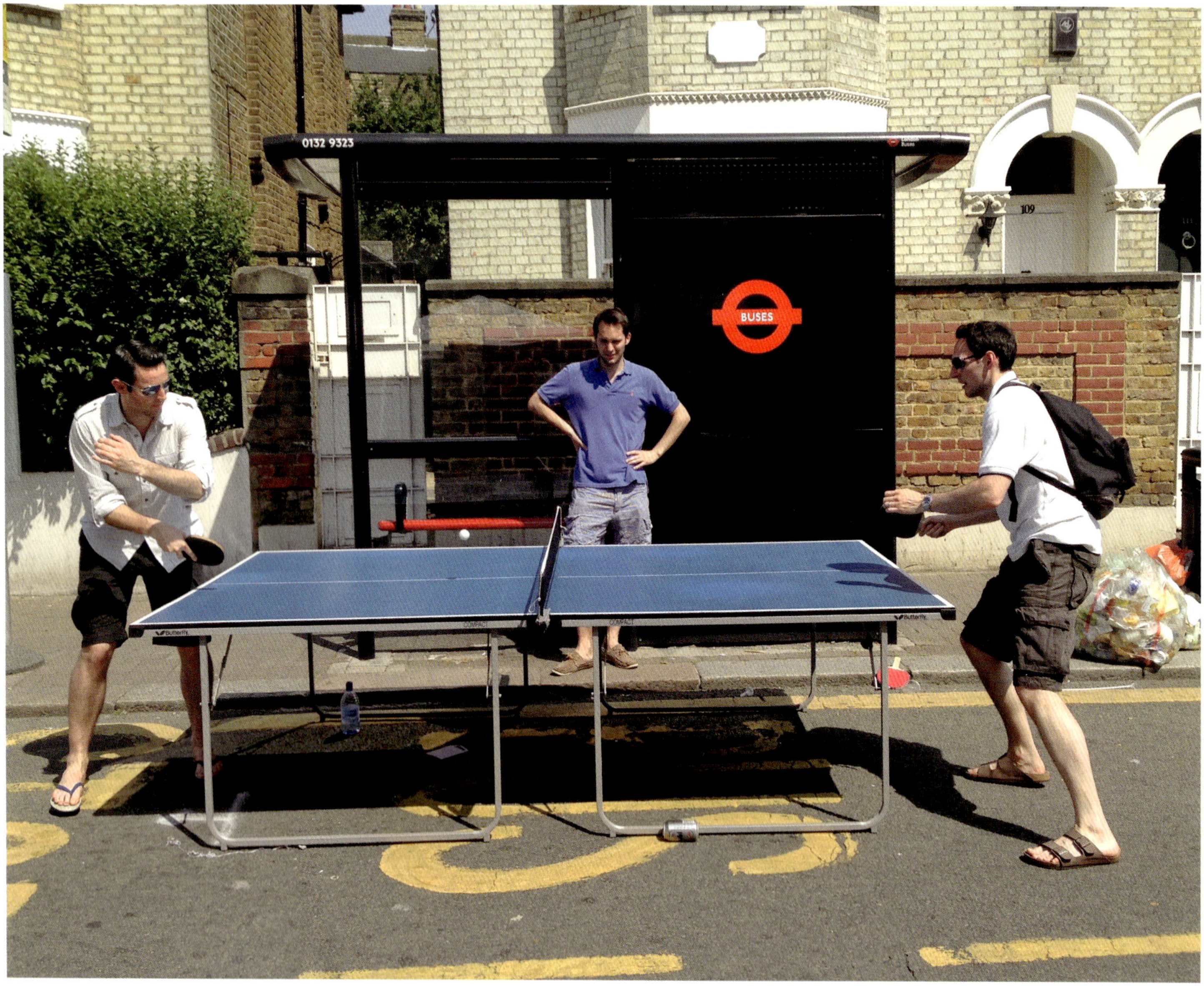

This page: Bus anyone? As the whole of Northcote Road was transformed for the day, even bus stops became areas for fun.

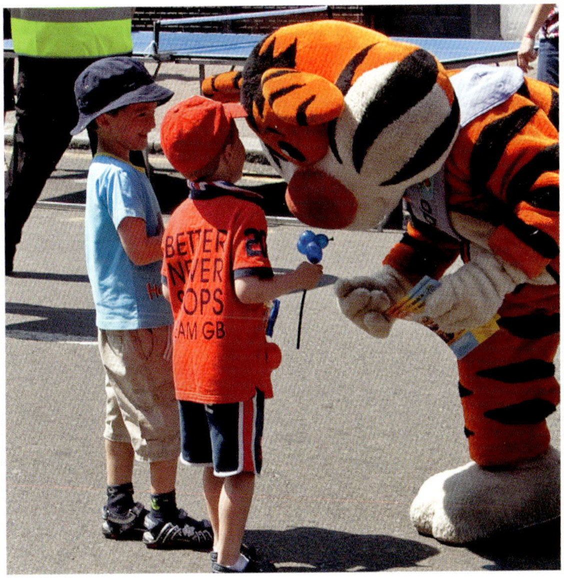
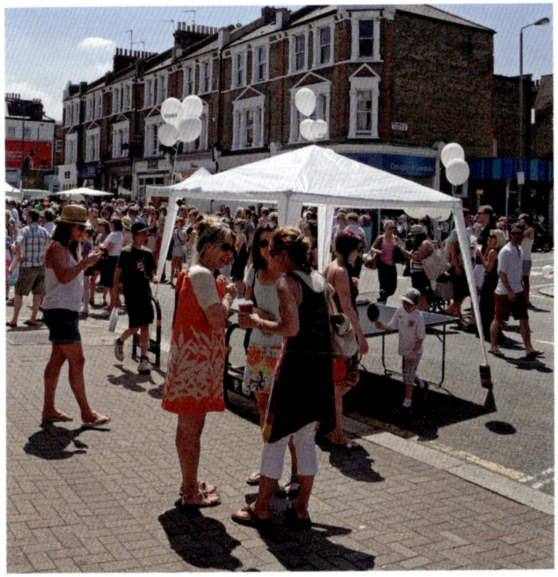
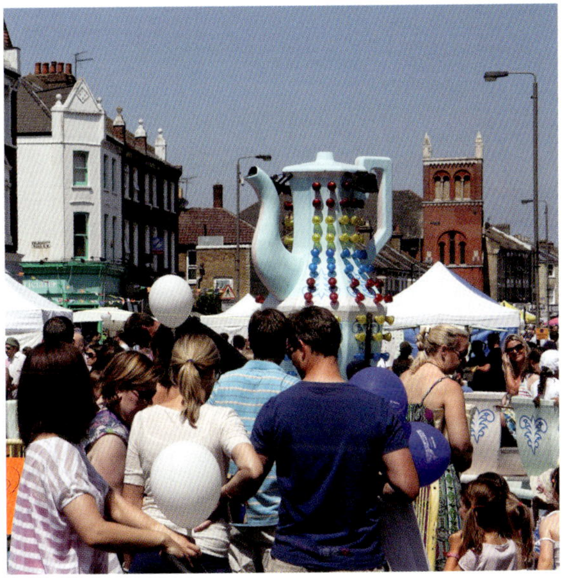
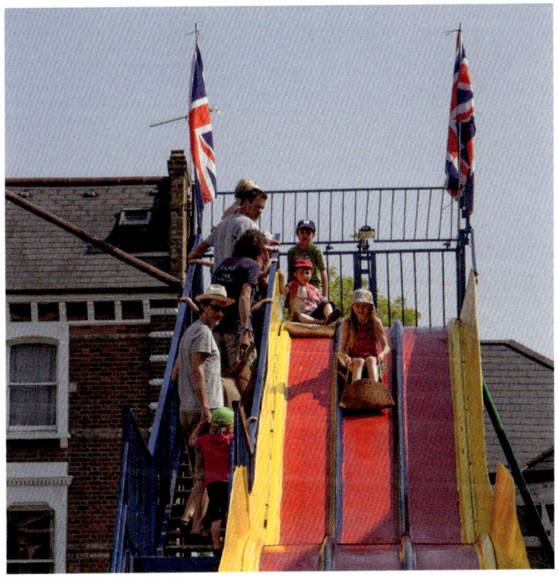

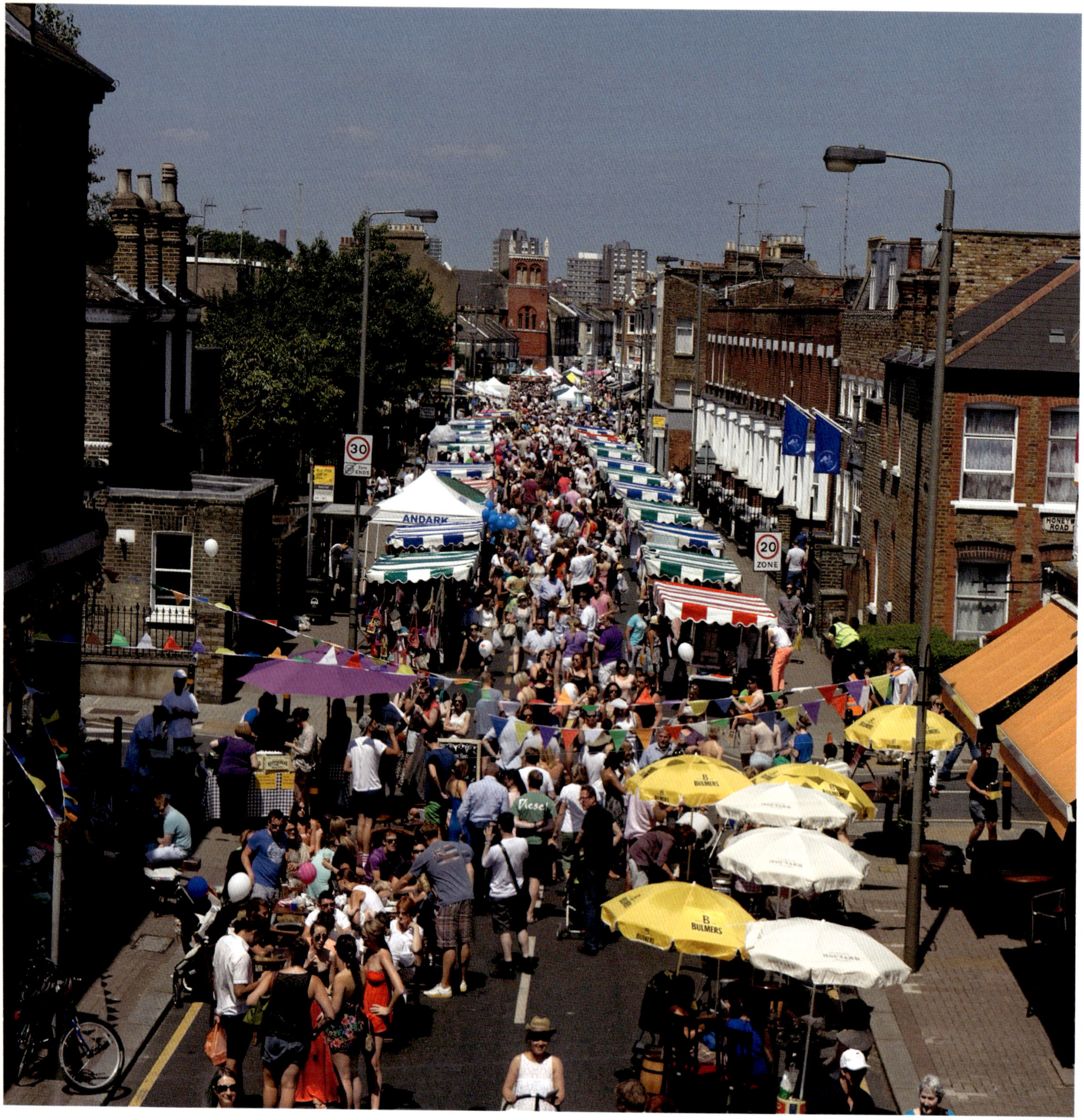
30
ANDARK
20
ZONE
BULMERS
BULMERS

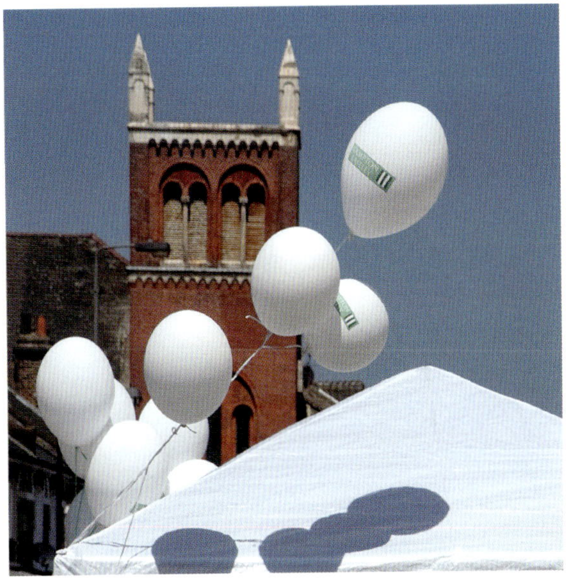

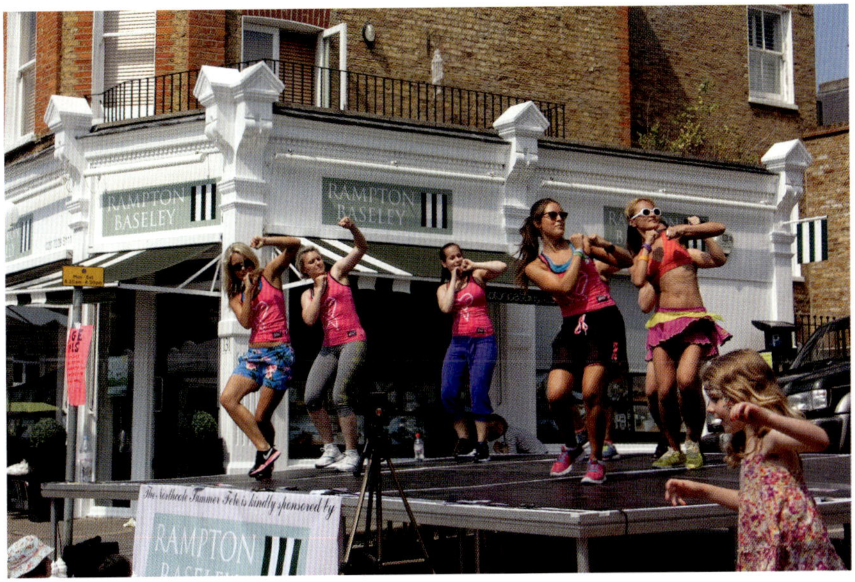

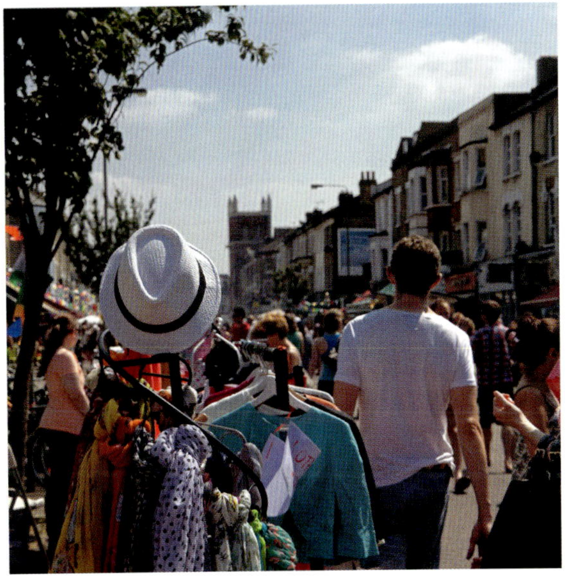

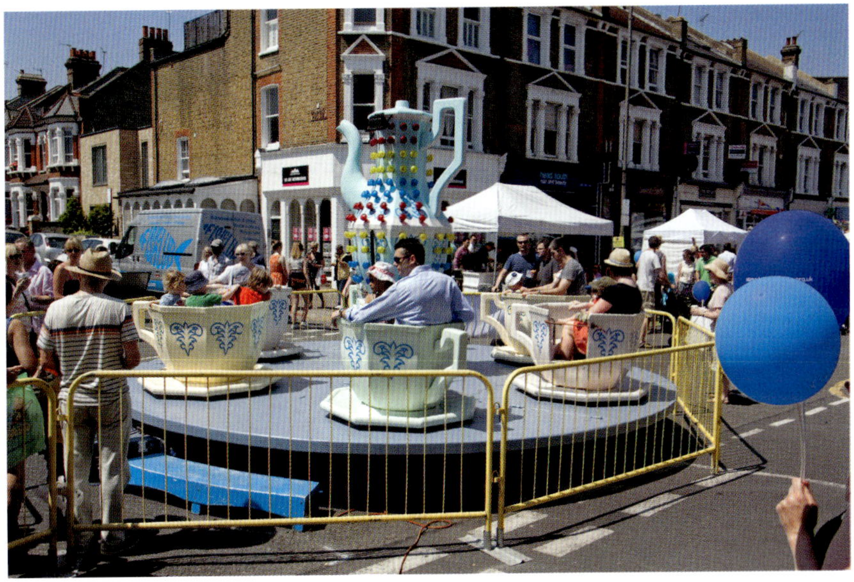

Opposite: At the southern end of the street they put up a monster slide and the guys running it kindly let me up to take some pictures.

Wandsworth Common

Wandsworth Common is slightly smaller than Clapham Common and very much more fragmented, as the railway line and Trinity Road cut right through the centre of it. Battersea West Heath, as most of it was once known, is no less loved though. In a chequered history, the most significant event was when its future was secured once and for all by its managevment being passed to Wandsworth Council in 1971. They have maintained and improved the space ever since and it is now a wonderful local resource. It has a large area given over to sport, two large ponds, a playground and a café.

Right: The large lake

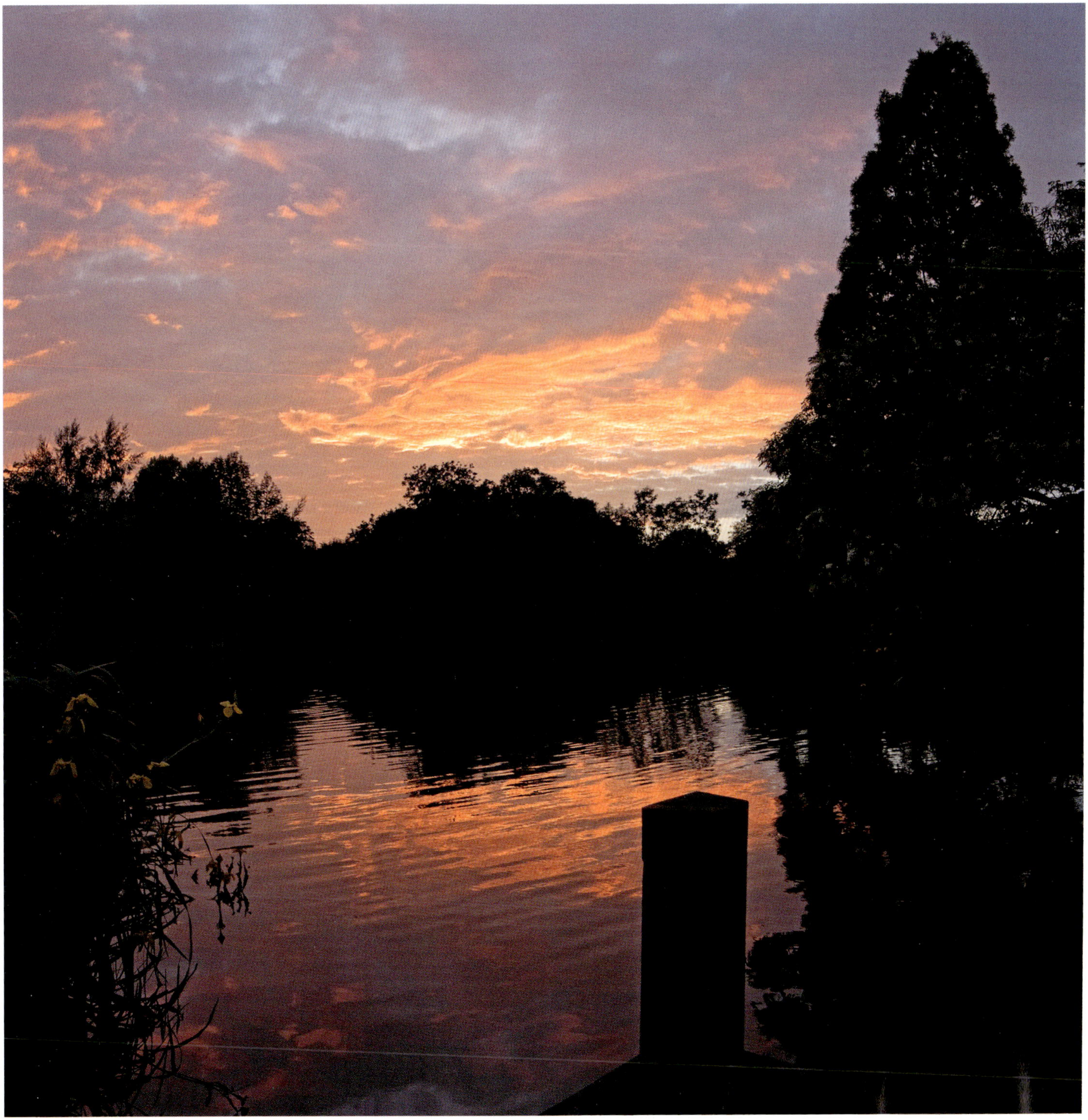

The Large Lake

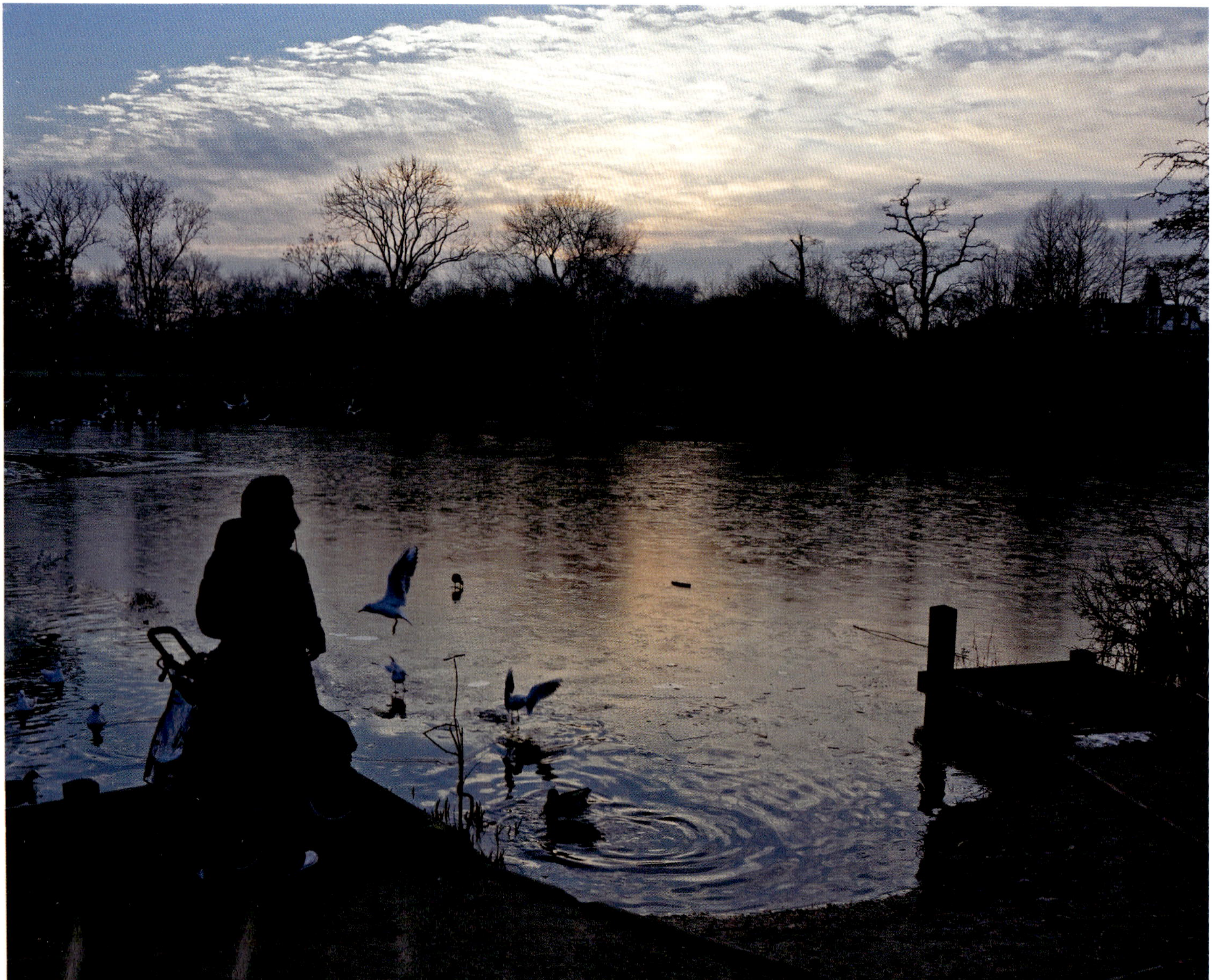

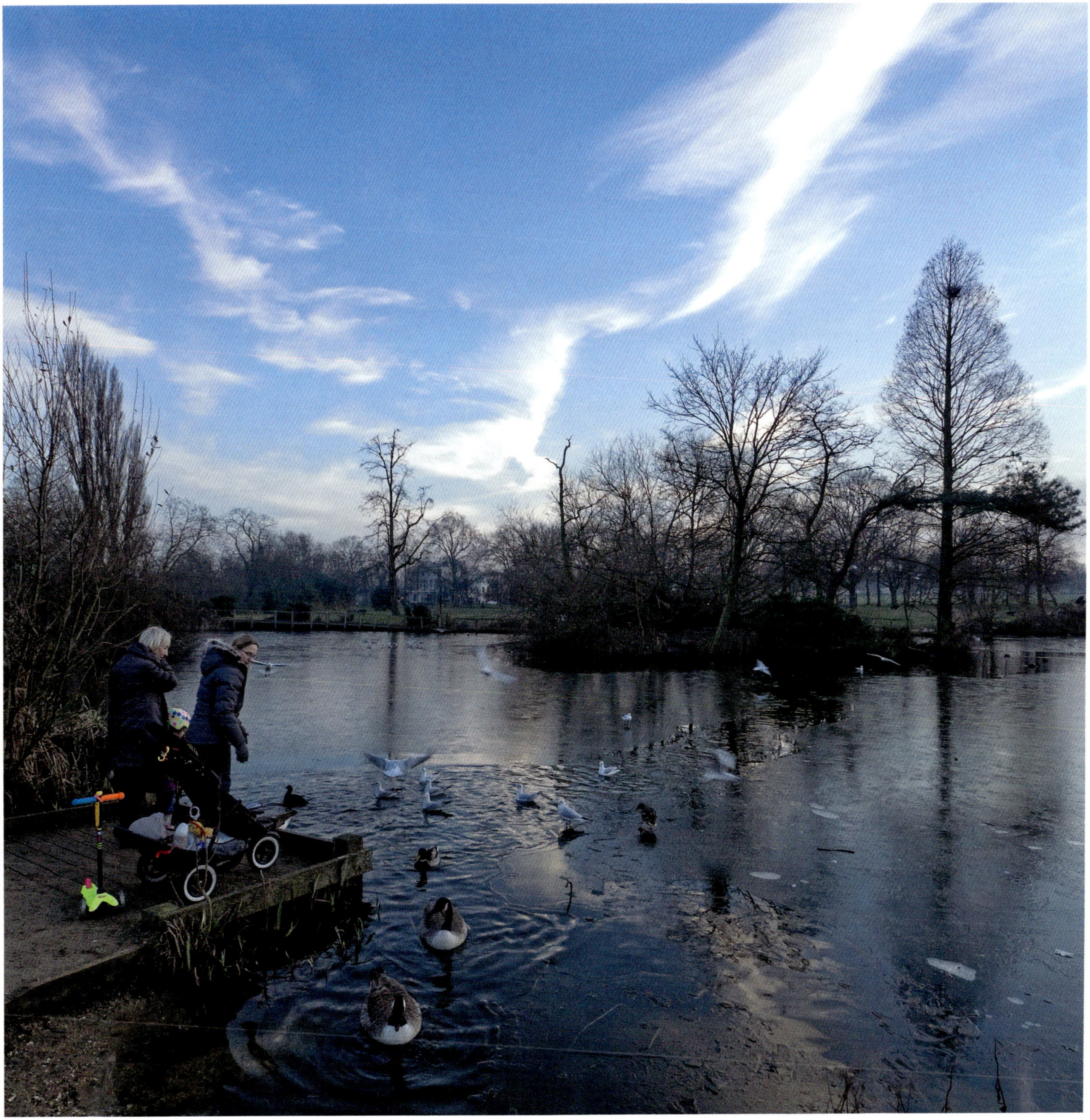

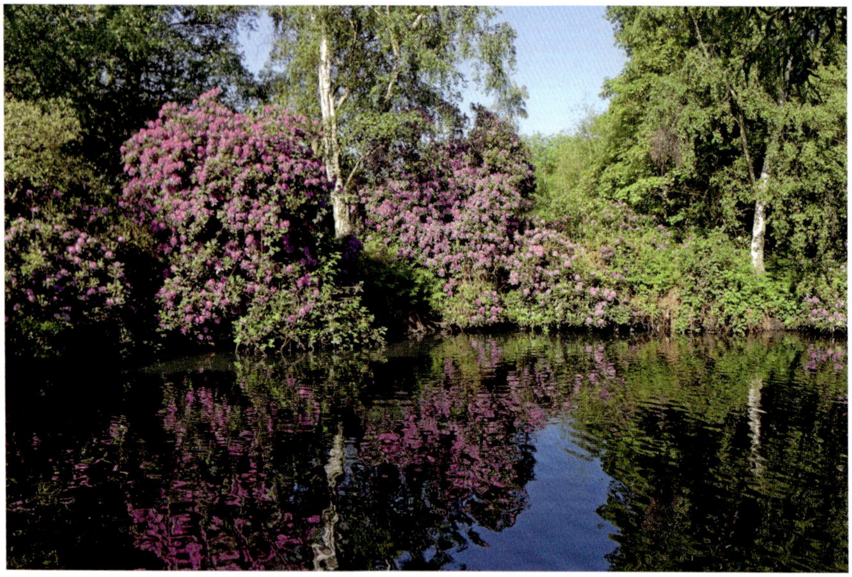

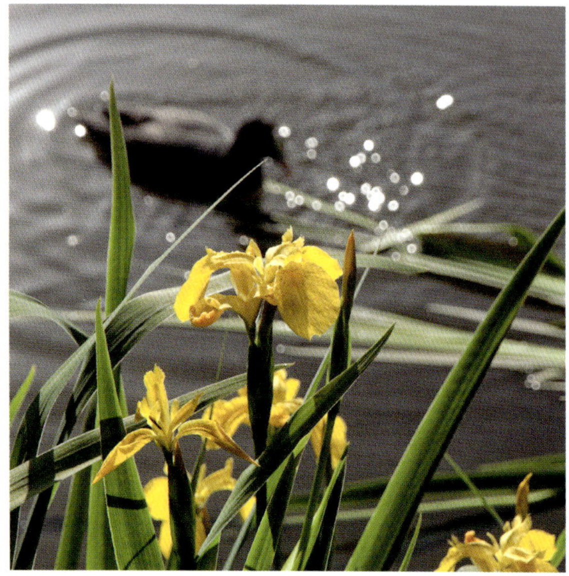

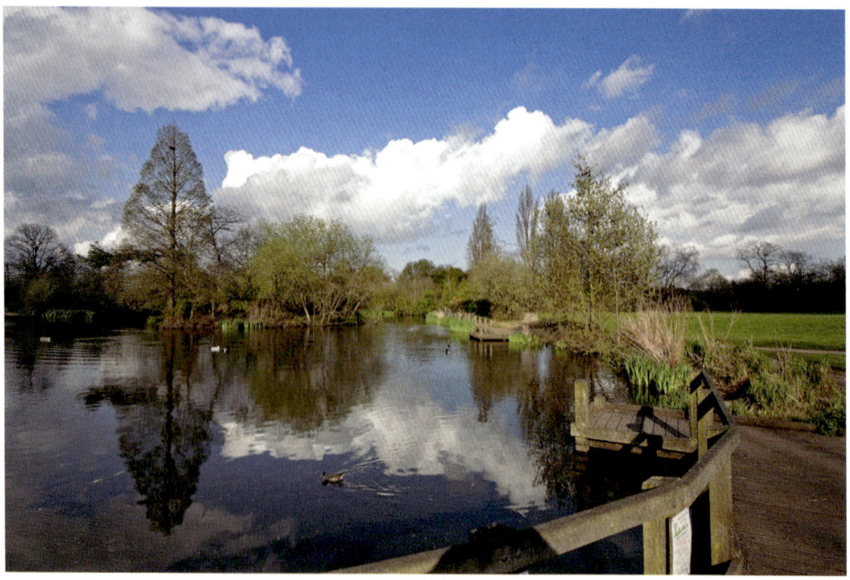

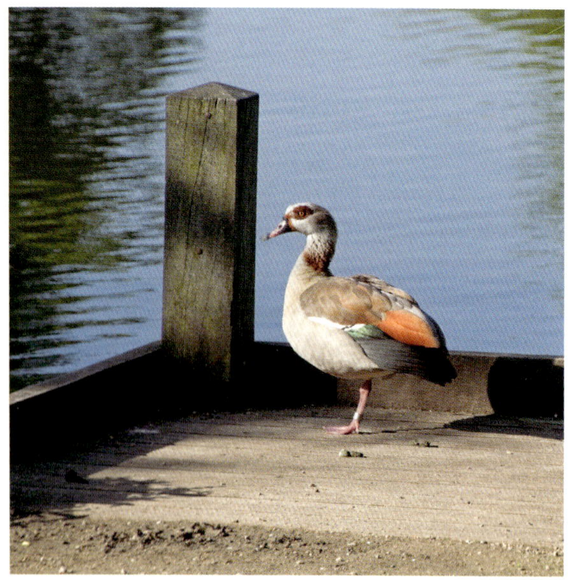

Top left: The lovely display of rhododendrons in summer.

Bottom right: Amongst a plethora of wild birds there are several pairs of Egyptian Geese.

Top right and opposite: The irises in late spring looked great.

Overleaf: The lake in late October 2013.

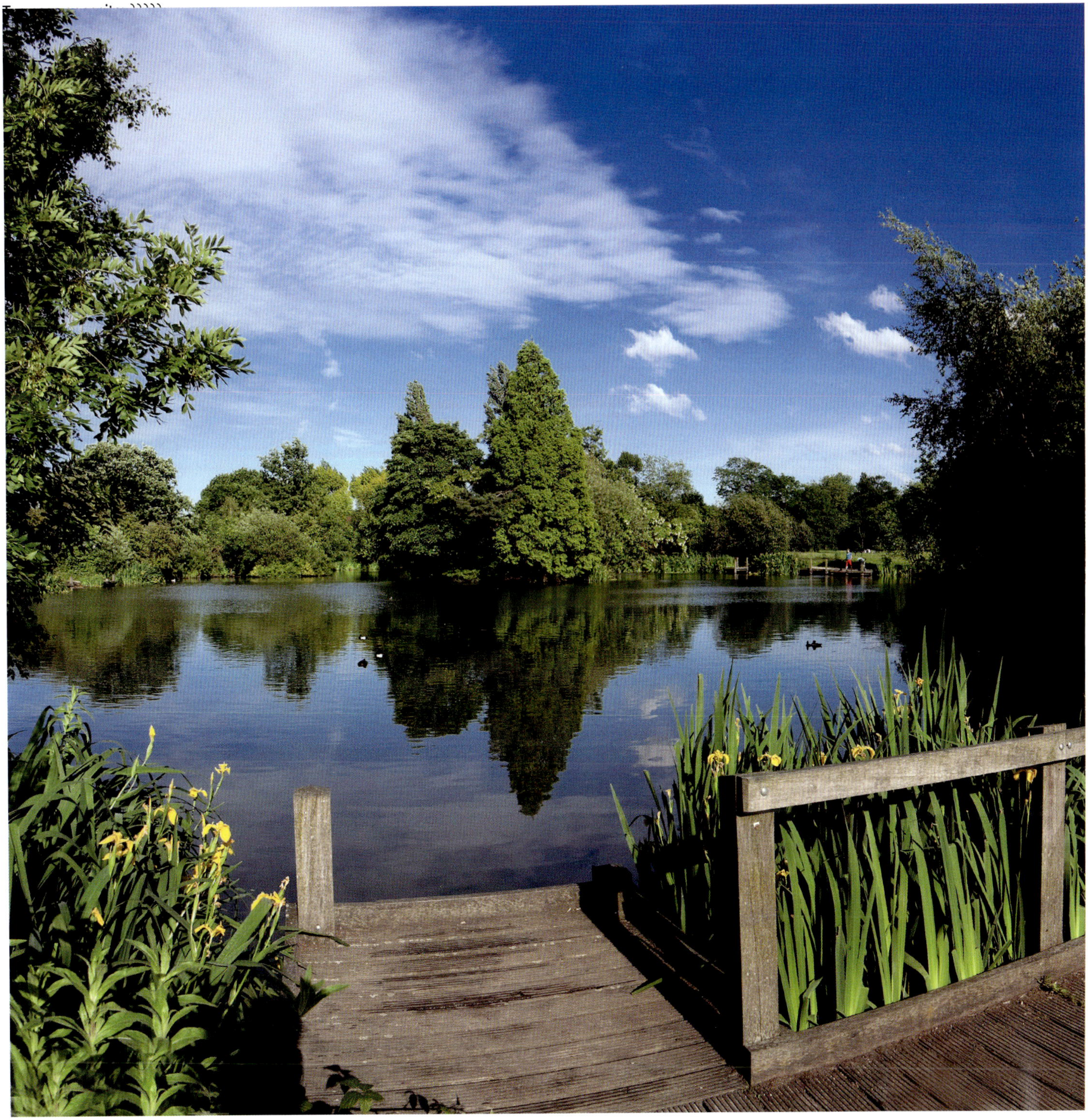

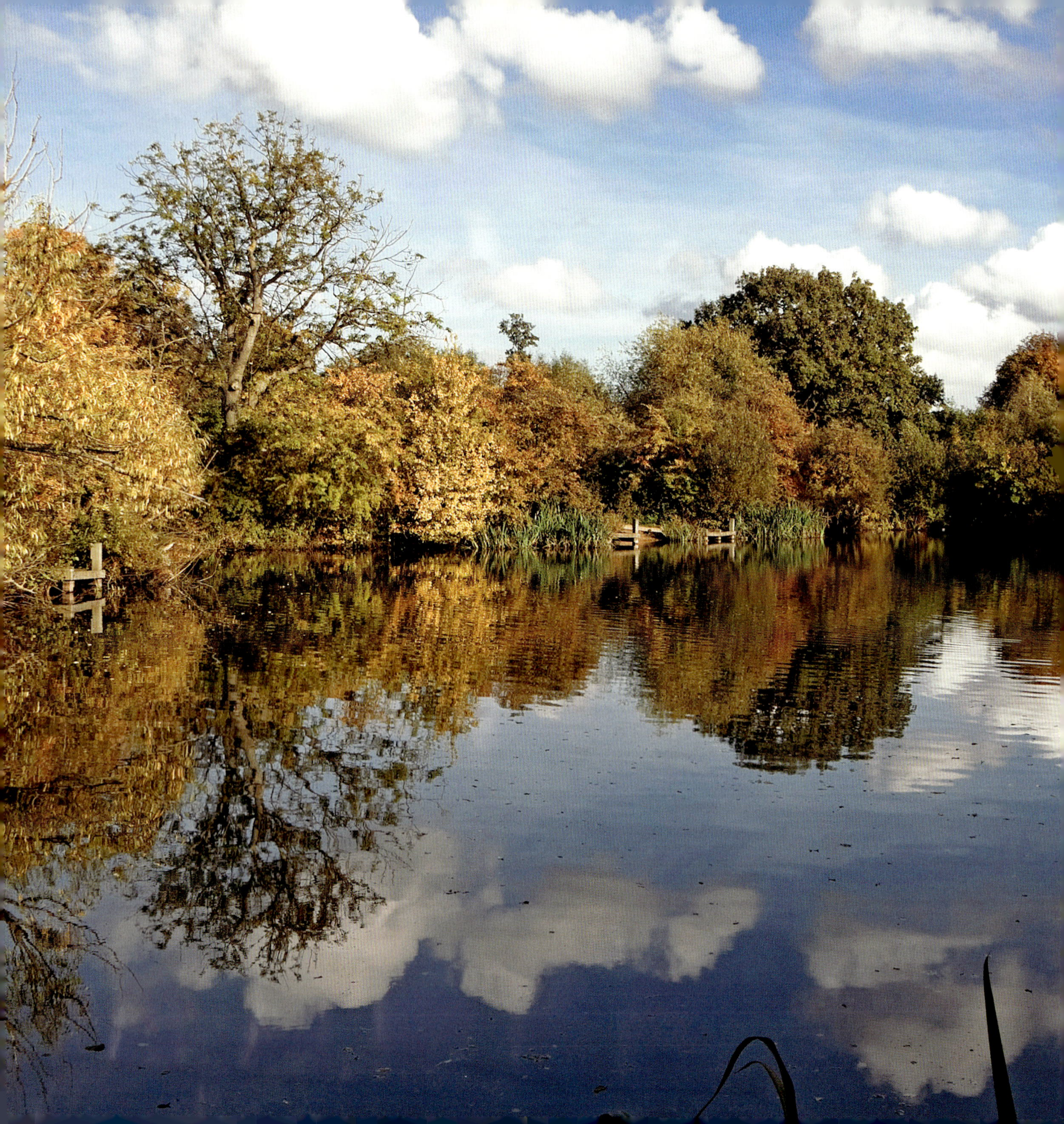

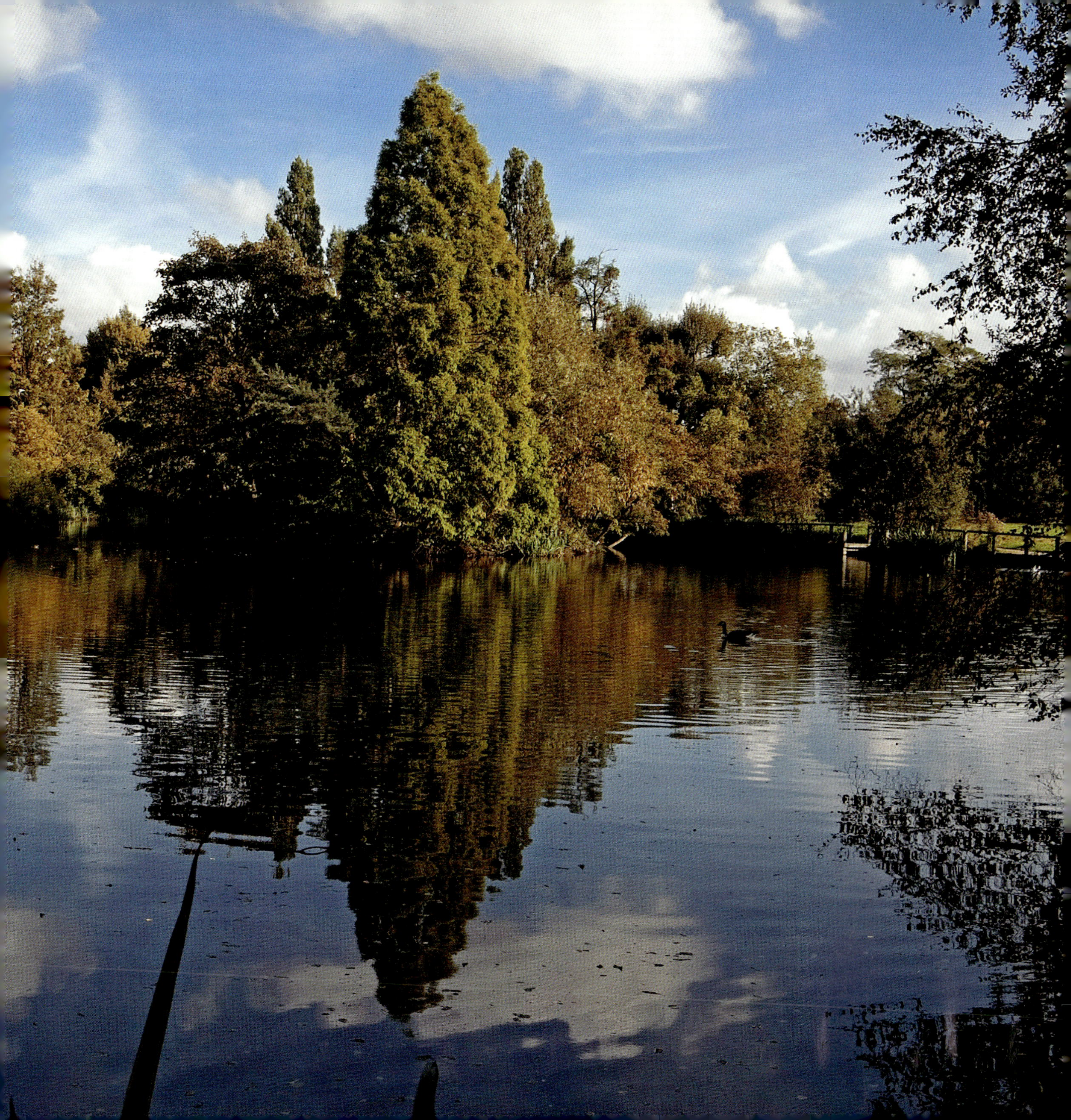

Neal's Nursery Garden Centre

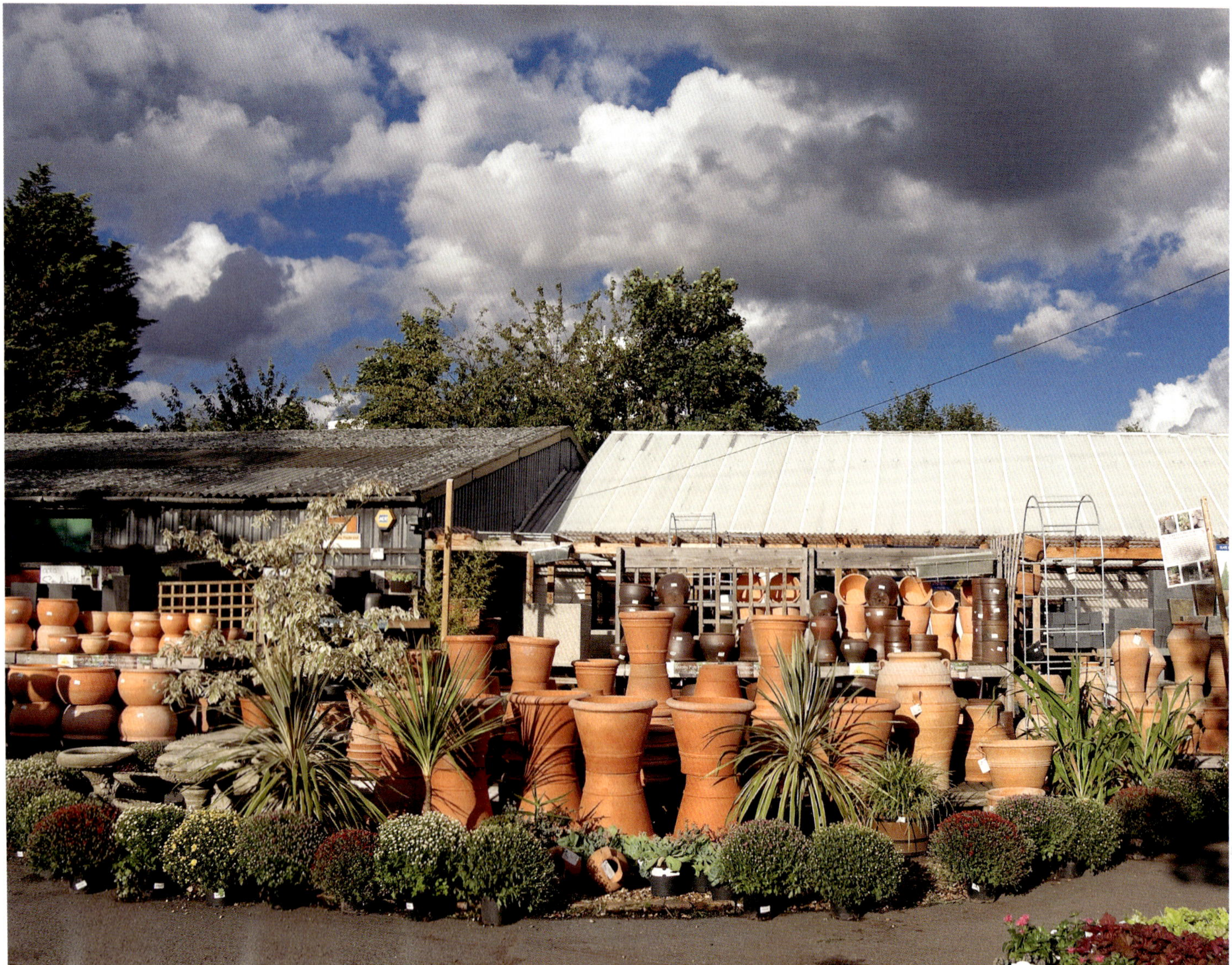

This page and opposite: Part of the Capital Gardens Group, who own four nurseries across London. This nursery, found on Heathfield Road, opposite the prison, is the largest plant centre in central London. A popular haunt for all local garden enthusiasts, Neal's can trace its history all the way back to 1850.

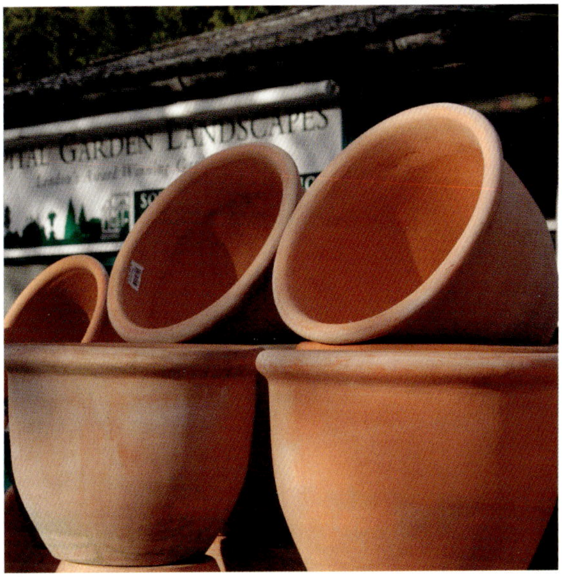

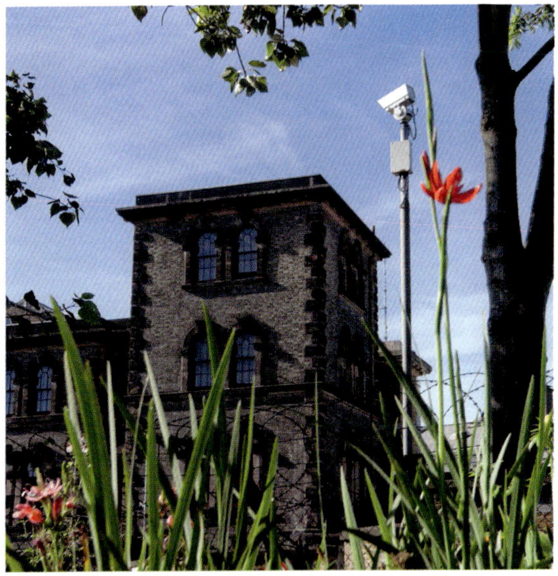

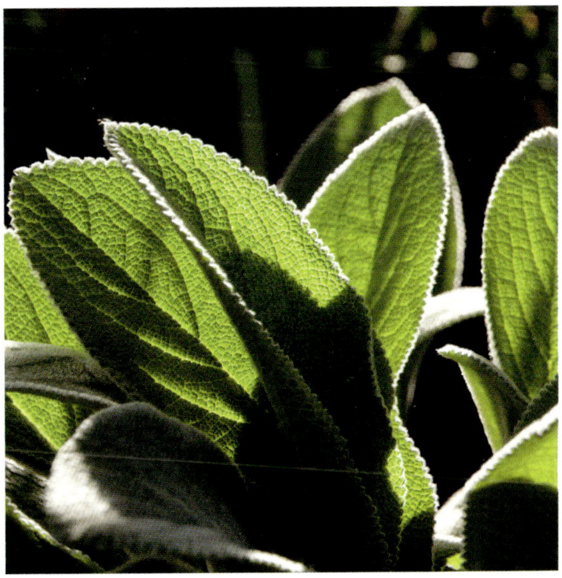

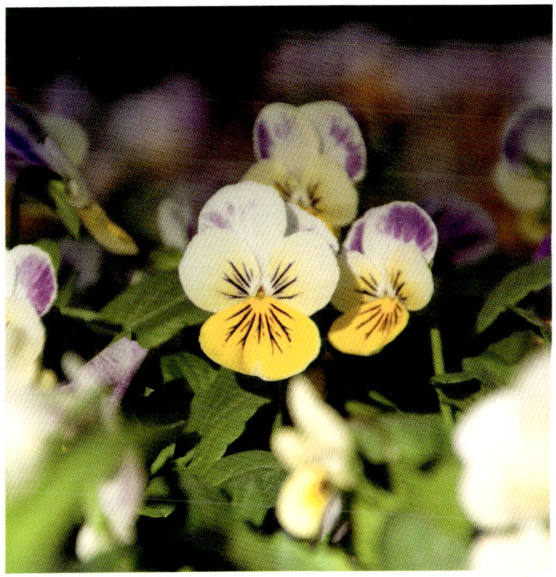

Royal Victoria Patriotic Building

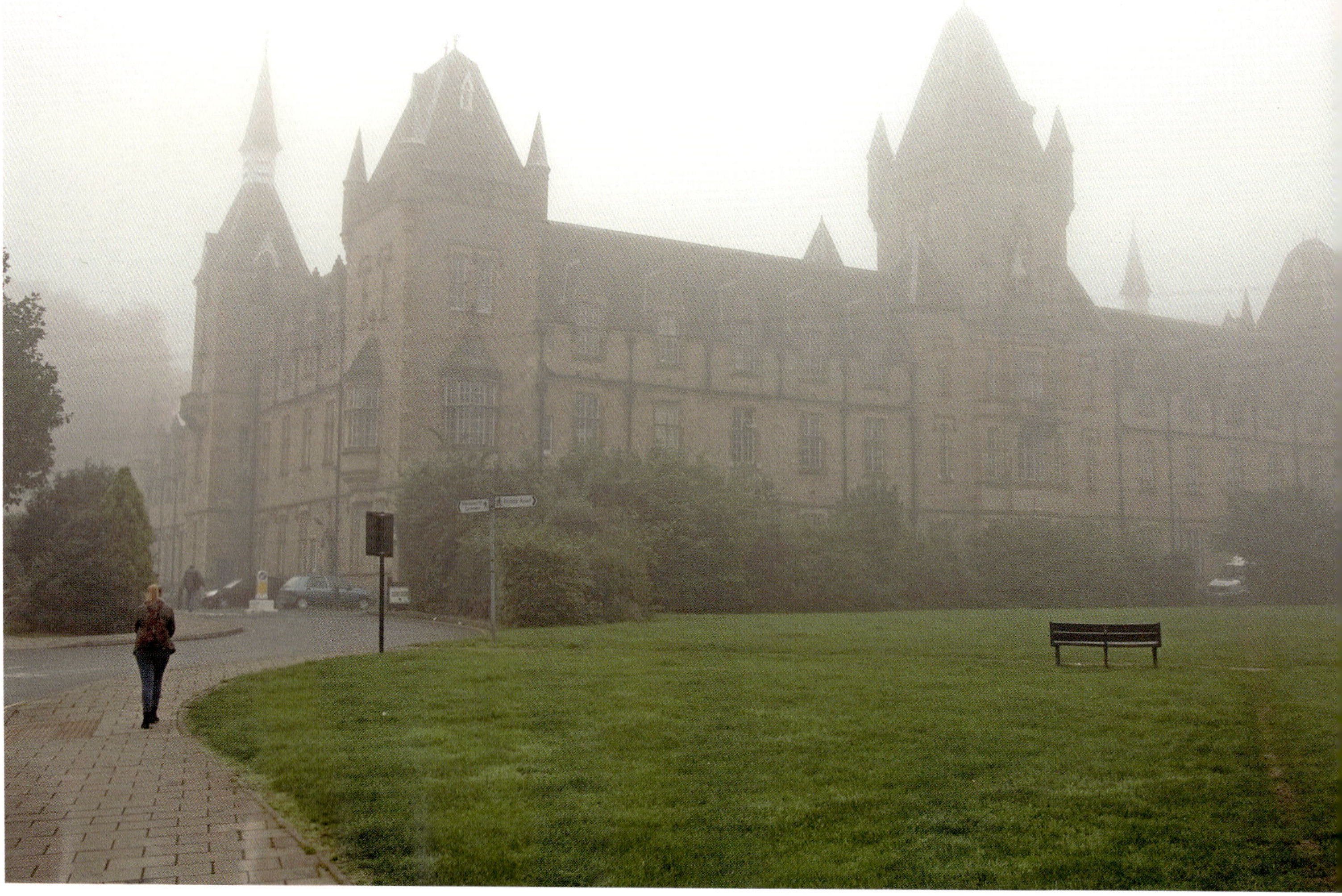

This page and overleaf:
Built in 1859 as an asylum for widows and orphans from the Crimean War, the building now houses offices, homes and a restaurant. Built in the Gothic style, the building was completely restored in the 1980s, which led to it winning several architectural awards. It is interesting to discover that Queen Victoria laid the Foundation Stone in 1857. I am grateful to the British Association for Local History for this snippet – *www.balh.co.uk*

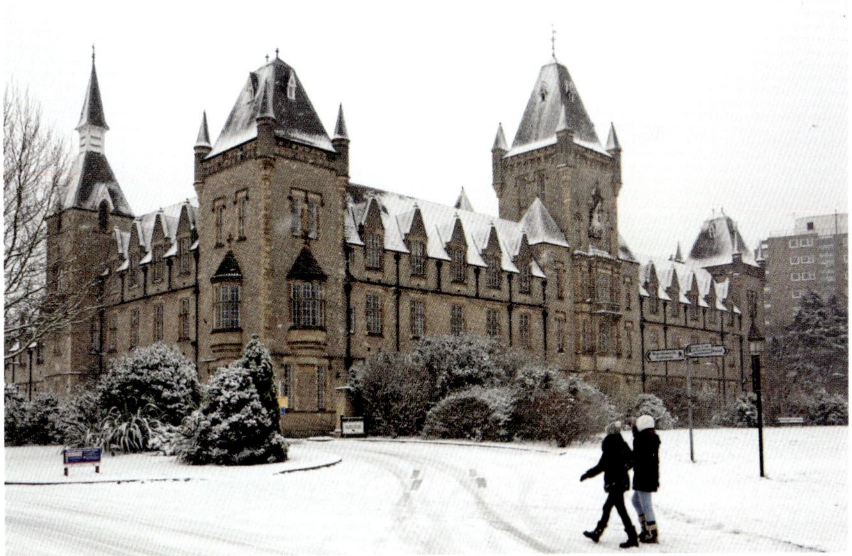

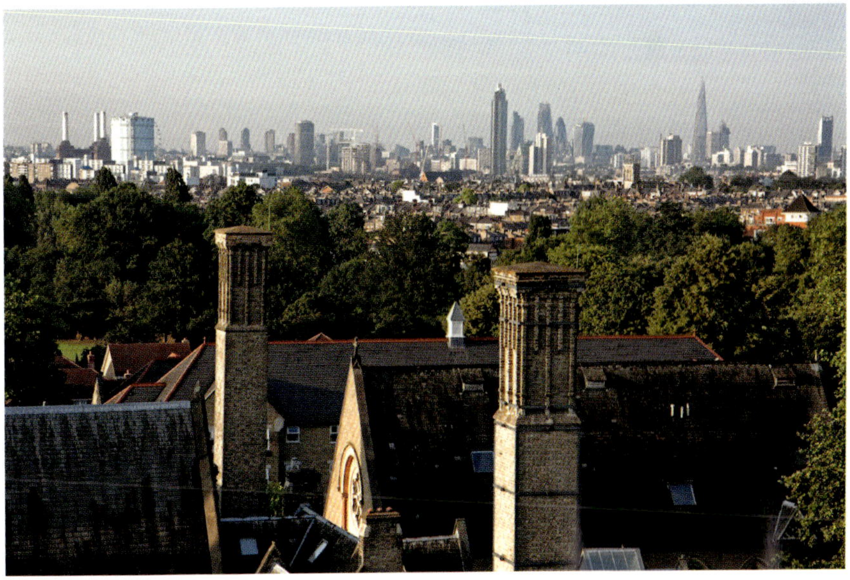

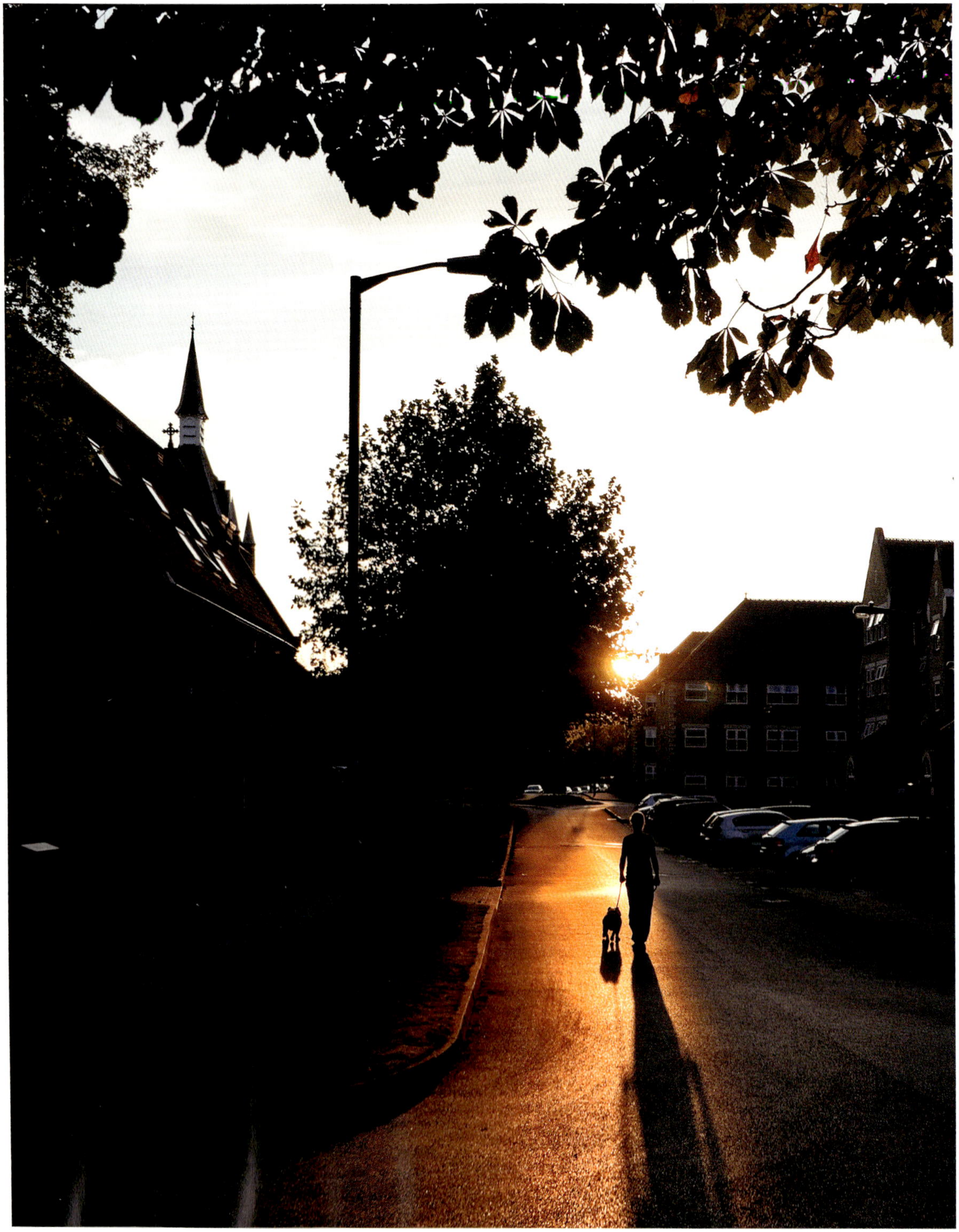

Left: John Archer Way late one summer's evening. In 1913 John Archer became the first black mayor in London, having been a Battersea councillor since 1906. His mother Mary Theresa Burns was Irish, so he can also be called the first Irish Mayor of Battersea!

Overleaf: The Royal Victoria Patriotic Building and London beyond from the large flats alongside. A huge thank you to Teresa and George from Morville House for letting me into their home one evening last summer to take this picture.

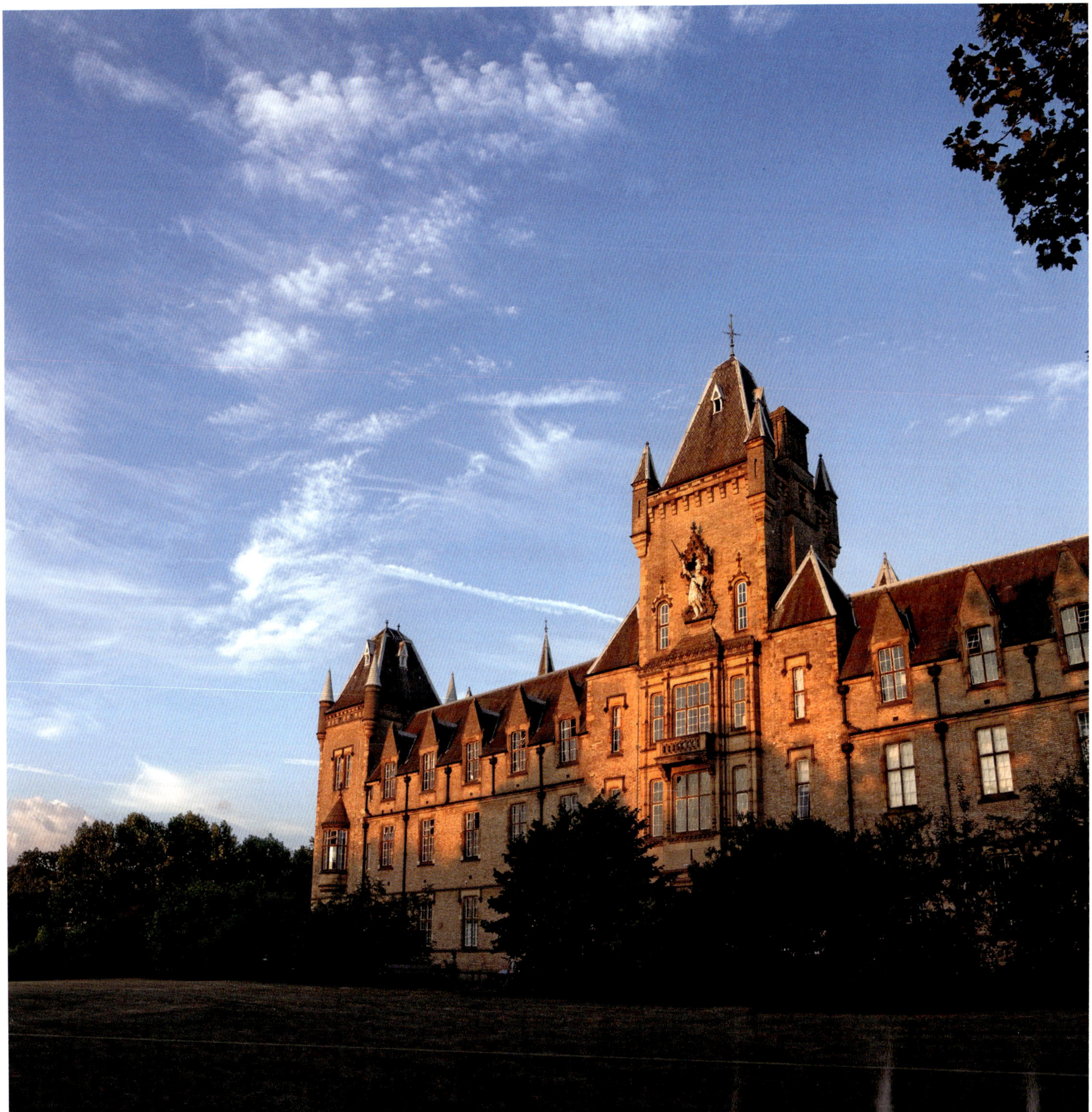

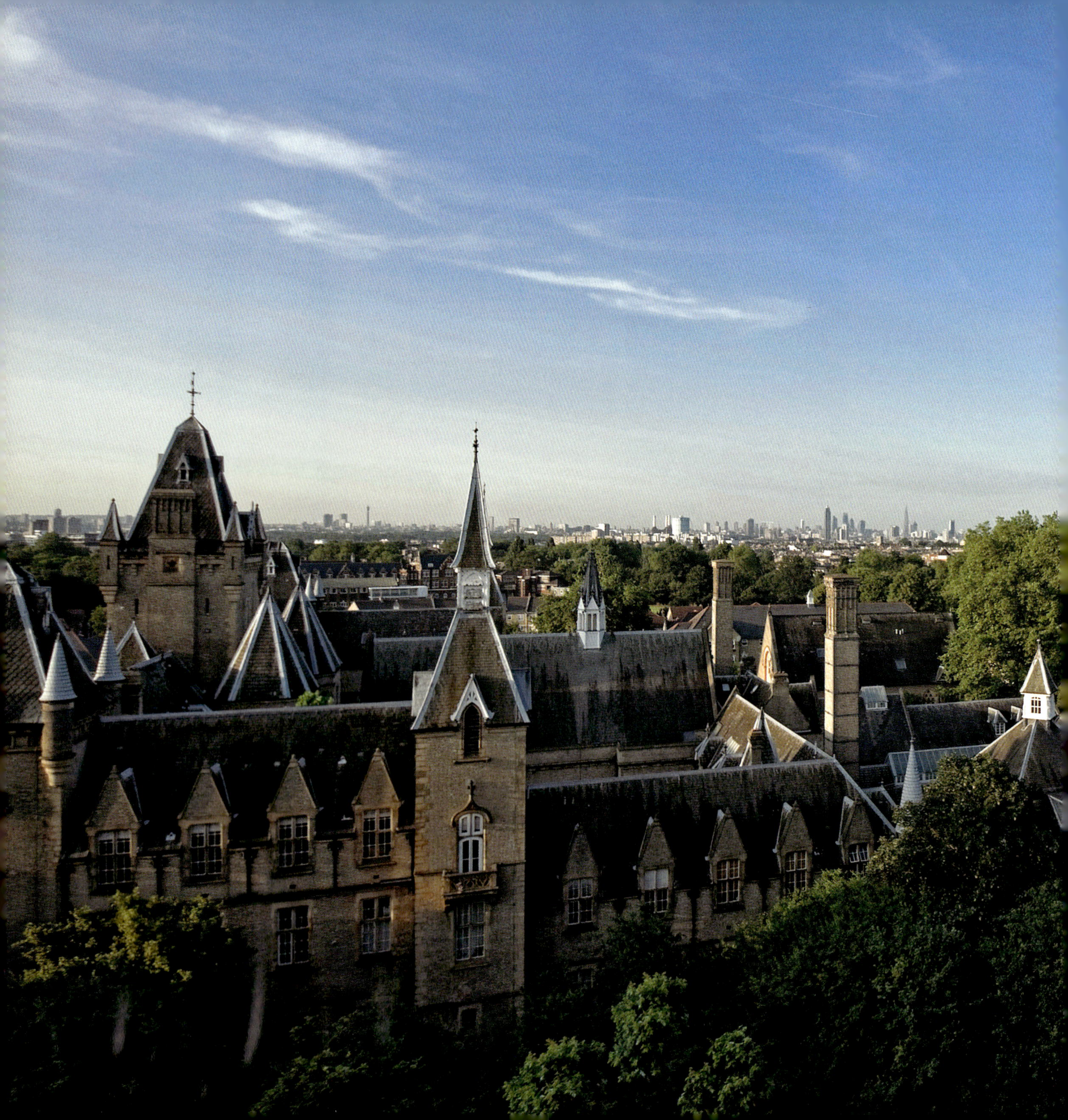

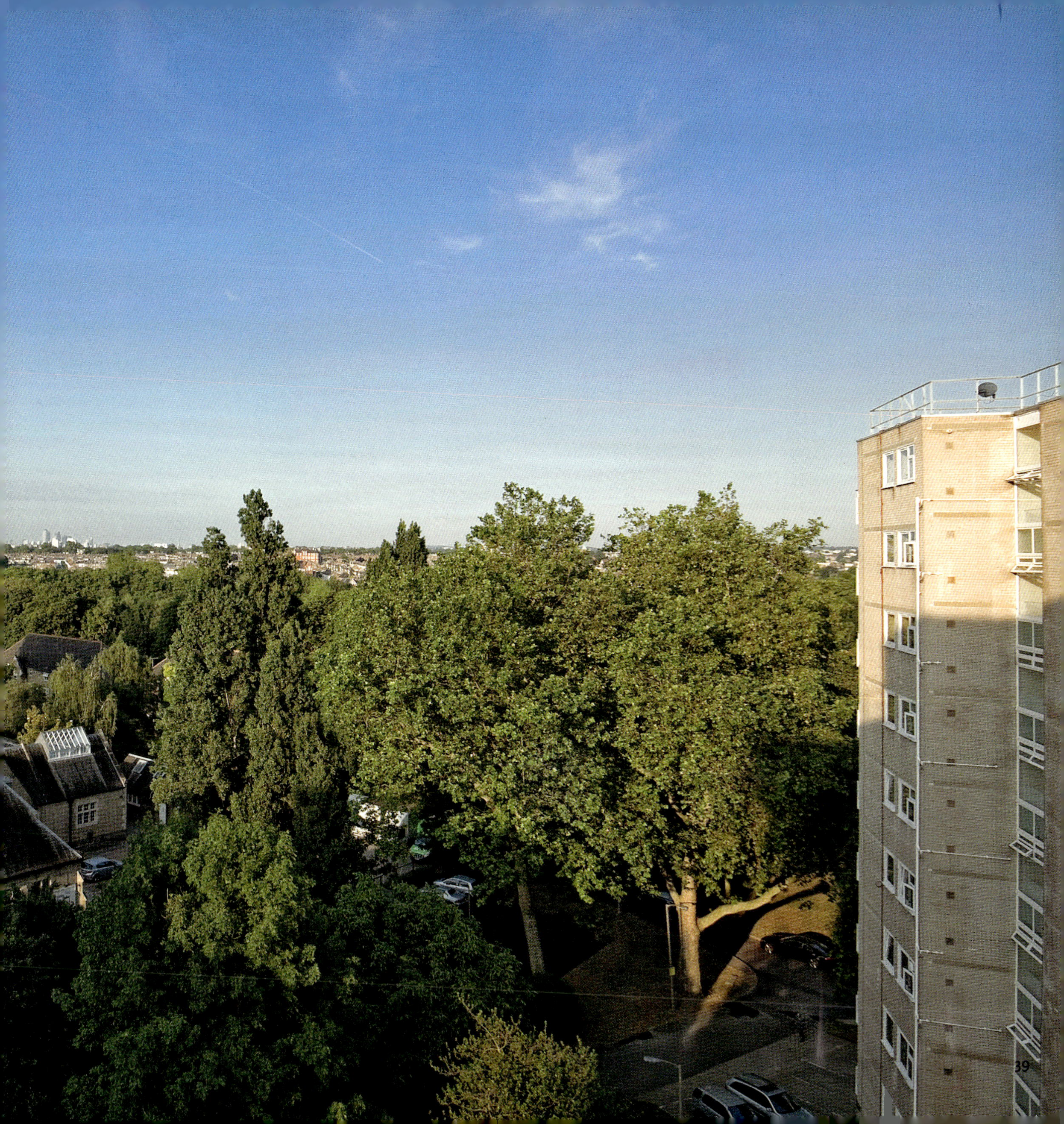

Trinity Road and Fields

This page: Trinity Road in summer and autumn.

Opposite and overleaf: Trinity Fields is great space for cricket and I am grateful to Nishit and the others from the Sinjun Grammarians Cricket Club for allowing me in to take these pictures of them at play. The club takes its phonetic name from the old Sir Walter St. John ('Sinjun') Grammar School, now known as 'Thomas's Battersea', on Battersea High Street.

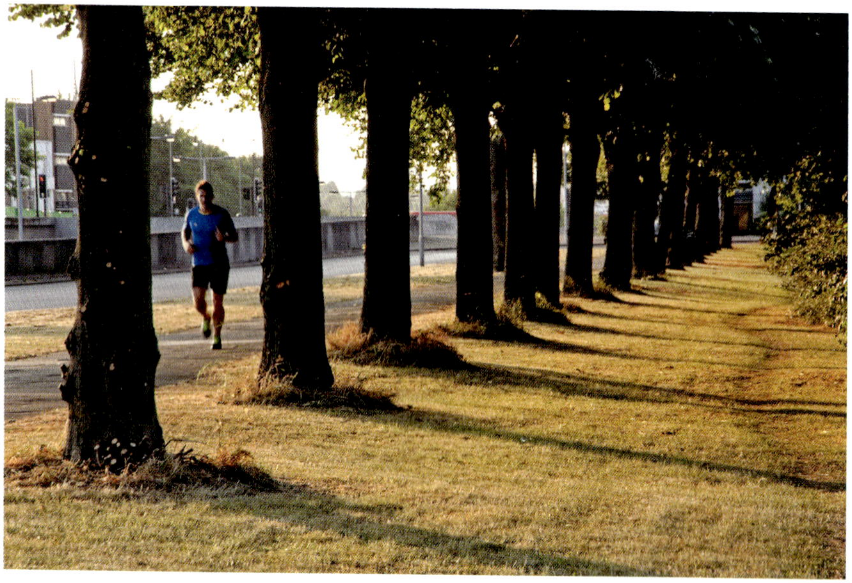

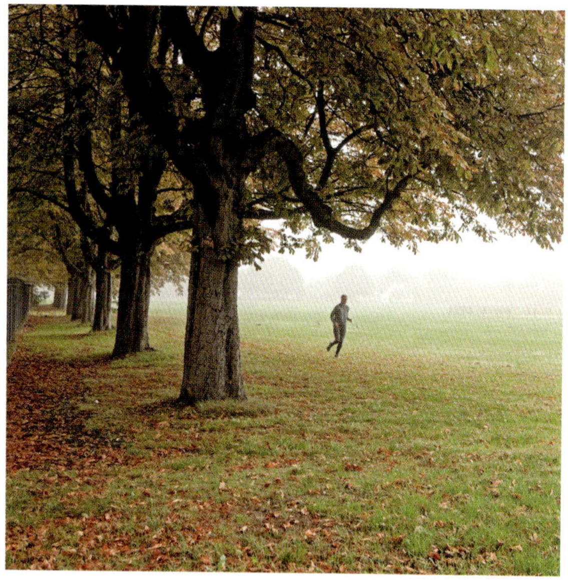

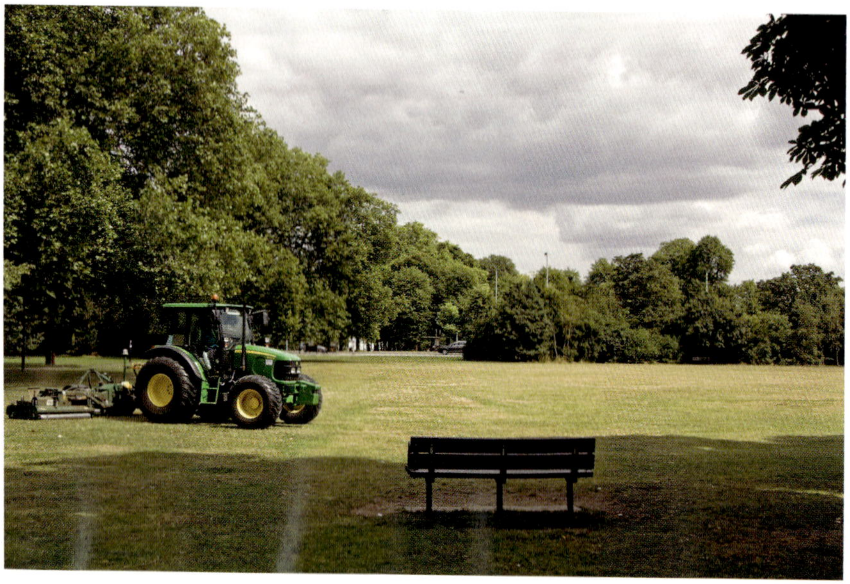

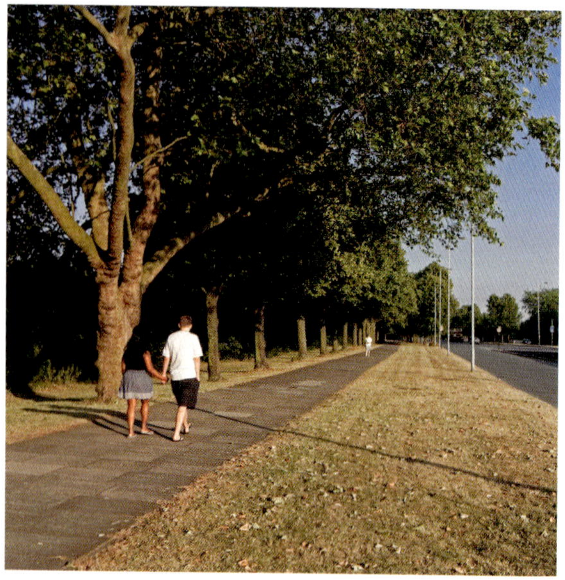

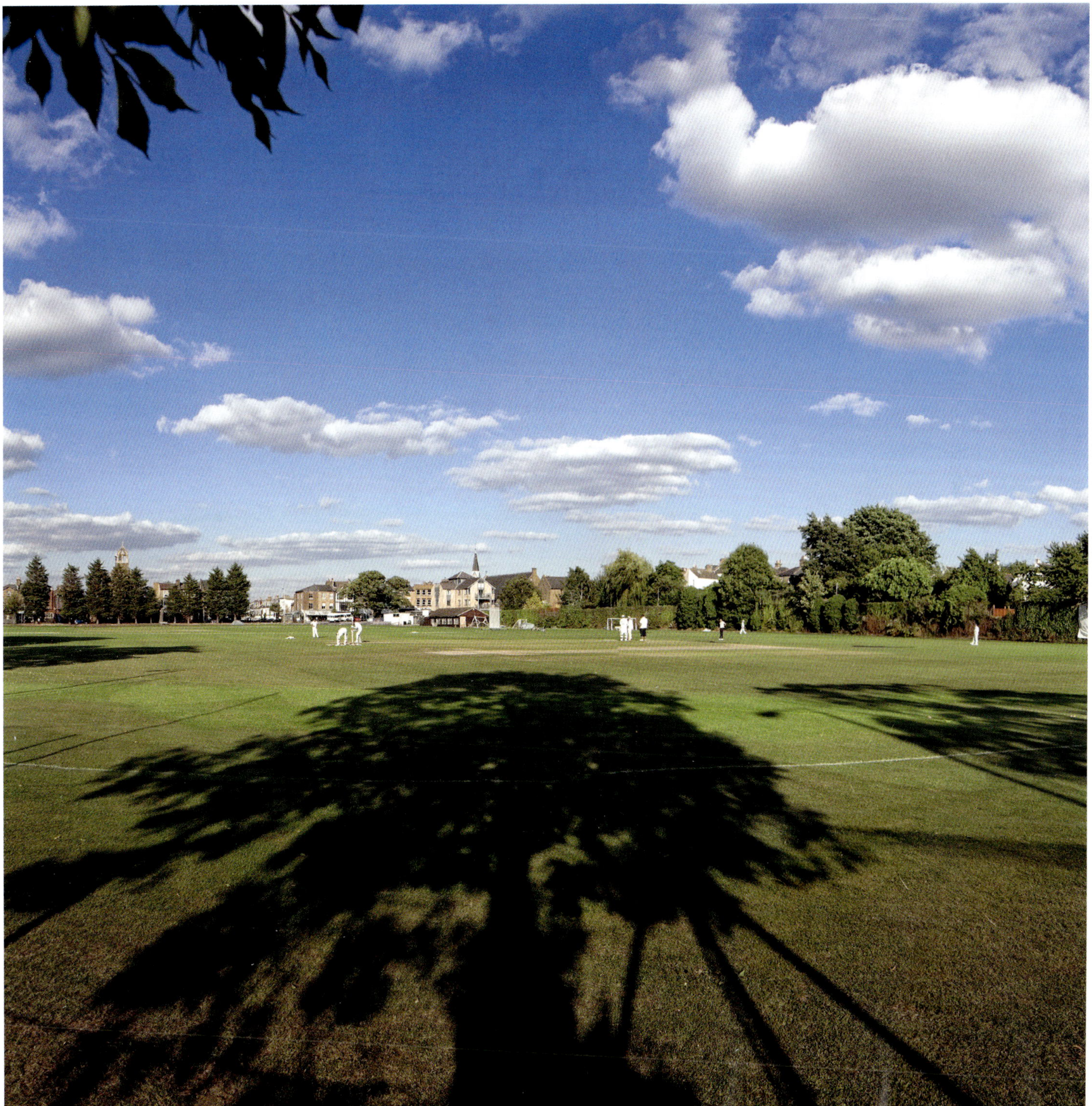

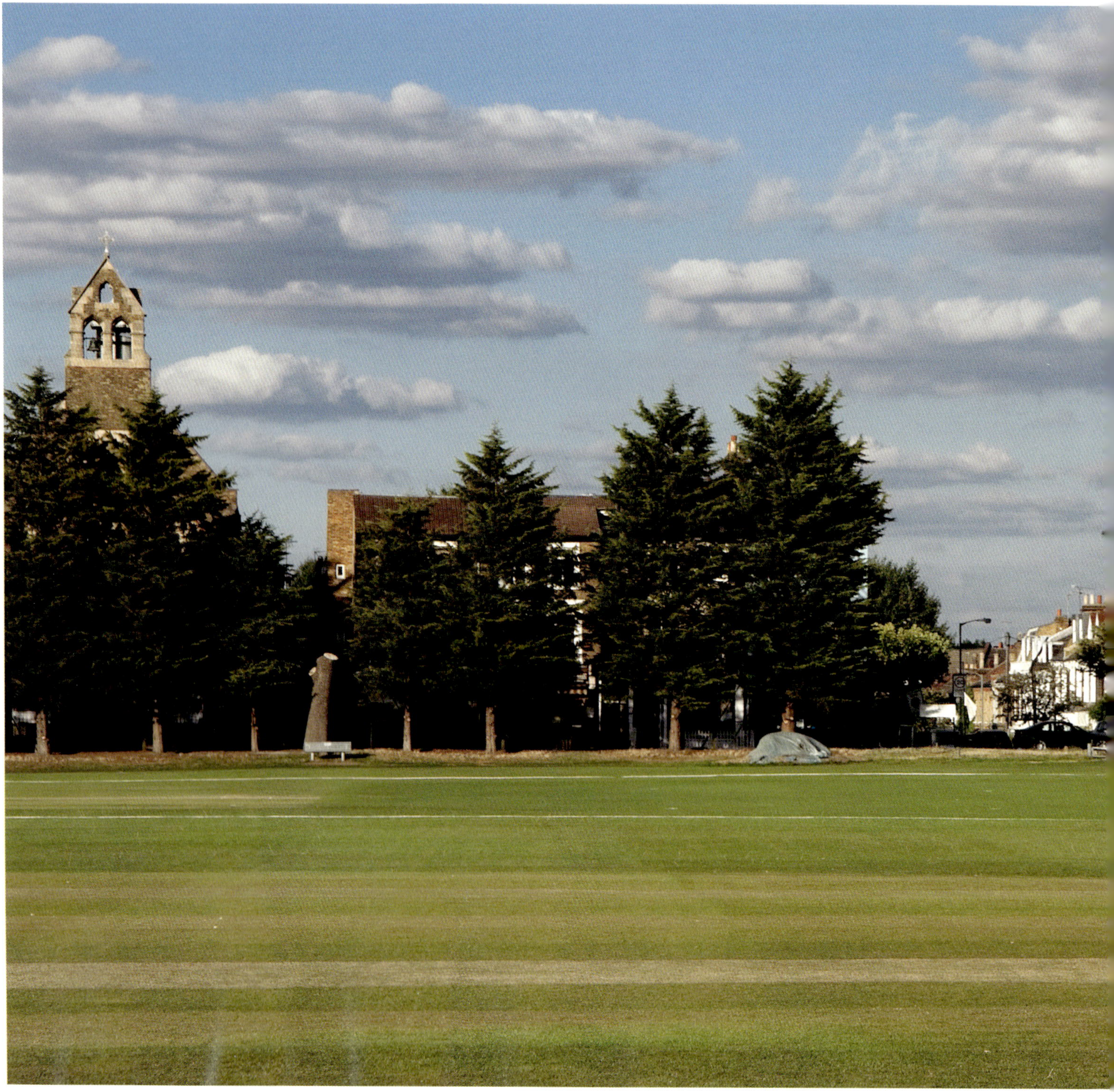

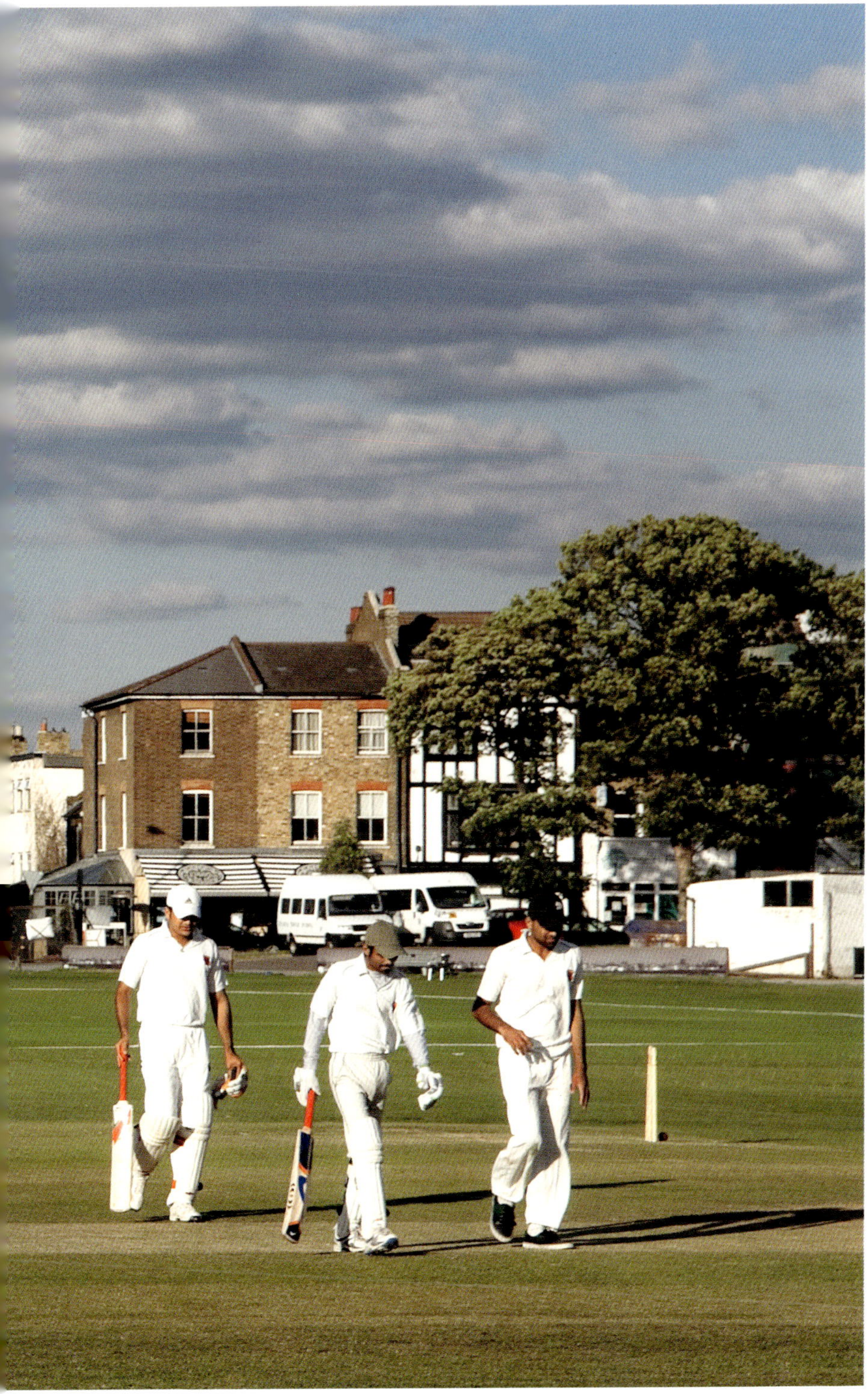

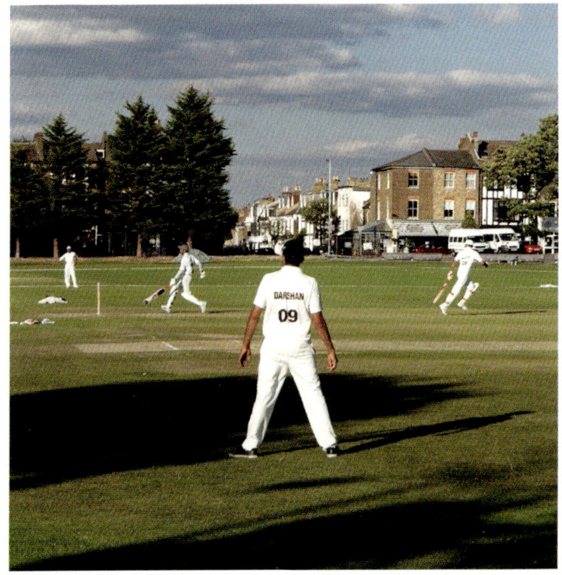

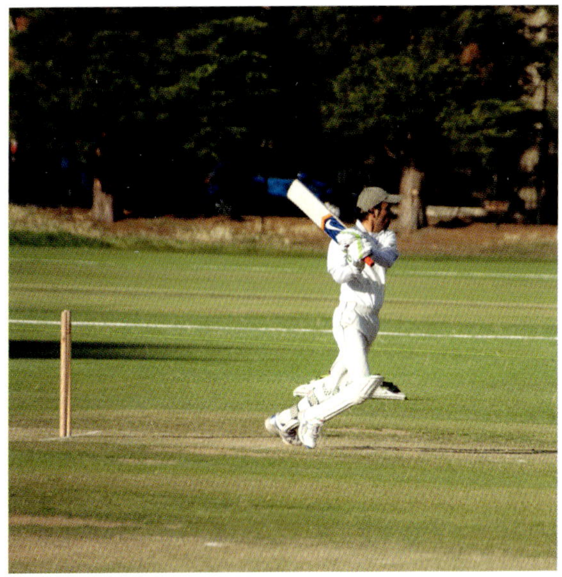

This spread: Cricket on Trinity Fields.

This page: A stormy sky on Trinity Road, looking east across Wandsworth Common.

Opposite top: Wandsworth Prison: Built in 1851, it was then known as the Surrey House of Correction. This is where in 1965 the notorious Great Train robber Ronnie Biggs escaped. Prone to the odd fantasy, I did wonder as I stood taking this picture if I was about to witness someone else coming over the wall and climbing into this fast car waiting outside.

Opposite bottom: The large towers of the Fitzhugh Grove Estate, alongside the Trinity Road and beside Wandsworth Common.

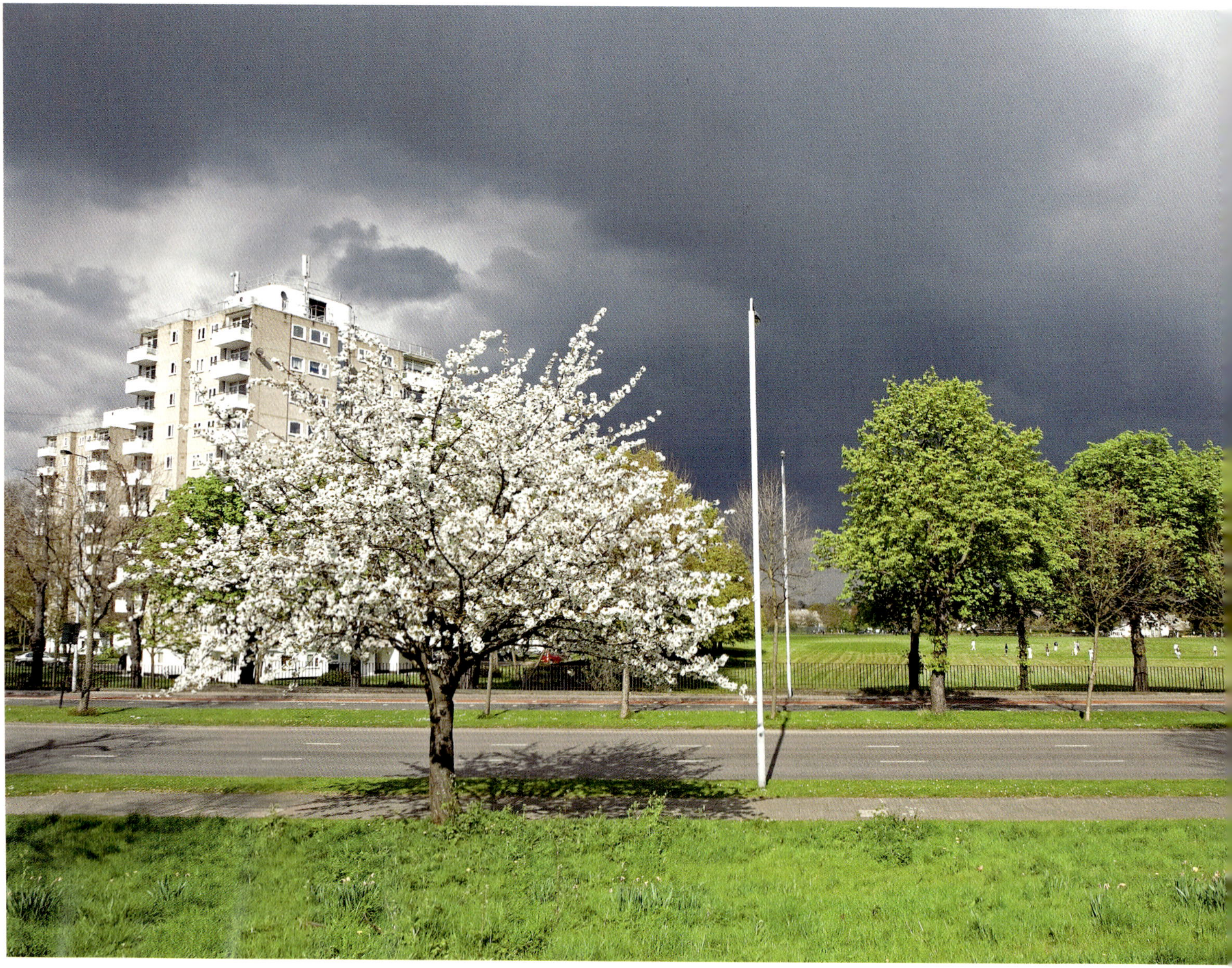

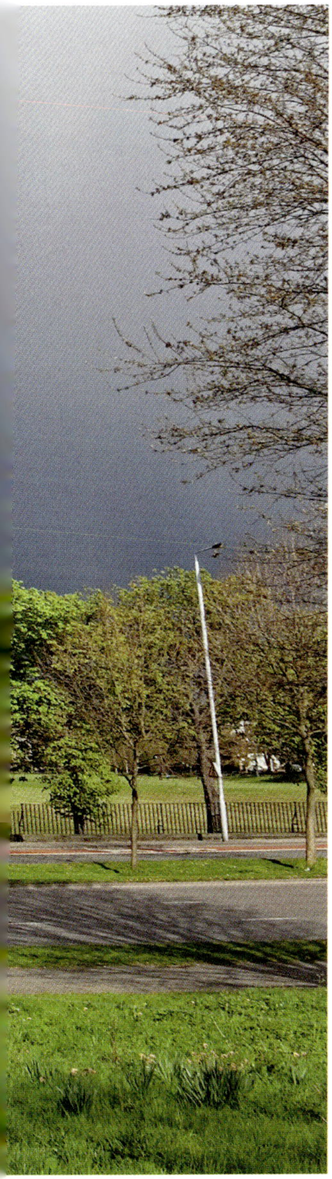

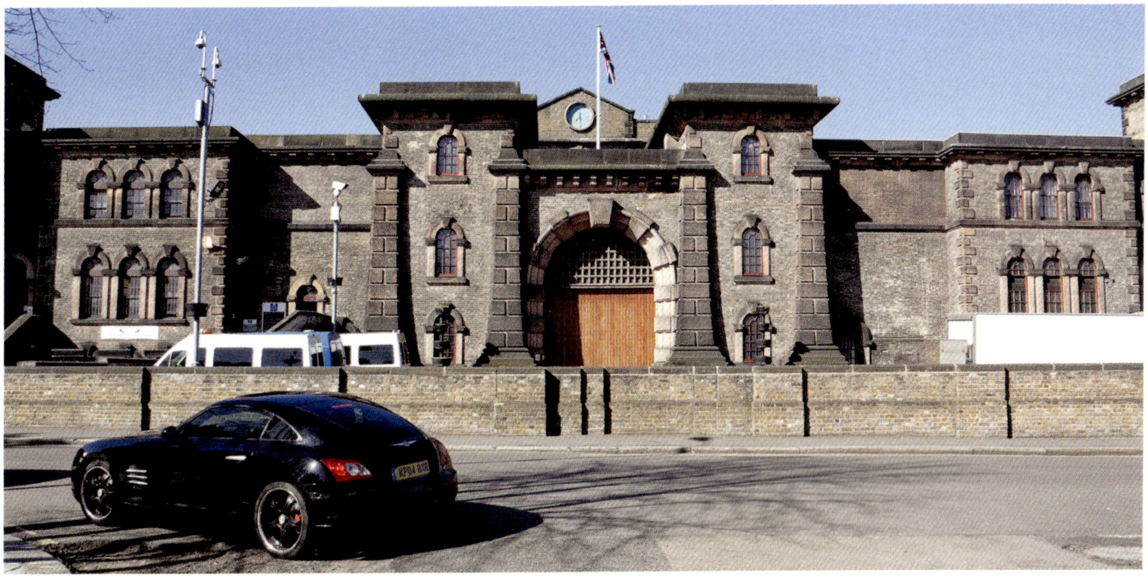

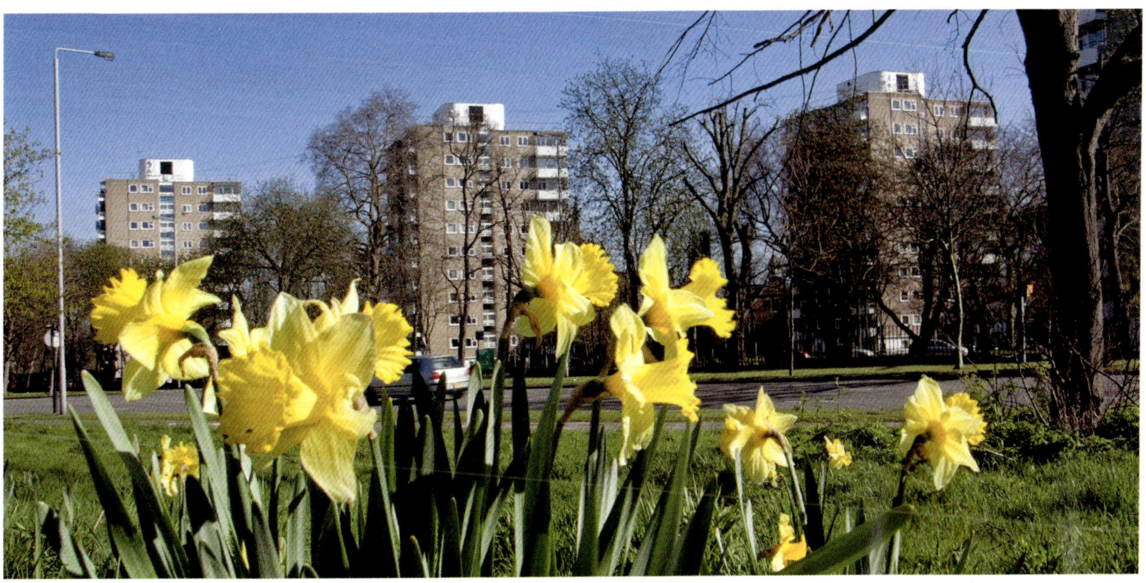

East of the Railway Line

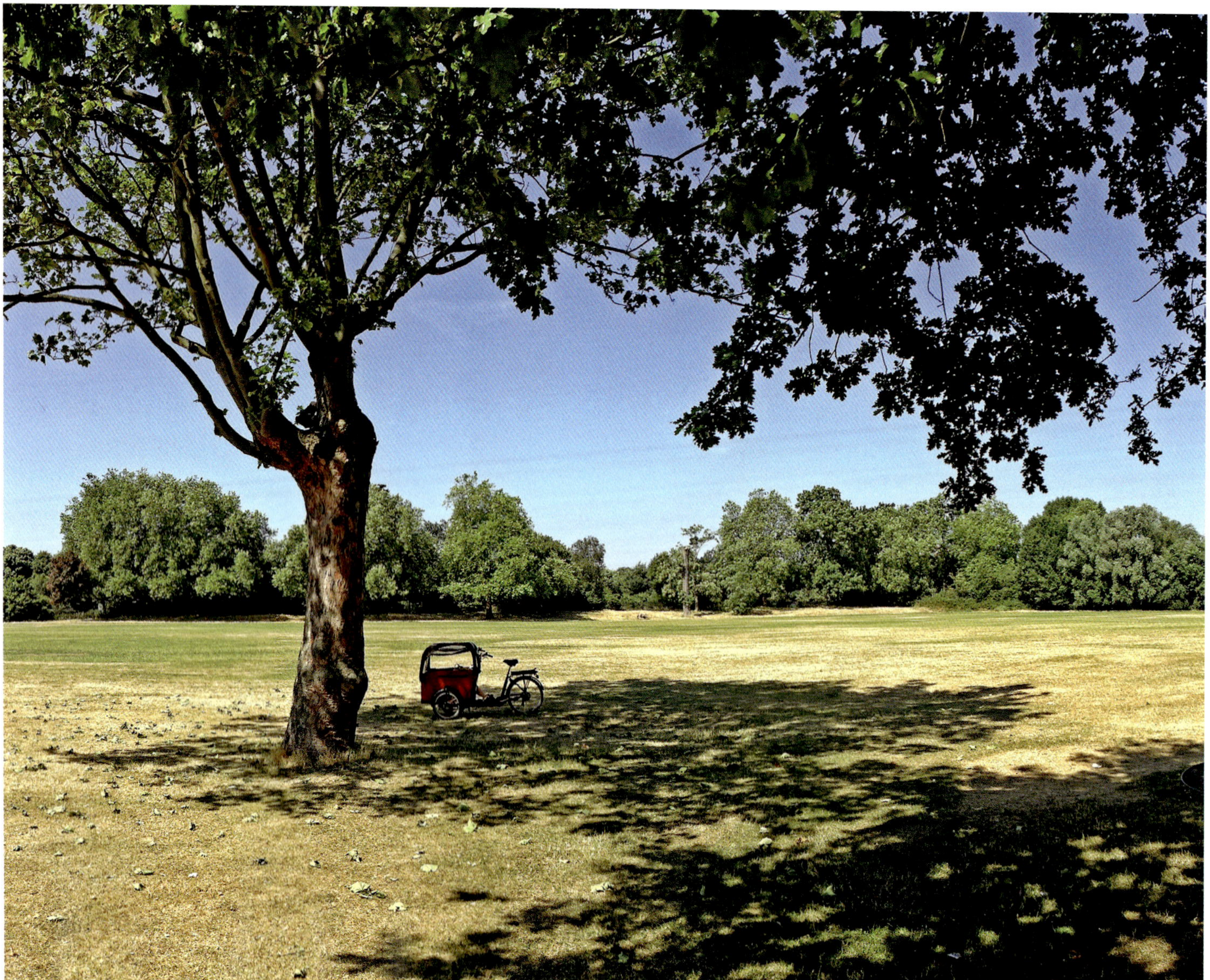

This page: We had a good summer in 2013, with a period of extremely hot weather in July, which made the common look very much like the Savannah. I love the way the council now cut the grass, with a machine spitting out huge bales. You could almost be in the country.

Overleaf: On Saturday mornings during the season you can always find lots of chidren playing extremely competitive football.

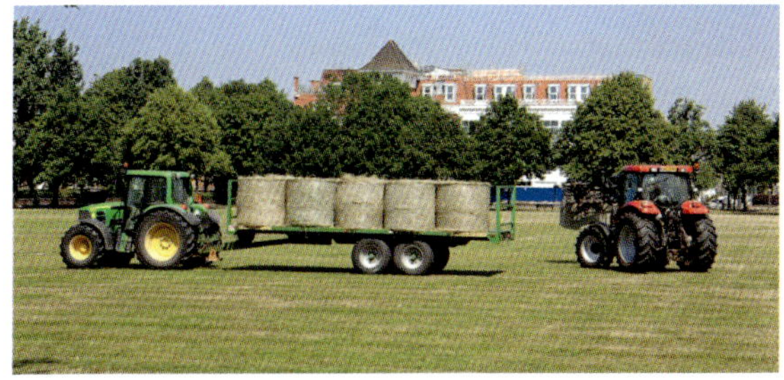

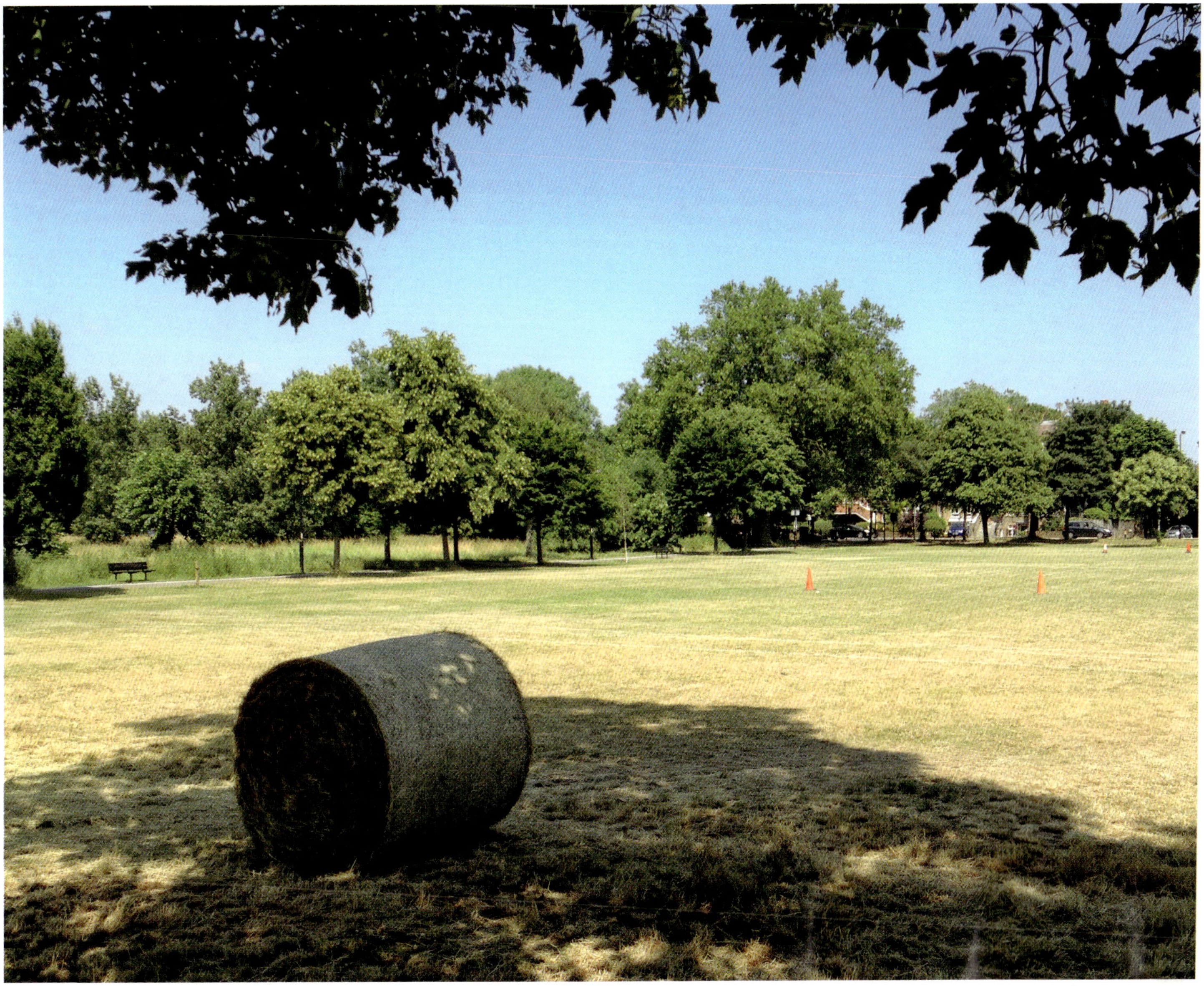

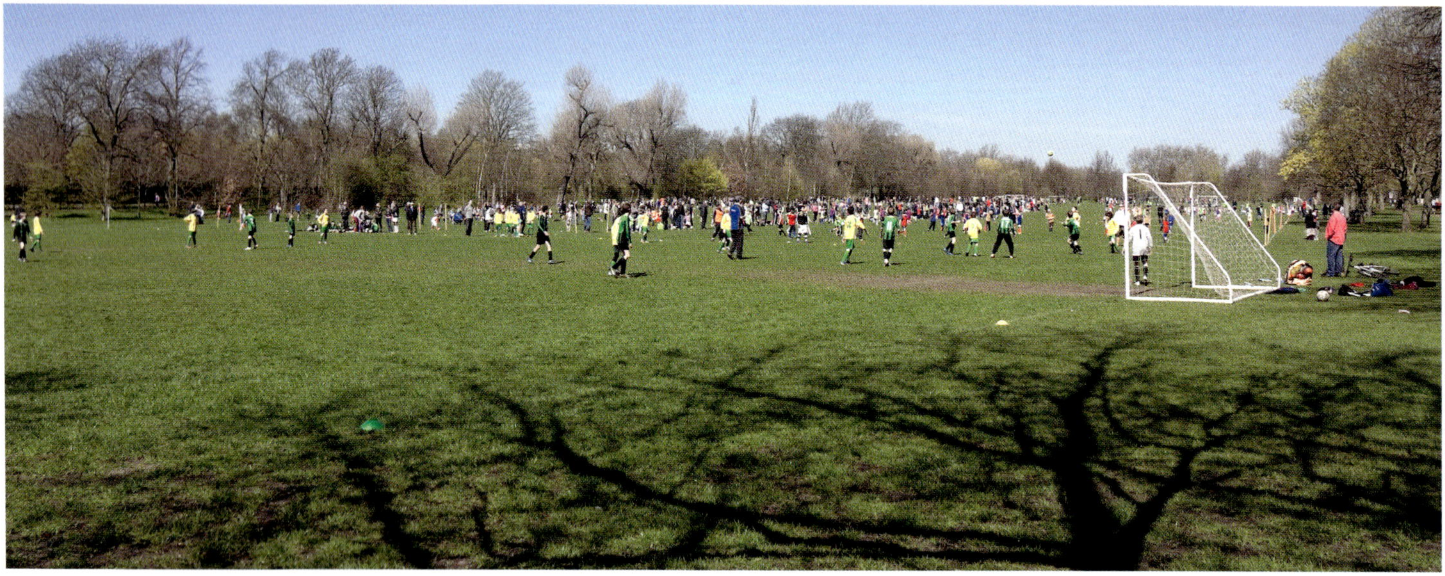

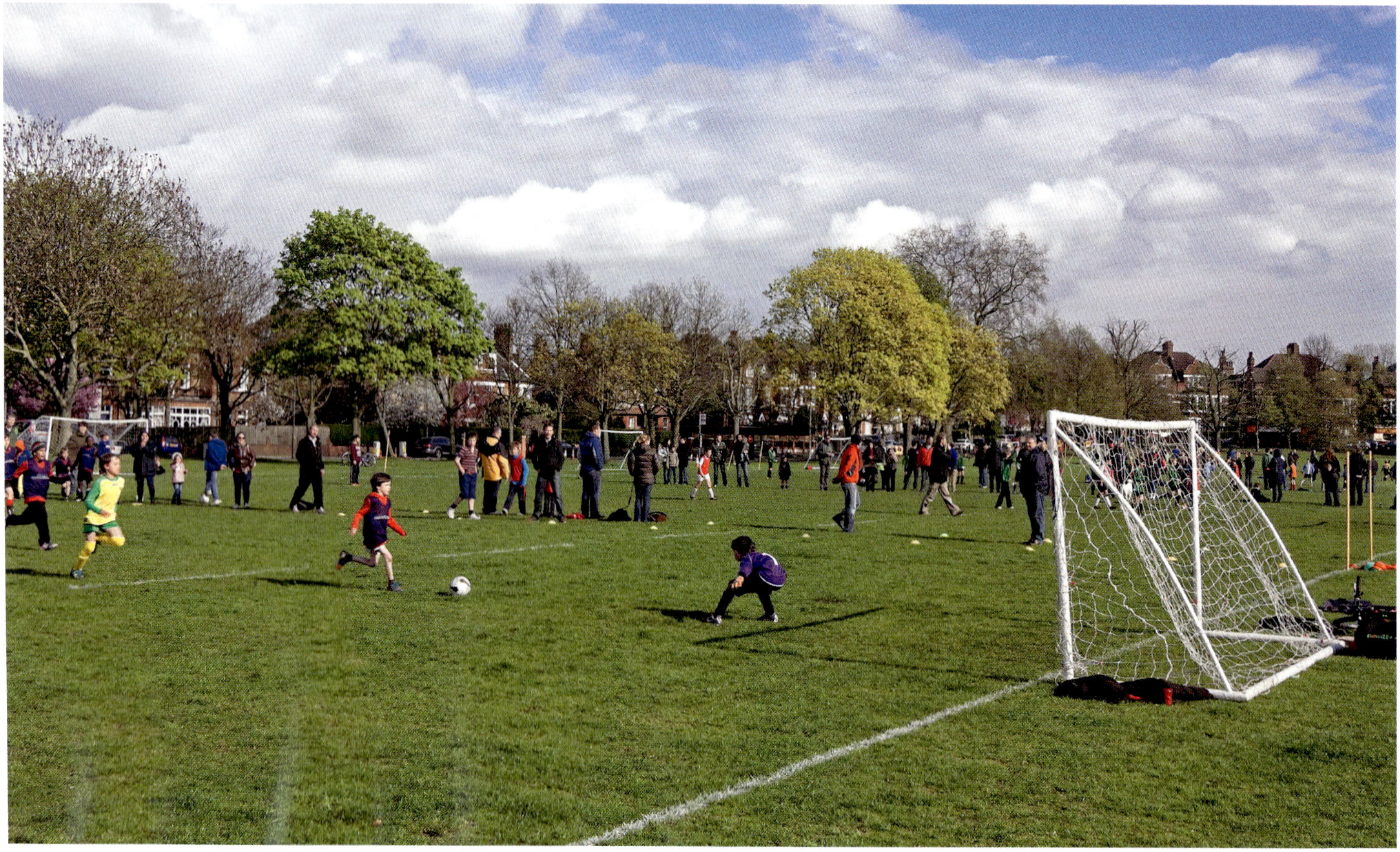

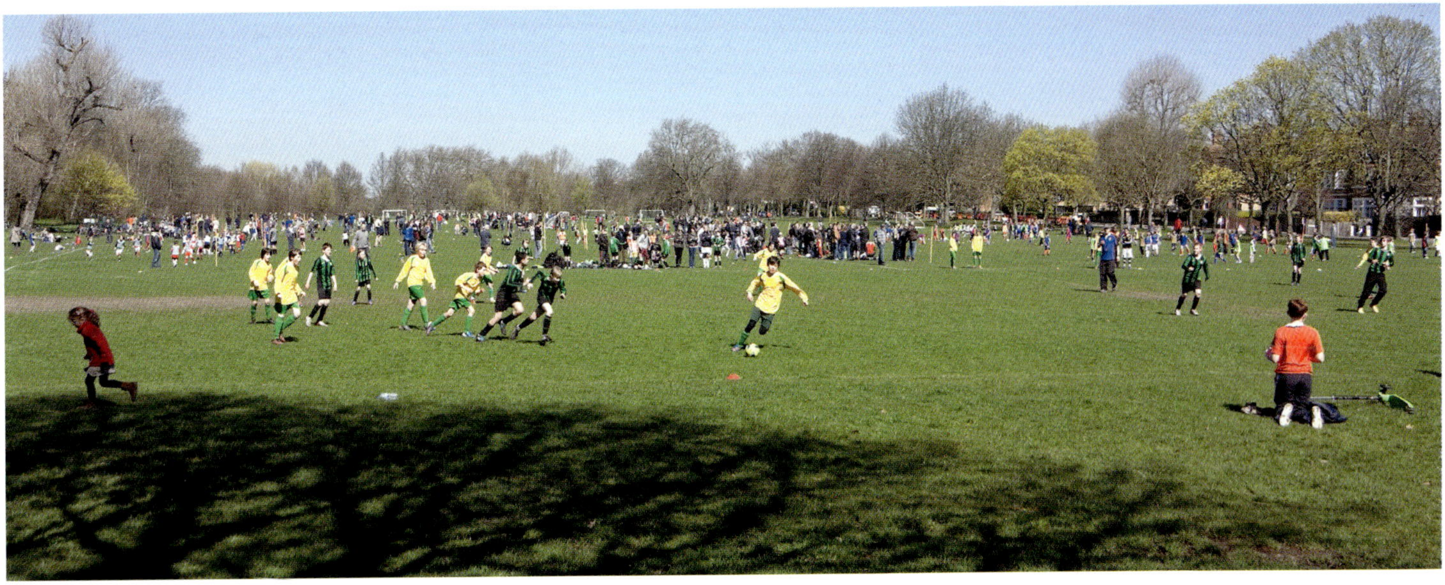

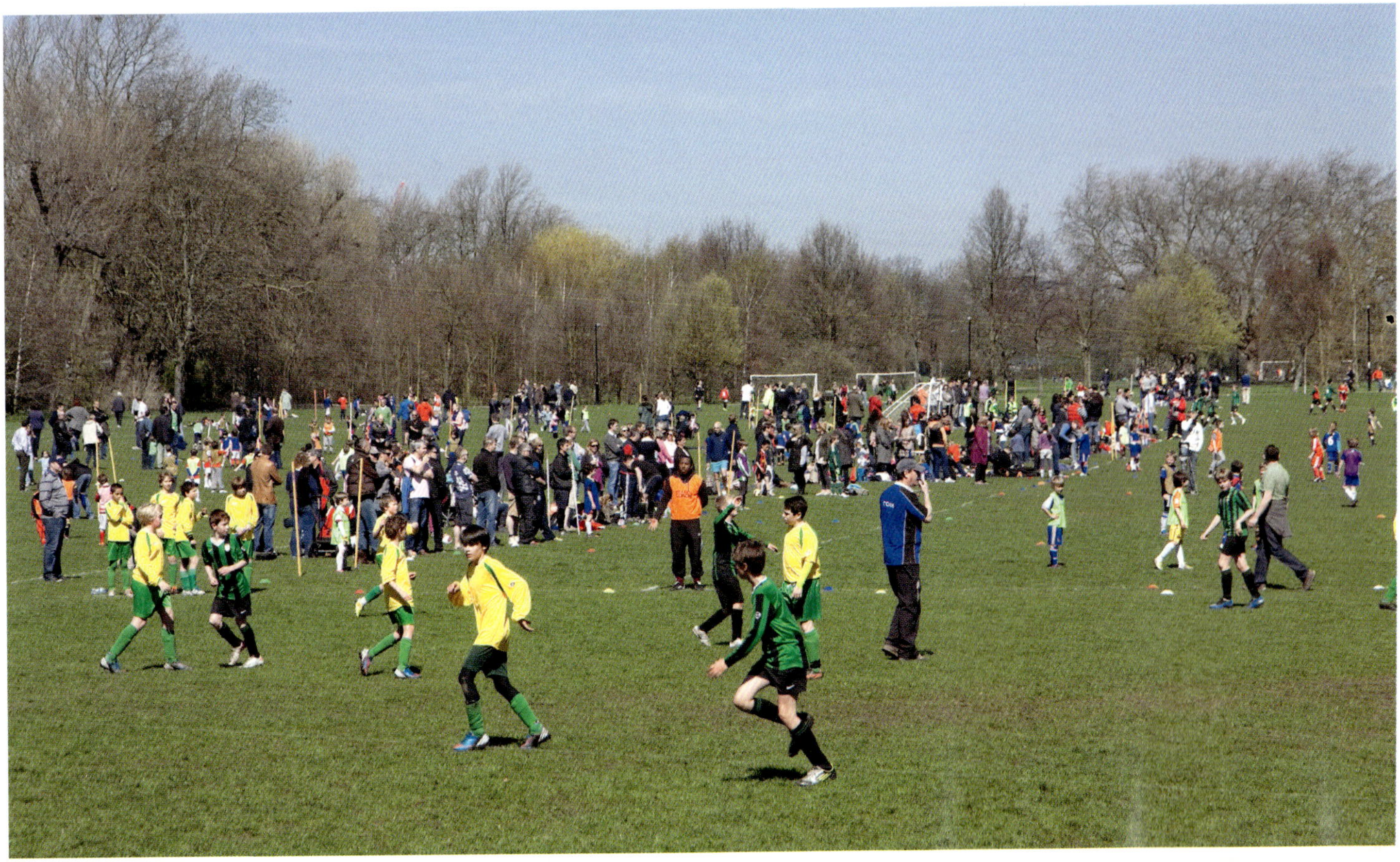

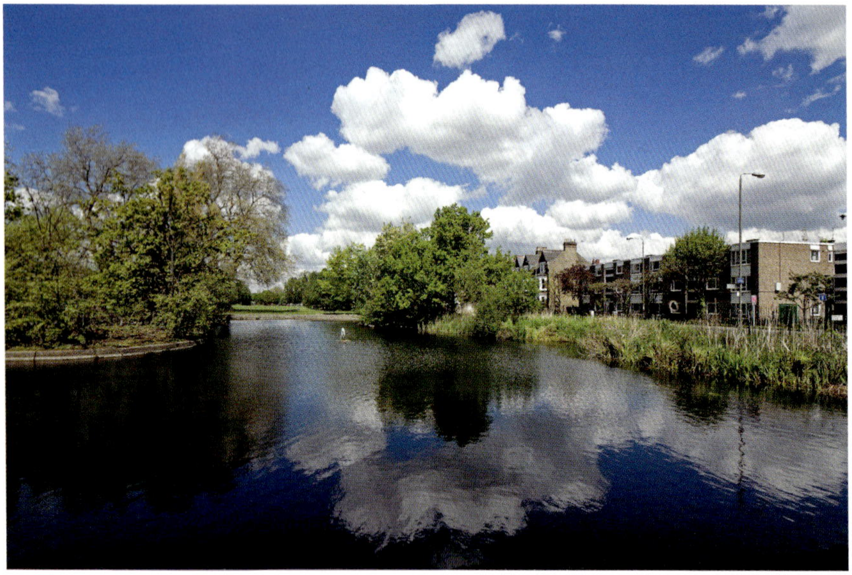

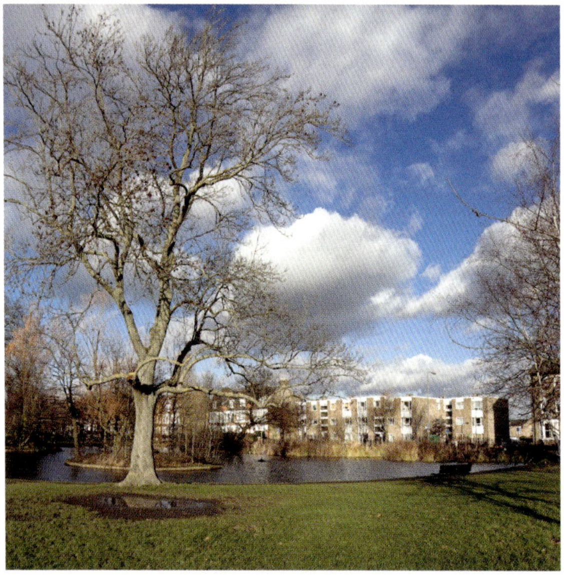

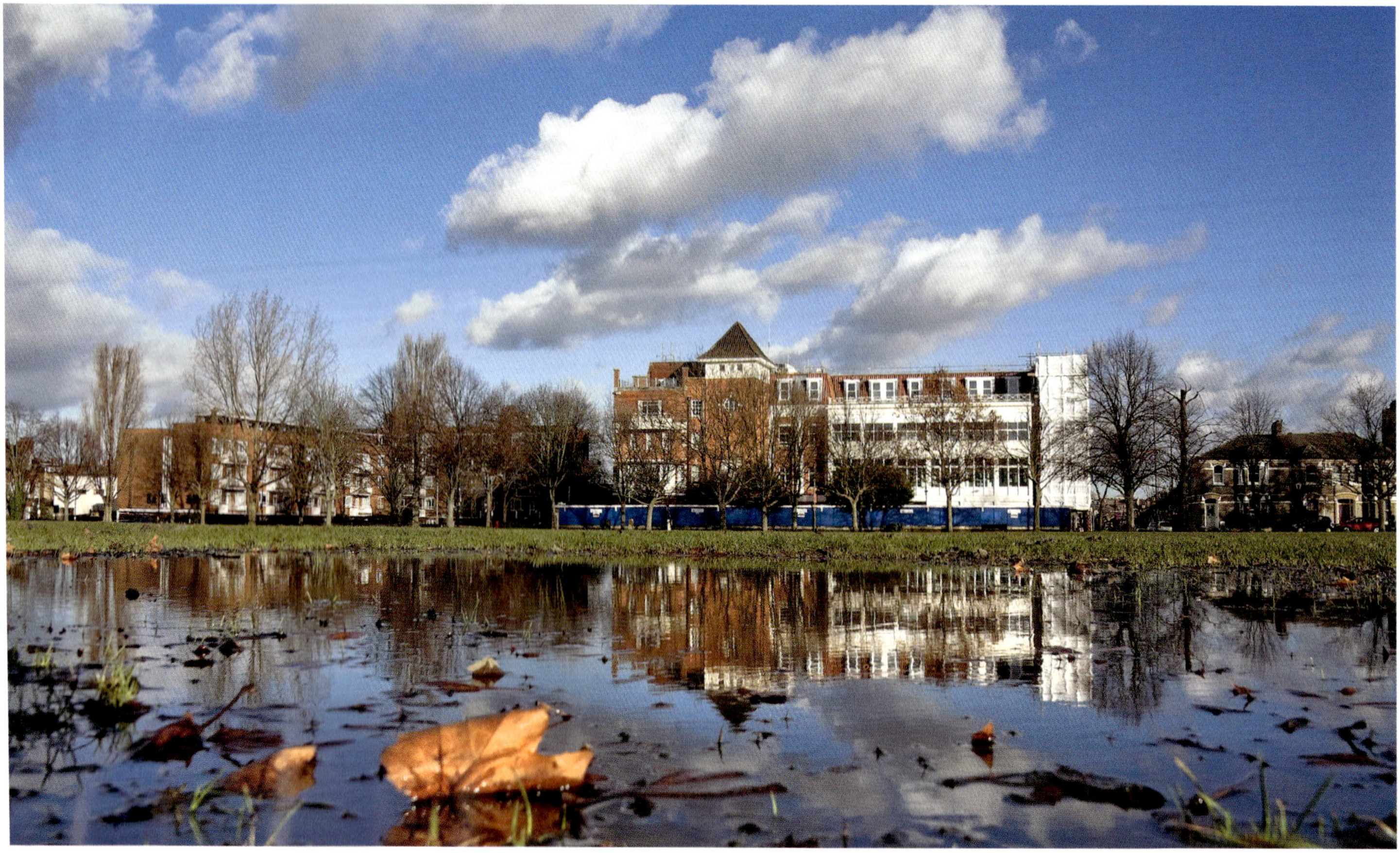

This page and opposite top: Bolingbroke Grove Stock Pond, through spring, summer and autumn.

Opposite bottom: Bolingbroke Grove with the old hospital now a school in the middle, as reflected in a puddle on the common. 2013 started very wet, which resulted in pools of water collecting on the common whenever it rained.

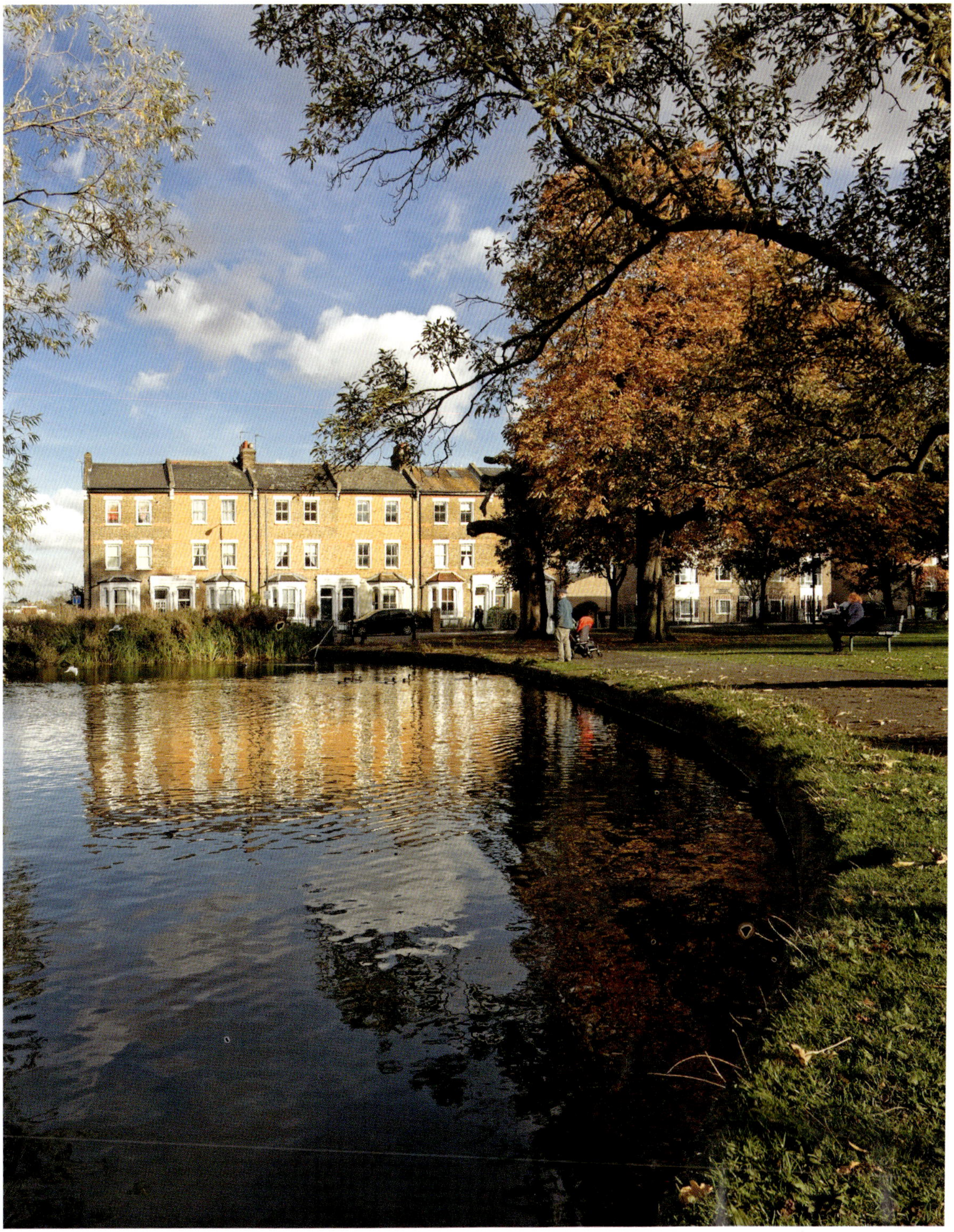

In the Snow

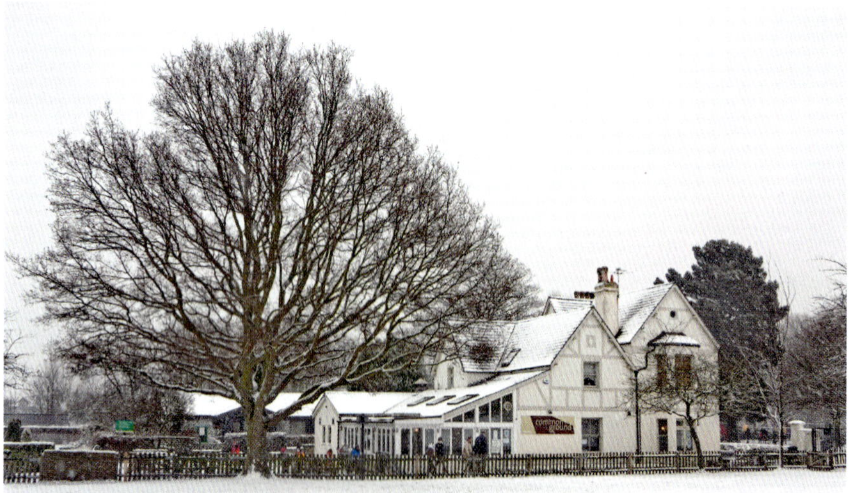

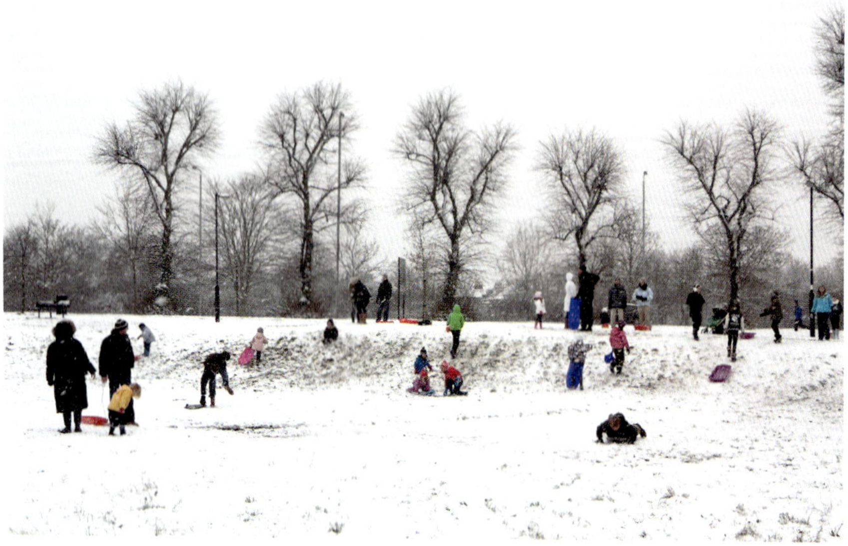

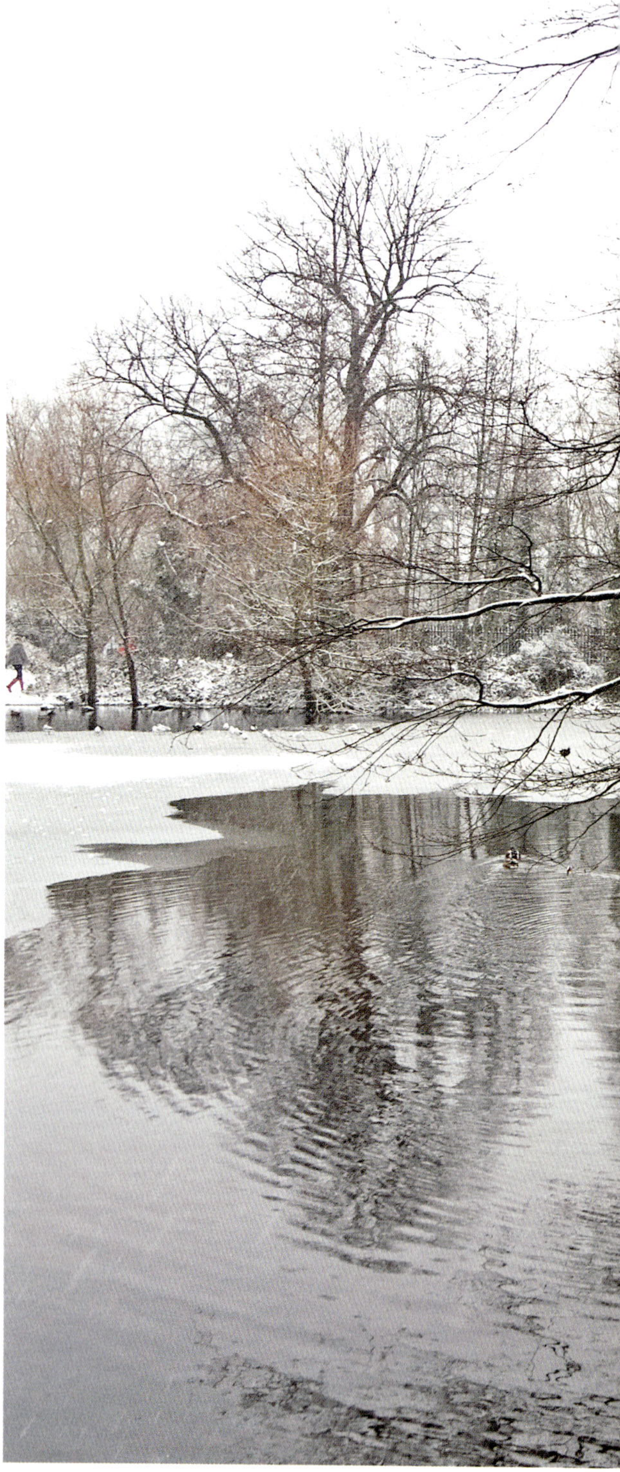

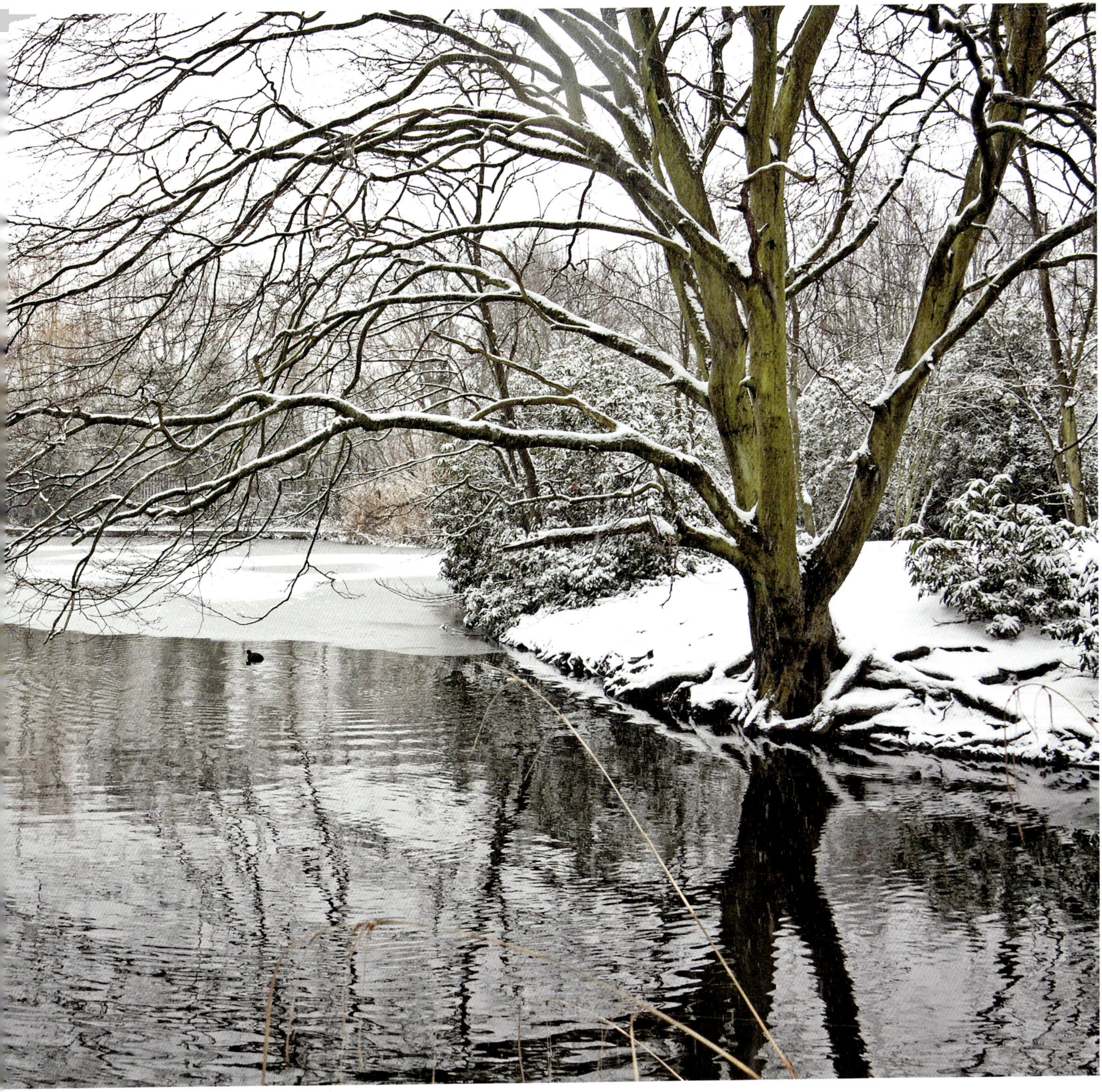

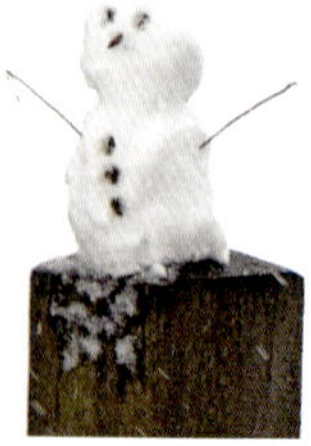

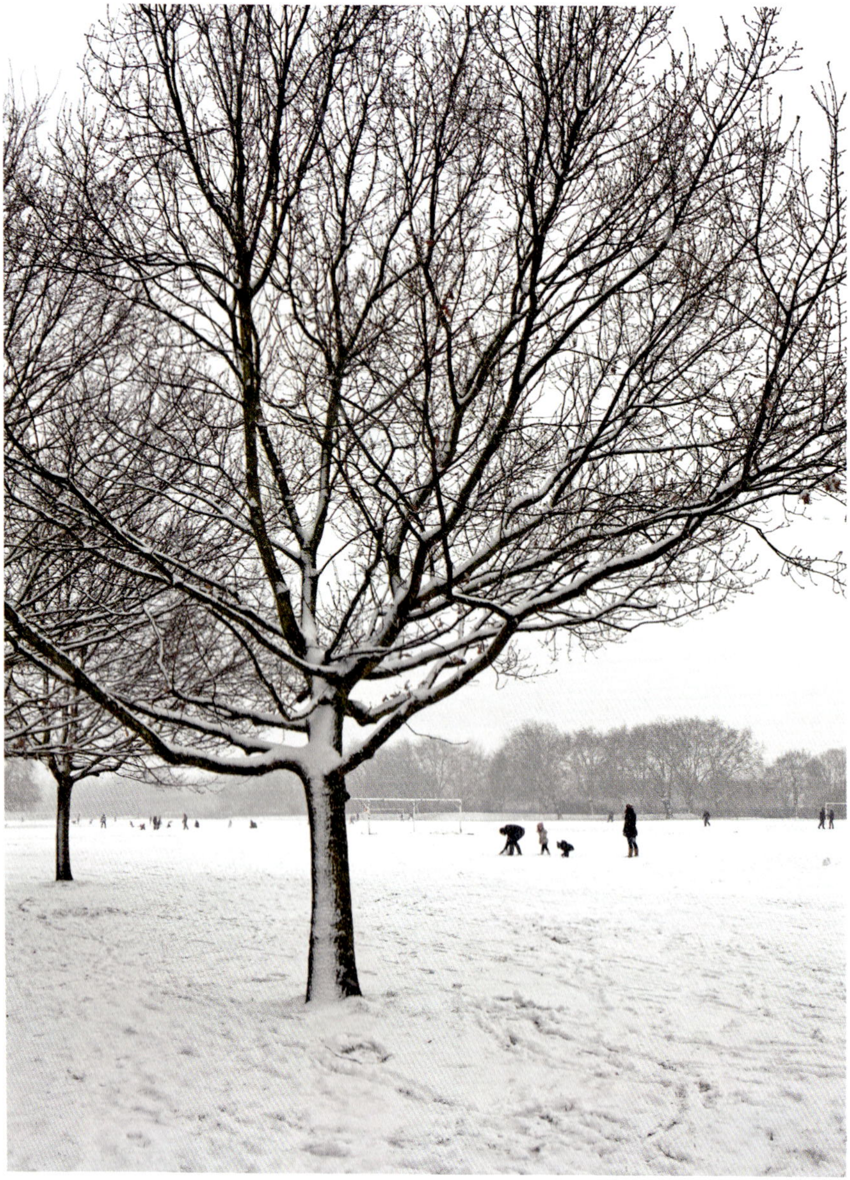

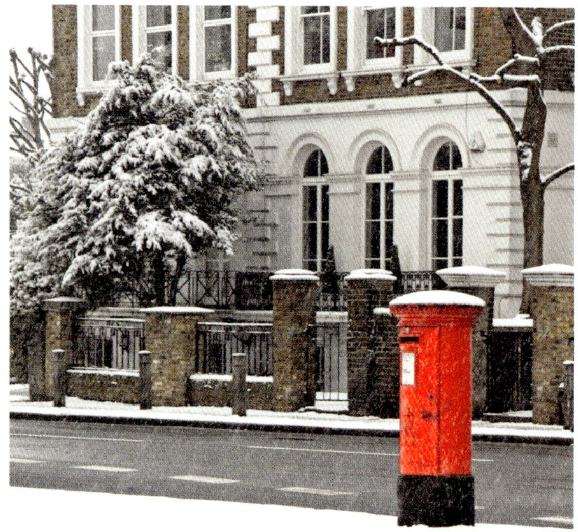

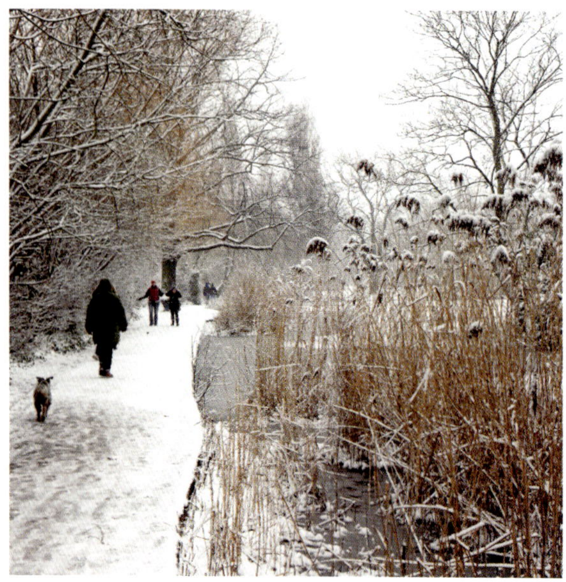

Previous page; main picture: The large lake.

Top left: The Common Ground cafe.

This spread: Wandsworth Common North Side.

Bottom: The large lake.

Below left: The stock pond.

Below right: the large lake, with its distinctive little bridge.

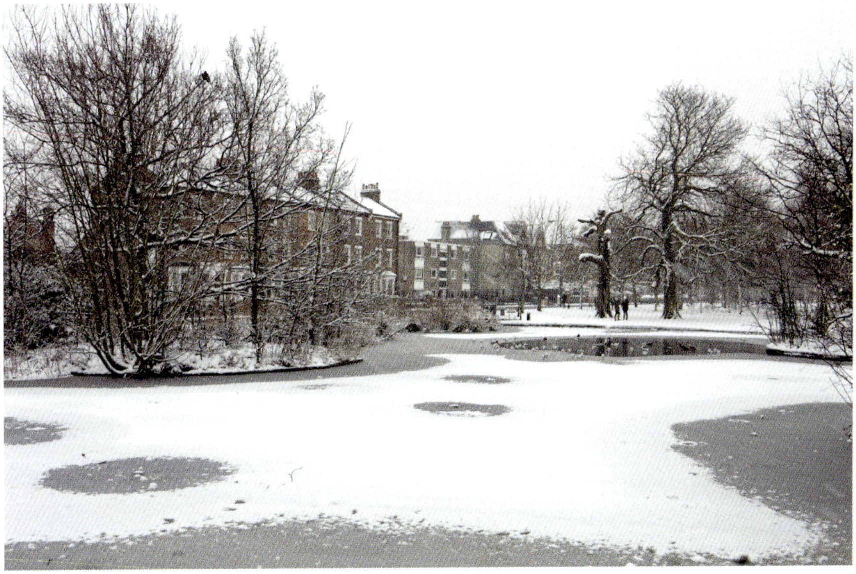

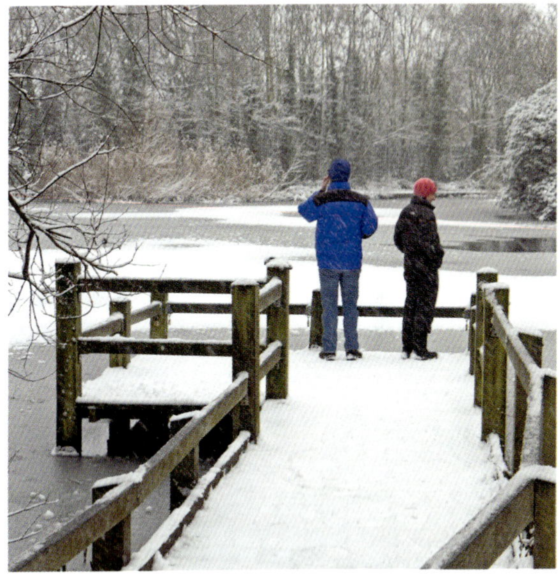

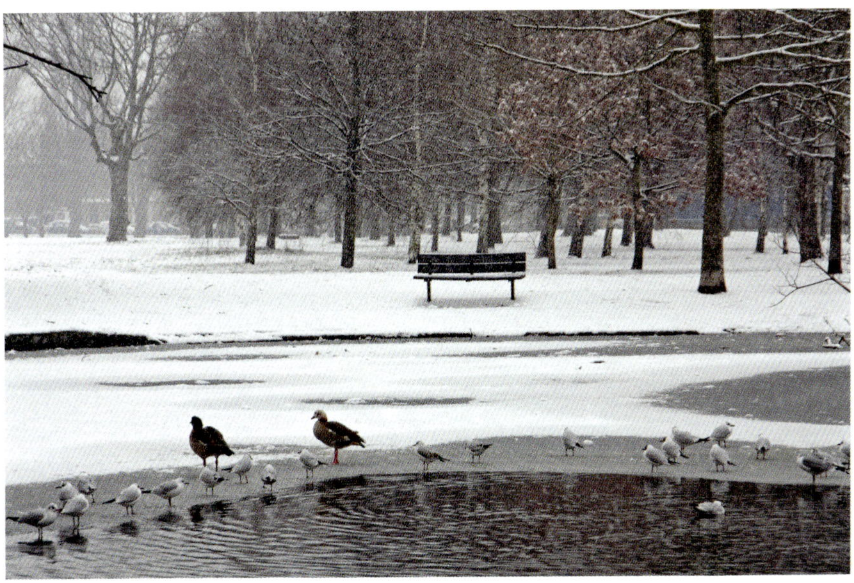

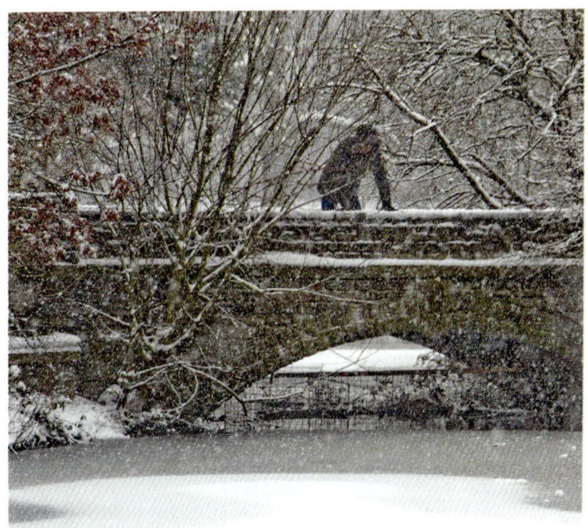

Wandsworth Common Westside

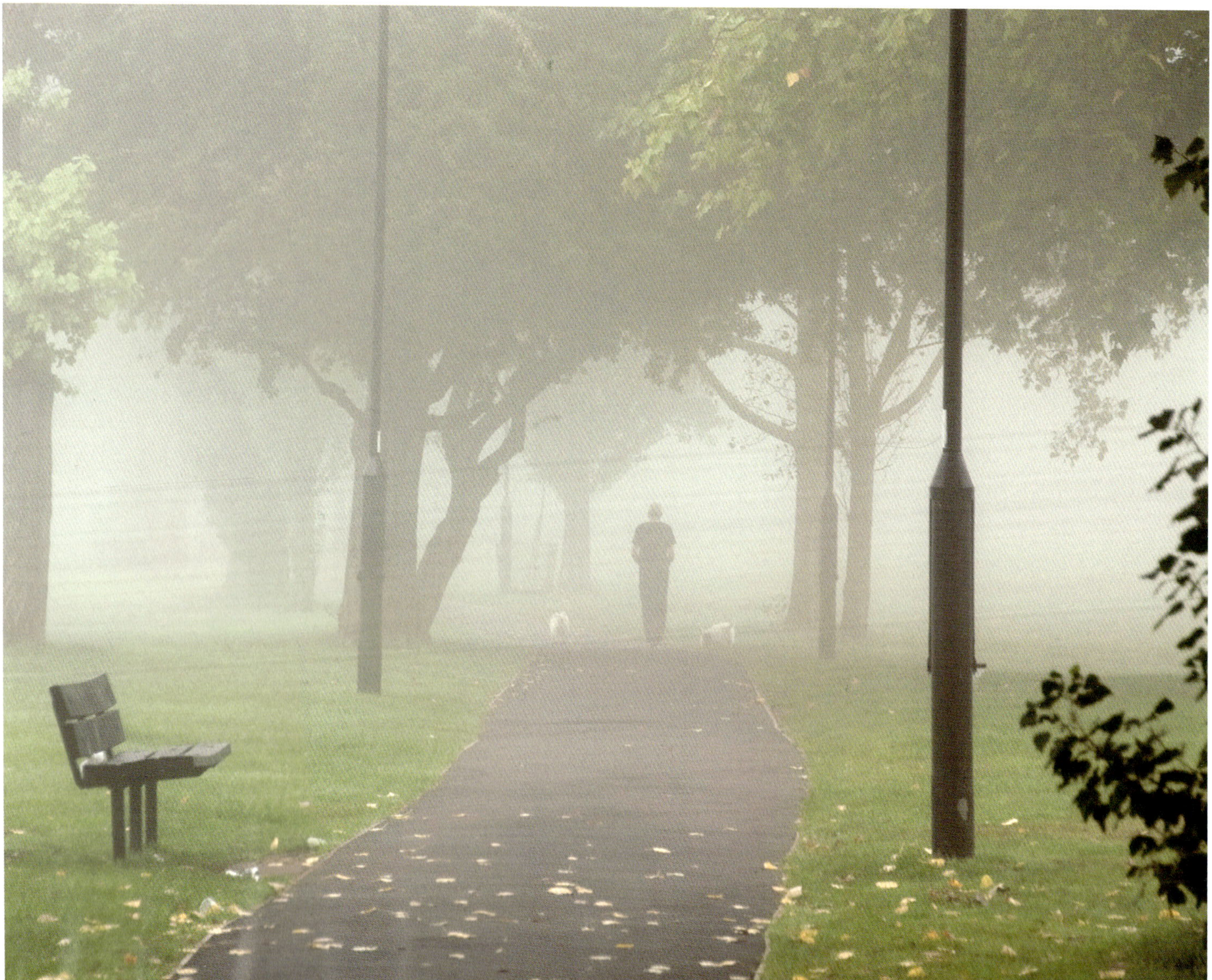

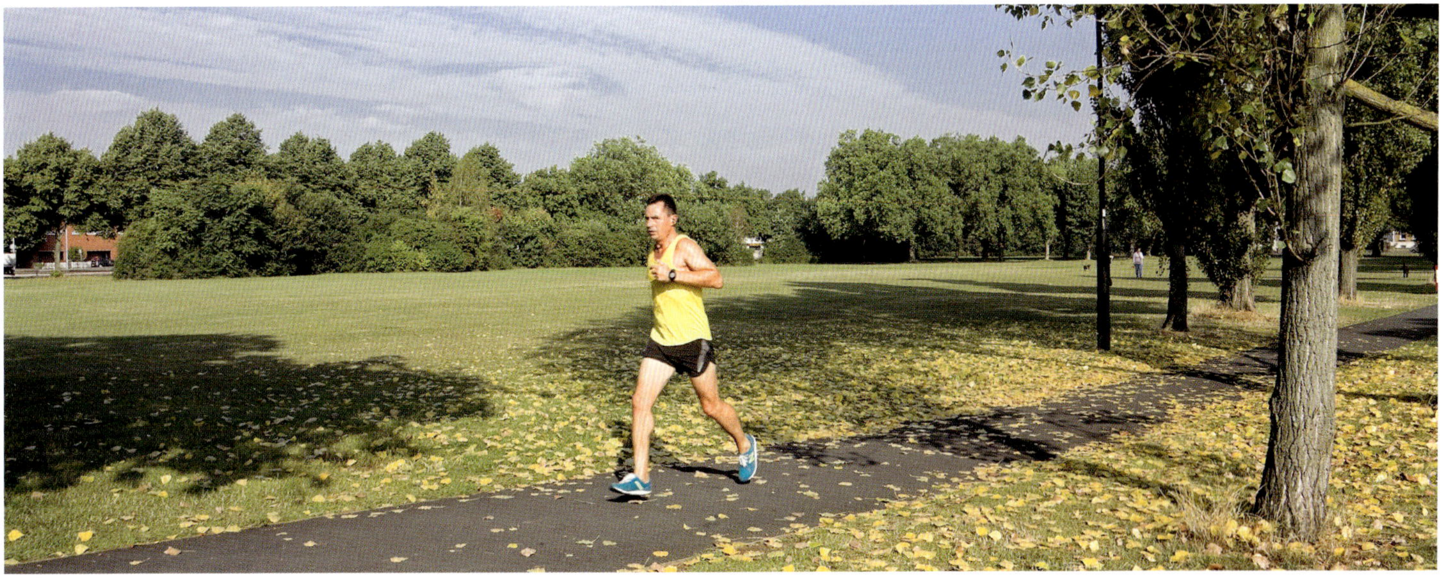

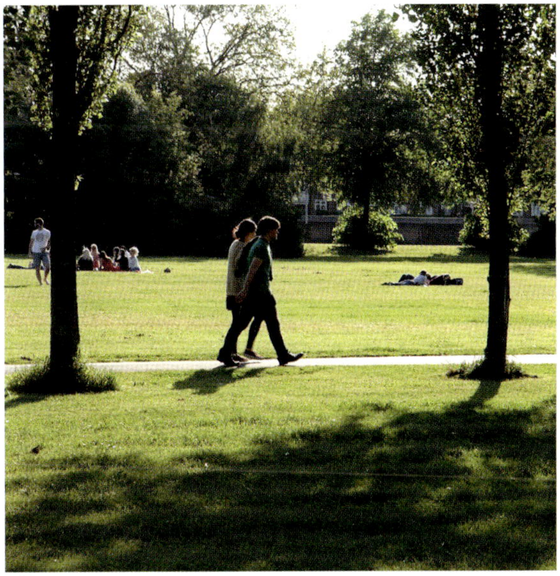

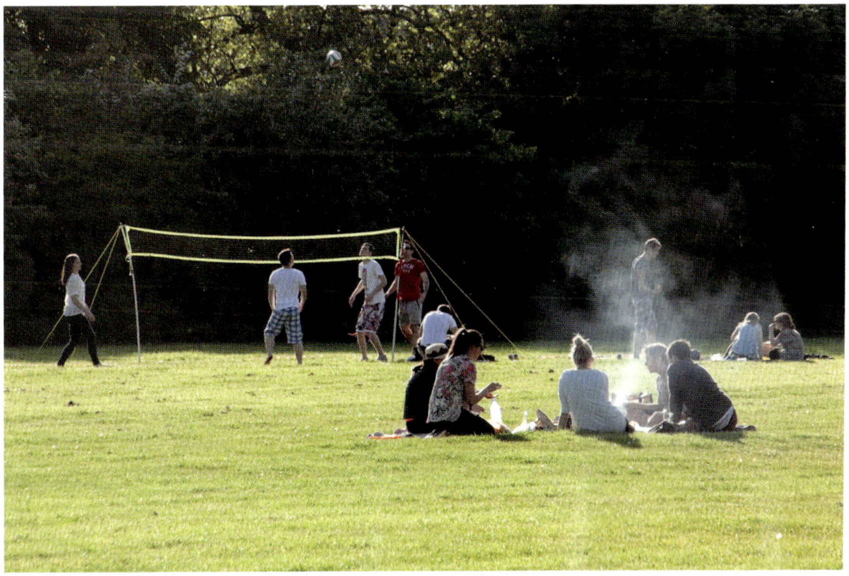

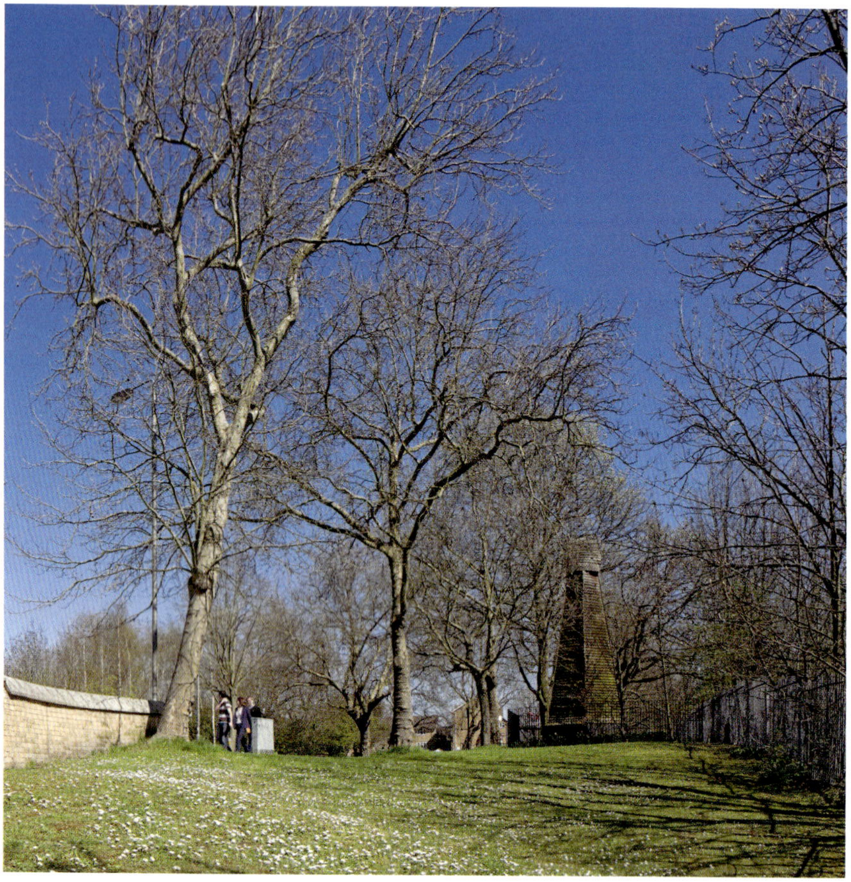

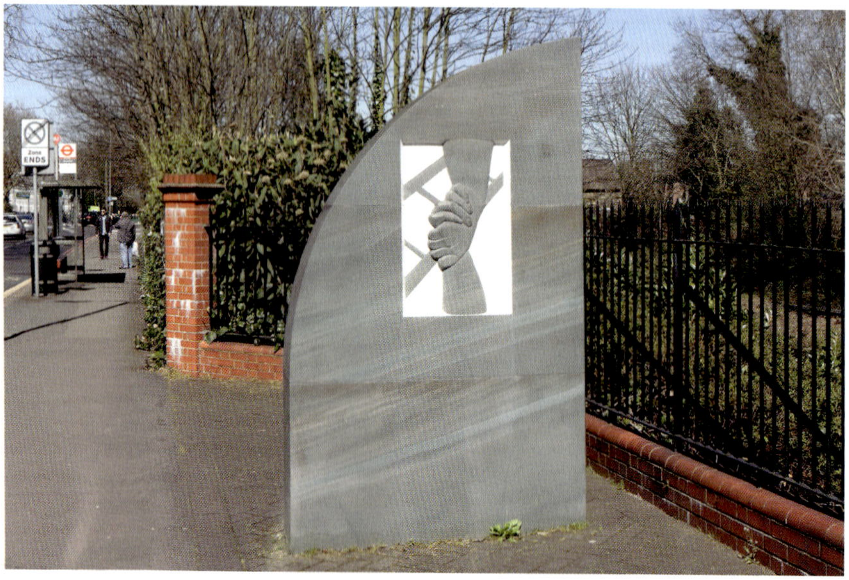

Top left: The Windmill on the common was built in 1837 as a pump to drain water from the railway cutting being built alongside. The resultant water was used to form a lake on the common, rather bizarrely called the Black Sea. However, this was filled in 1884, the pump was no longer needed and they rather disappointingly took away its sails.

Bottom left: On December 12th 1988 there was an awful train accident on the line just outside Clapham Junction, where 35 people lost their lives and over 500 were injured. On Windmill Road you can find this rather striking memorial.

Opposite: Across the centre of the common runs a magnificent line of poplar trees.

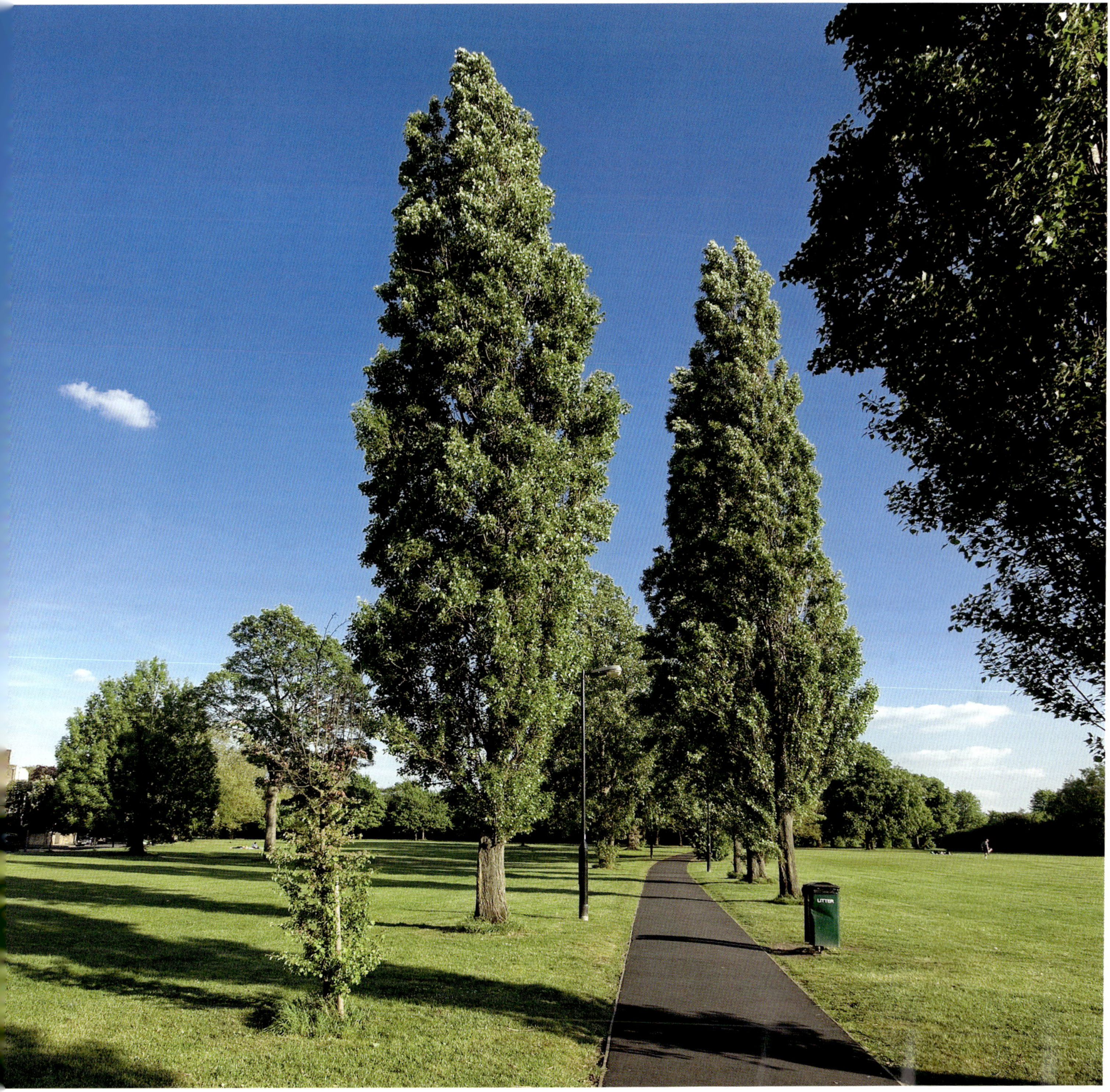
LITTER

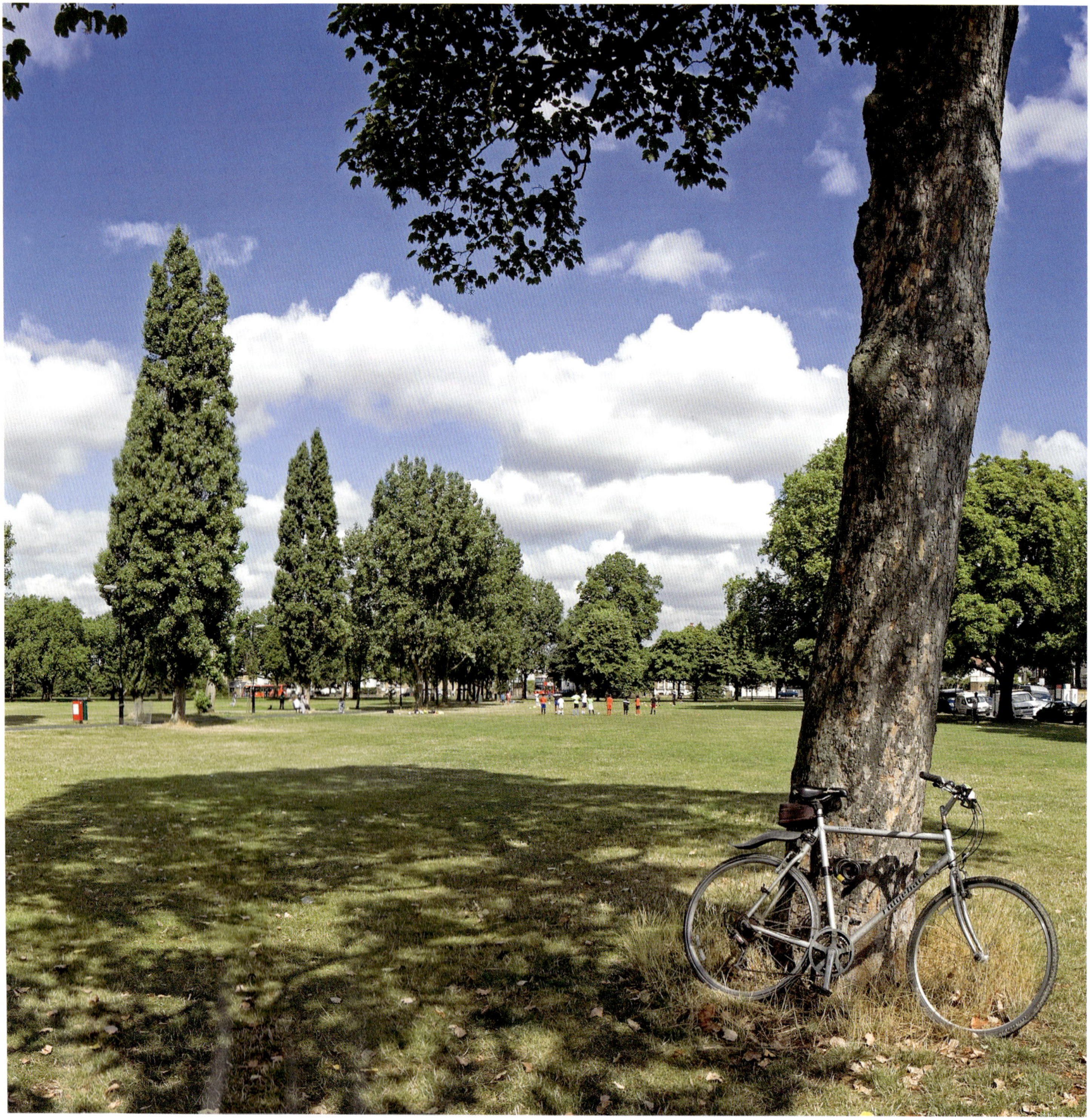

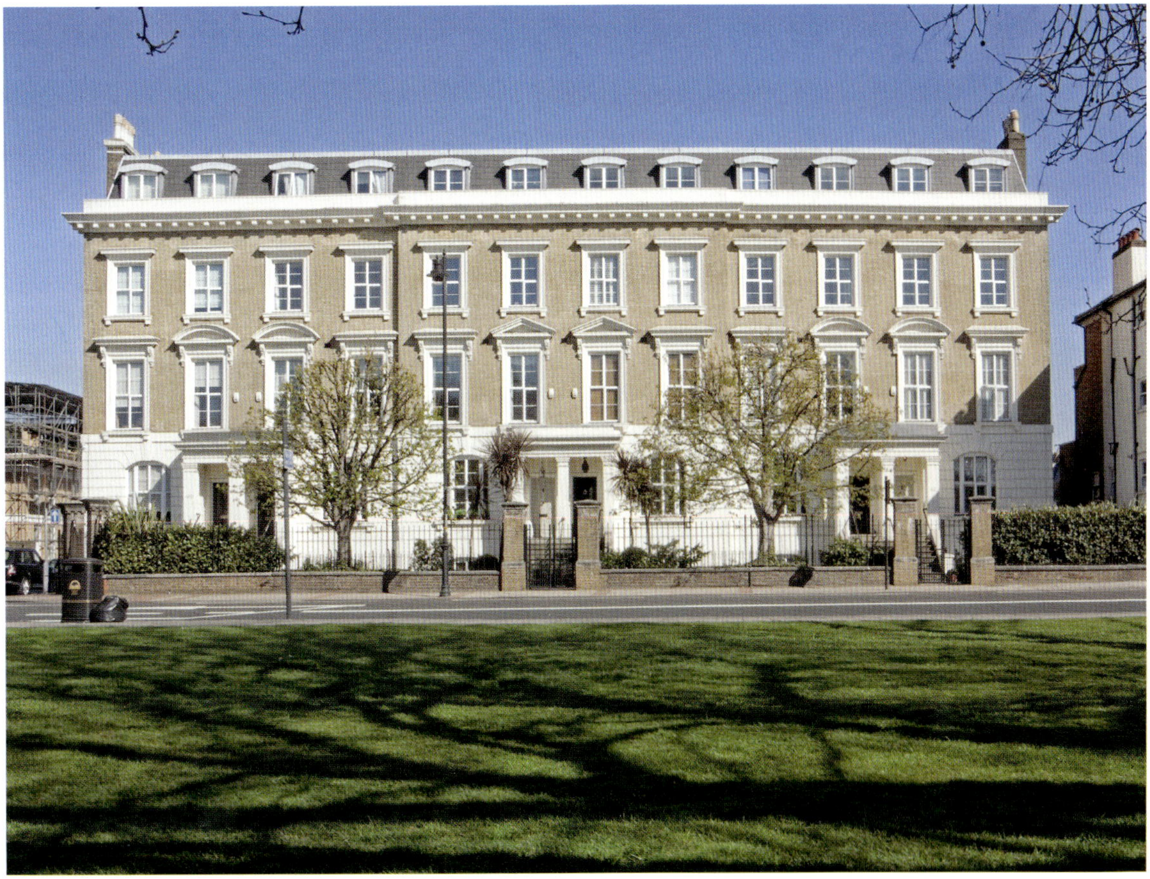

This page and overleaf: The common with its poplar trees.

Top left: Wandsworth Common North Side.

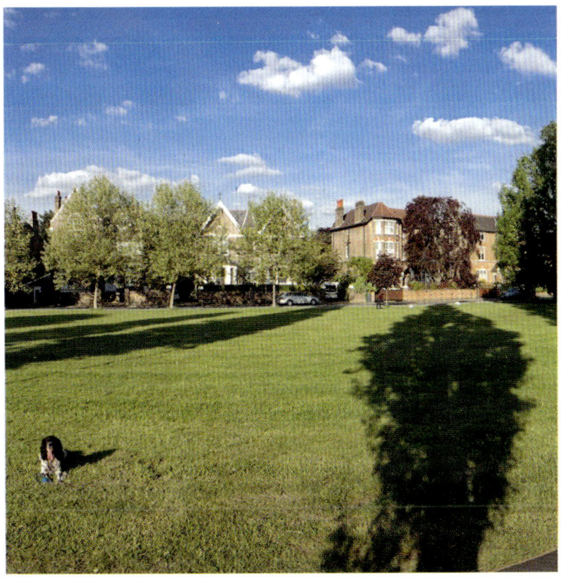

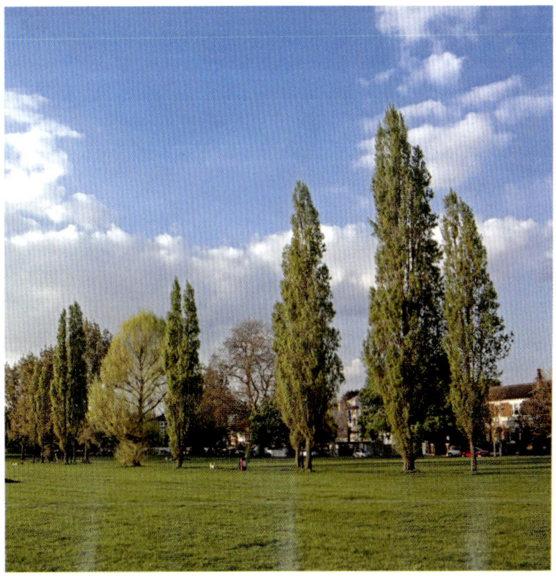

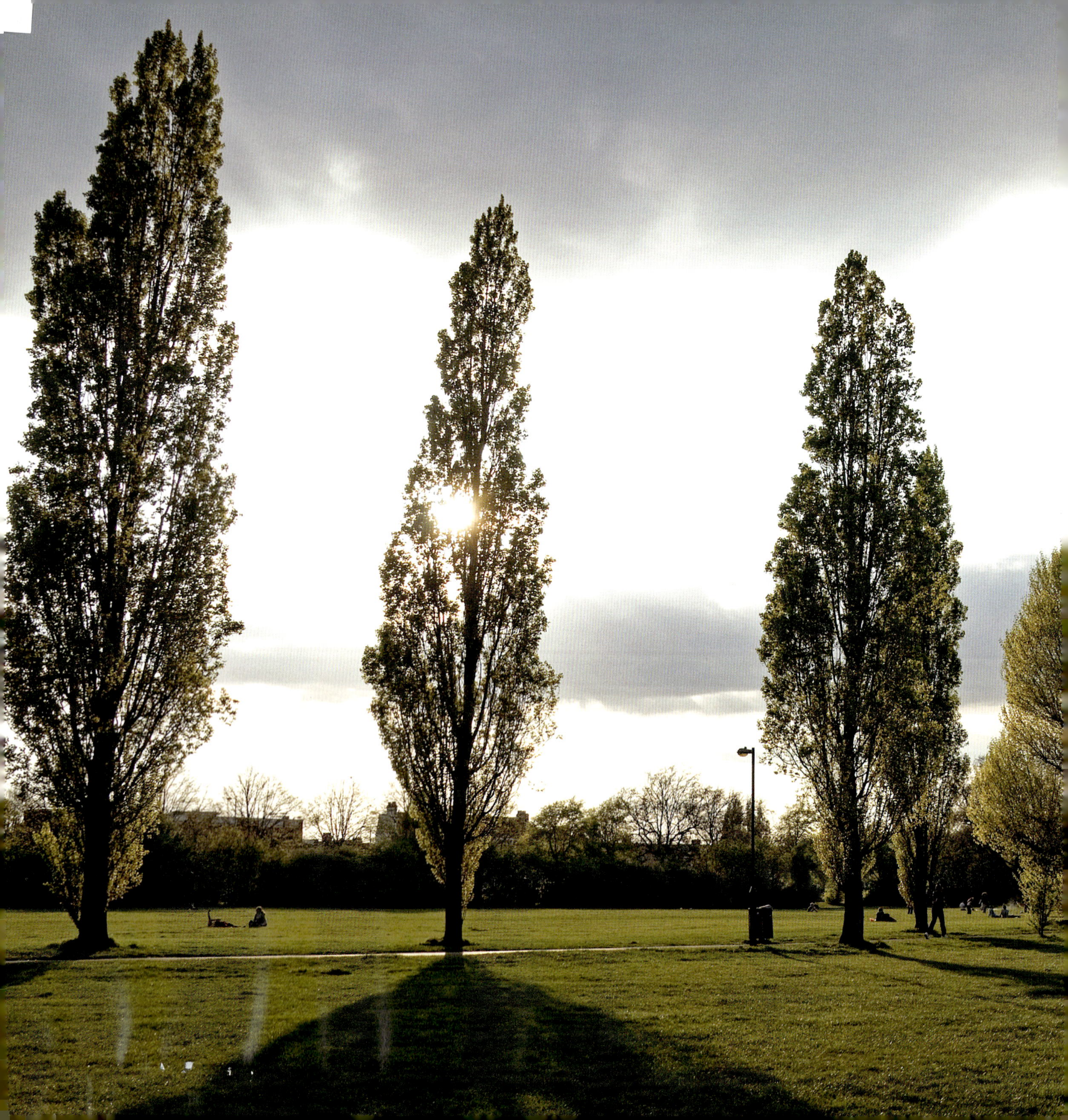

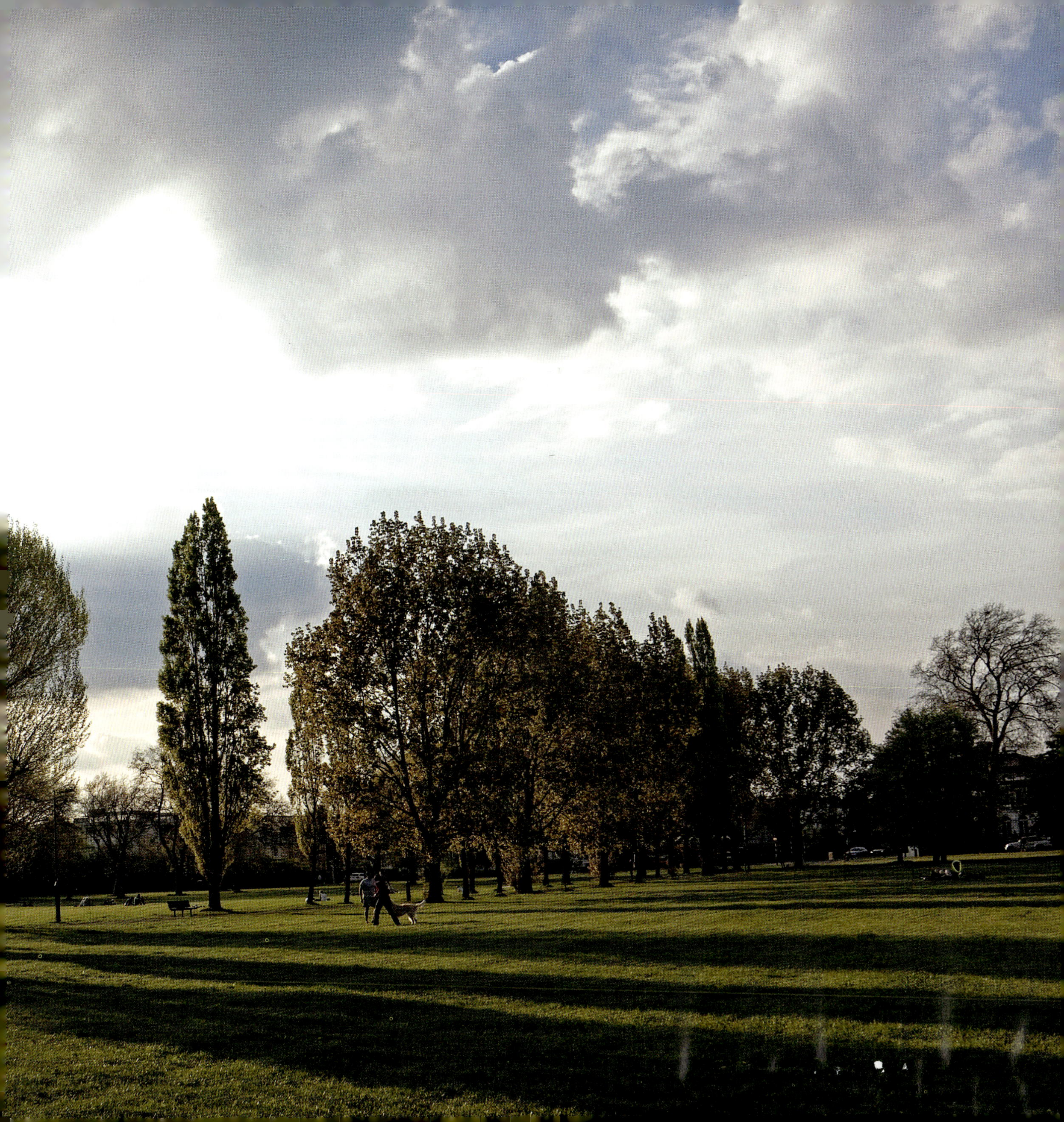

Wandsworth Common Station

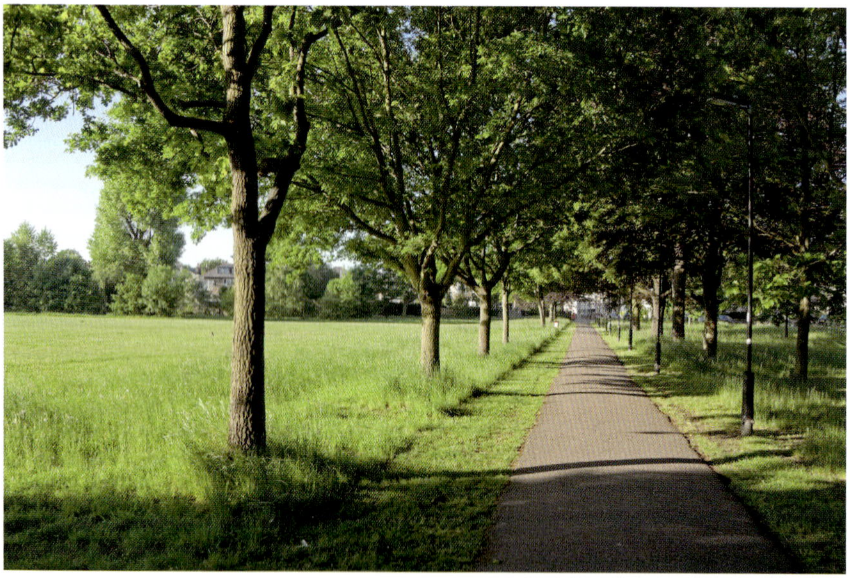

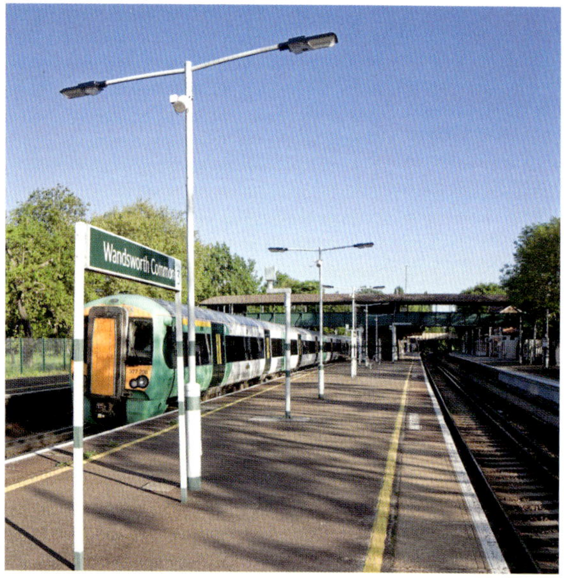

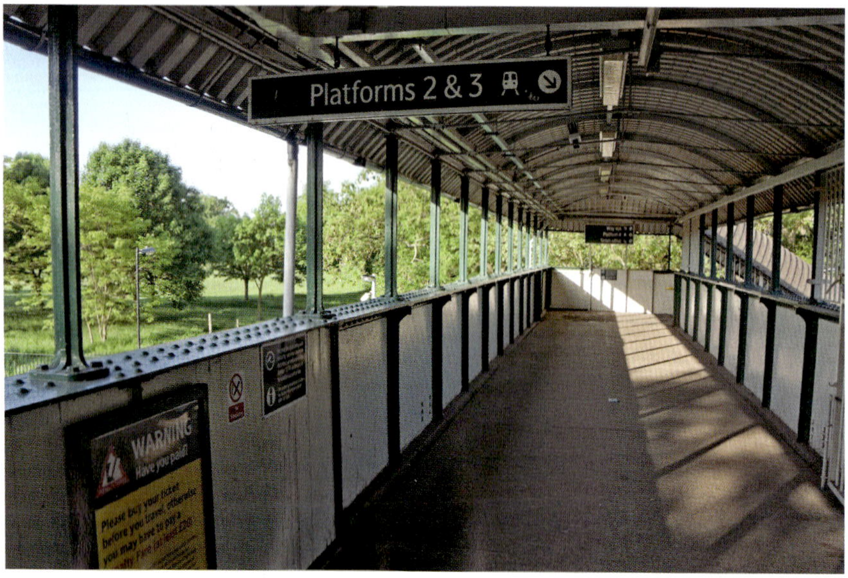

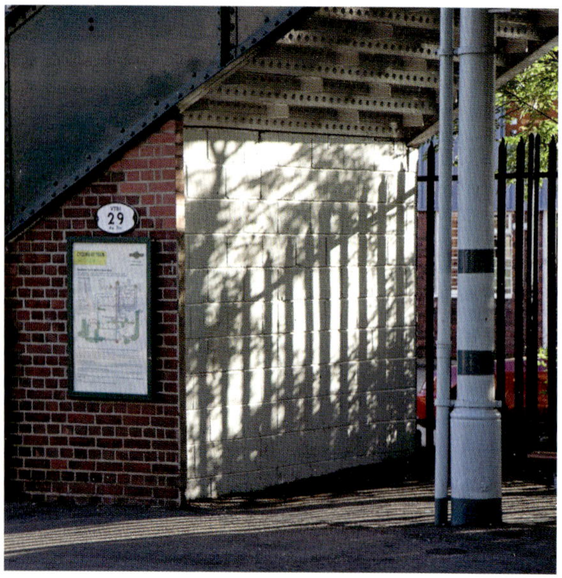

This page: Standing on the platform of Wandsworth Common station (built 1869), you could almost be in the countryside.

The station was built on land that formed the southern most part of Battersea parish, jutting southwards from Bellevue Road and Nightingale Lane.

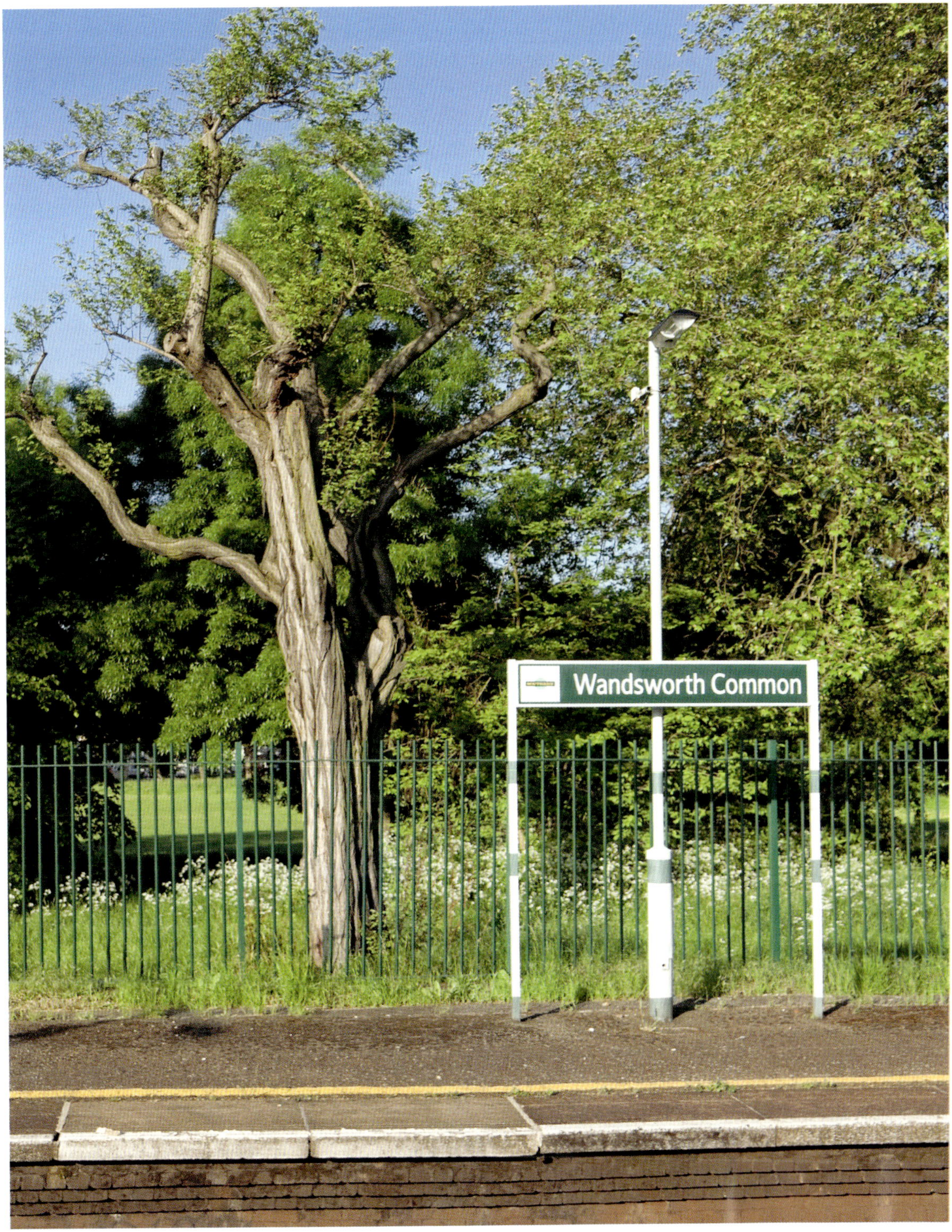

Common Ground

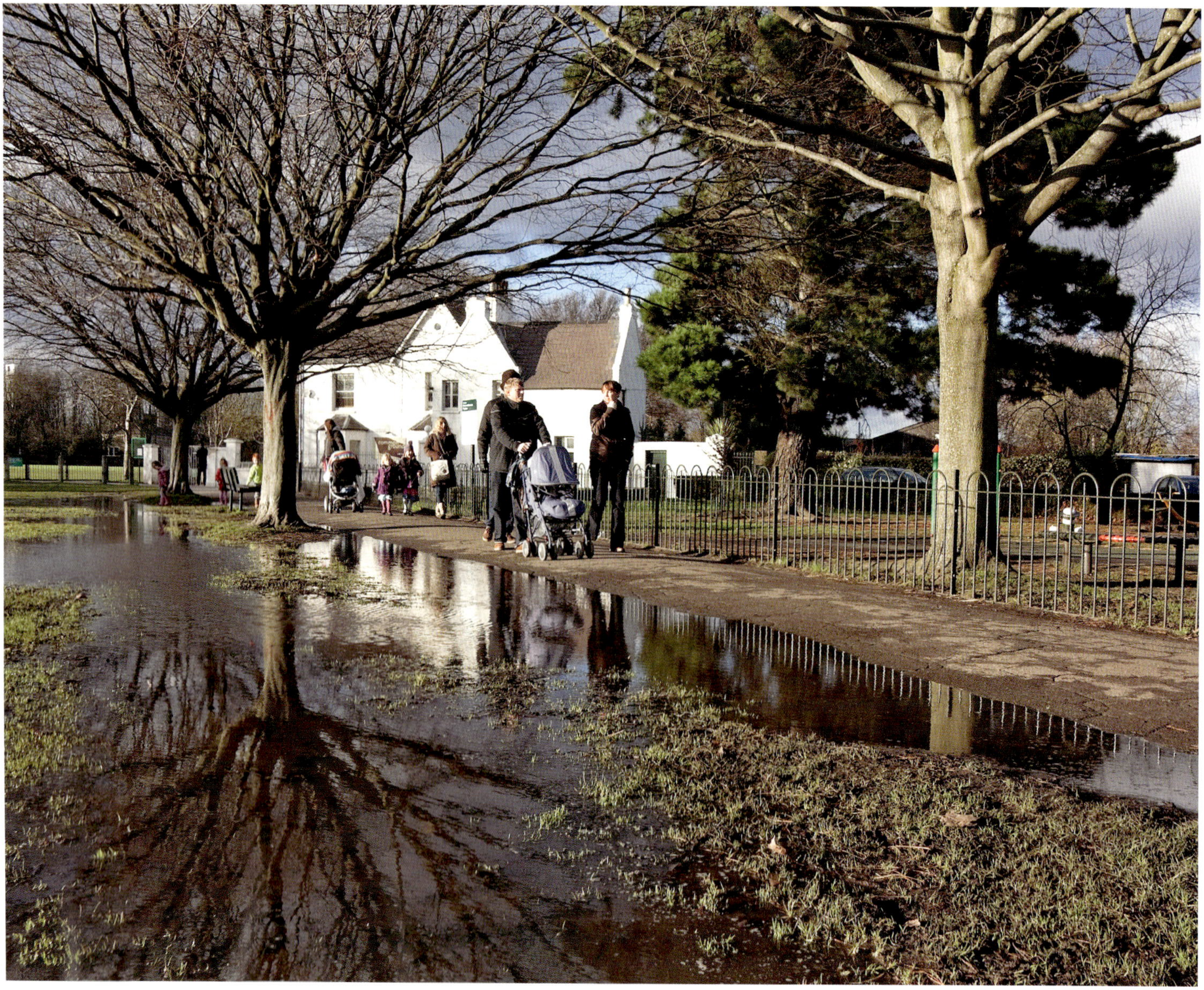

Opposite: The Common Ground café, which can be found in the centre of the common, very near the tennis courts (top right). Thank you to the guys from All Star Tennis for letting me take some pictures.

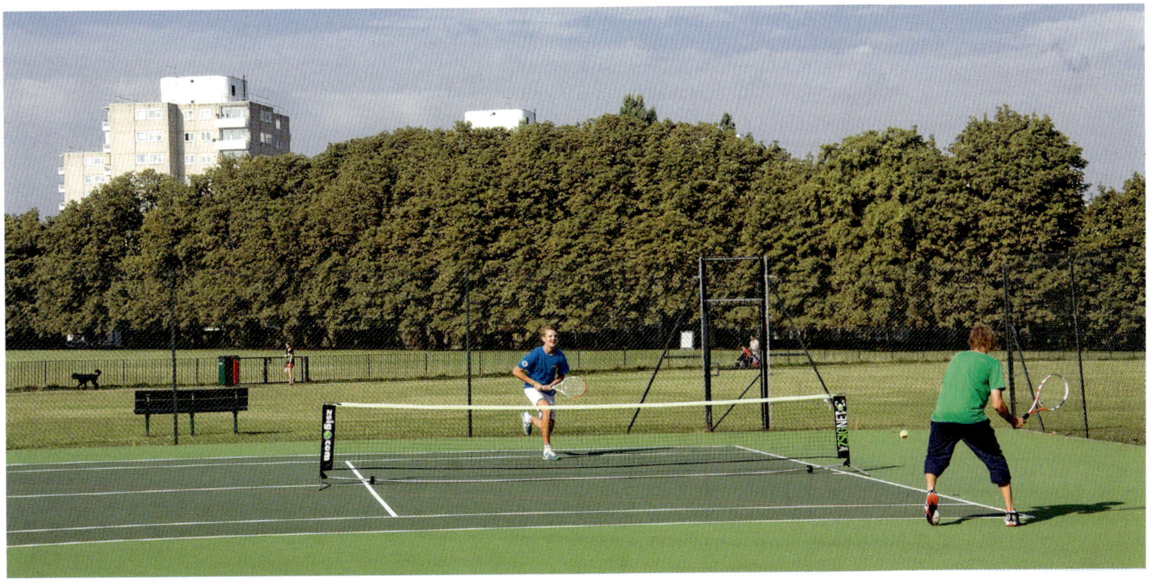

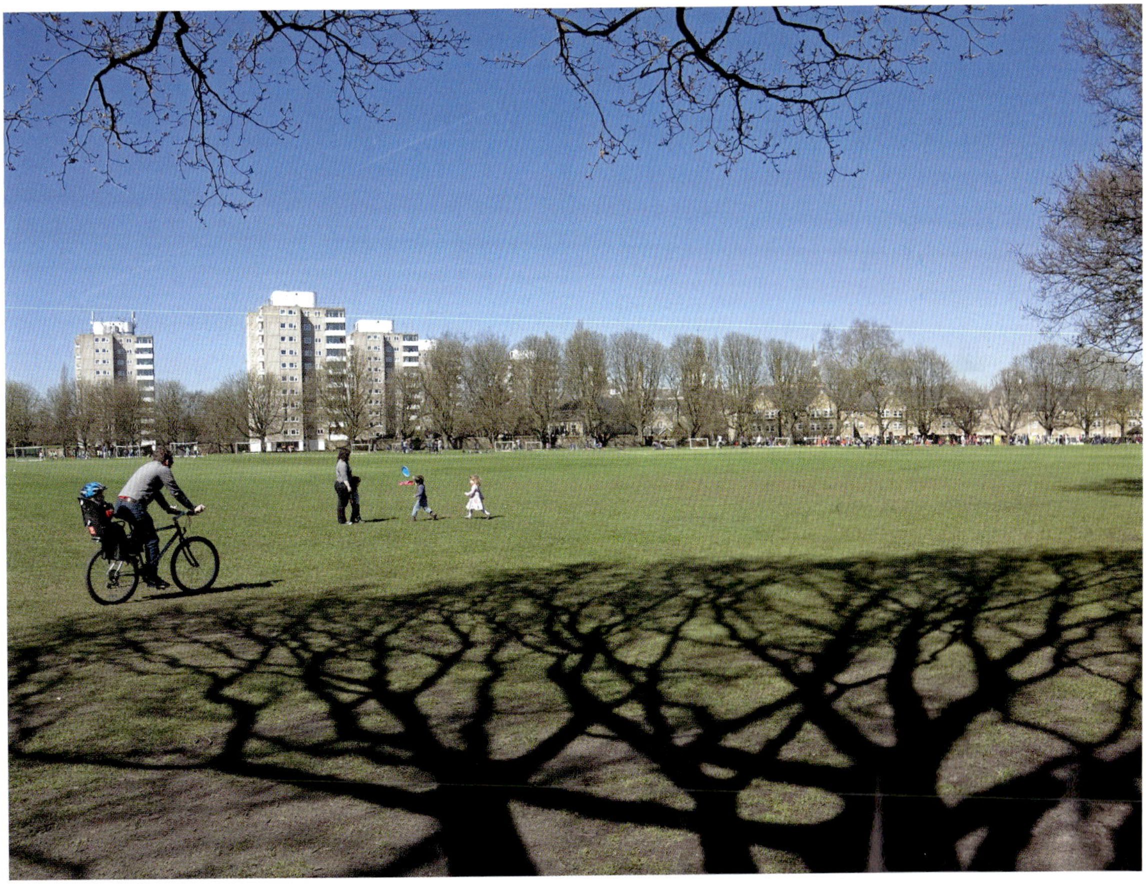

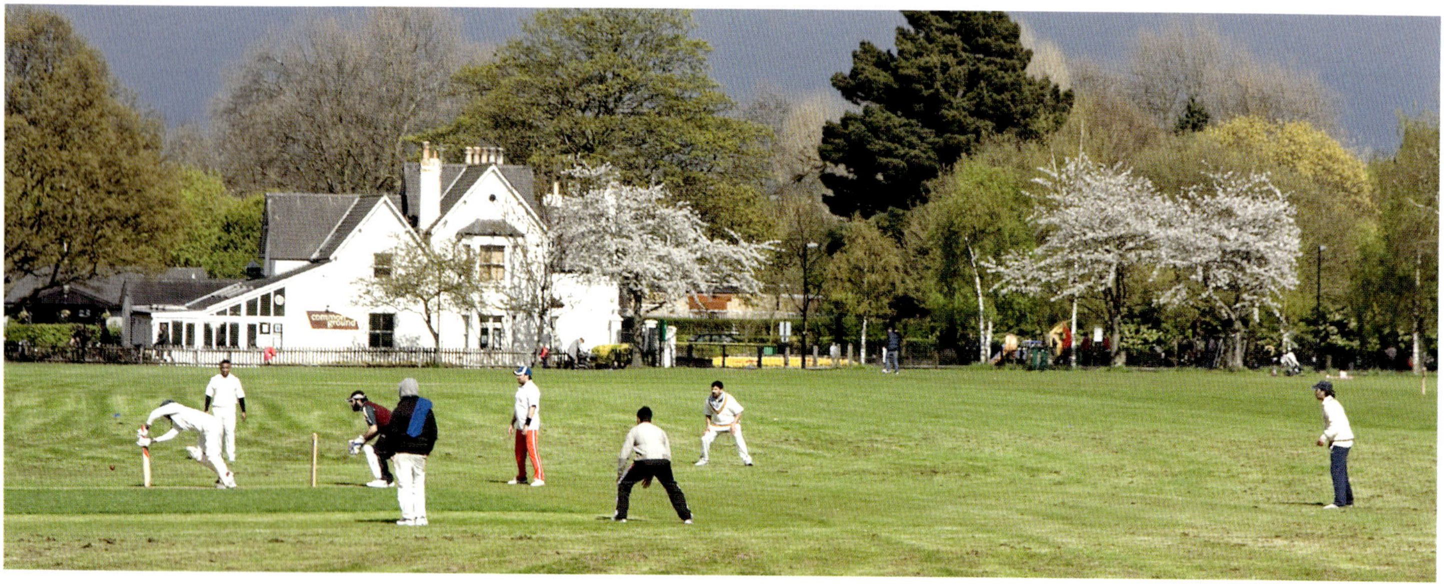
common ground

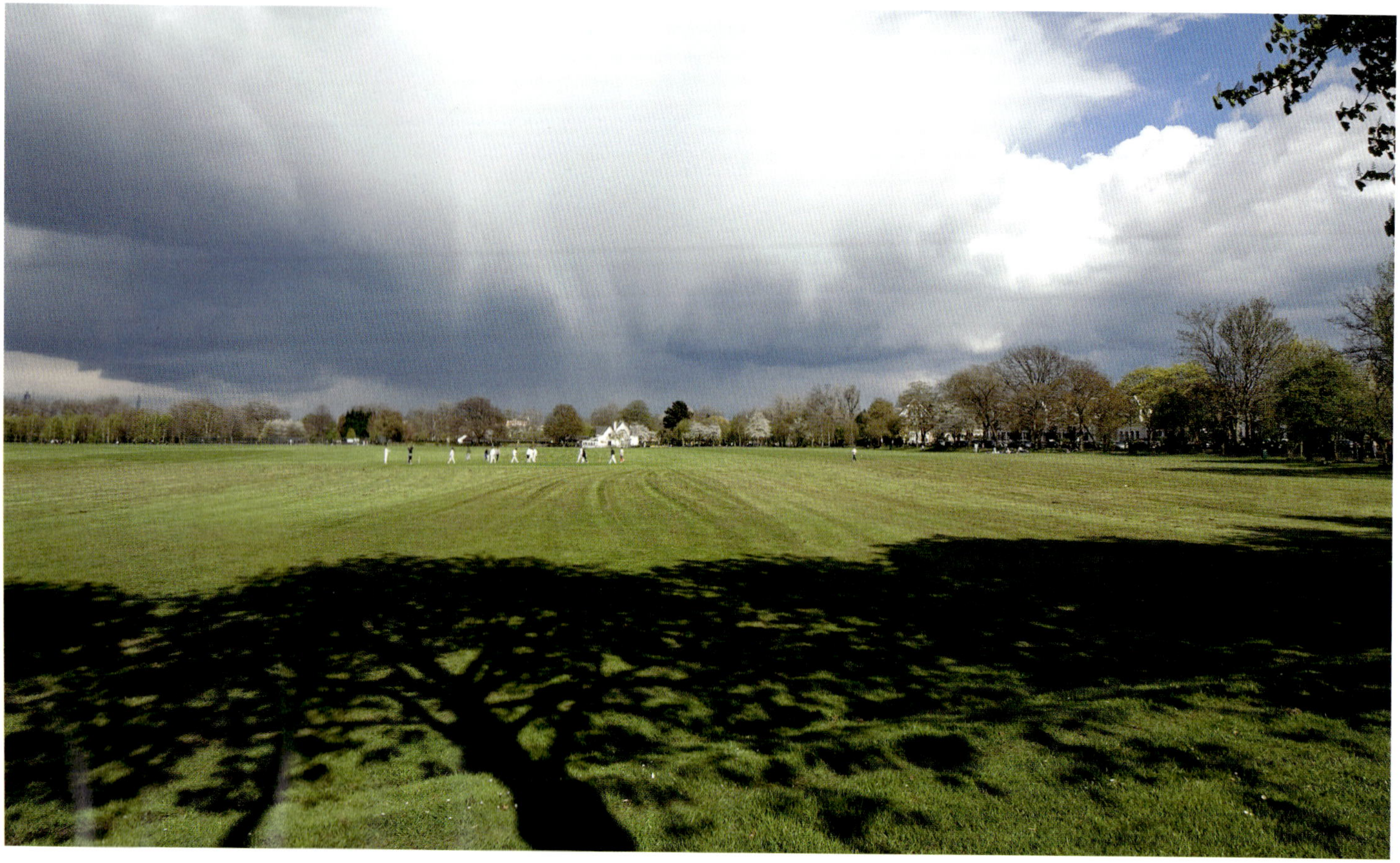

This page: Besides cricket and tennis, the common also has a rather smart bowls green.

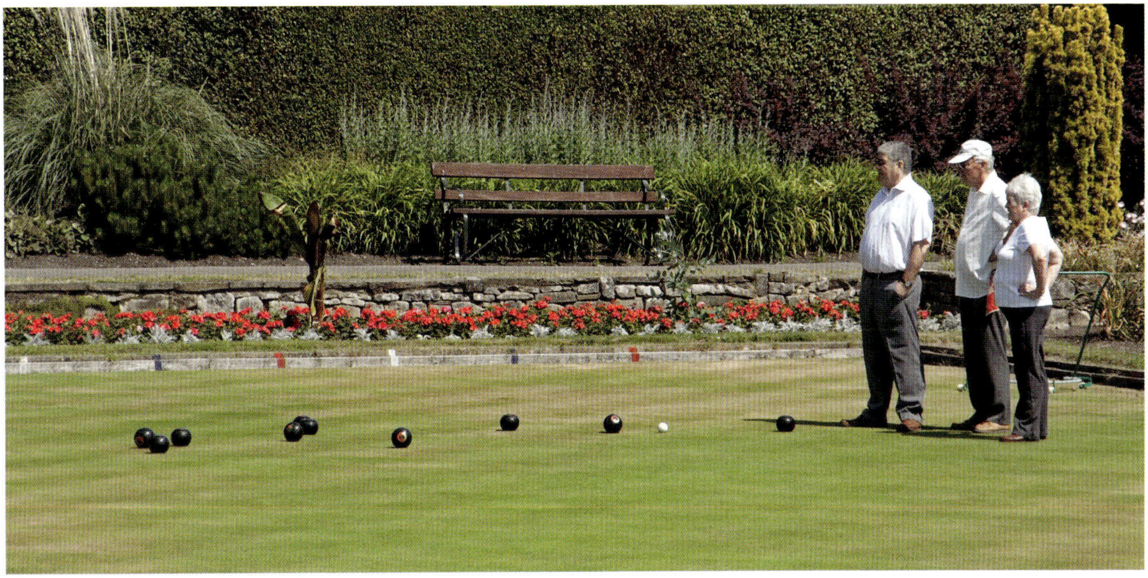

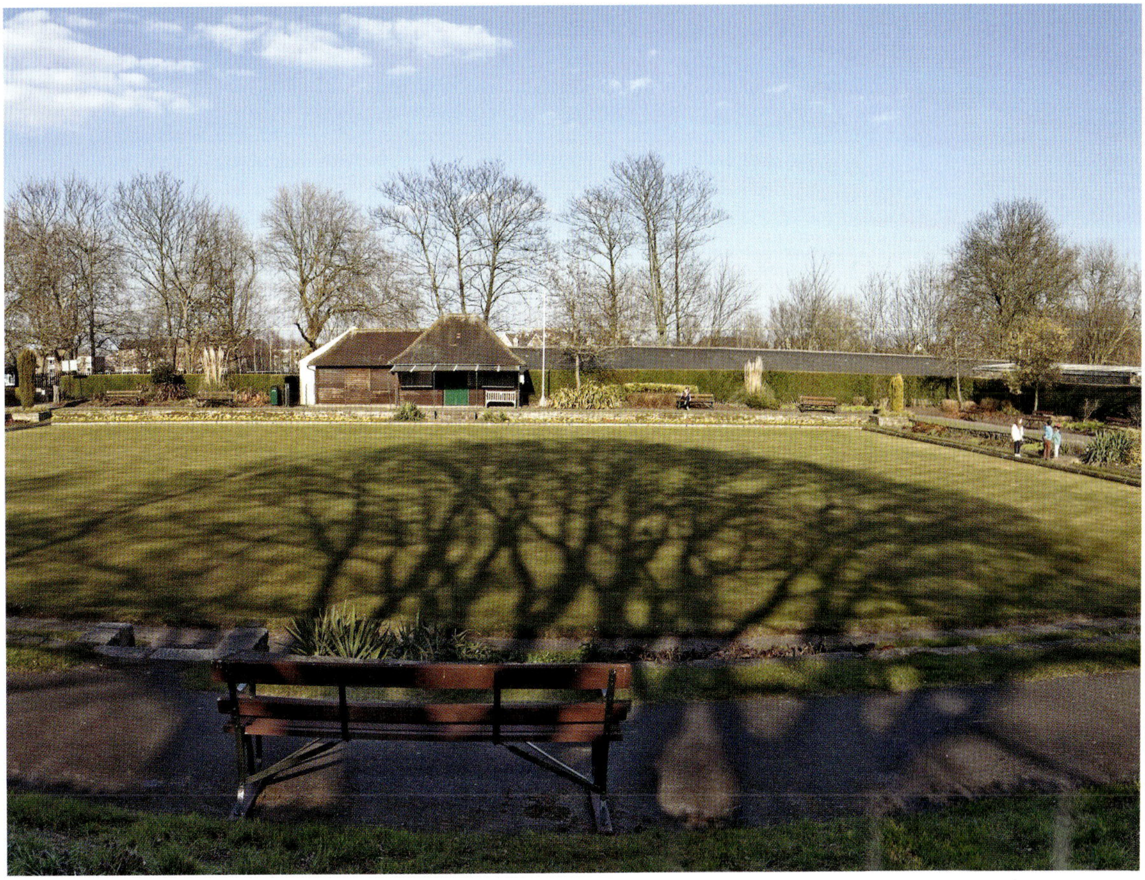

The Toast Rack

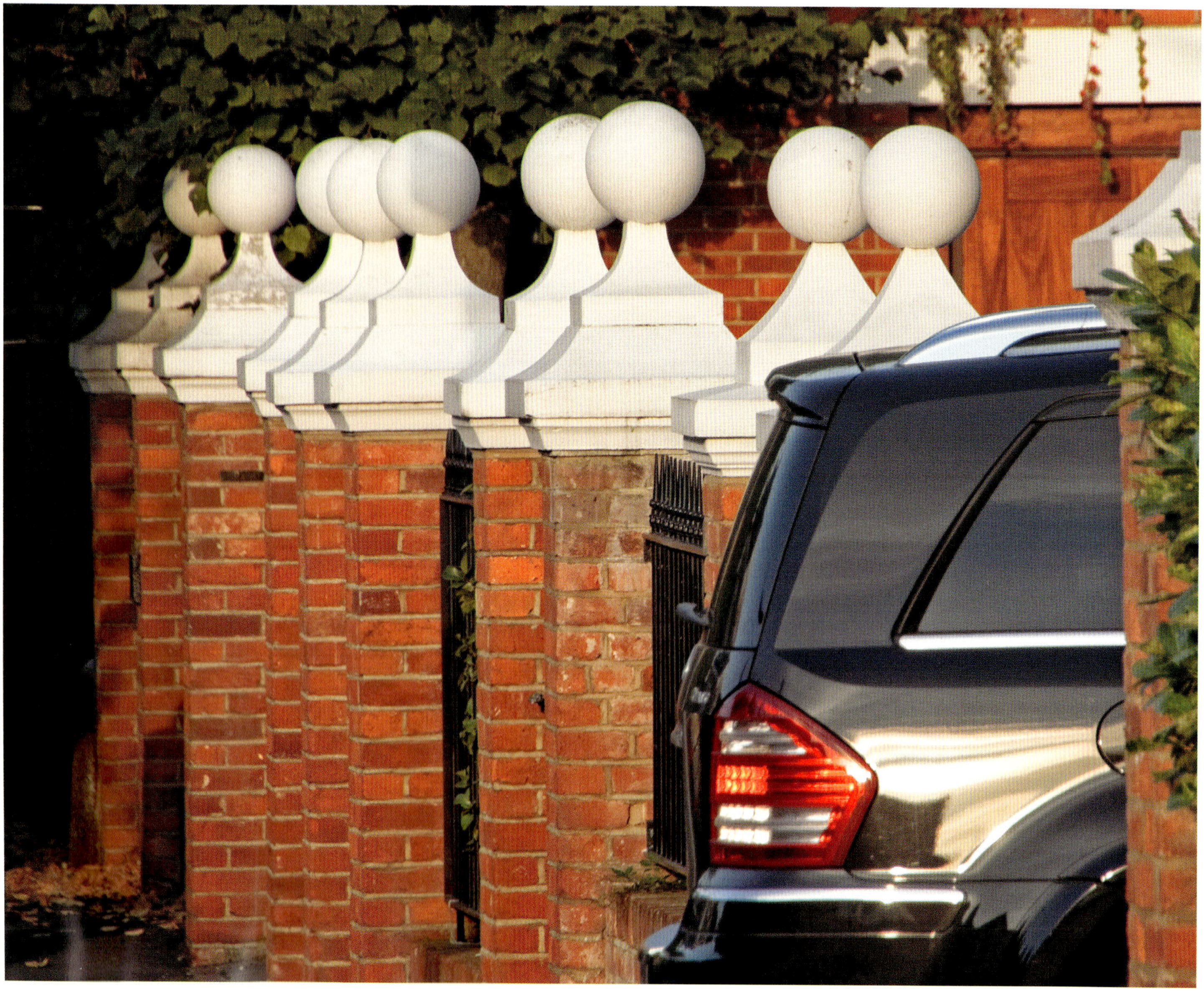

This page: Alongside the common and entered via Trinity Road can be found a series of roads known locally as the Toast Rack, on account of the way the streets are laid out. It was interesting to discover that David Lloyd George had once lived here on Routh Road.

Bottom right: Many of the houses in Baskerville Road have these rather ornate entrances.

Overleaf: Bolingbroke Grove from the common.

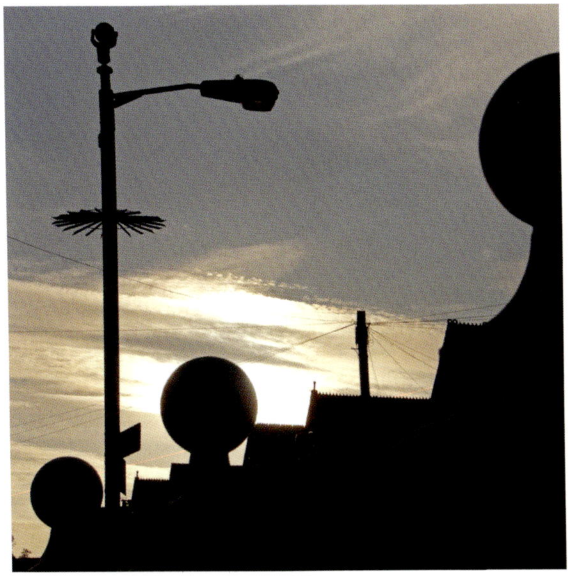

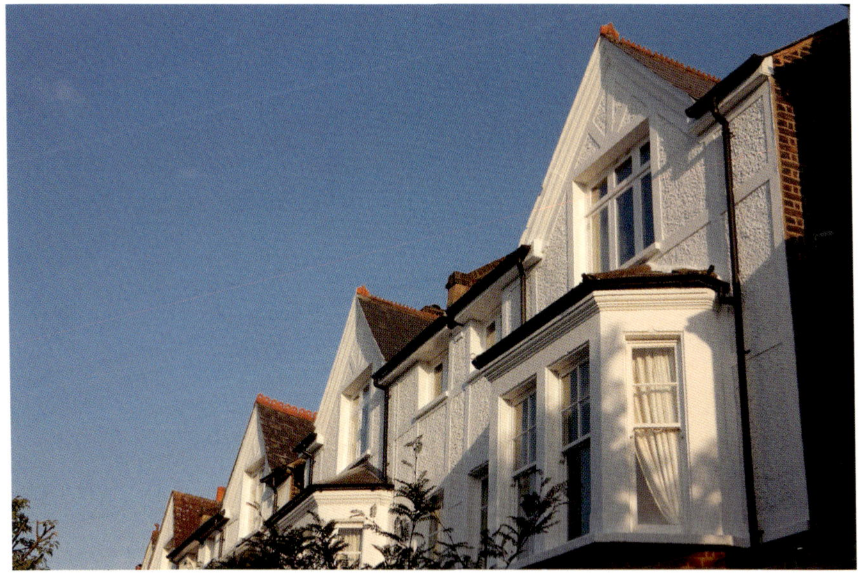

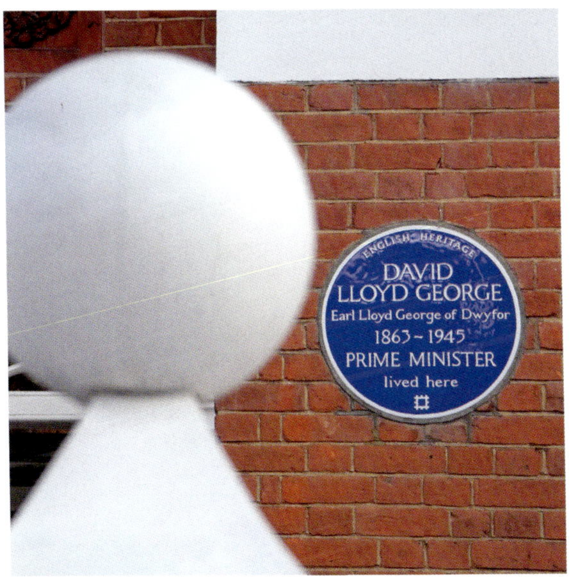

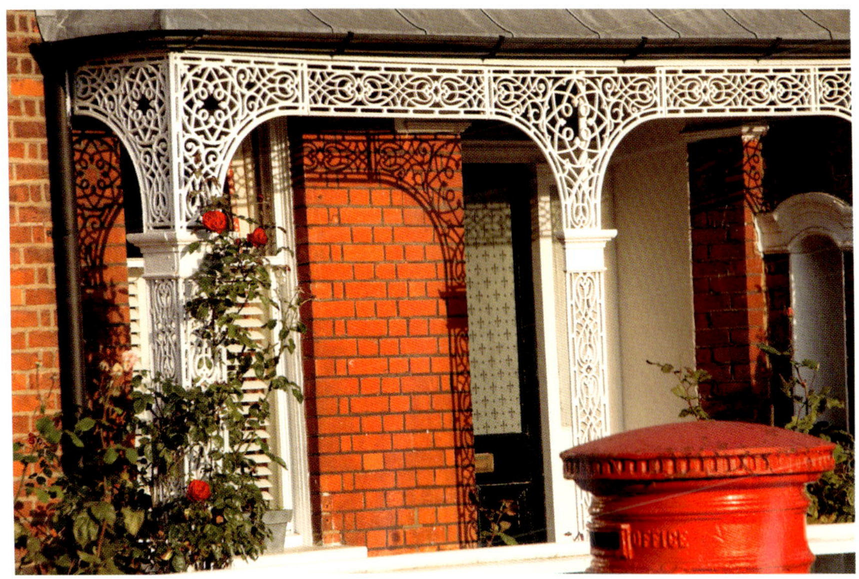

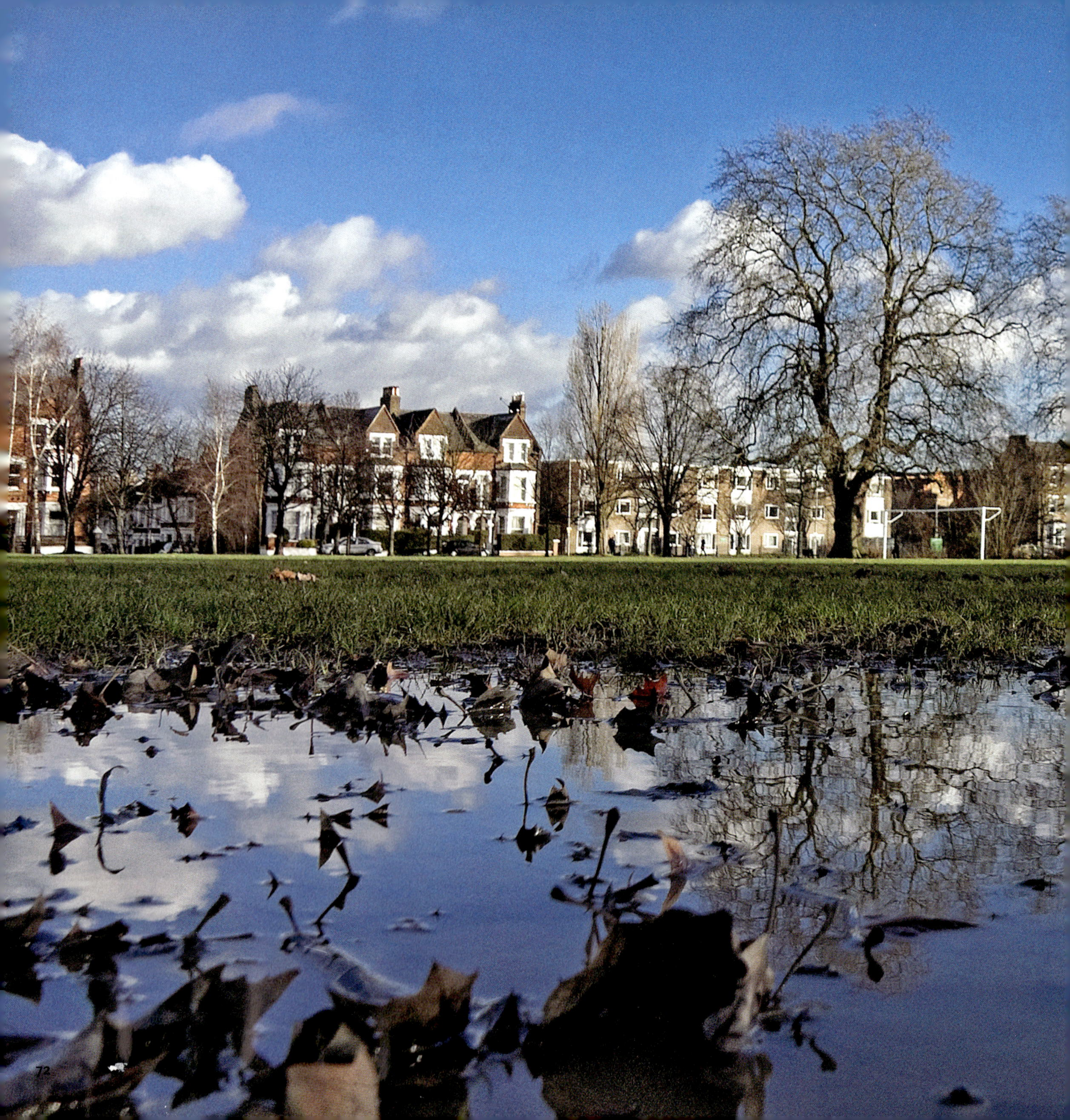

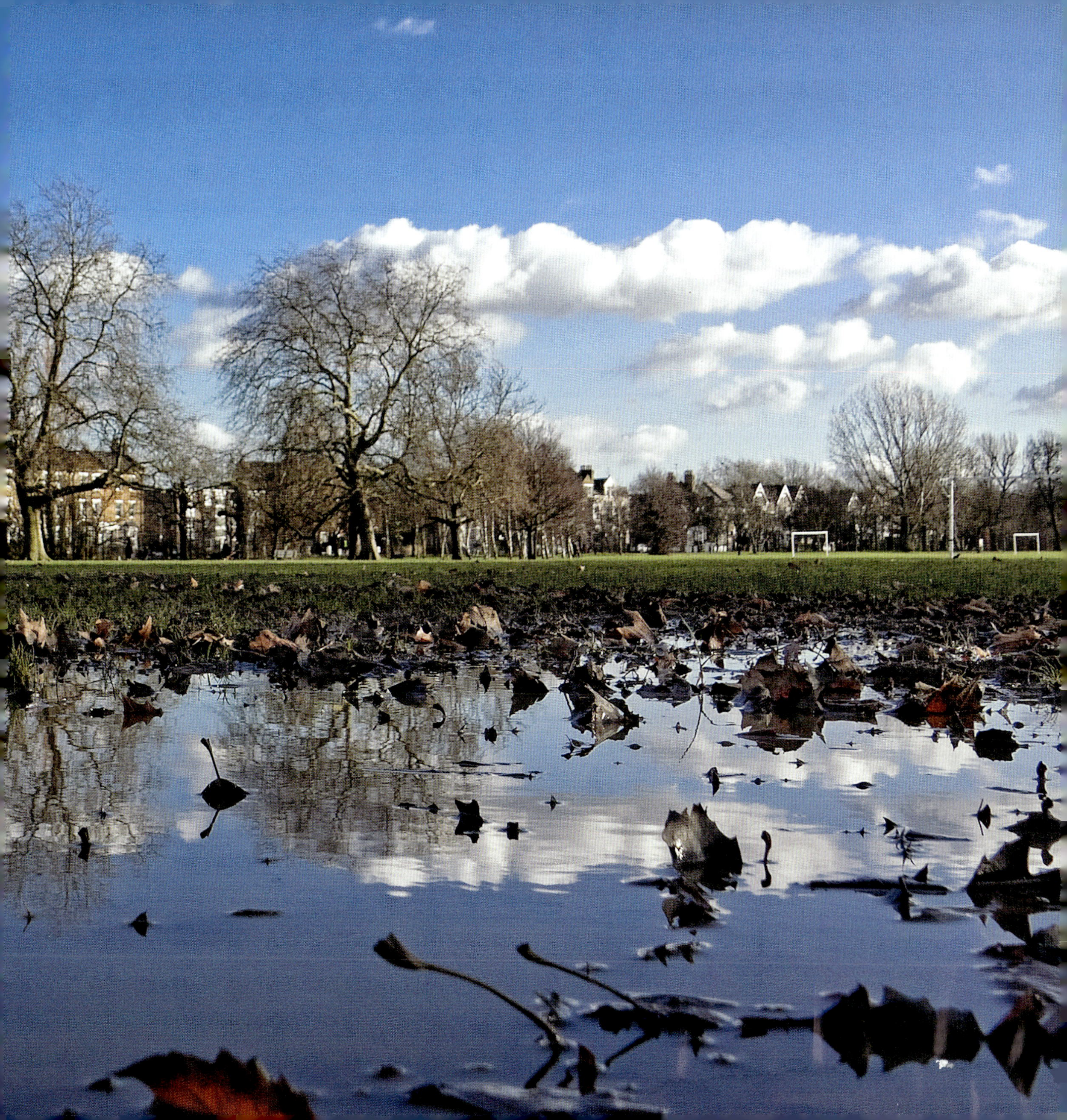

Street Life

South Battersea or 'Between the Commons' has at its centre the Northcote Road, which by a freak of nature is situated in a perfect valley (the old route of the Falcon Brook) with roads running off of it east and west. 'The Junction', as it was referred to for most of the 20th century, has completely transformed over the last 20 years. As the wealth of London has grown, so have the suburbs, as residents found new places to live. The area also benefits from being well supported by green spaces, with two of London's larger parks bordering the area east and west. Although some might question the changes, no one could deny that this is a much improved area to live in thankfully some of the characters still remain on the high street to remind residents of times gone by.

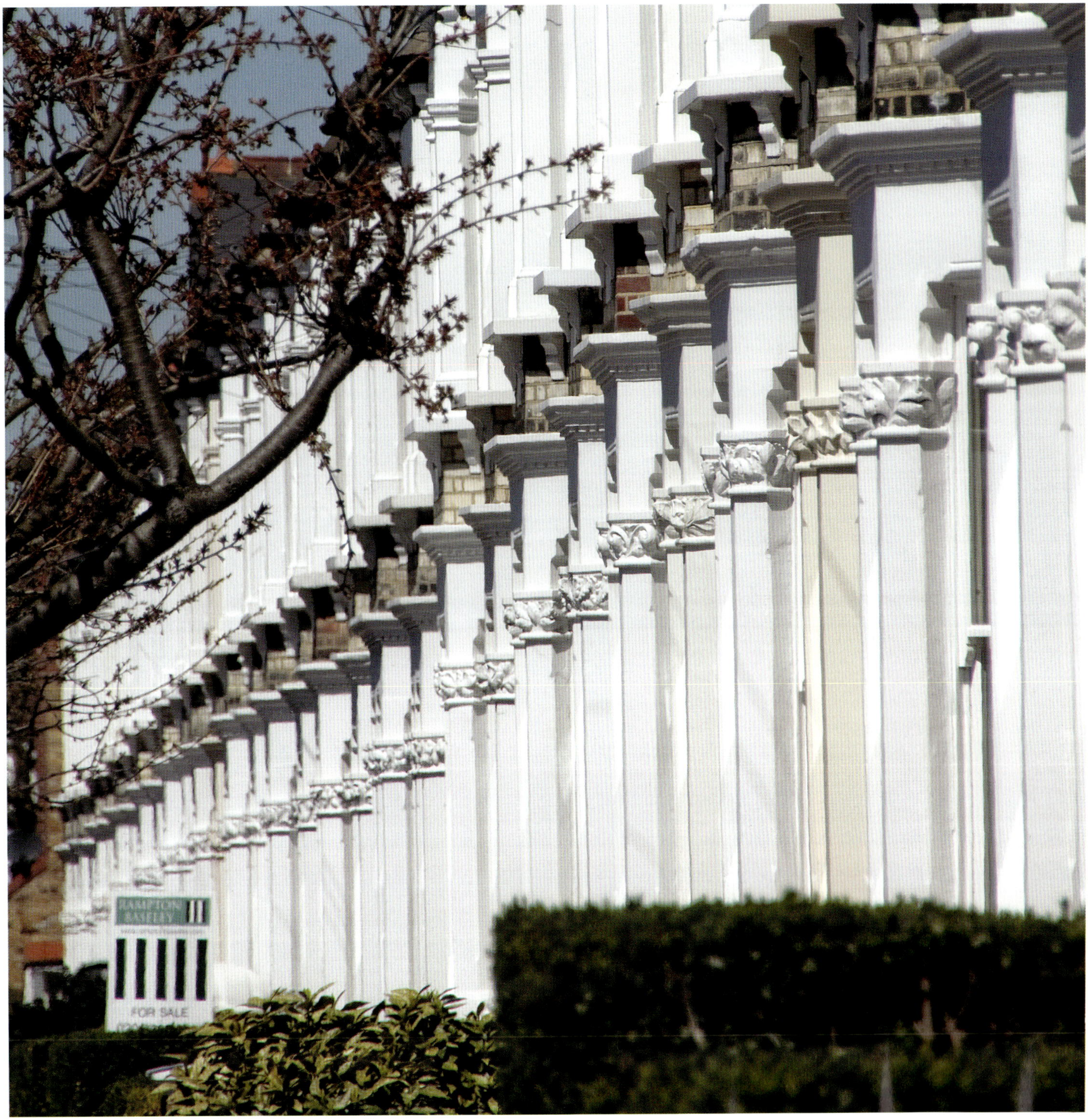
FOR SALE

Battersea Rise

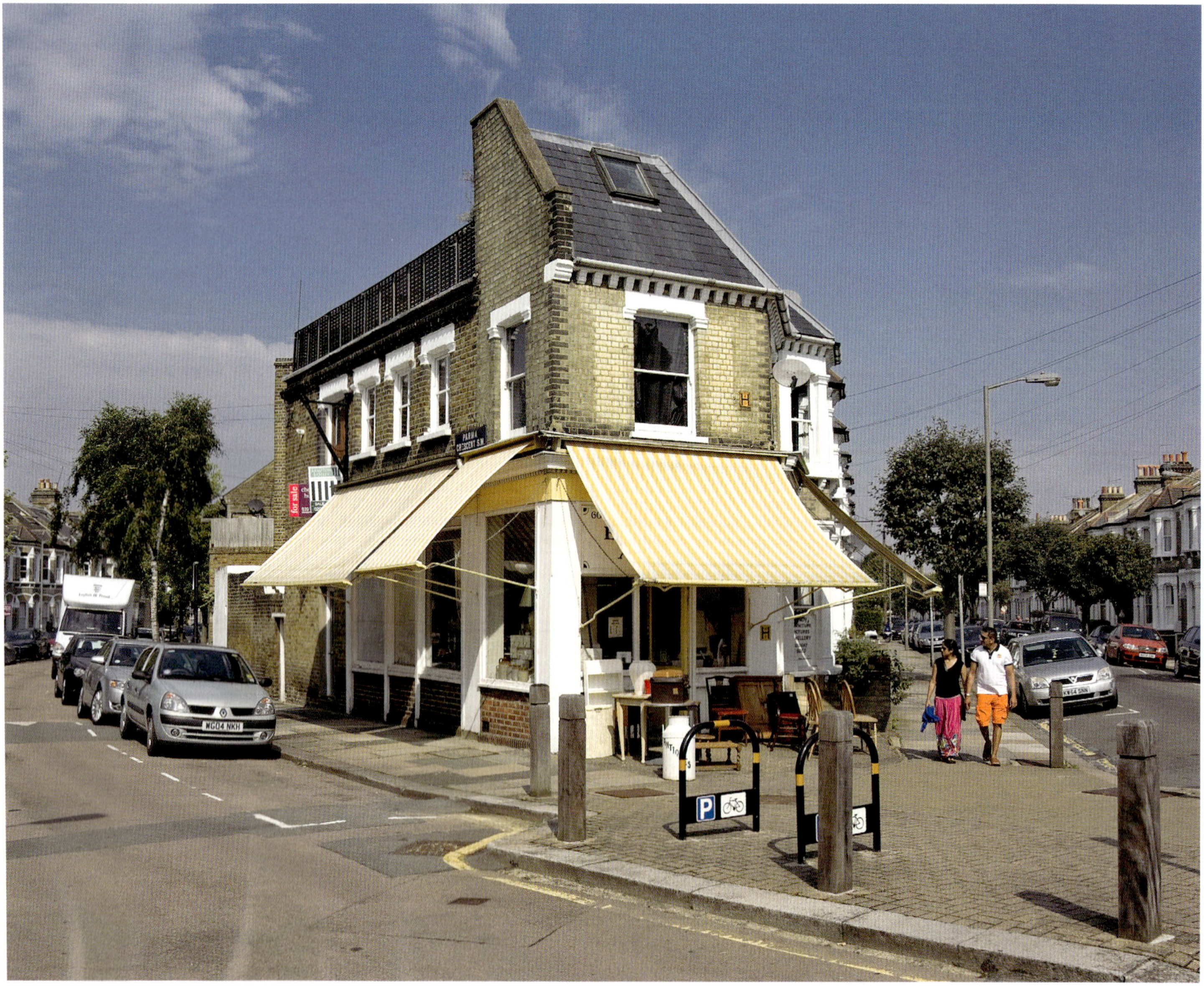

Top left, bottom left and opposite: Just off Battersea Rise you can find Eccles Road and this rather splendid antiques shop with its wonderful canopy.

Bottom right: There are some nice independent clothes shops along Battersea Rise; here a hat I saw displayed in the window of Katharine Bird's shop.

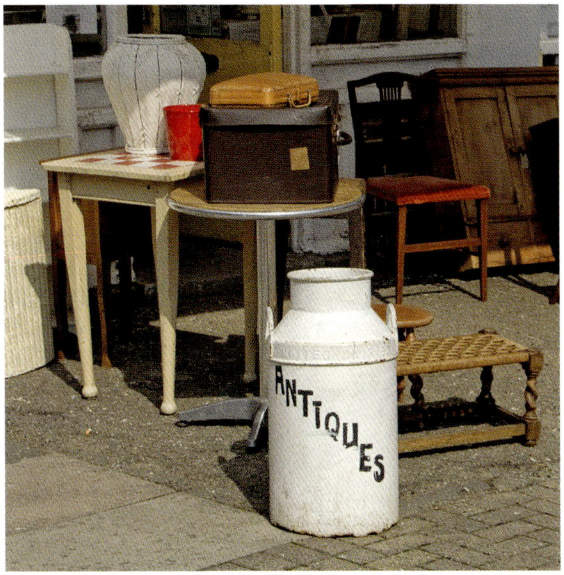

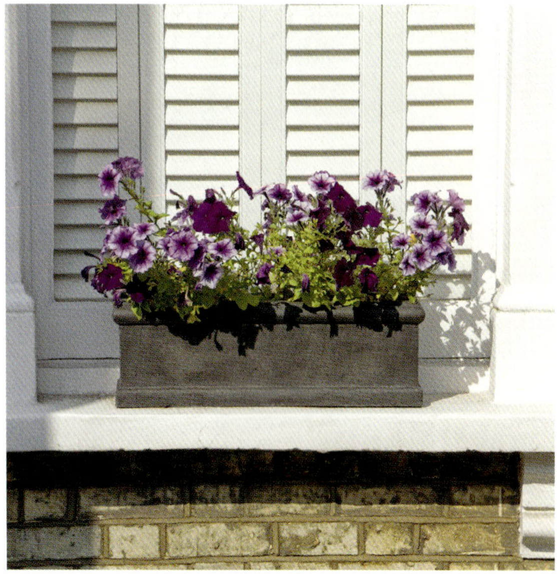

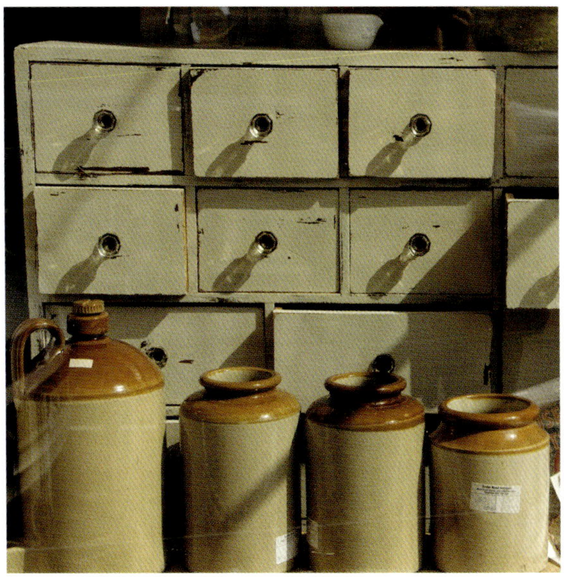

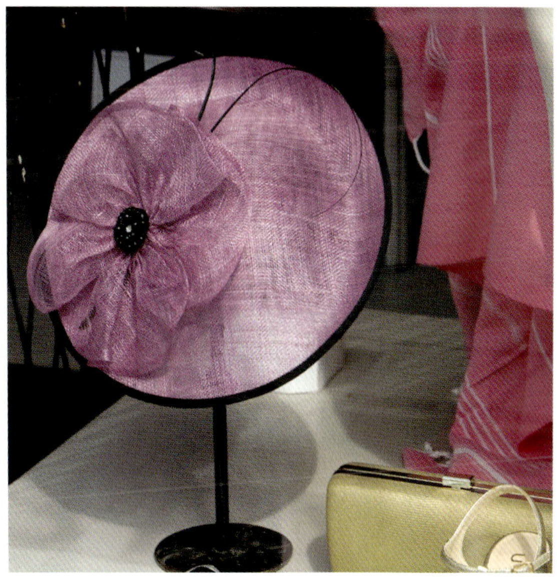

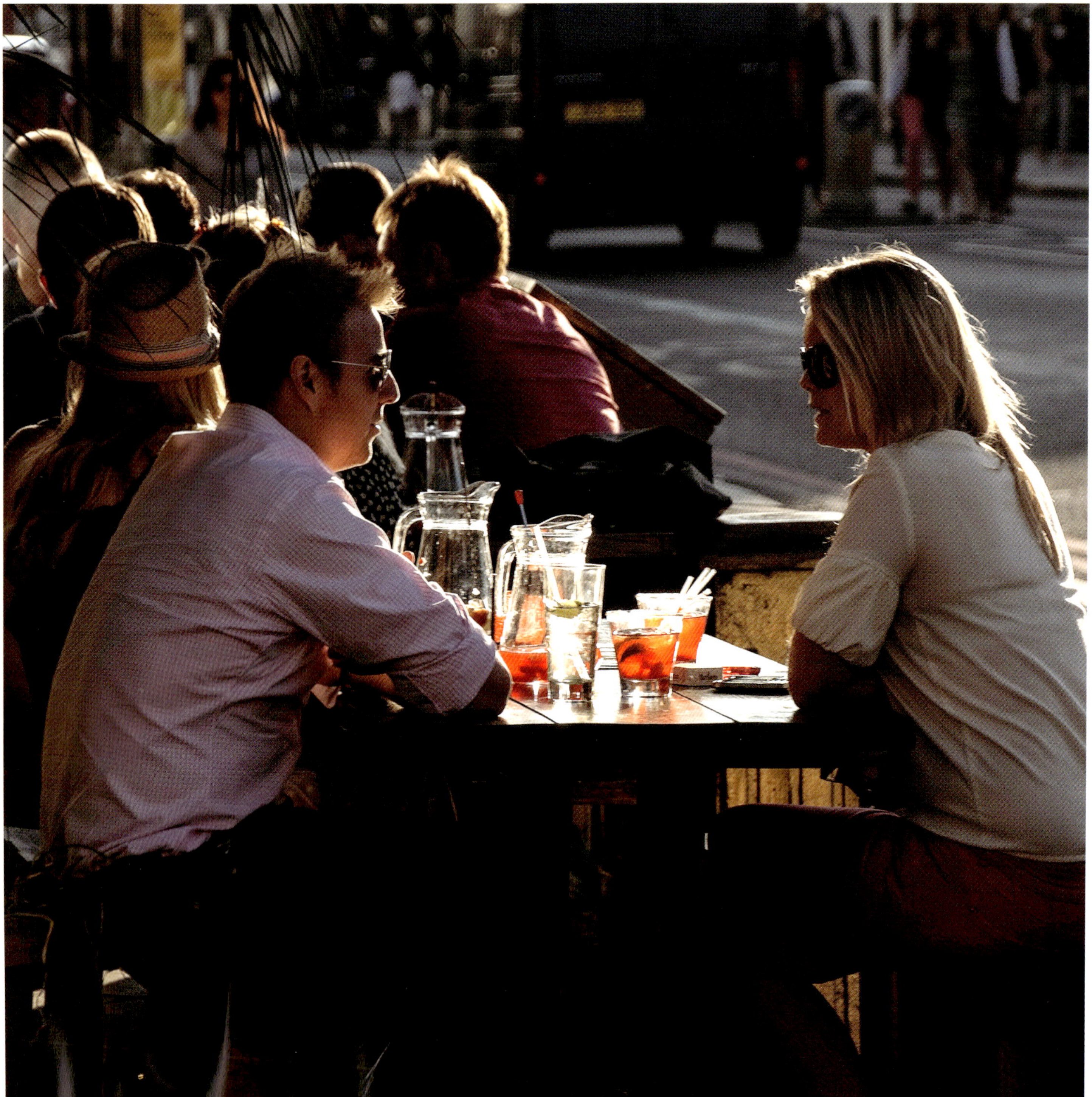

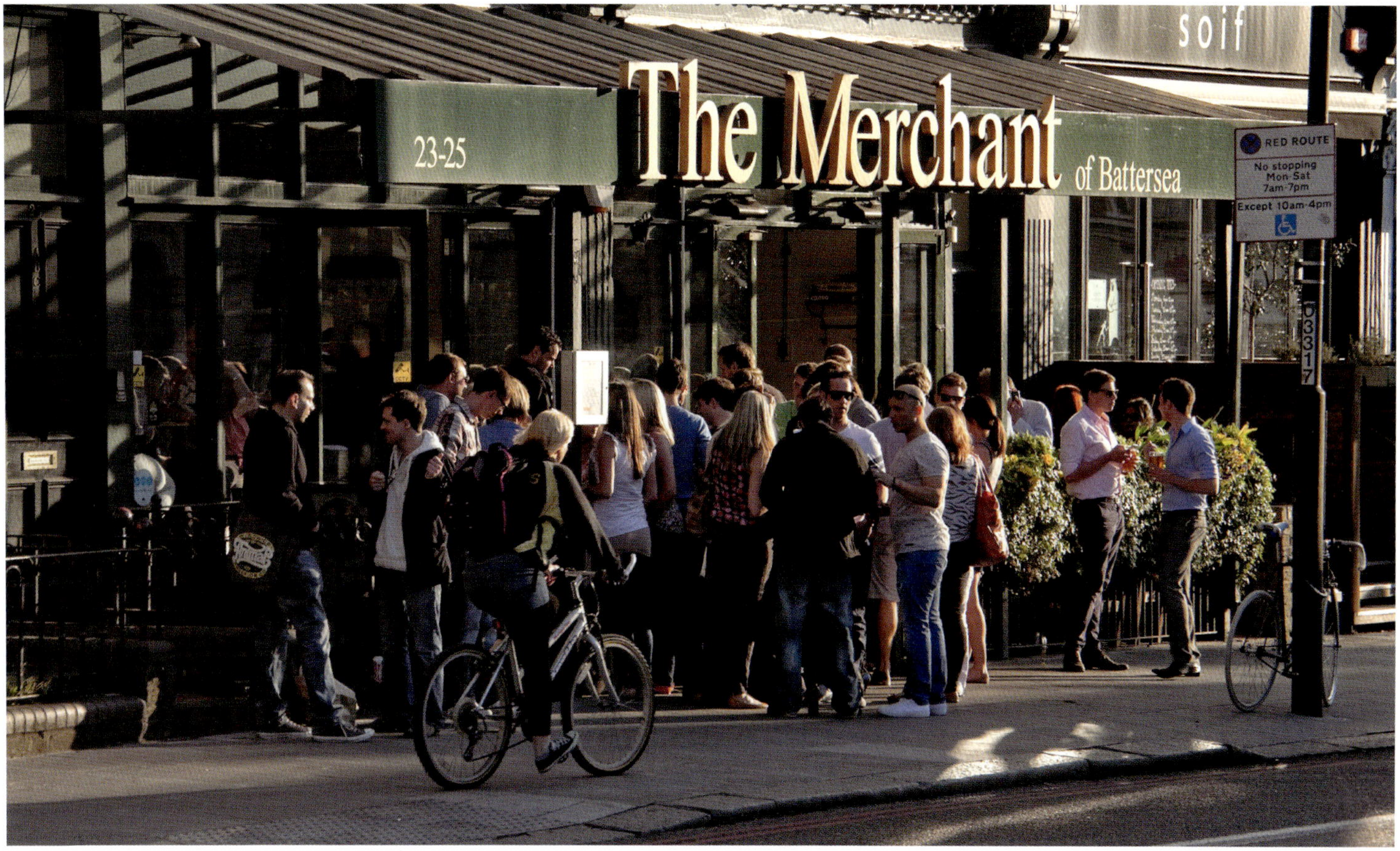

This page: Battersea Rise has some excellent bars and restaurants, especially in summer when you can sit out. There are regularly queues on the weekend at The Breakfast Club (bottom left).

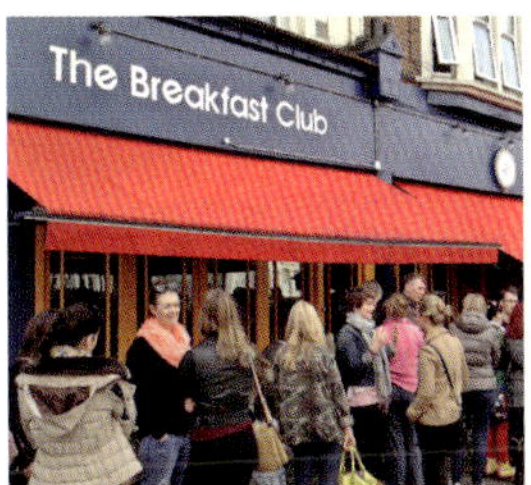

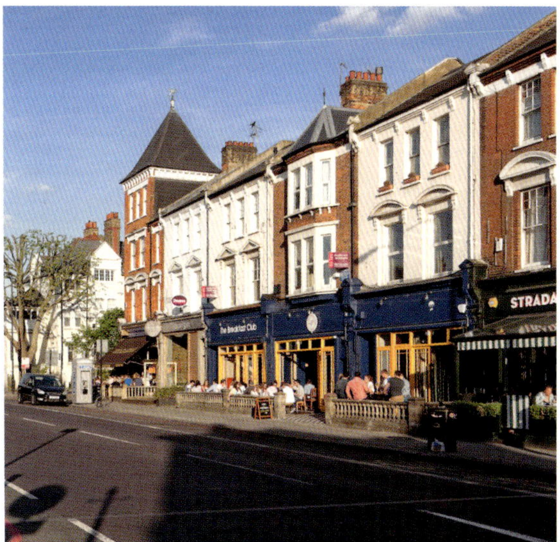

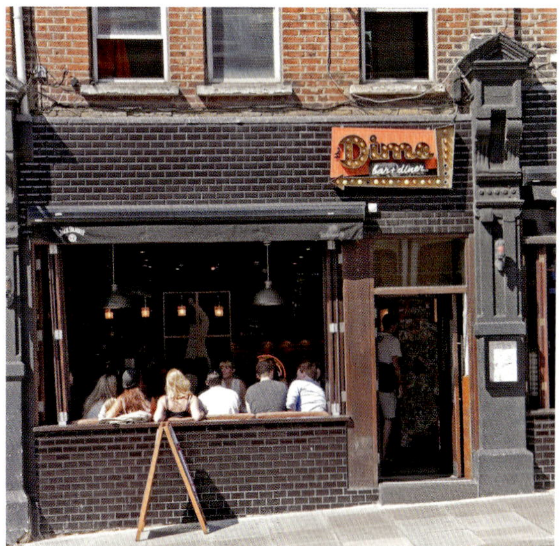

Clapham Junction Station, Battersea

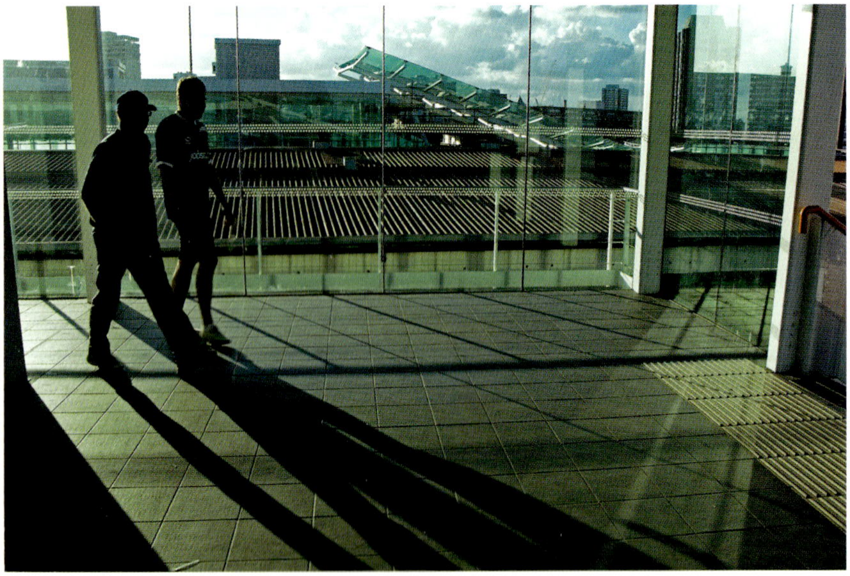

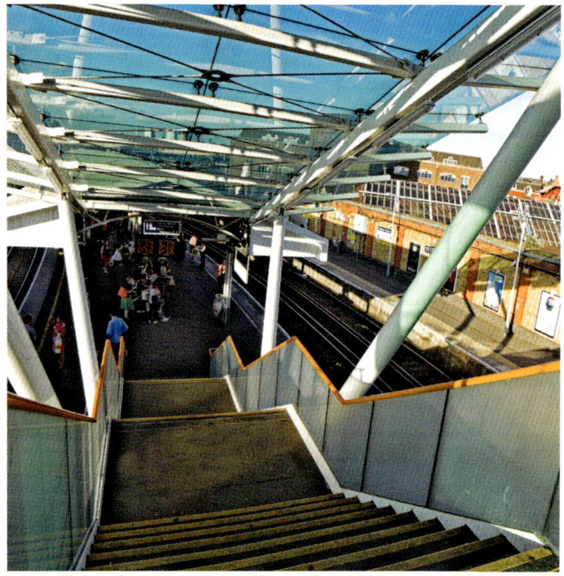

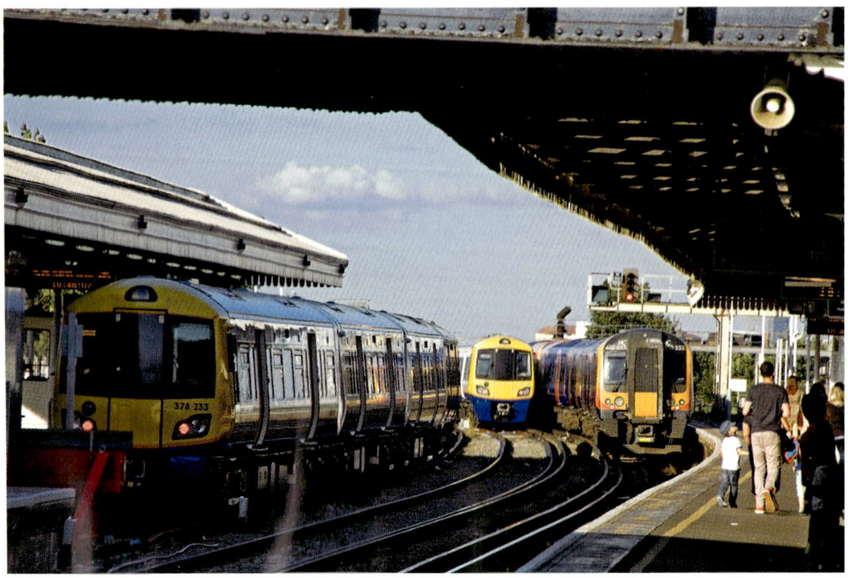

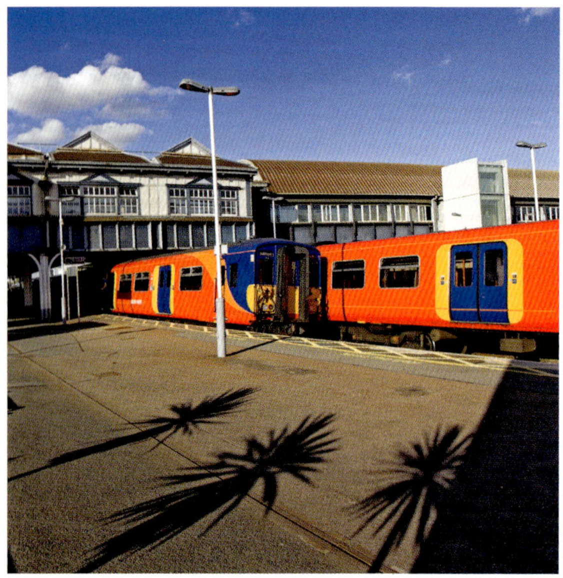

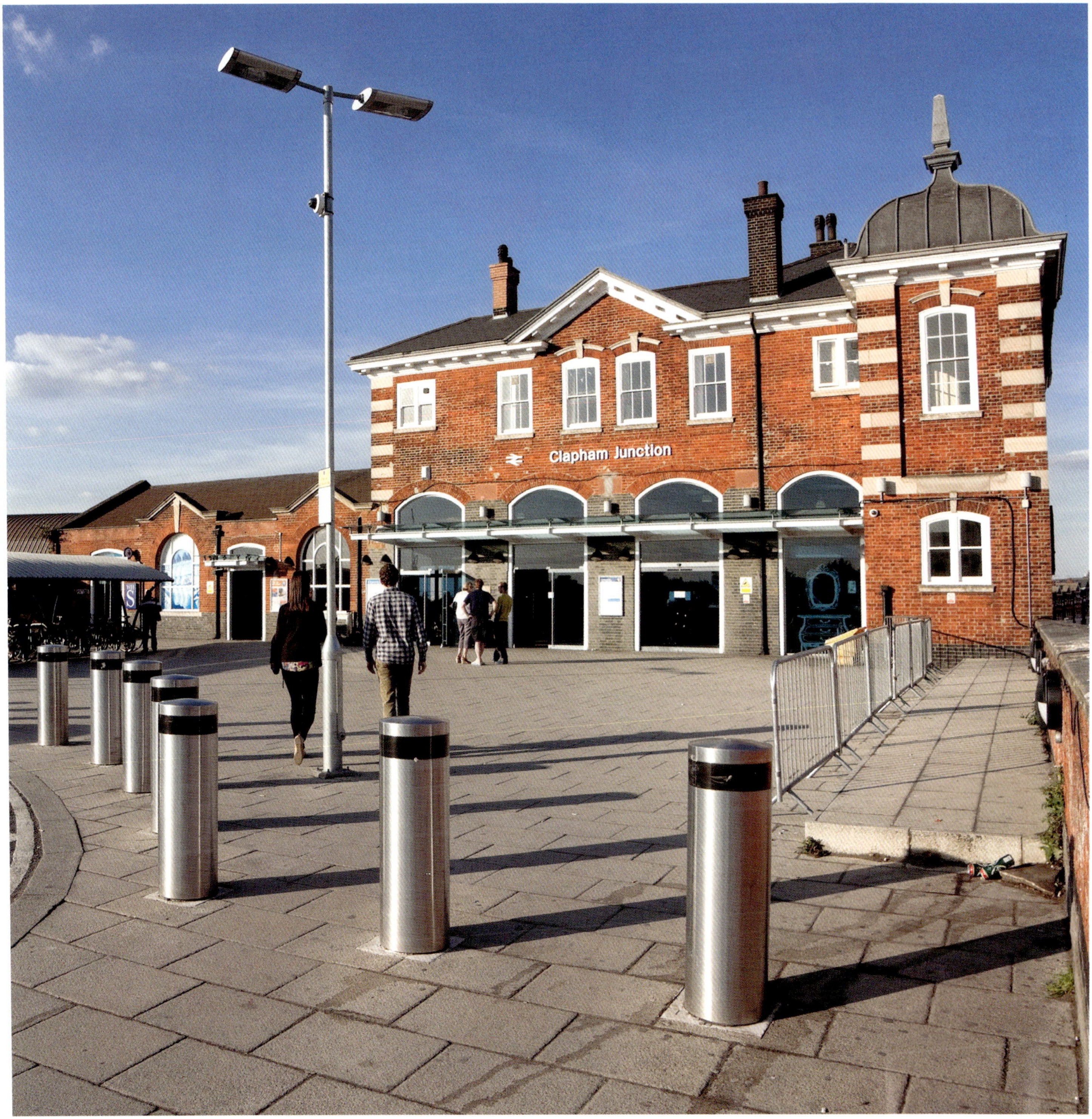
Clapham Junction

Clapham Junction is one of Europe's busiest stations, with over 100 trains an hour outside peak times. Opened in 1863, it is interesting to note that although in Battersea, the train owners at the time plumped for the grander name of Clapham, as Battersea was a much poorer district back then. Before the coming of the railway, the area was very rural and specialised in growing Lavender, hence Lavender Hill. My thanks to South West Trains, who operate the station, and the staff at the station, for allowing me to take these pictures.

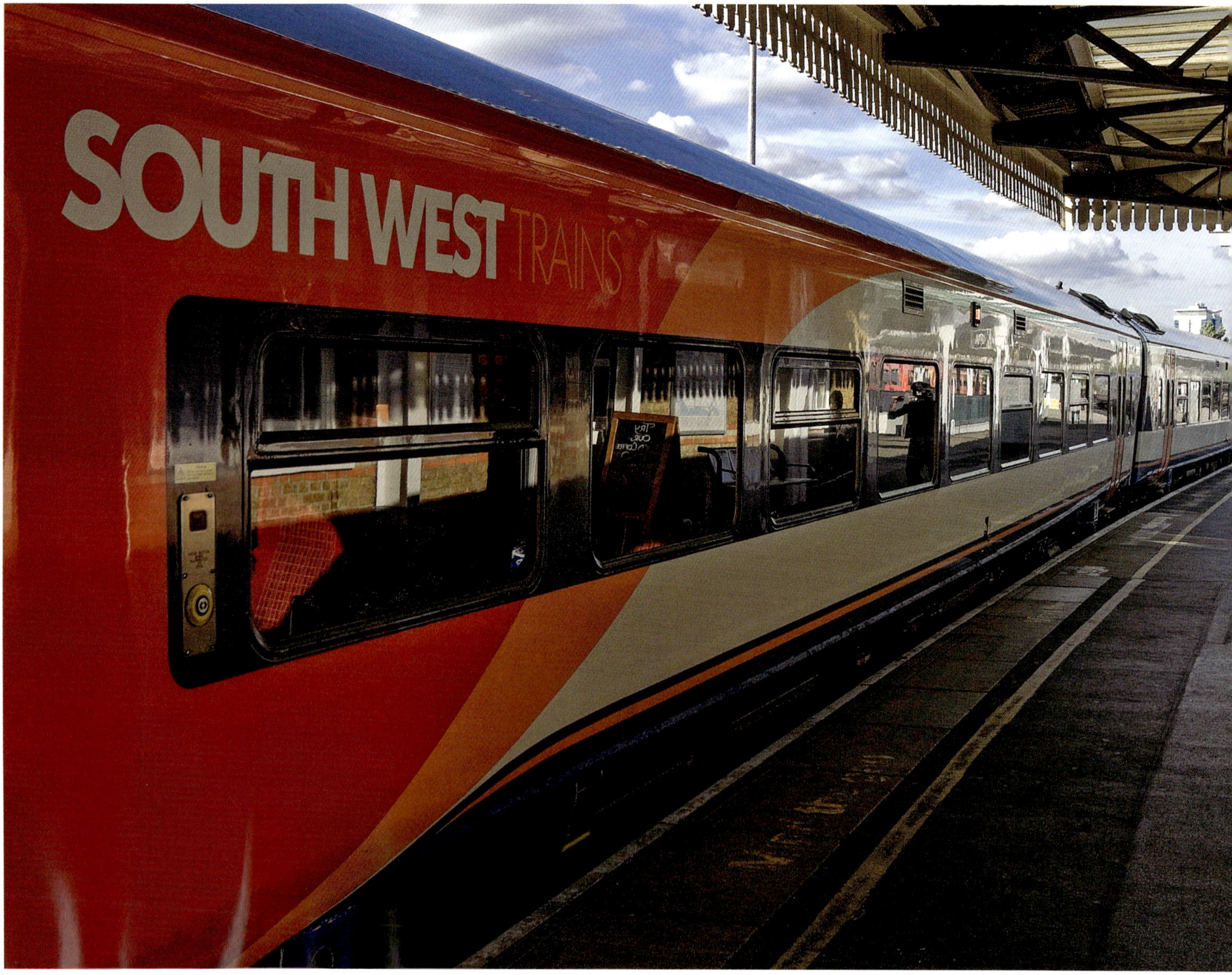

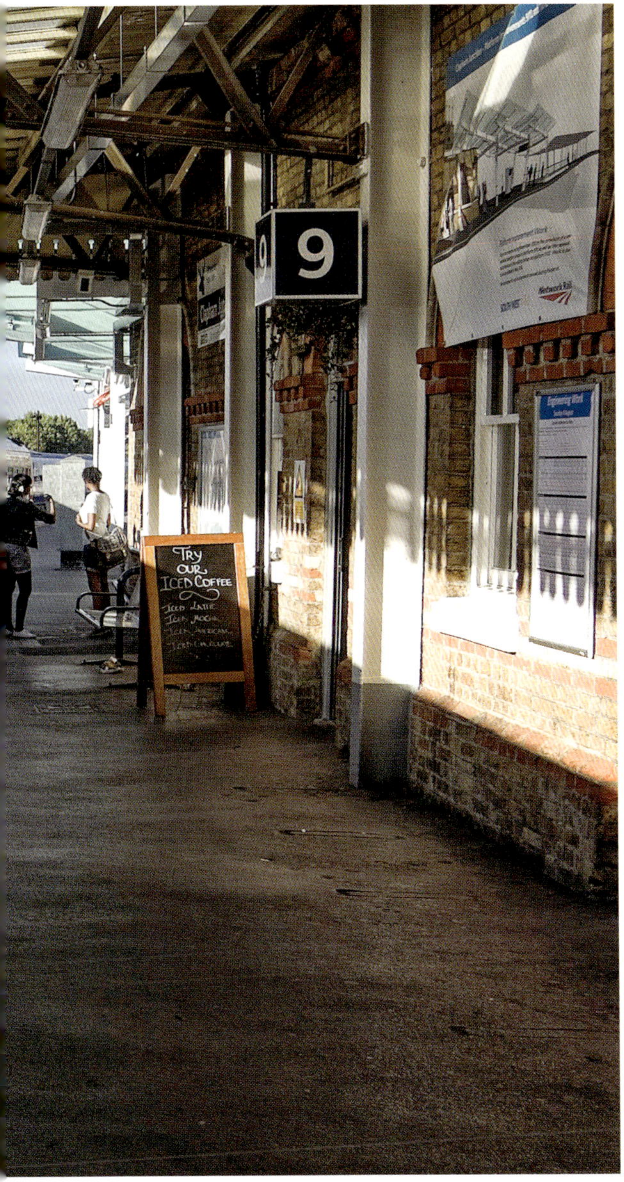
9
TRY
OUR
ICED COFFEE
Network Rail
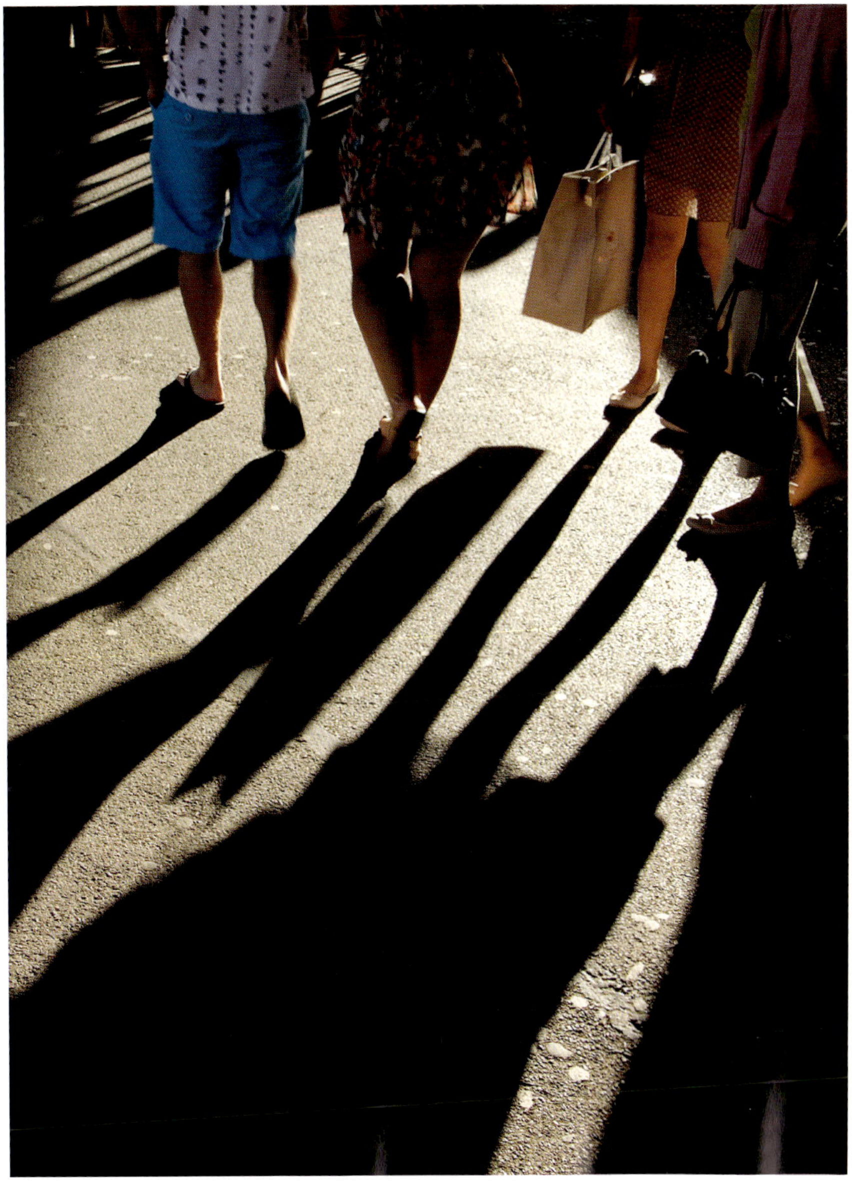

From West to East

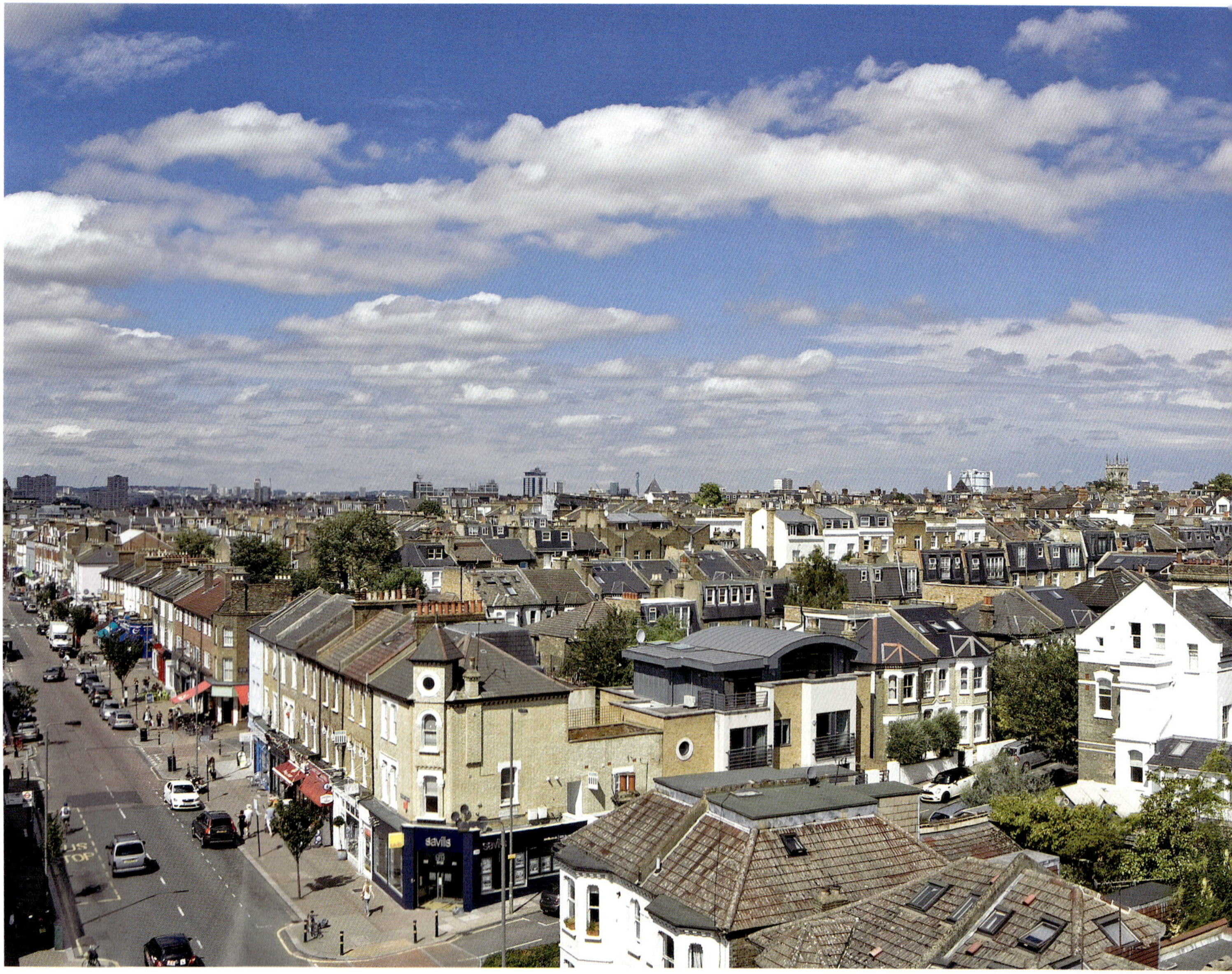

Northcote Road in Battersea lies within a valley, with roads climbing up either side, many of which directly connect Wandsworth Common with Clapham Common – west to east. This page, the view of Northcote Road left and Wakehurst Road right from the tower of Northcote Road Baptist Church. My thanks to the Rev Nick Morris for letting me up on the roof one fine afternoon last August. Nick had never been up there himself and I soon discovered why, as to gain access you have to climb through a hatch in the roof. There is a ladder but the hatch is not directly above and you have to reach up and dangle in the air to get through. I'm not known for putting myself in any form of danger, but Nick led the way, and I finally scrambled up to enjoy the spectacular view from the roof.

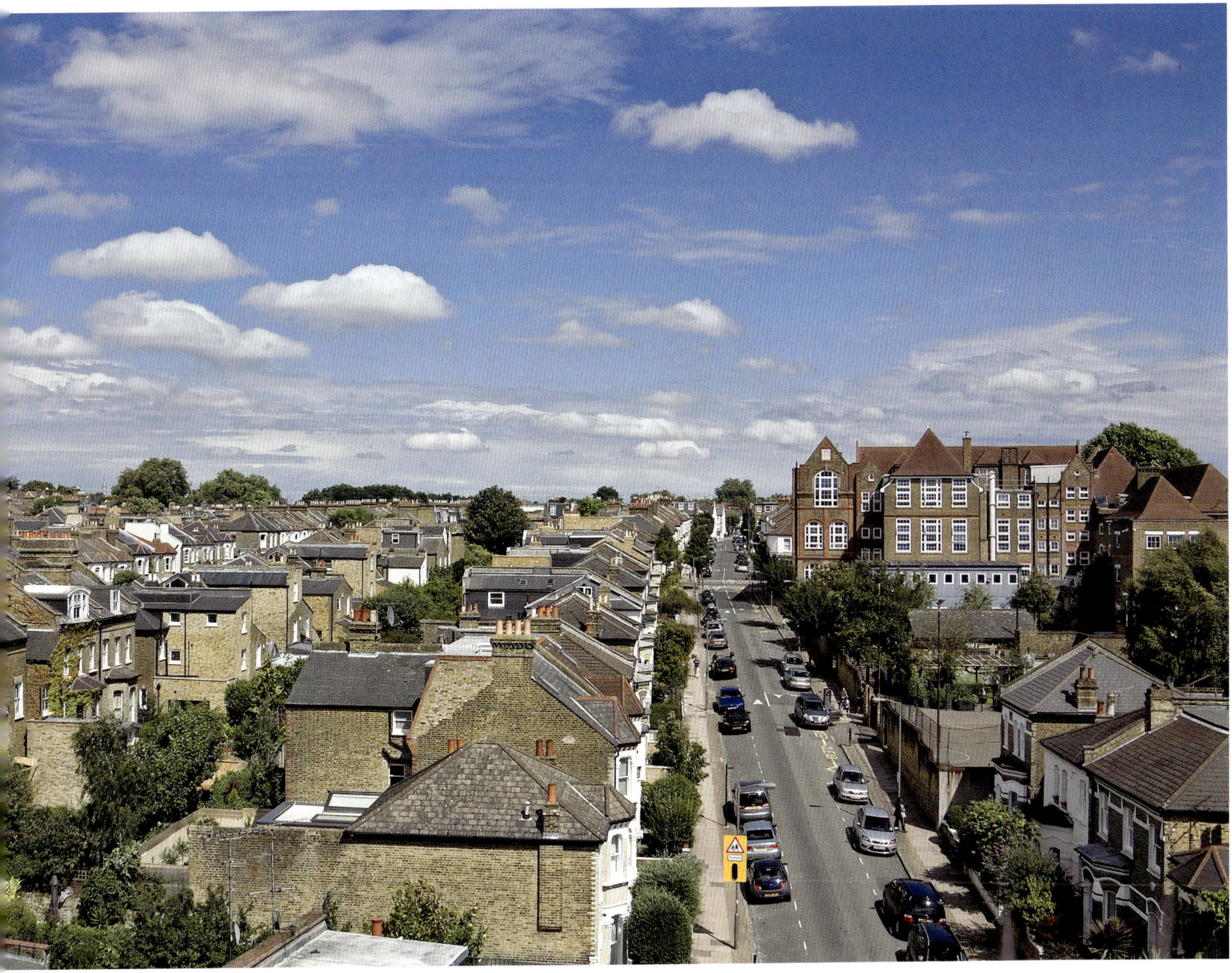

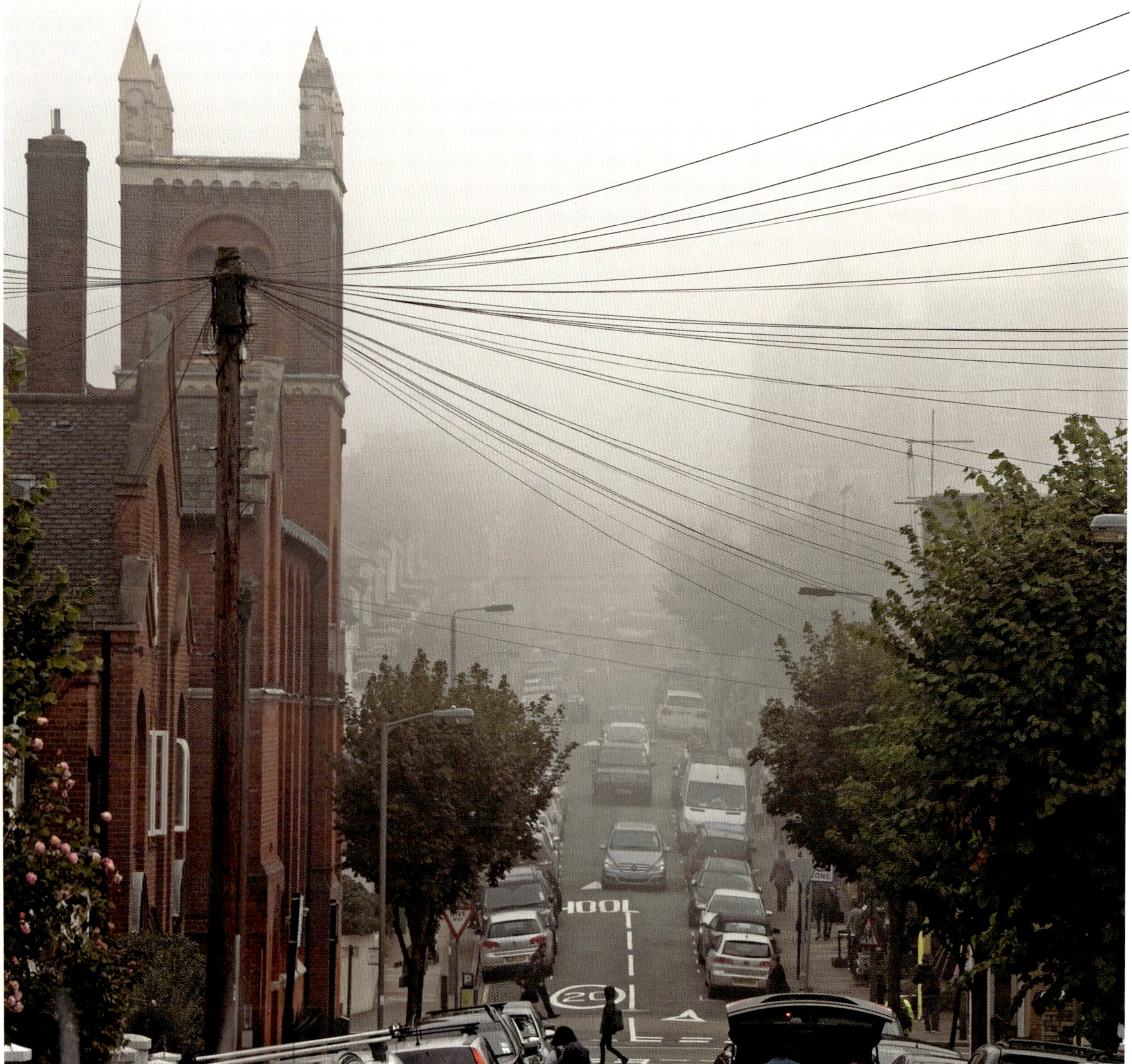
20

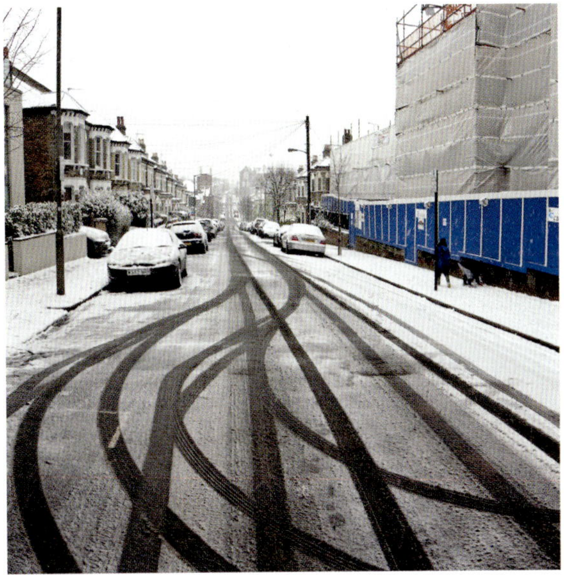

Opposite: Wakehurst Road.

Left: Wakehurst Road.

Right: Honeywell Road.

Bottom: Bramfield Road.

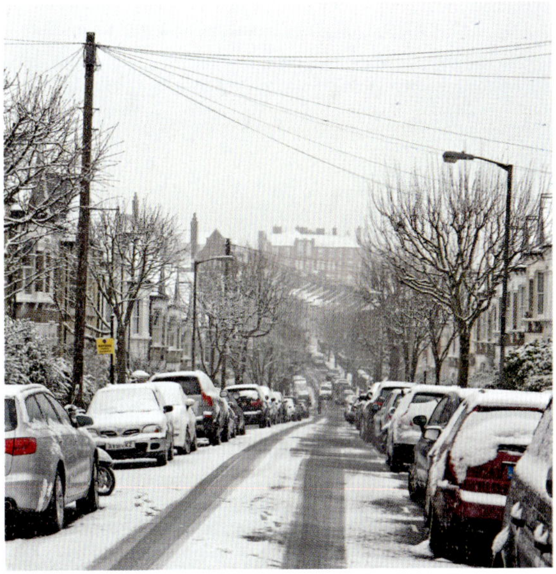

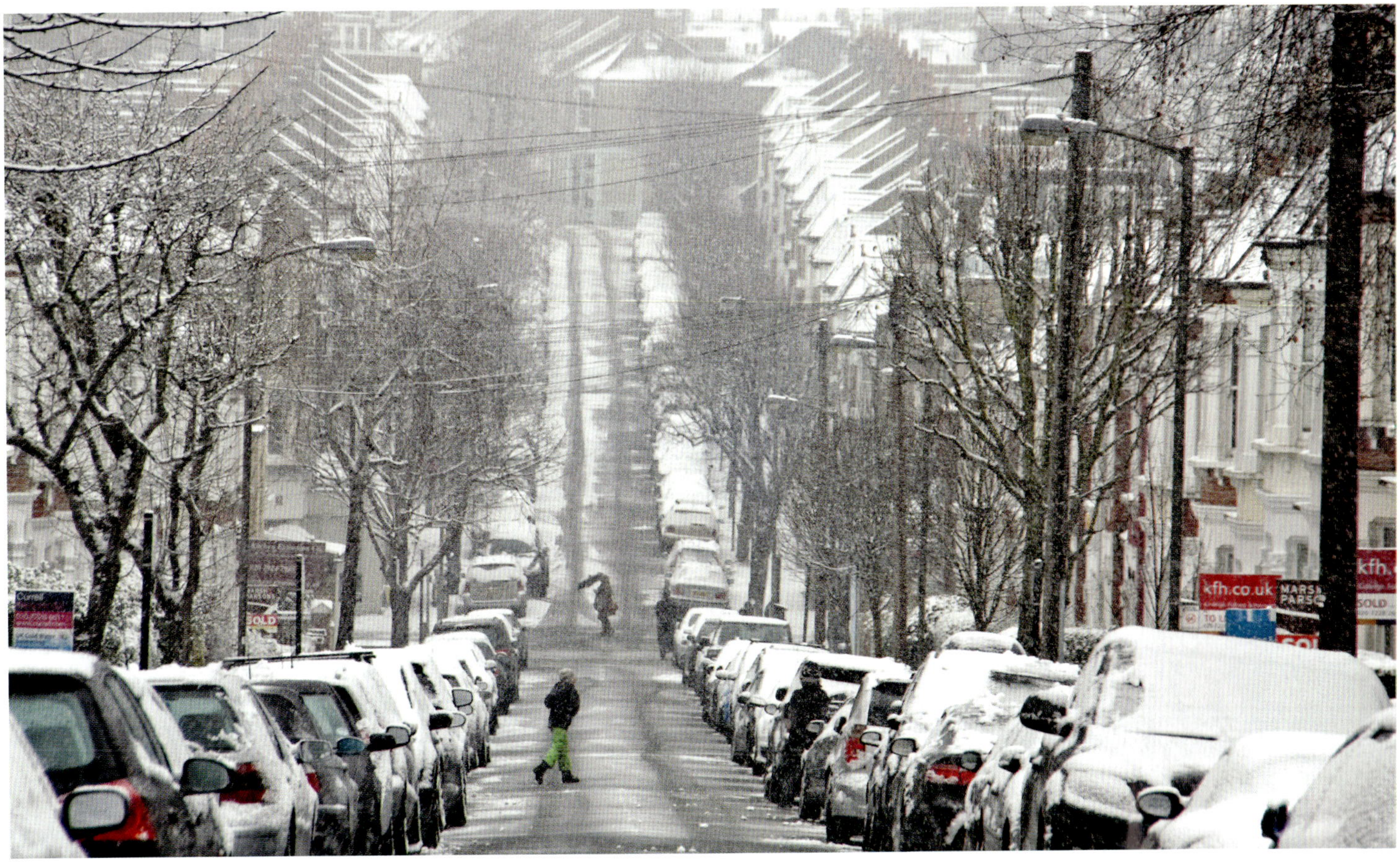

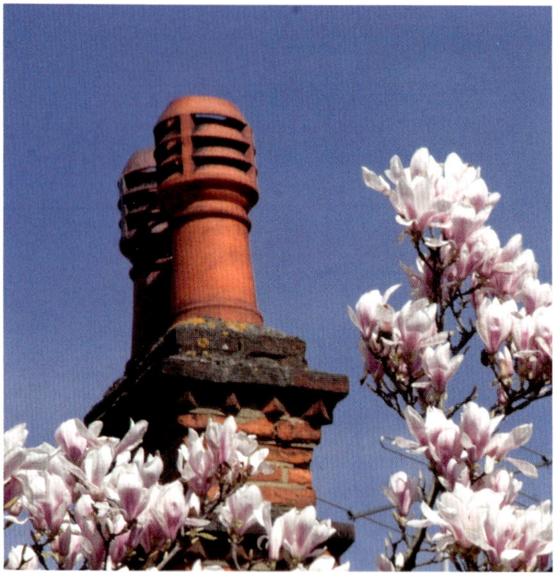

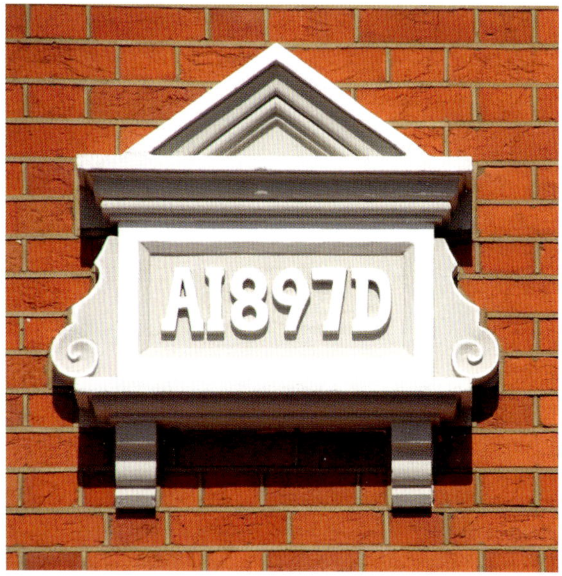

Top left and right, and opposite: Thurleigh Road has some particularly fine houses. The church at the top of the road is St. Luke's Battersea.

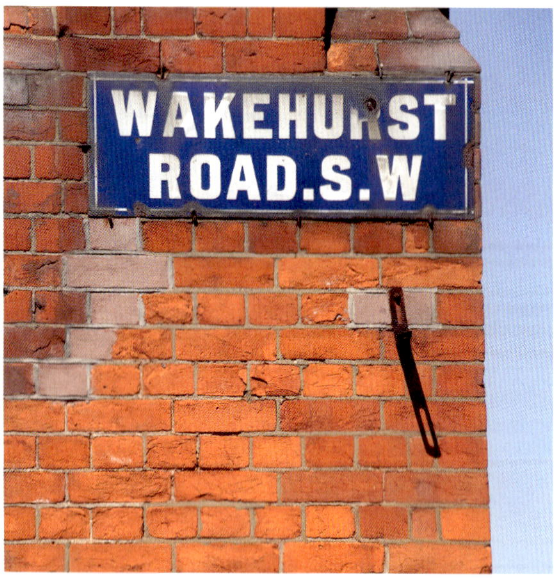

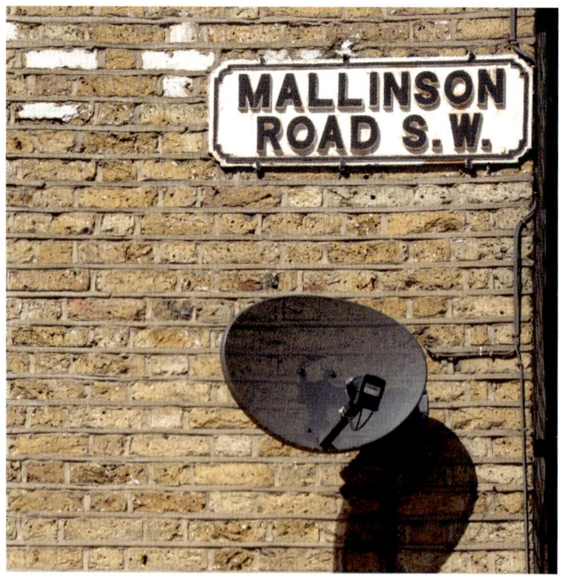

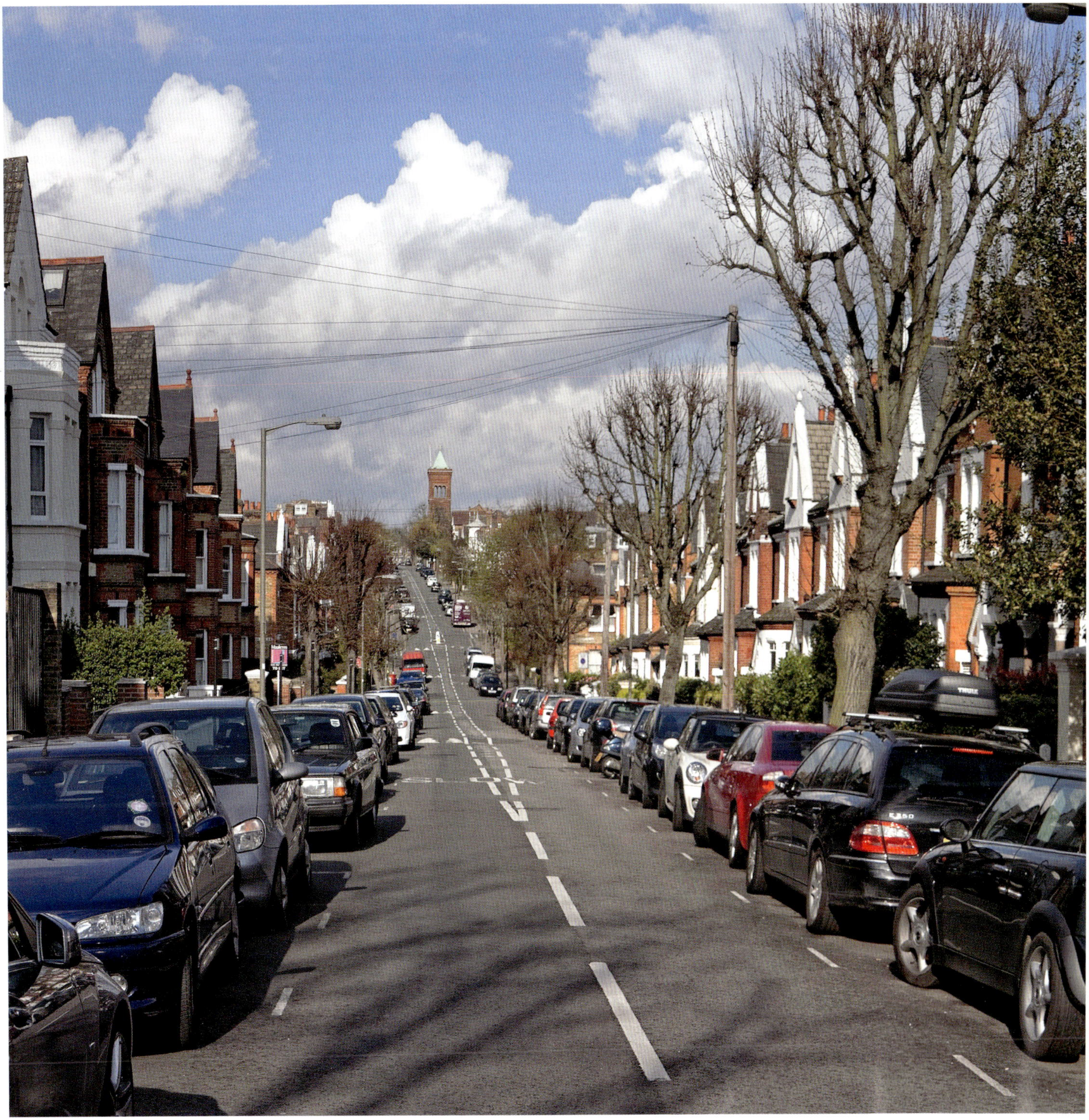

Lavender Hill

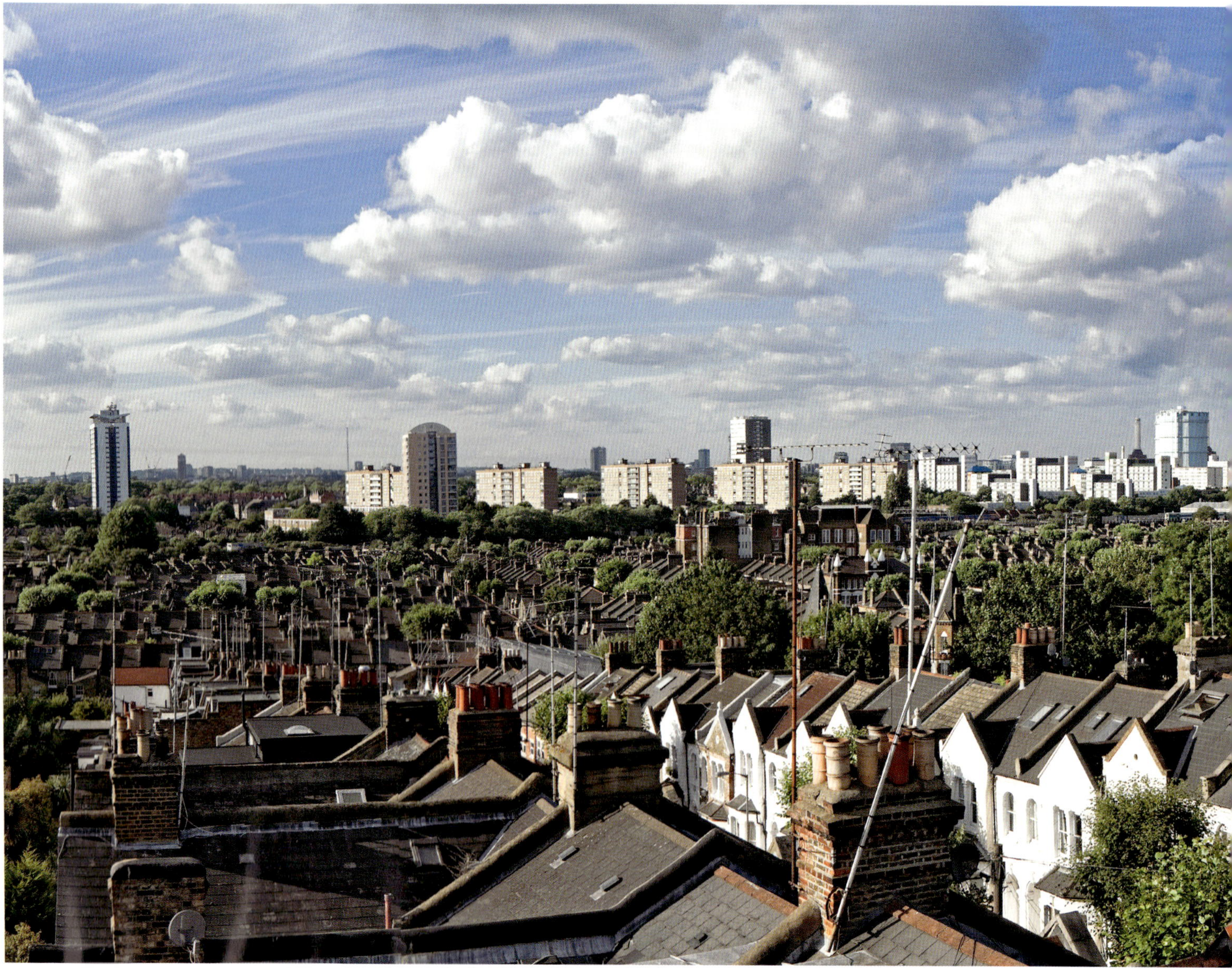

Main picture: I am grateful to George Bramble for letting me into his home on Lavender Hill one fine summer's evening to admire the view from his roof terrace and take this picture.

Right: Battersea Library.

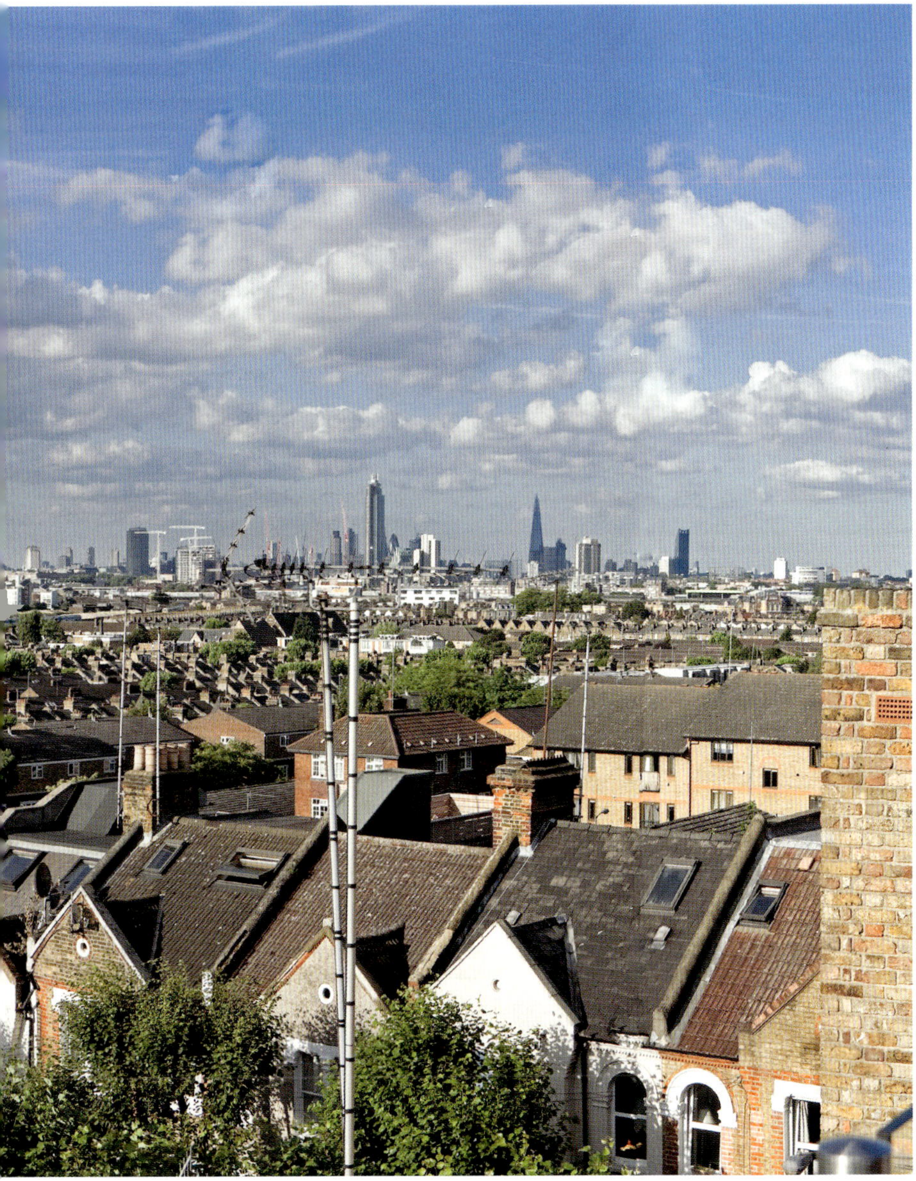

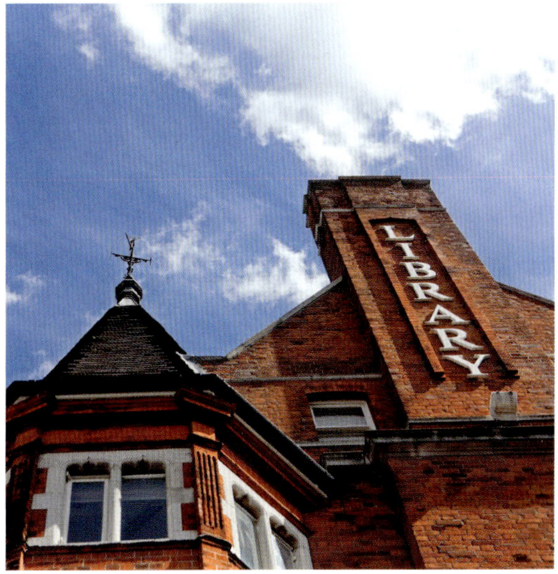

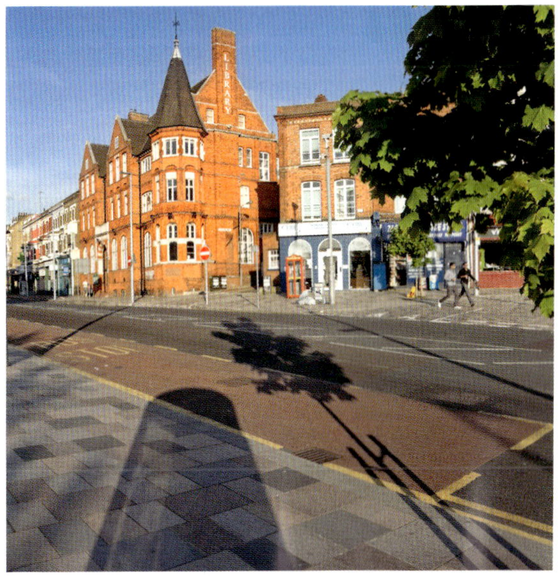

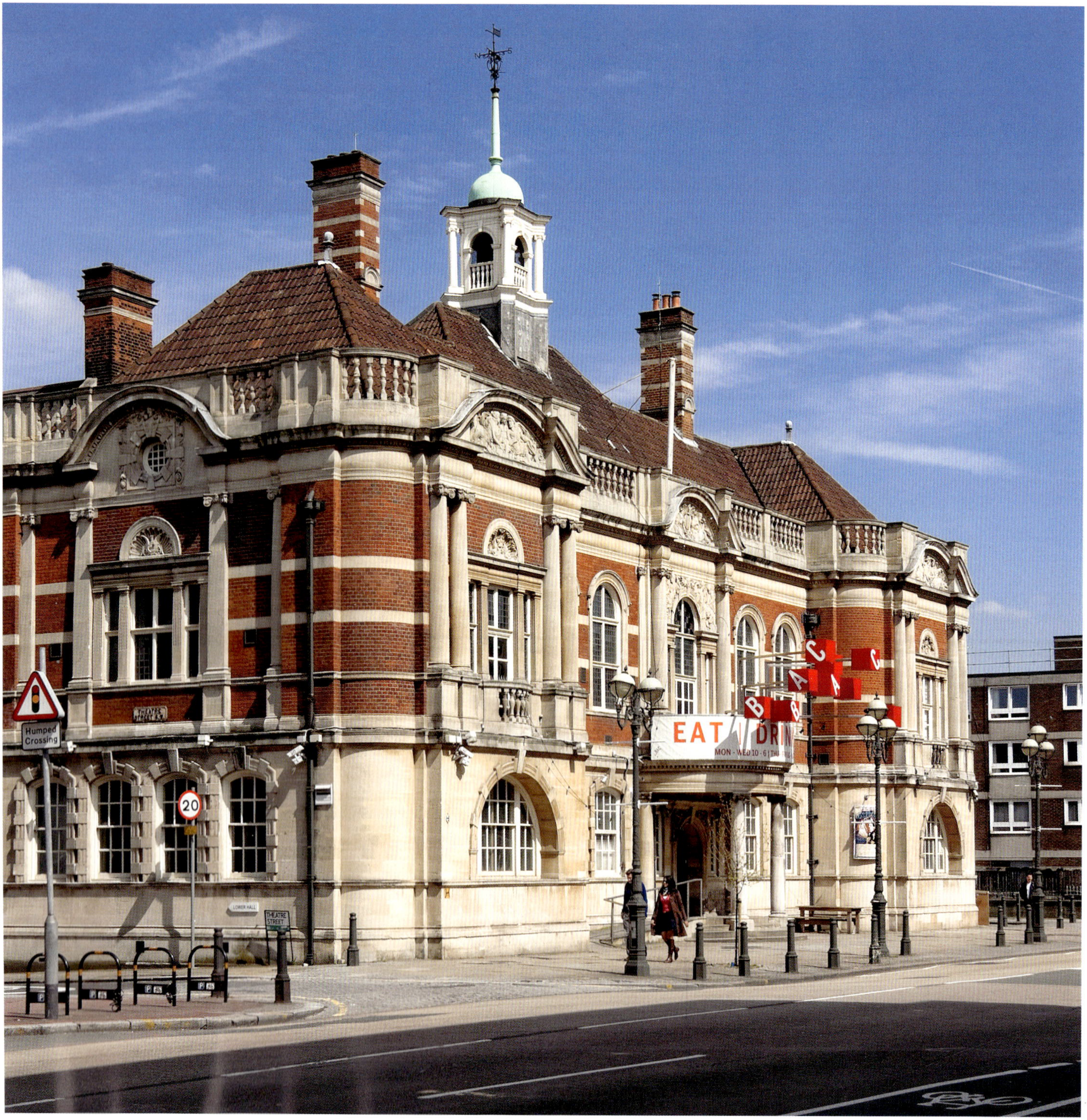
Humped Crossing
20
EAT

This spread: The Battersea Arts Centre. Built in 1893, this is the former Battersea Town Hall. When in 1965 the Borough of Battersea was absorbed by Wandsworth, the building was threatened with development. Thankfully it was saved by the efforts of a local campaign and the building was subsequently Grade II listed in 1970.

Overleaf: On the intersection of Lavender Hill and St John's Road can be found the old Arding & Hobbs department store, now a Debenhams. Arding and Hobbs started as a drapery store in Wandsworth High Street in 1867 but moved to this better site in 1885. Following a fire in 1909 the present building was completed in 1910. I am grateful to the website for British Listed Buildings for these facts.

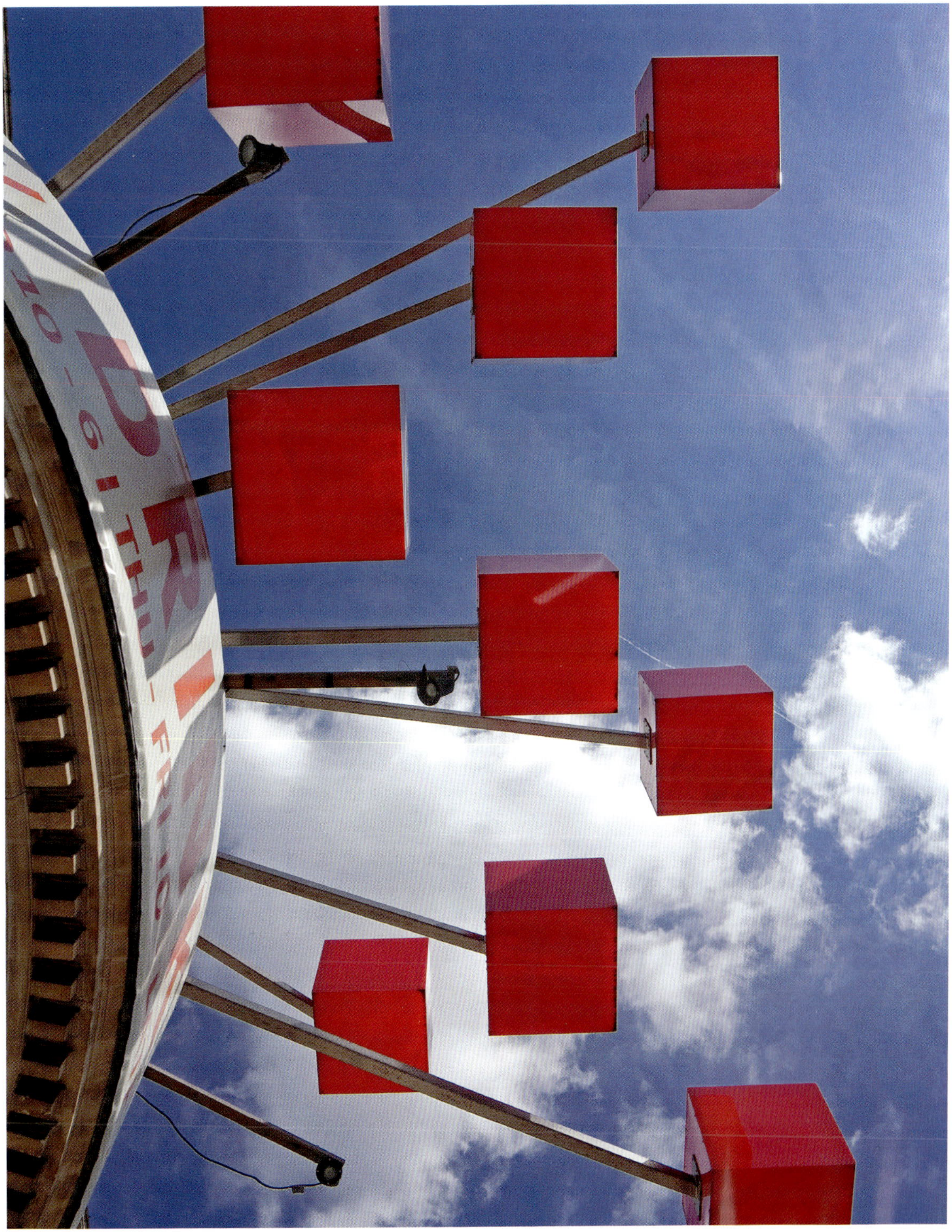

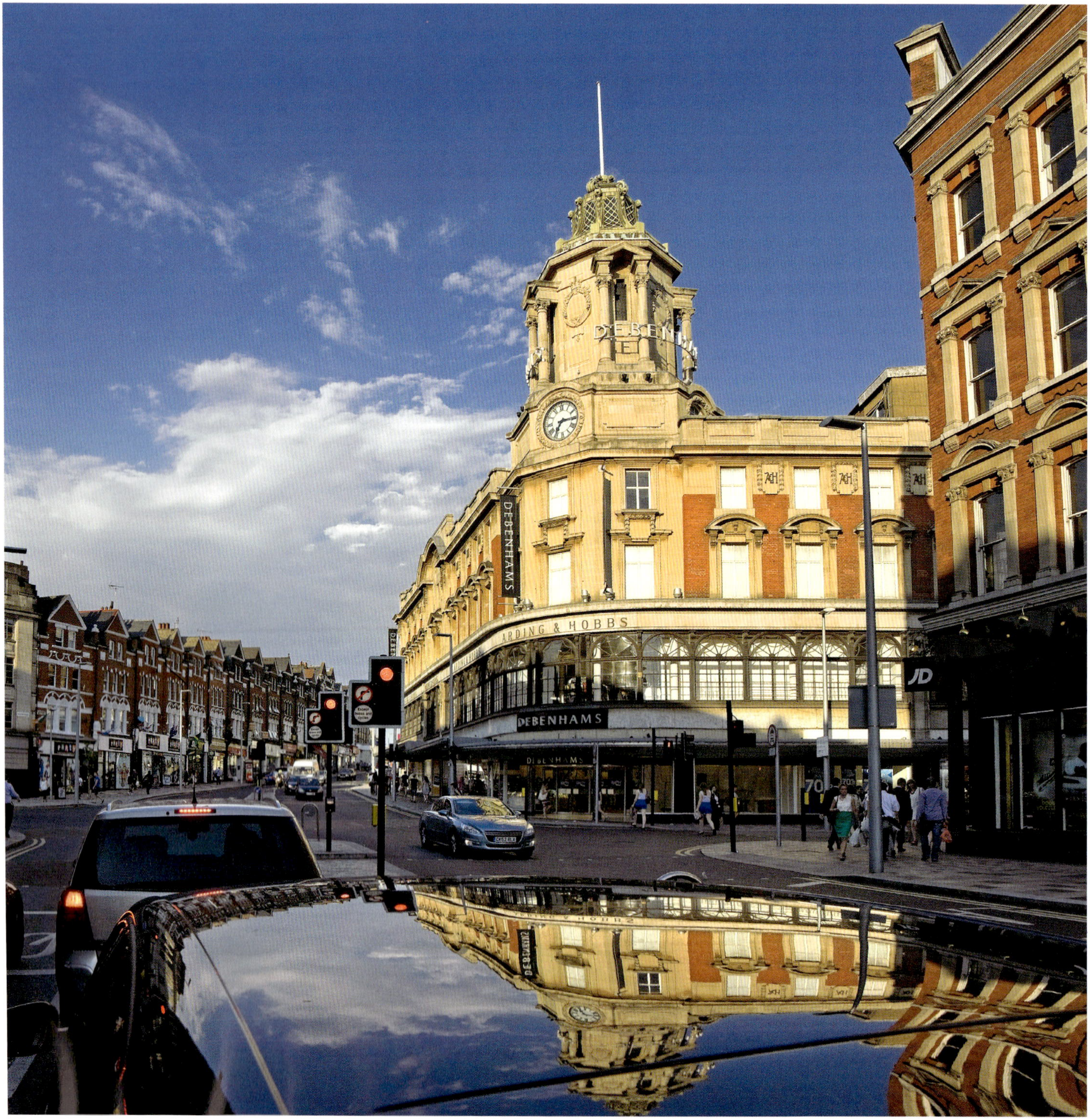
DEBENHAMS
ARDING & HOBBS
DEBENHAMS
JD

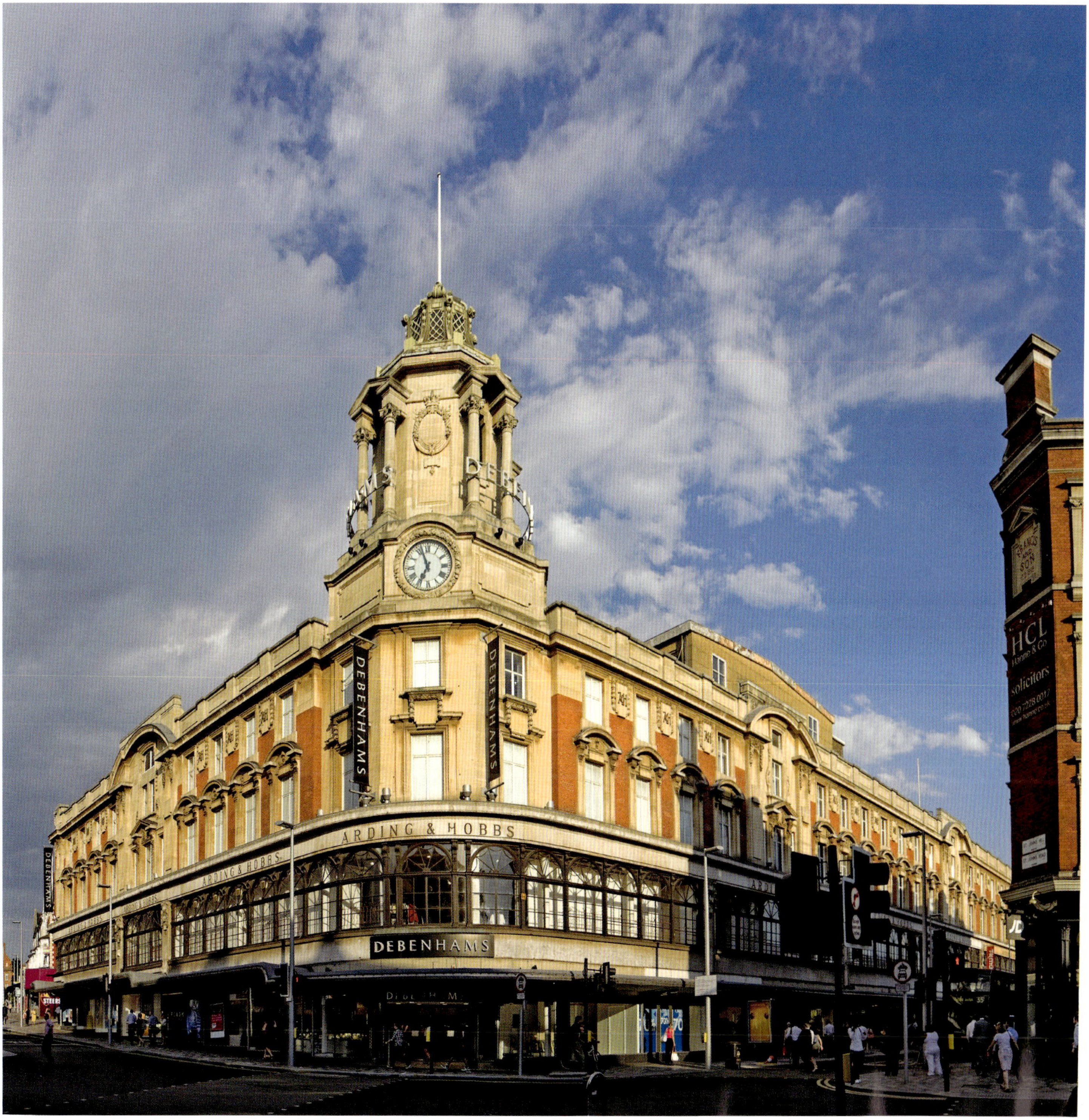
DEBENHAMS
DEBENHAMS
ARDING & HOBBS
ARDING & HOBBS
DEBENHAMS
HCL
solicitors

Bellevue Road

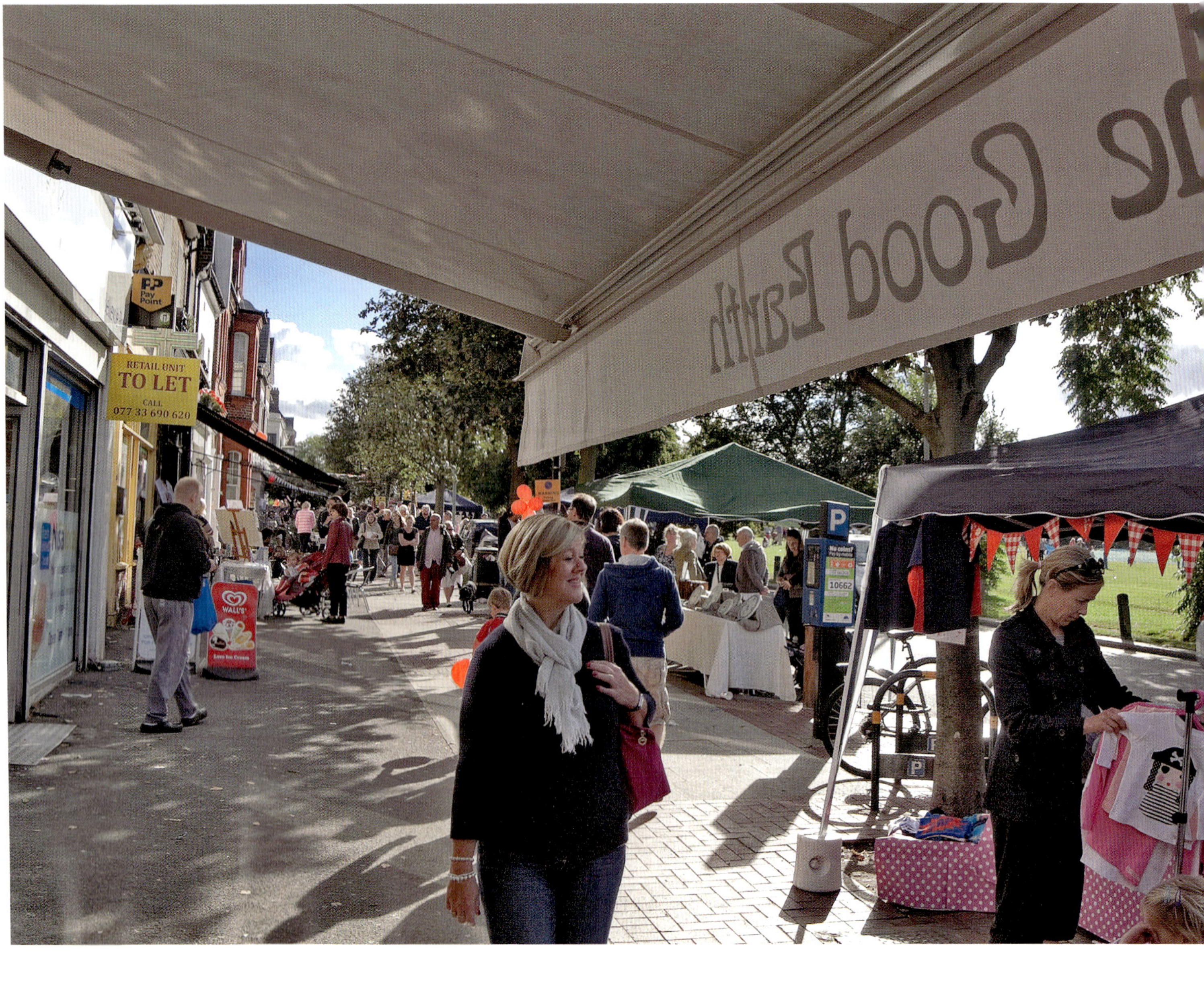

This page and overleaf: On the south side of Wandsworth Common, near the station can be found this lovely row of shops. Unlike many of London's shopping streets, it's only built up on one side and looks right out onto the common. In September 2013 they held their annual Summer Fair, with stalls along the side of the road and numerous activities out on the common. Although cloudy it fortunately didn't rain, but it's a shame they couldn't have closed the road for the day, like they do with Nightingale Lane.

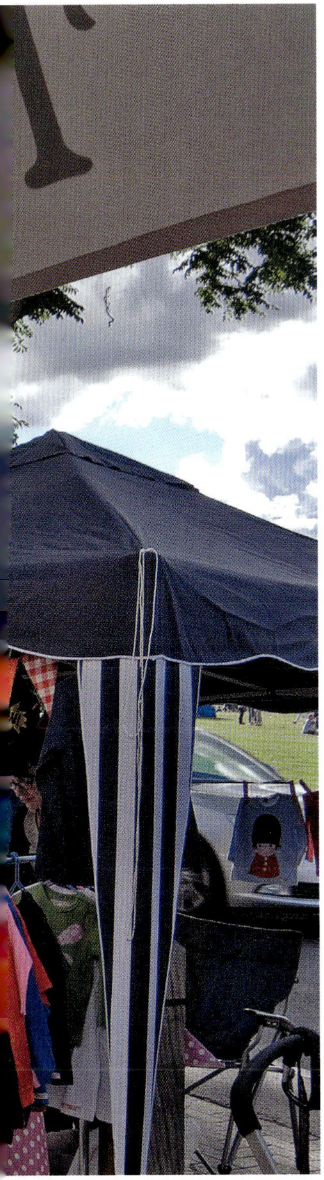

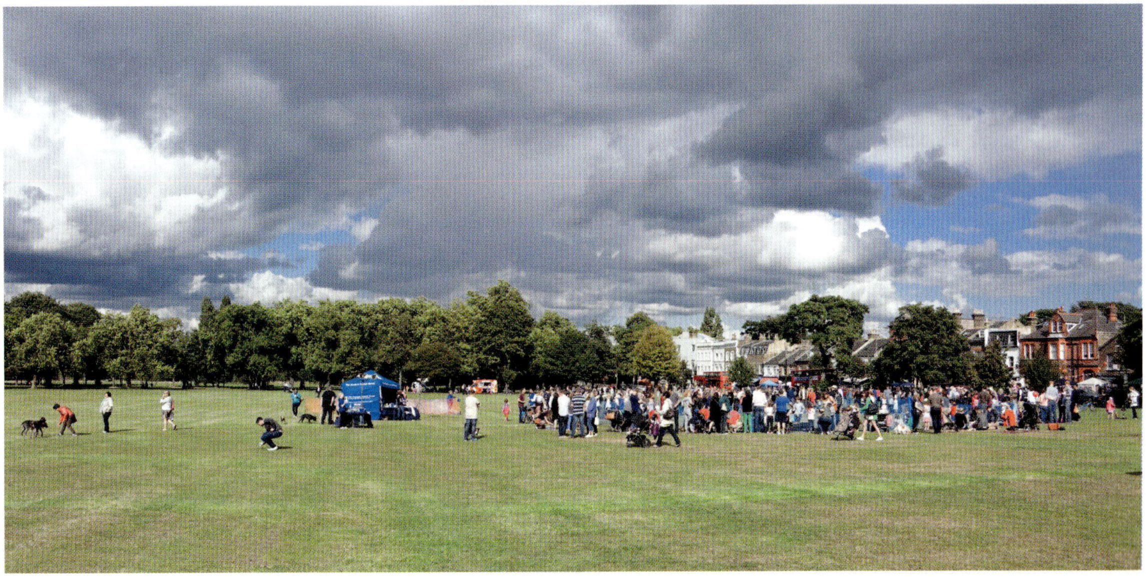

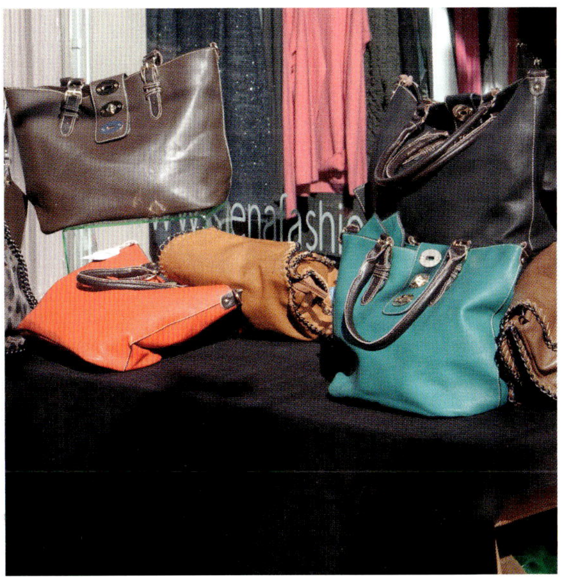

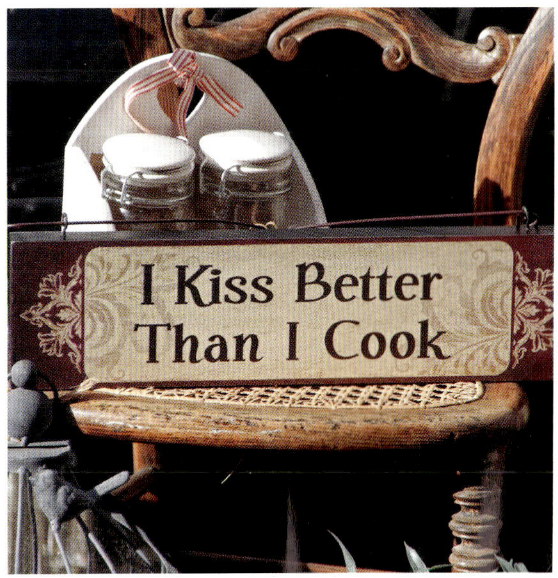

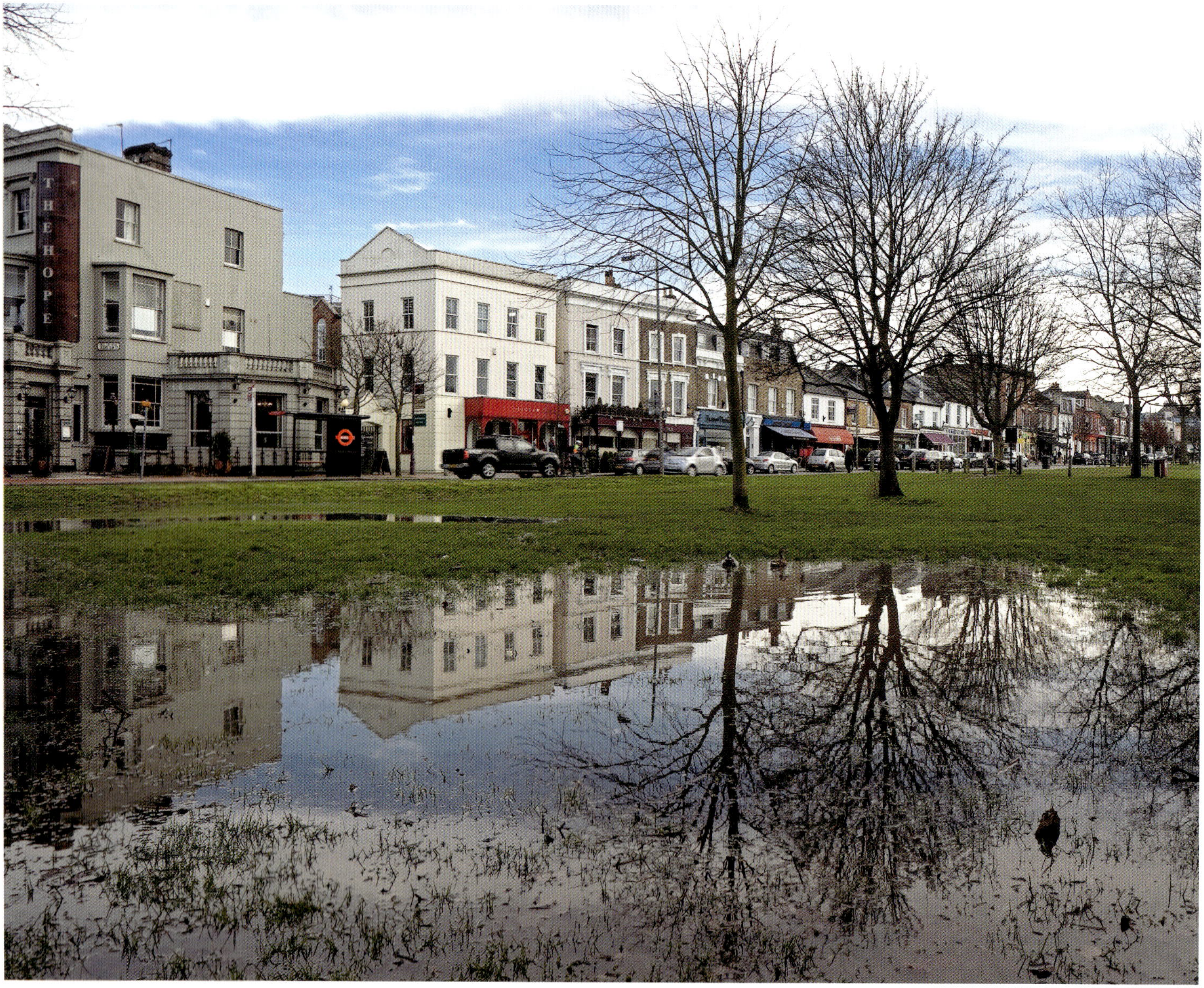
THE HOPE

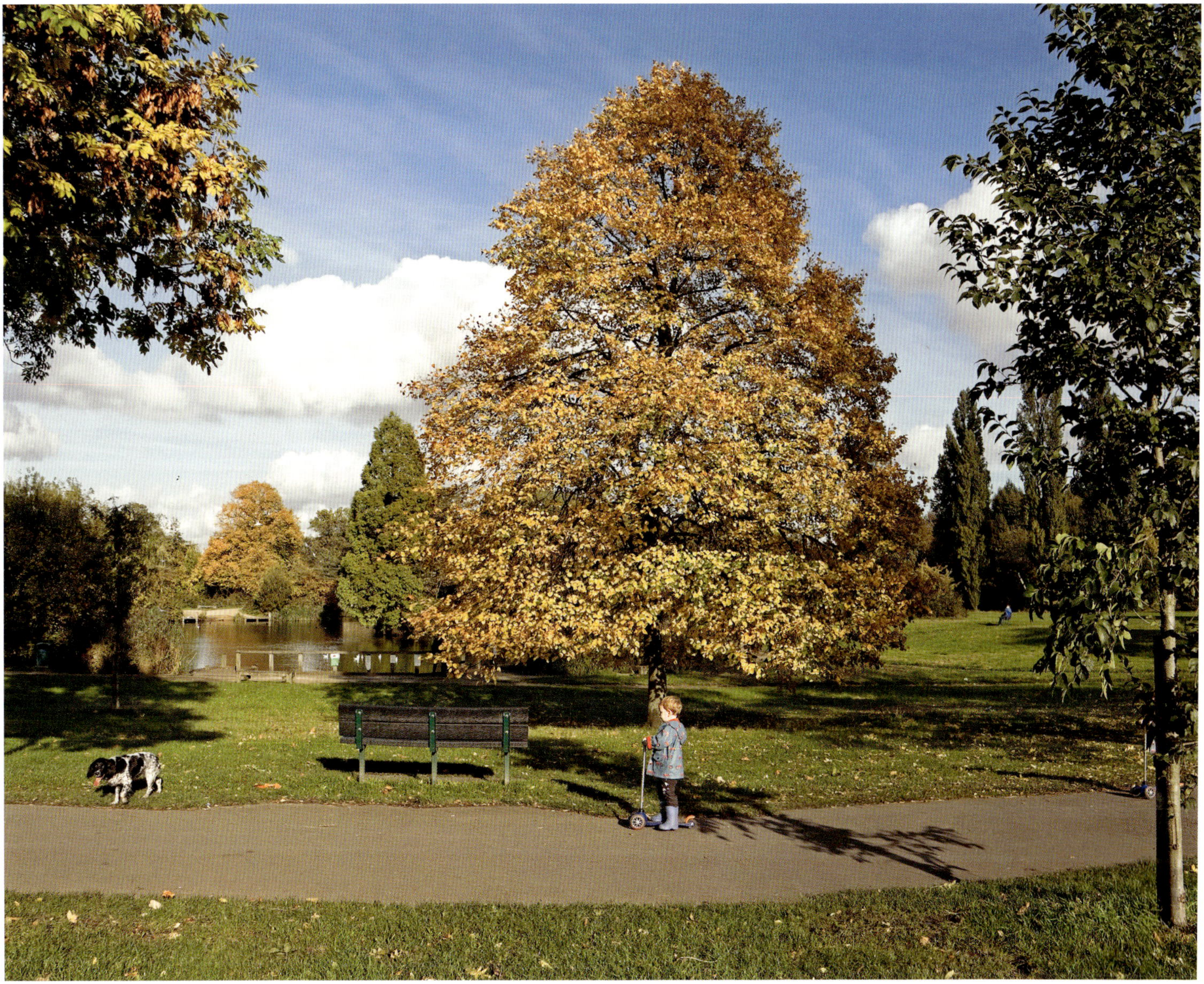

Opposite: Bellevue Road in early 2013.

This page: The common October 2013. Autumn came very late this year with October being very mild.

Nightingale Lane

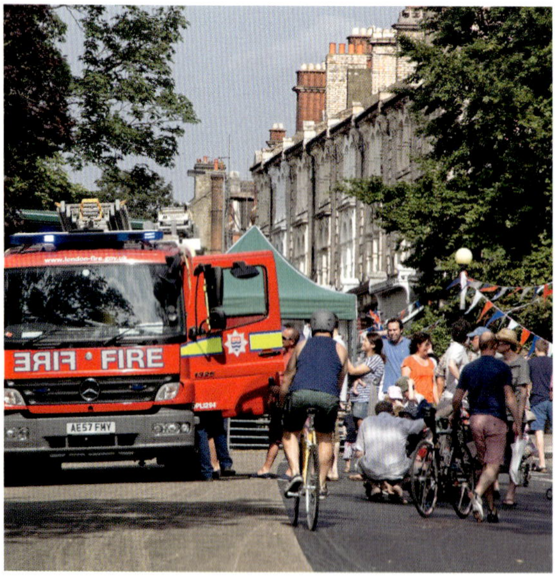

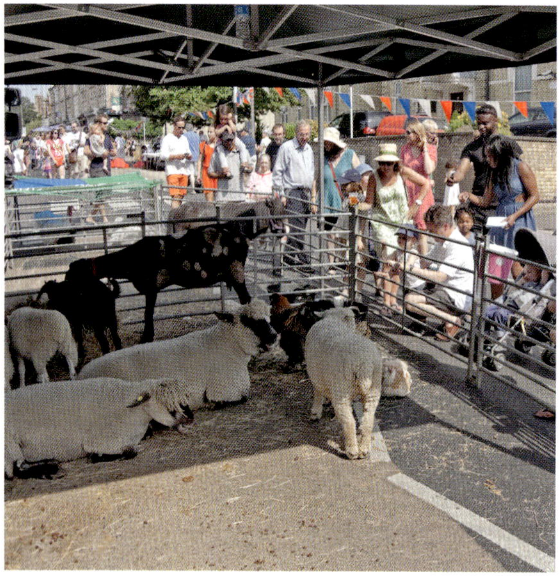

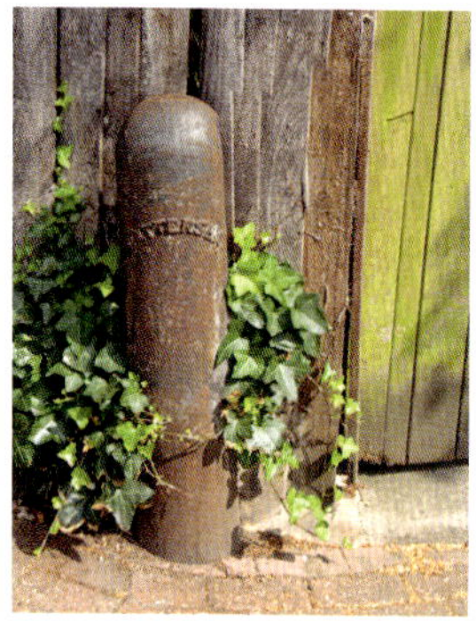

Each summer, Nightingale Lane hosts the Between the Commons Country Fayre. A lovely day – with the road closed, everybody could had a fun time with the usual array of stalls, rides on the Young's Brewery shire horses, and even some livestock. Nightingale Lane is part of the southern boundary of Battersea (pictured above).

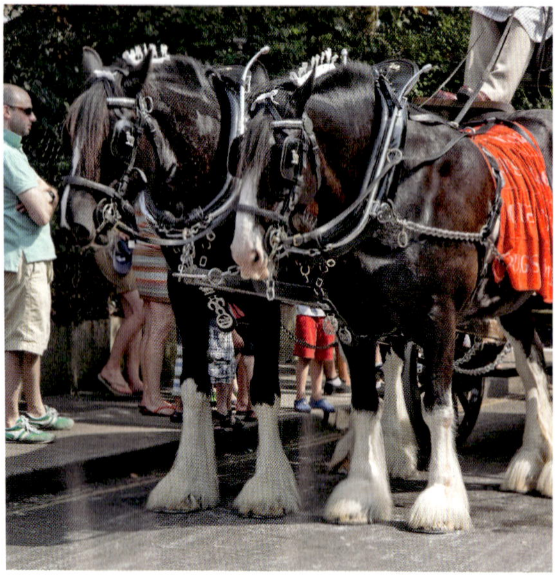

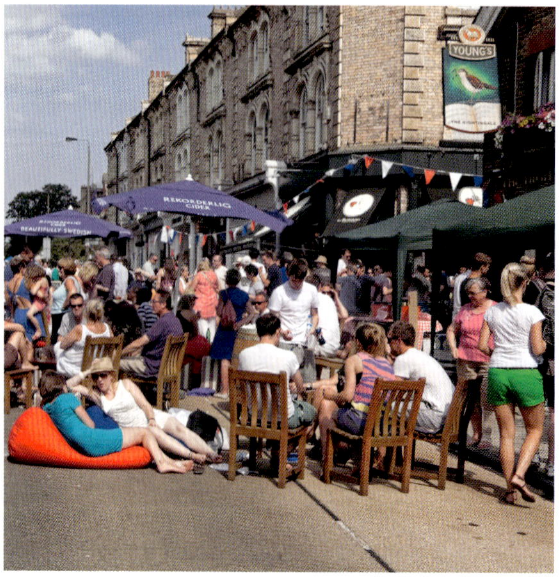

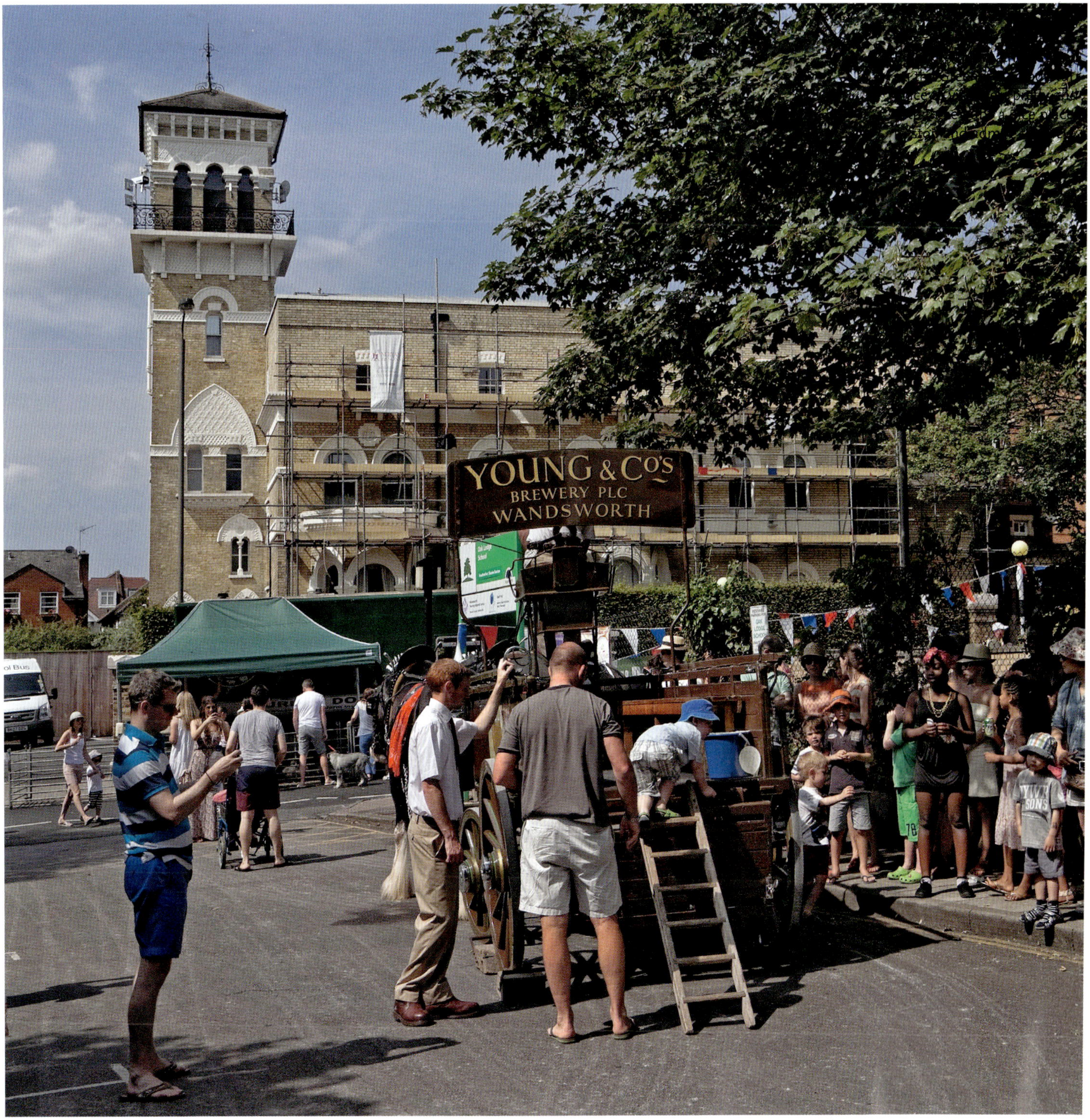
YOUNG & Co's
BREWERY PLC
WANDSWORTH

Northcote Road

Over the last 20 years or so Northcote Road has changed radically, and become the bustling, thriving street you find today. Mary Portas, as part of her recent report to The Government regarding the future of our high streets, refers to them needing to change. You could say that Northcote Road is a good example of that. These days it is every bit as much a destination as it is a shopping street. With countless bars and restaurants as well as many shops it is wonderful place to visit. They also hold an amazing annual fair in the summer (see page 14 for more on this). Northcote Road is sometimes referred to as Nappy Valley, and a valley it most certainly is, given it runs along what was once the Falcon Brook. The brook is still there but covered over.

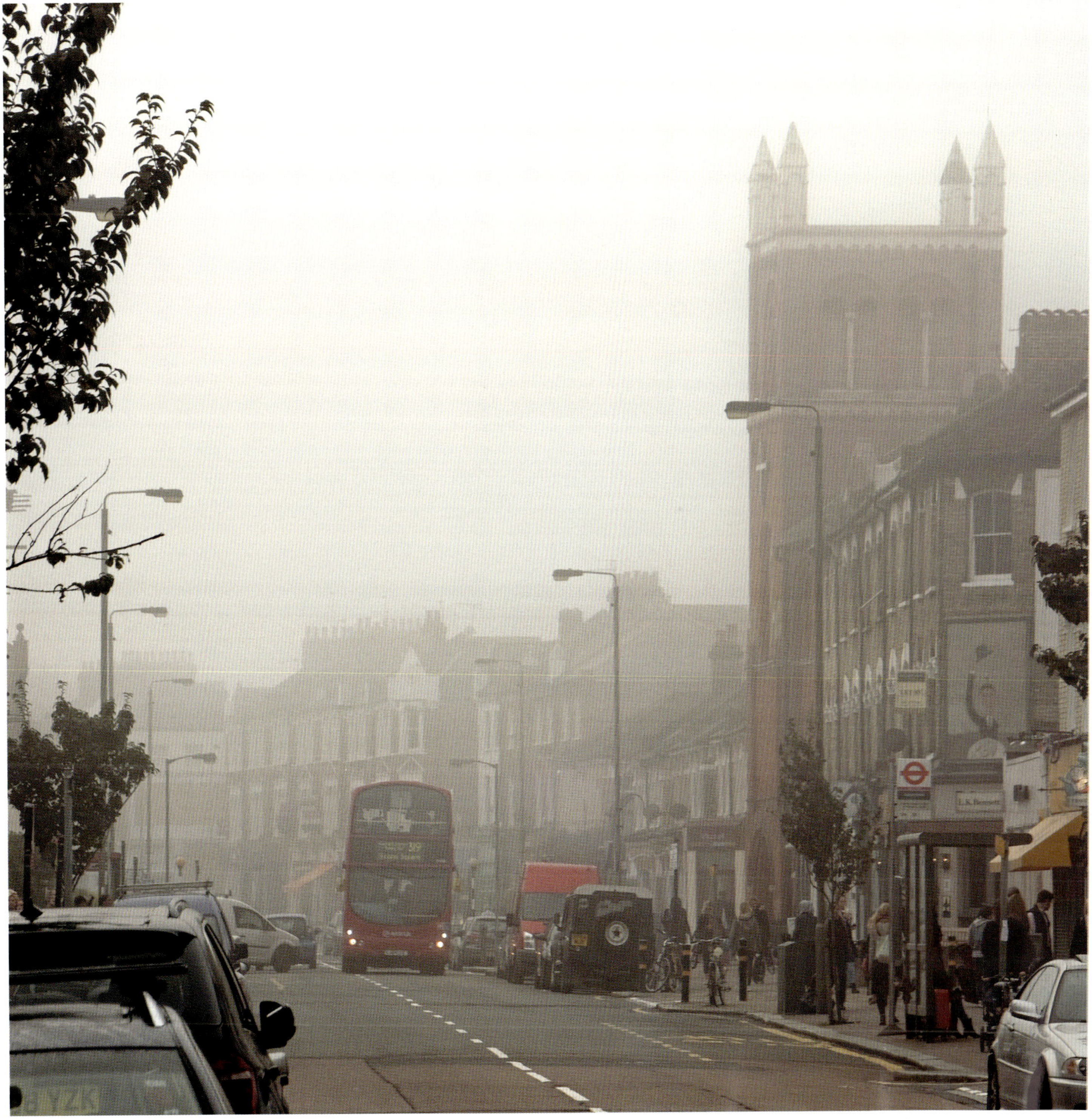

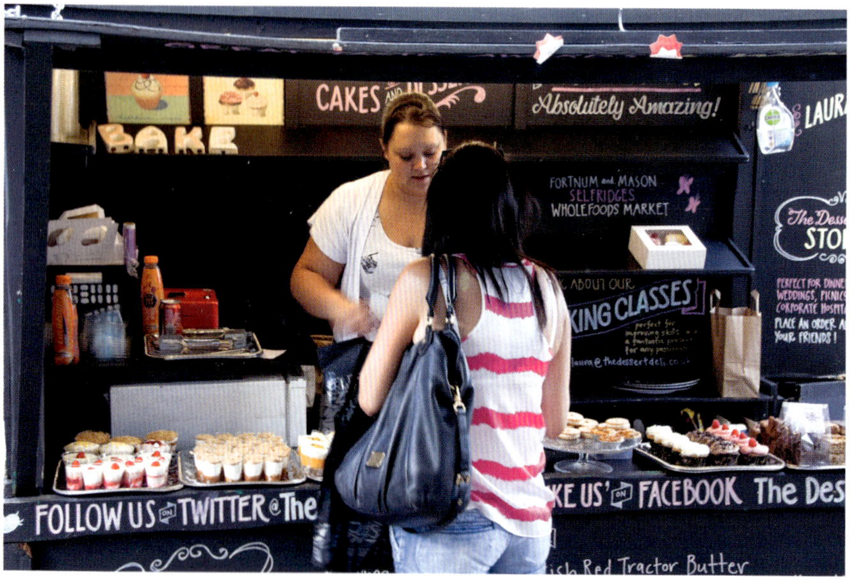

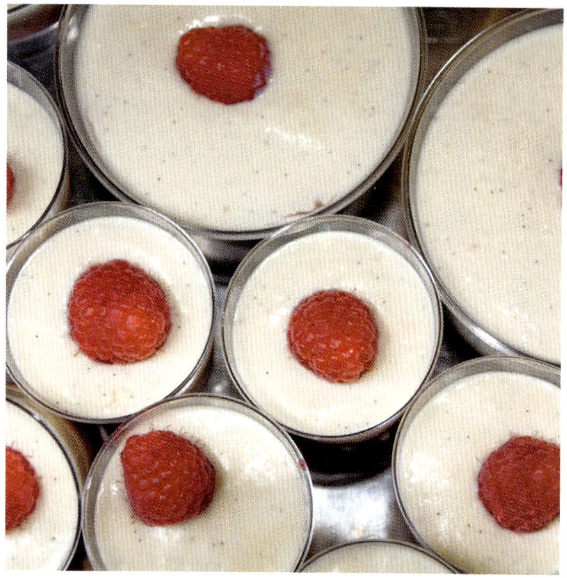

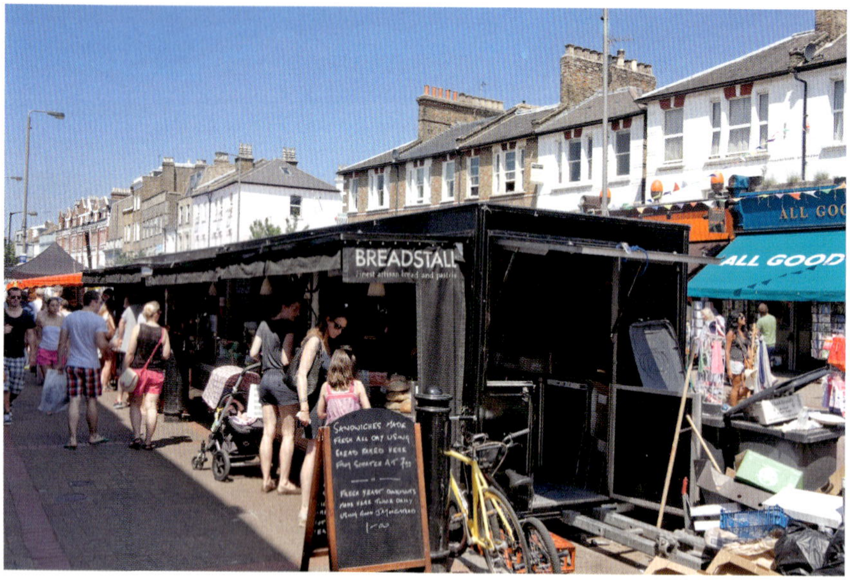

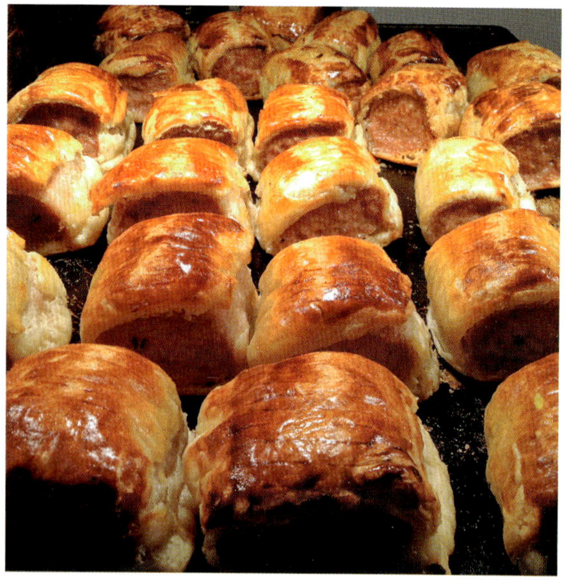

This page: Although not as many as years gone by, Northcote Road still has the odd market stall, especially on a Saturday.

Top right and left: Laura who runs The Dessert Deli, has a stall every Saturday and sells some mouthwatering delights.

Above: The Breadstall is open every day and sells almost everything, sweet and savoury. I heartily recommend the amazing sausage rolls, like no other I can assure you.

Opposite: The Byron Restaurant is very popular.

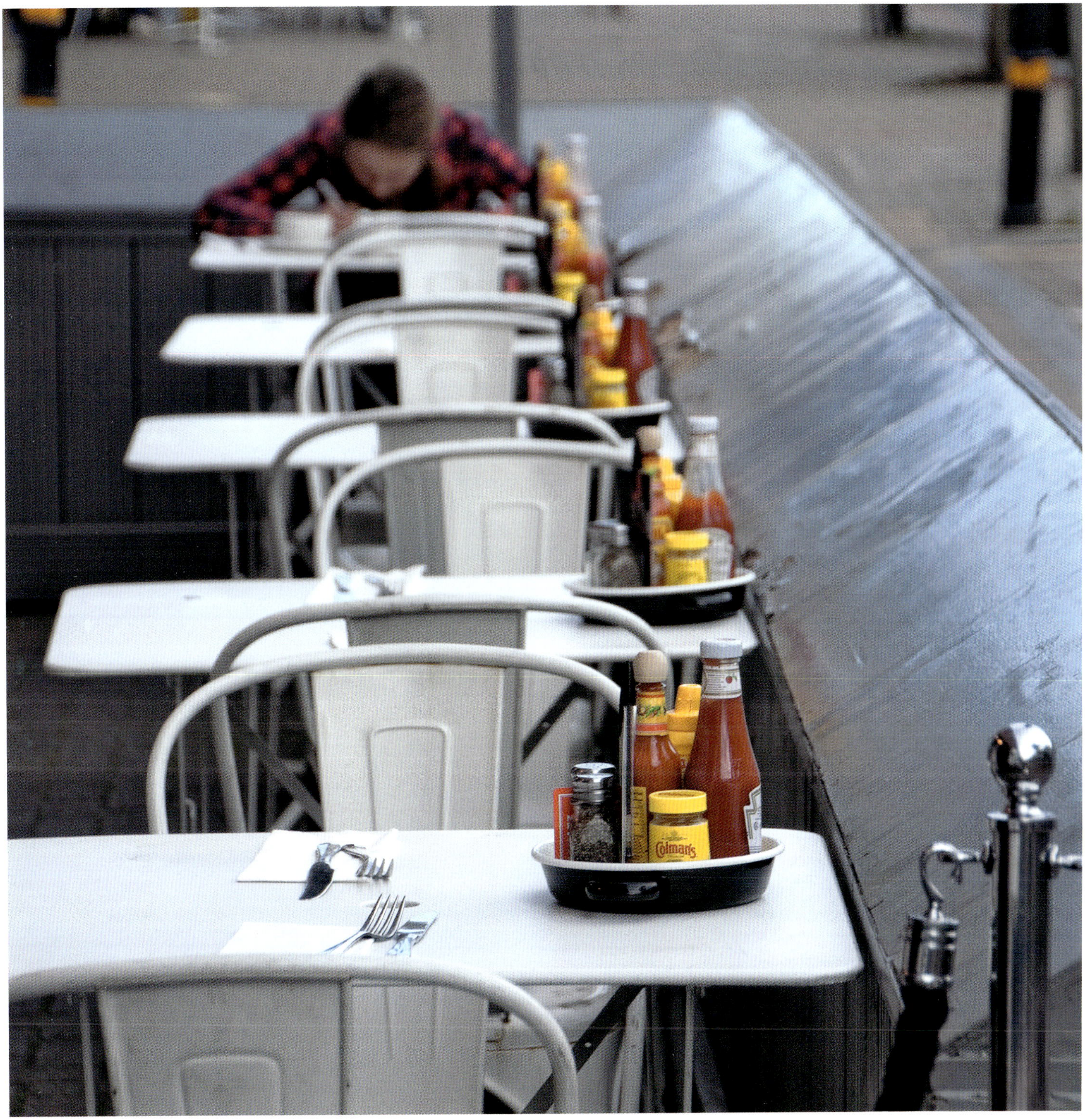
Colman's

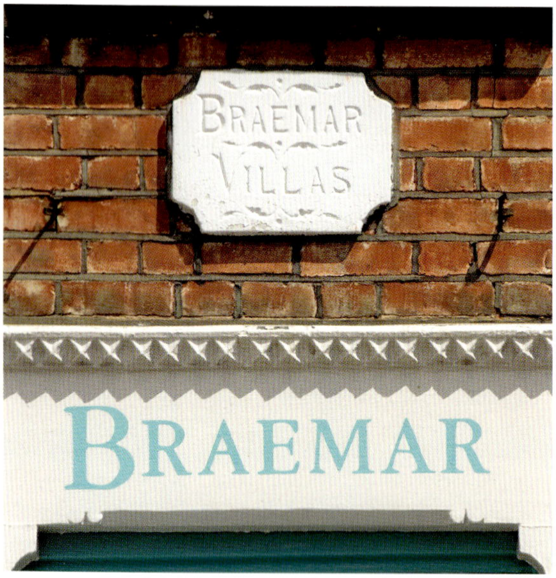
BRAEMAR
VILLAS
BRAEMAR

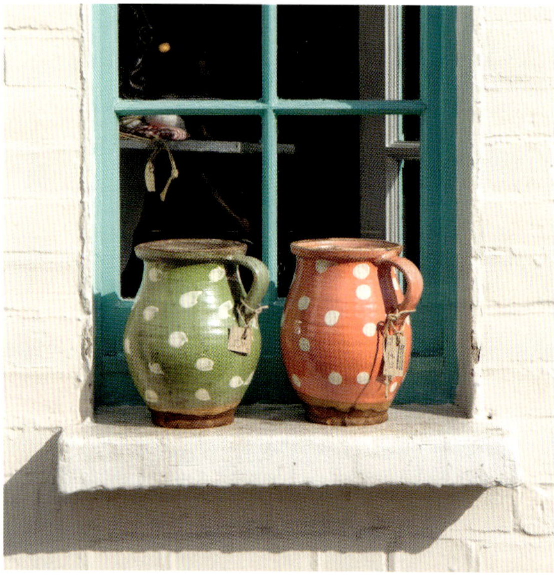

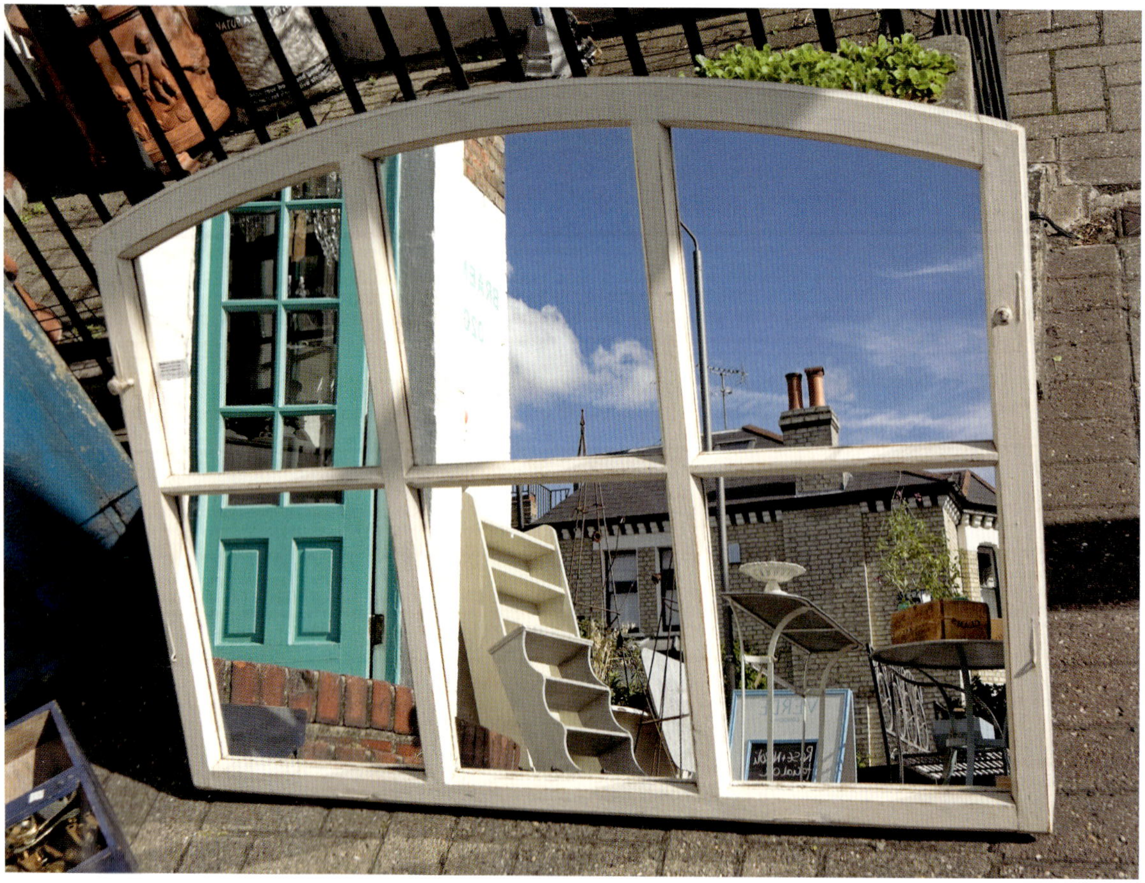

Opposite: Braemar Antique shop has been on the Northcote Road for 18 years and is owned by the fantastically named Marlies Ramos De Deus.

Top left: All Good Gifts was one of the first of the smarter shops to come onto the Northcote Road 25 years ago, Lorinda the local town centre manager tells me. Jackie, who owns it with her son, Matt, was originally only there to help out but given she was so good at it was asked if she might like to buy the shop, which she did, firstly taking a share before buying it outright.

Top right: I rather like these sheep that the Merino Kids store puts out – clever thinking as the kids always want to stop and play with them.

Bottom: The Hive Honey Shop.

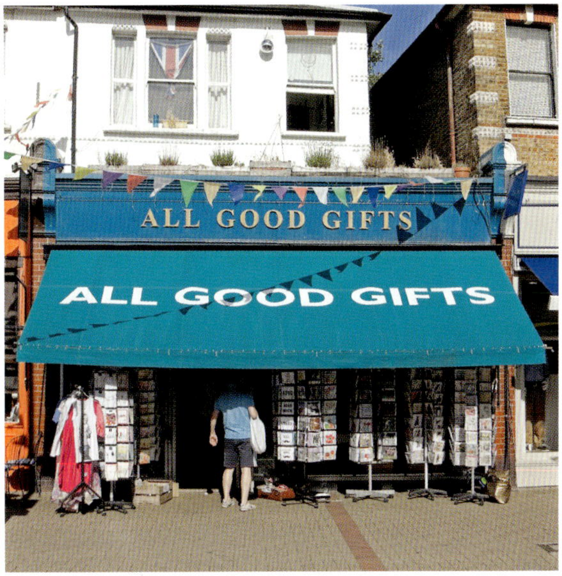

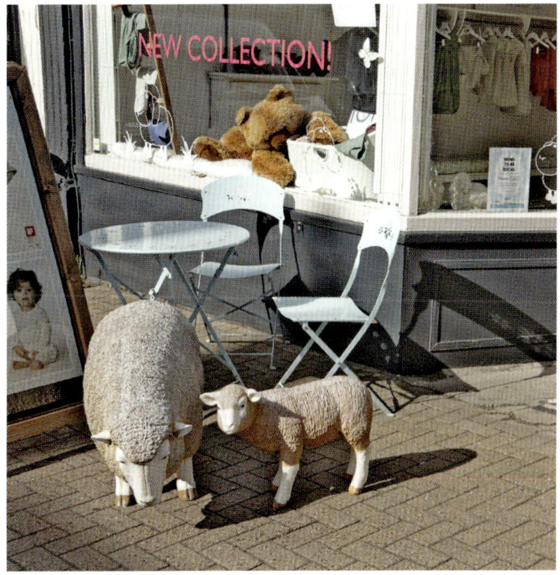

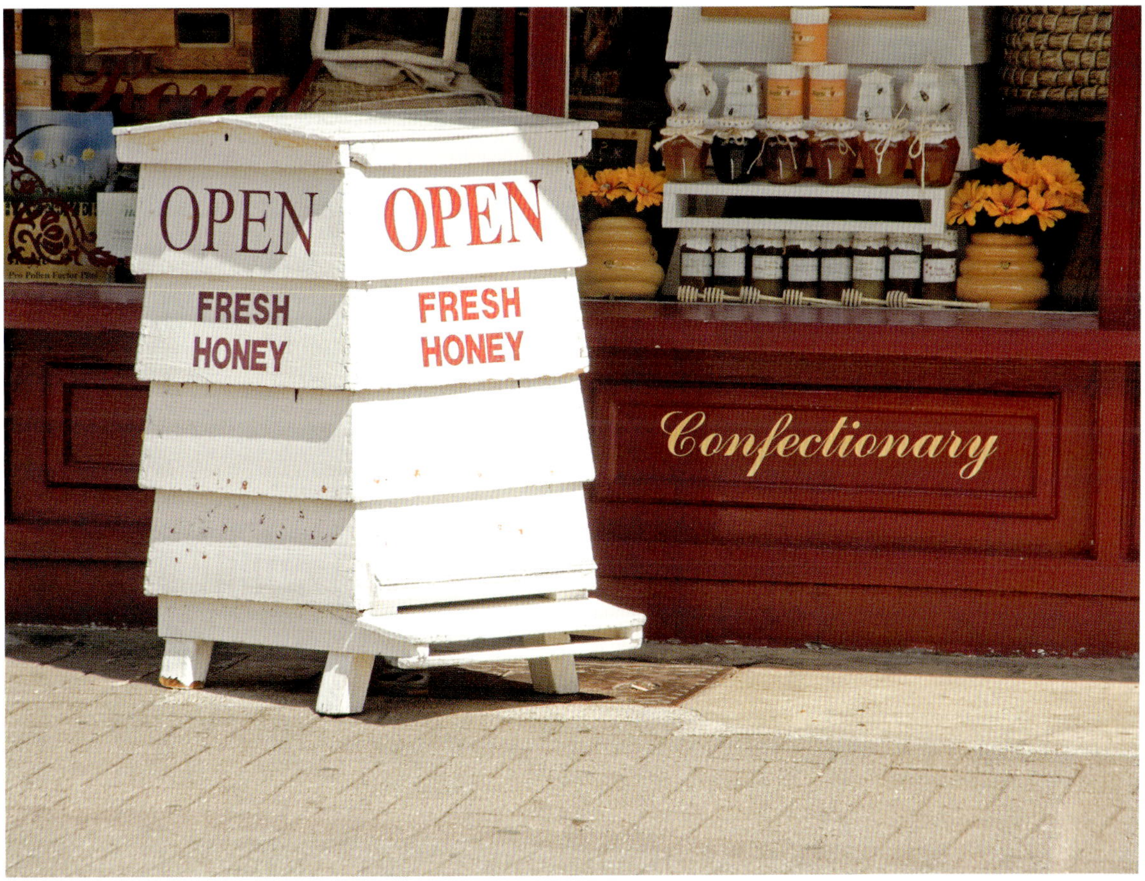

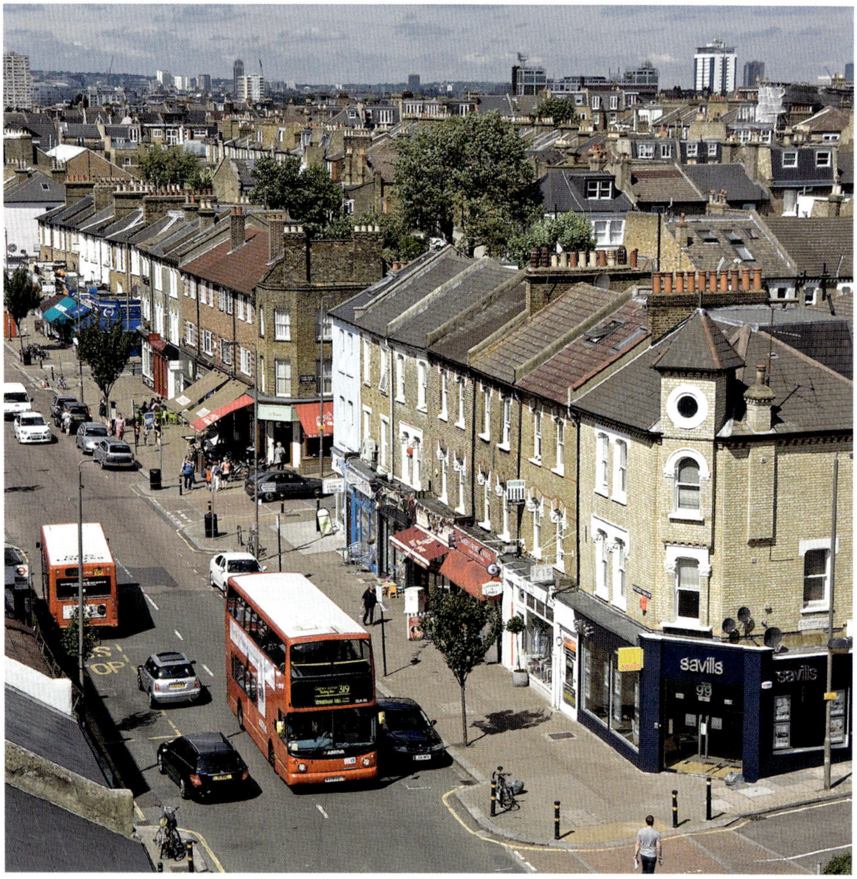

Northcote Road from the air.

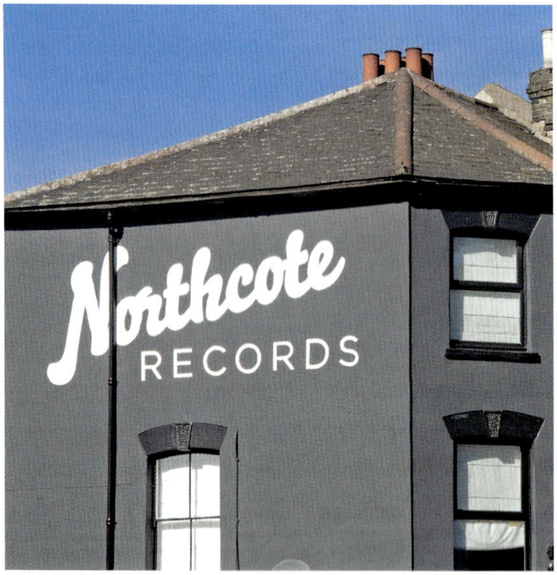

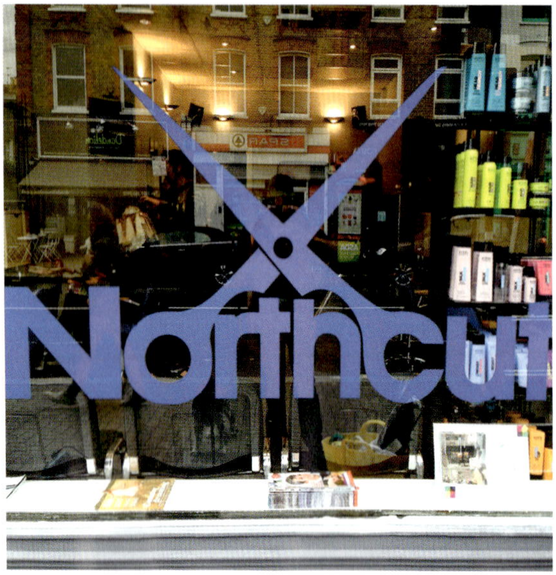

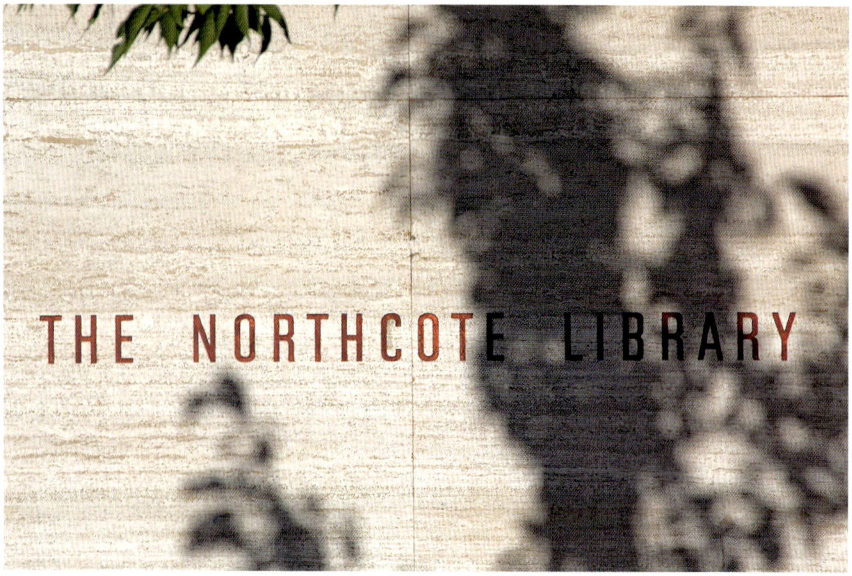

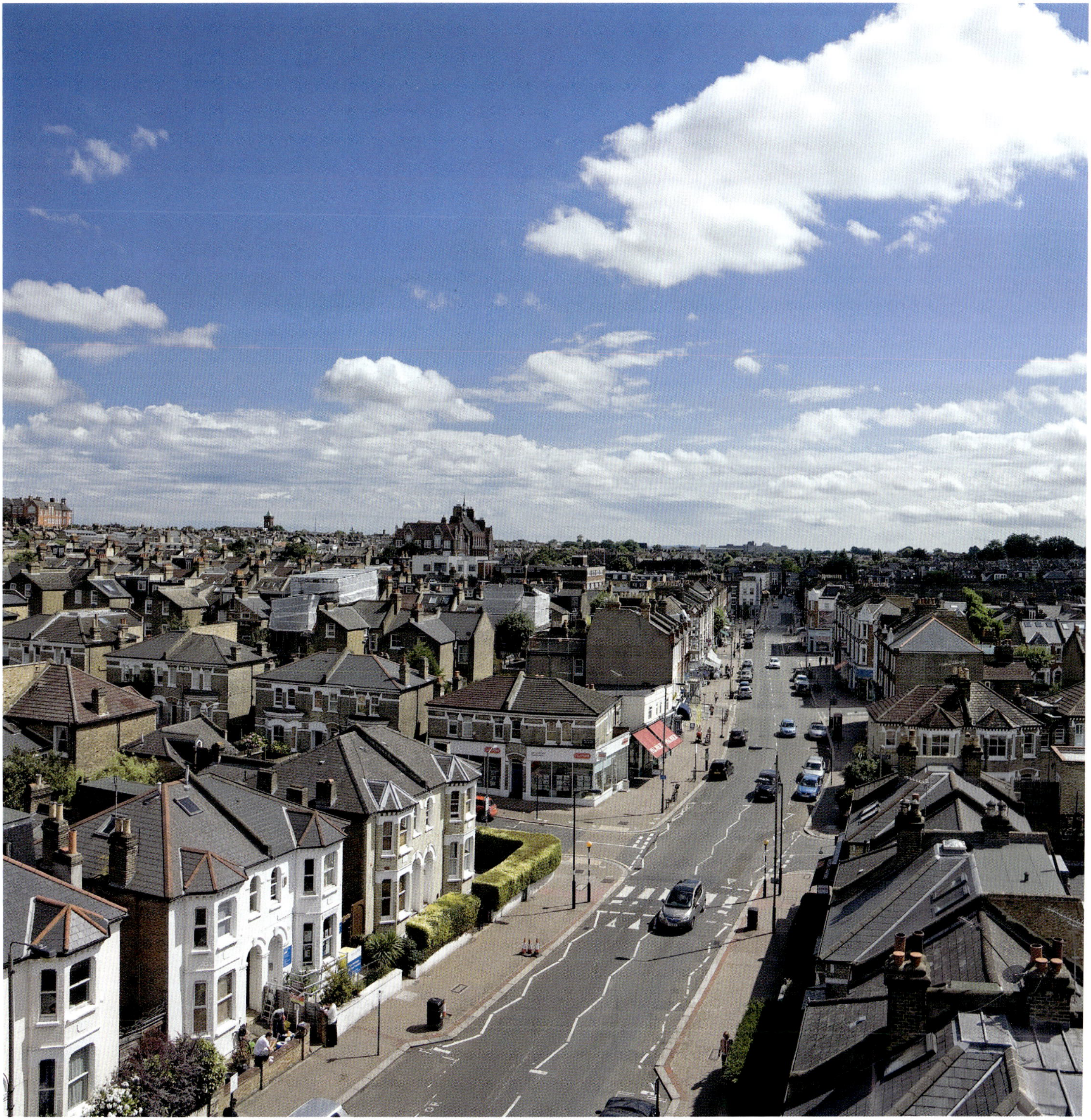

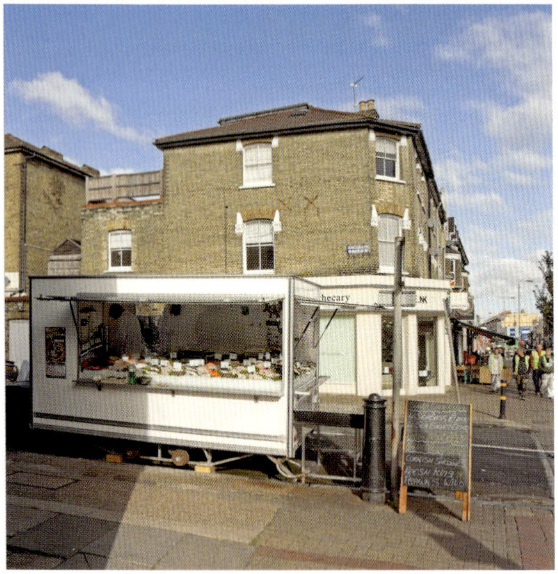

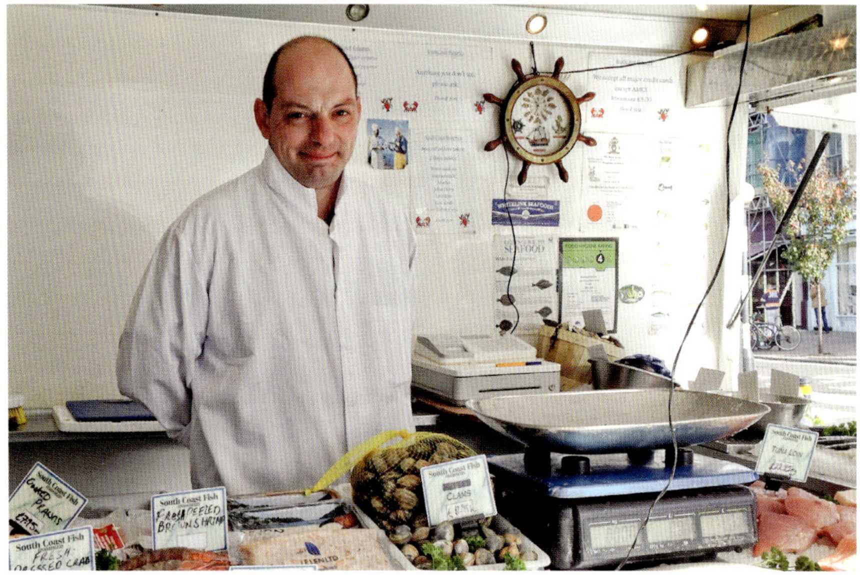

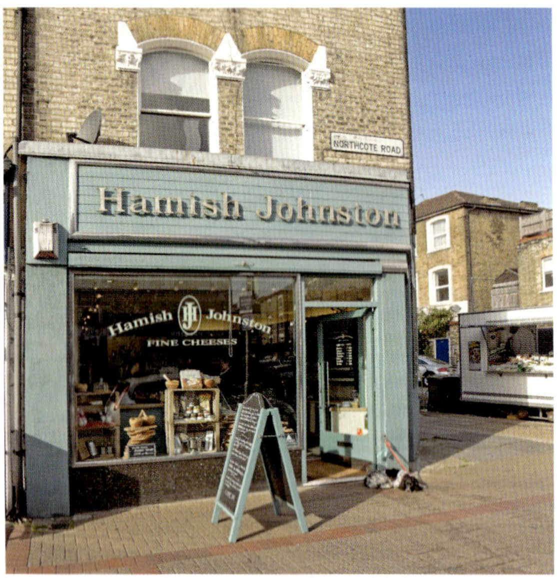

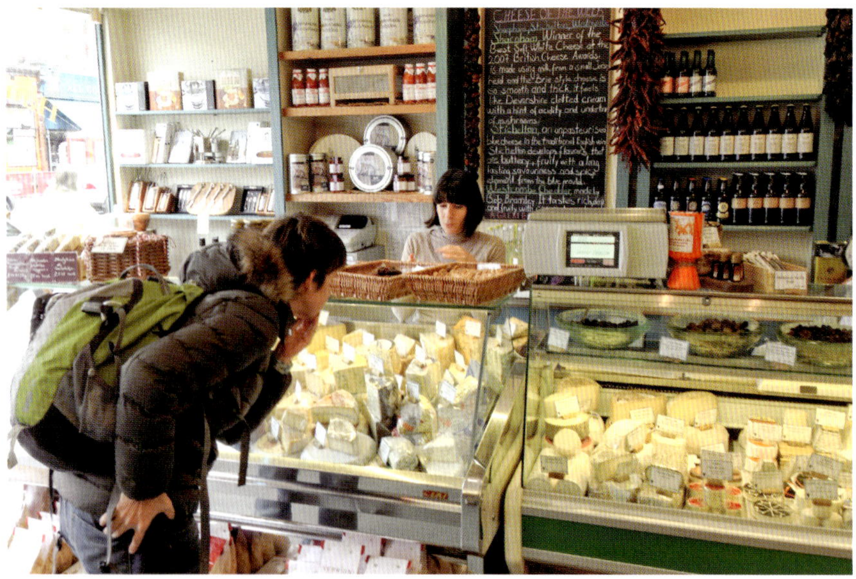

Top: Another of the last remaining permanent stalls is the one selling fish, which is run by Tony and Jim. They used to have a shop but down-sized to the stall to save money seven years ago. Most of their fish comes either from Billingsgate or the day boats from Rye in Sussex.

Bottom: Another of the foodie shops is the Cheese Shop, run by Will Hamish Johnston and Mark Newman. Other than cheese I was intrigued to see they stock a range of beers from a local brewery called Belleville. The company was set up by some fathers from Belleville school, hence the name I presume.

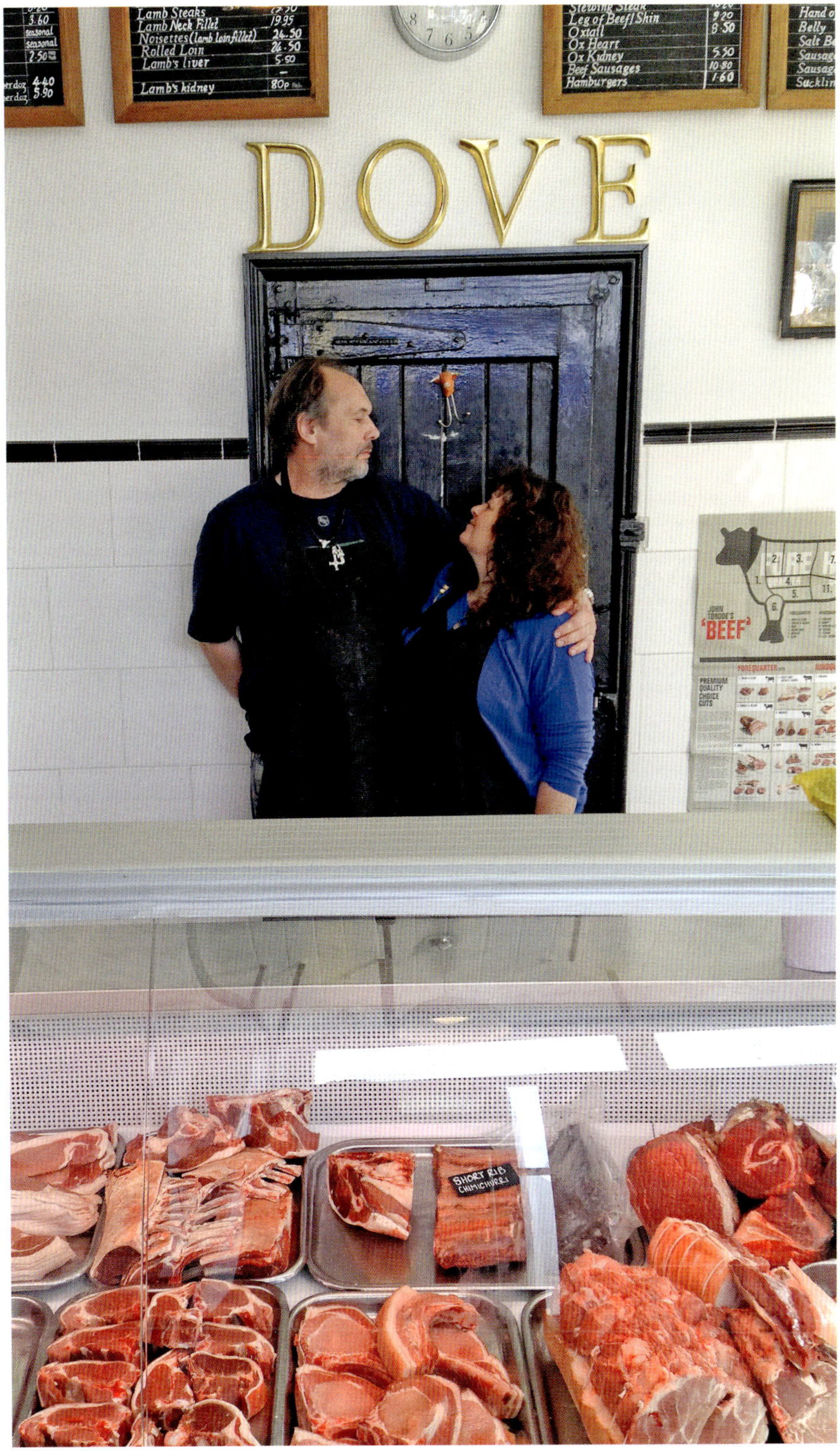

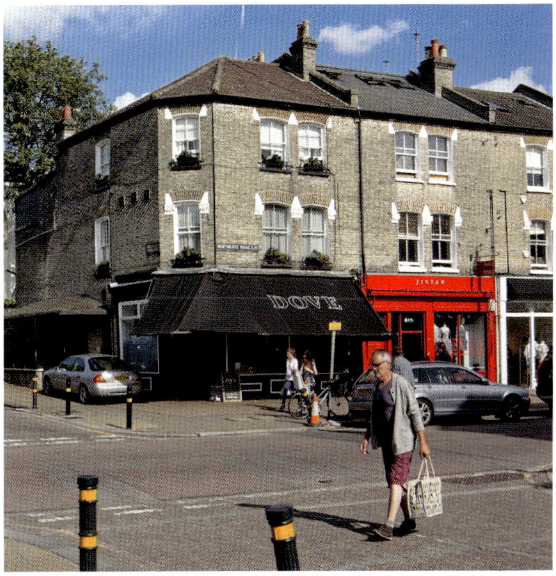

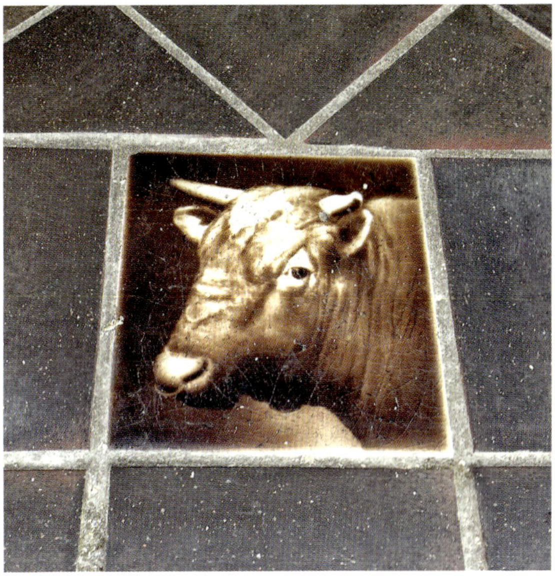

This page: The dove from above. Dove the butchers has been on Northcote Road for over 100 years; Bob having taken over the business from his father. It is never easy running a small shop these days but I was pleased to see that he was putting on a brave face when we met and actually had much to celebrate as he and Jo, pictured right, have just got married. Congratulations to them both. As you enter the store do look out for this most striking tile they have on the floor, above, most appropriate for a butchers.

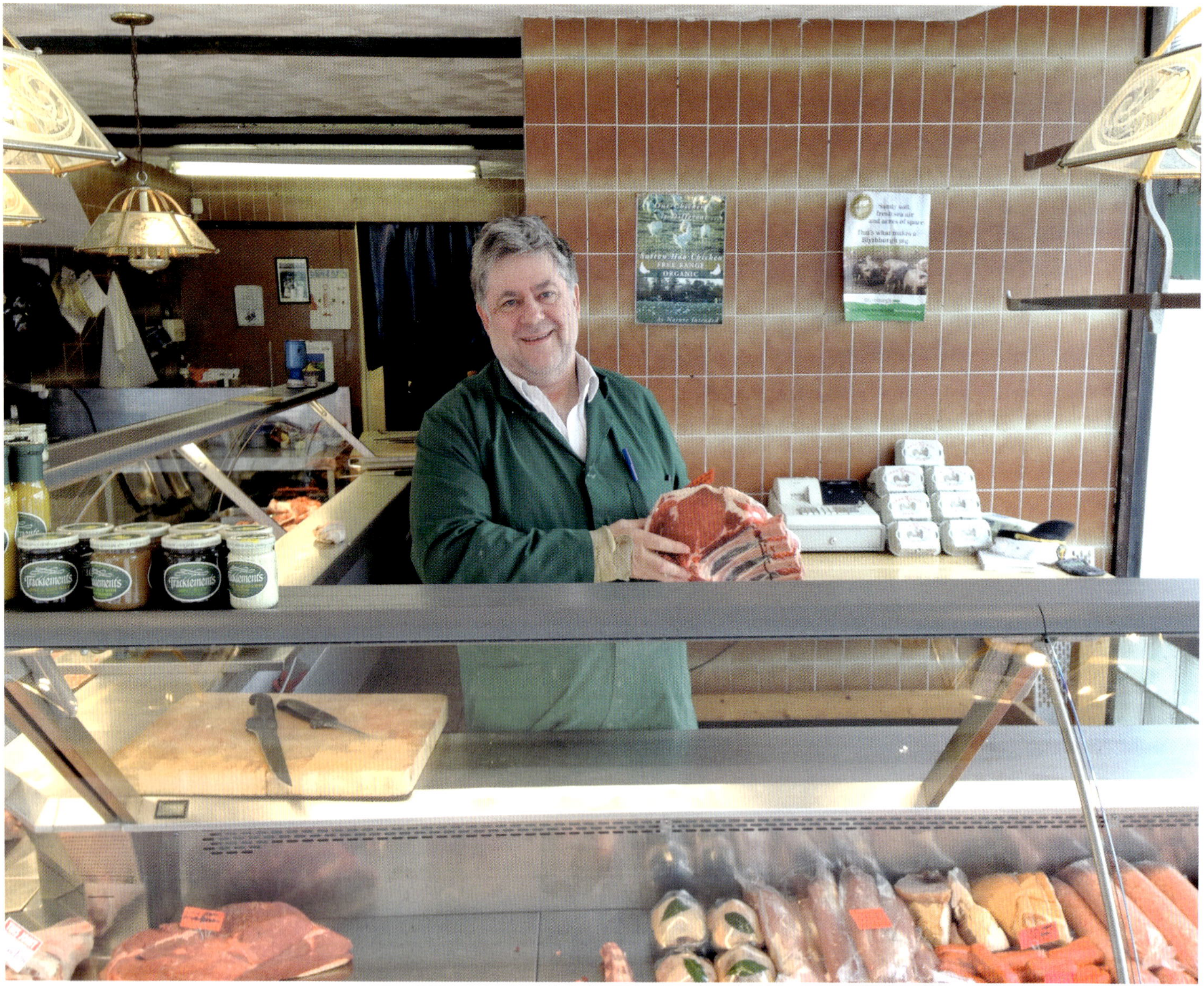

This page and opposite bottom left: Northcote Road used to have many butchers but these days just two. Hennessey's is run by Gary, above, who has been with the business since 1968, when he started as a Saturday boy. Local through and through, Belleville School and everything, I was astonished to see that besides meat he also has a piano in the shop, which is for the kids he tells me – they can't resist playing on it.

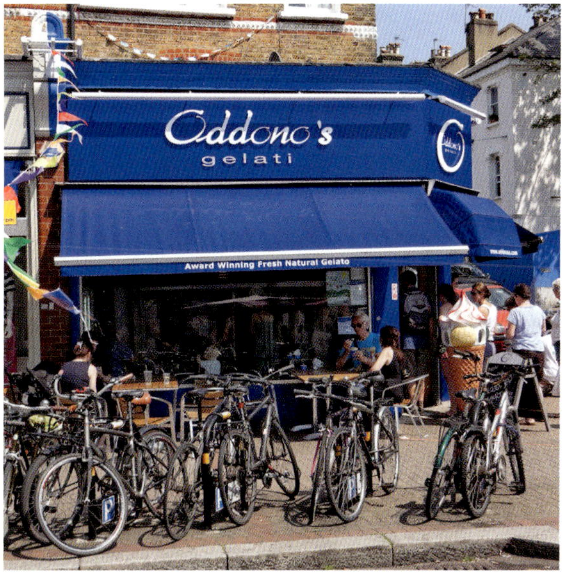

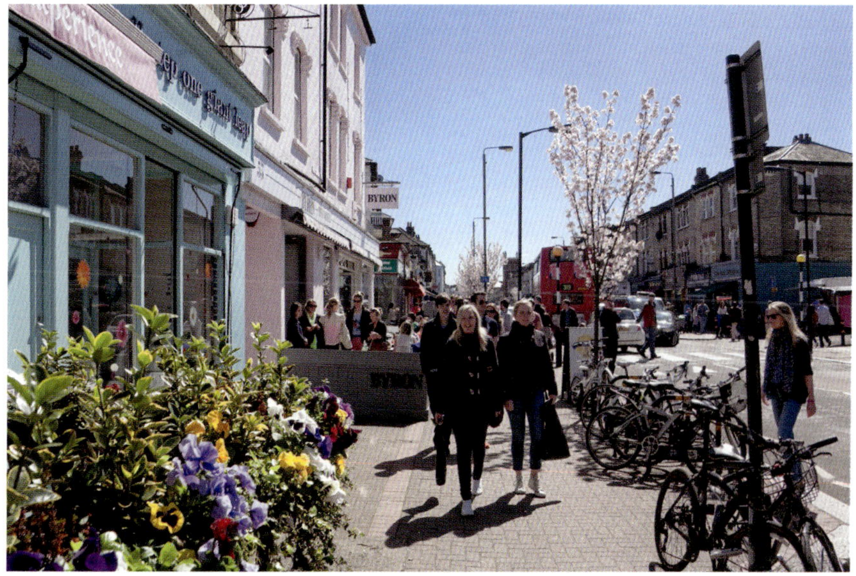

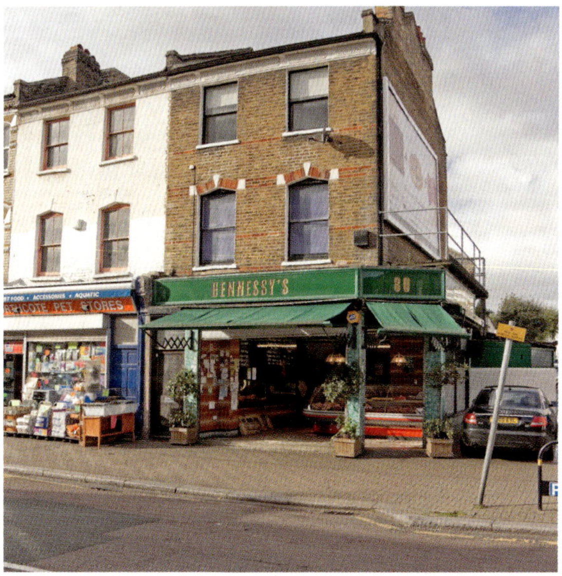

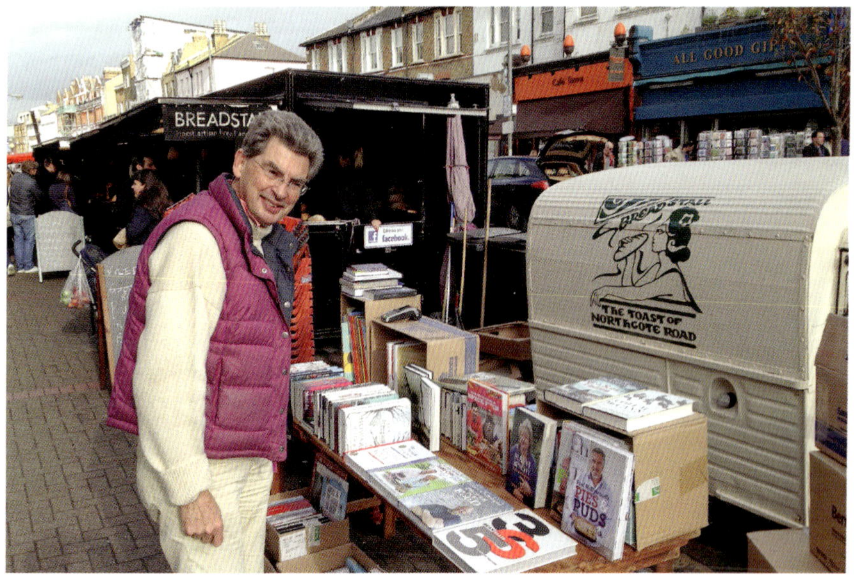

Top left: Oddono's Gelati Italiani started in 2004 in South Kensington and now can be found on Northcote Road, as well as all over London. Started by Christian Oddono and the help of three friends, they make their ice cream, or should I say gelato, fresh every day. I personally recommend you try it with coffee.

Bottom right: Unfortunately, the independent Bolingbroke Bookshop in Northcote Road was forced to close earlier in 2013 but I am pleased to see that Michael Gibbs has made a return taking a stall next to The Breadstall – I wish him luck and that the weather remains fine for him and all the others.

St. John's Road

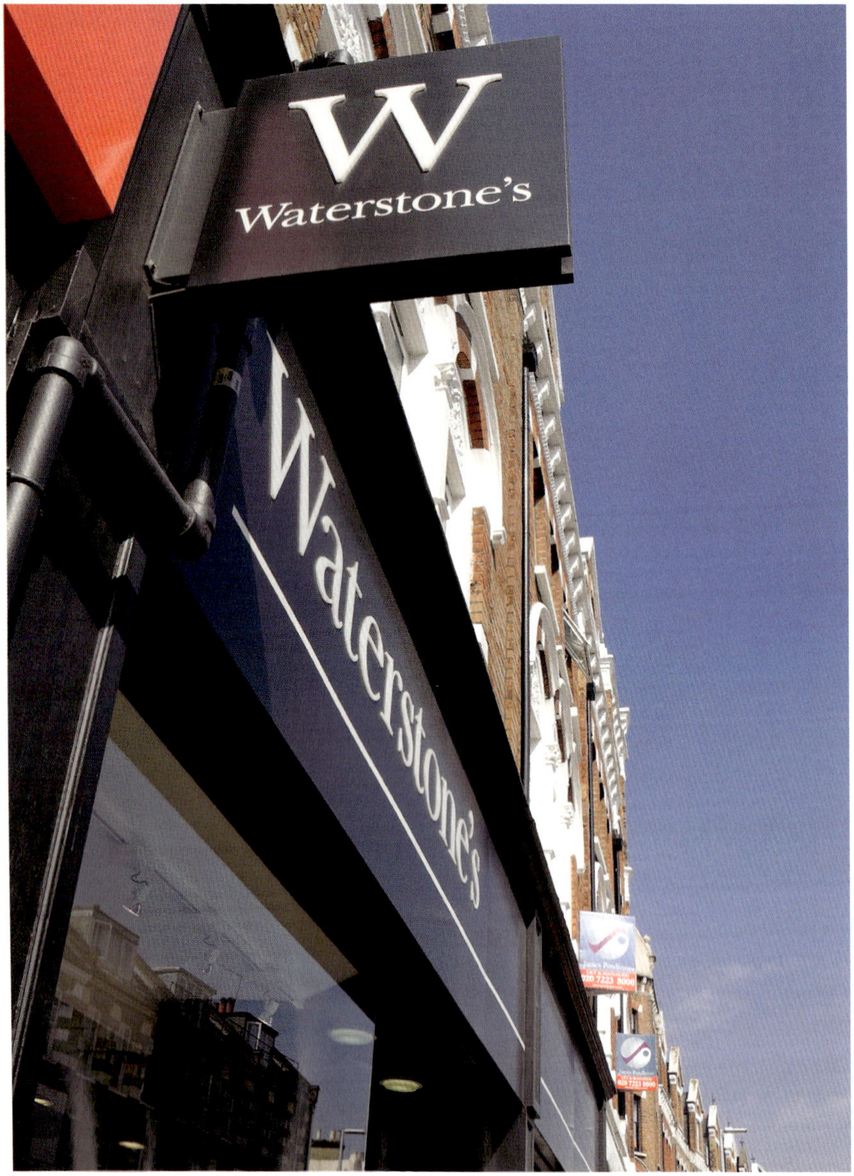

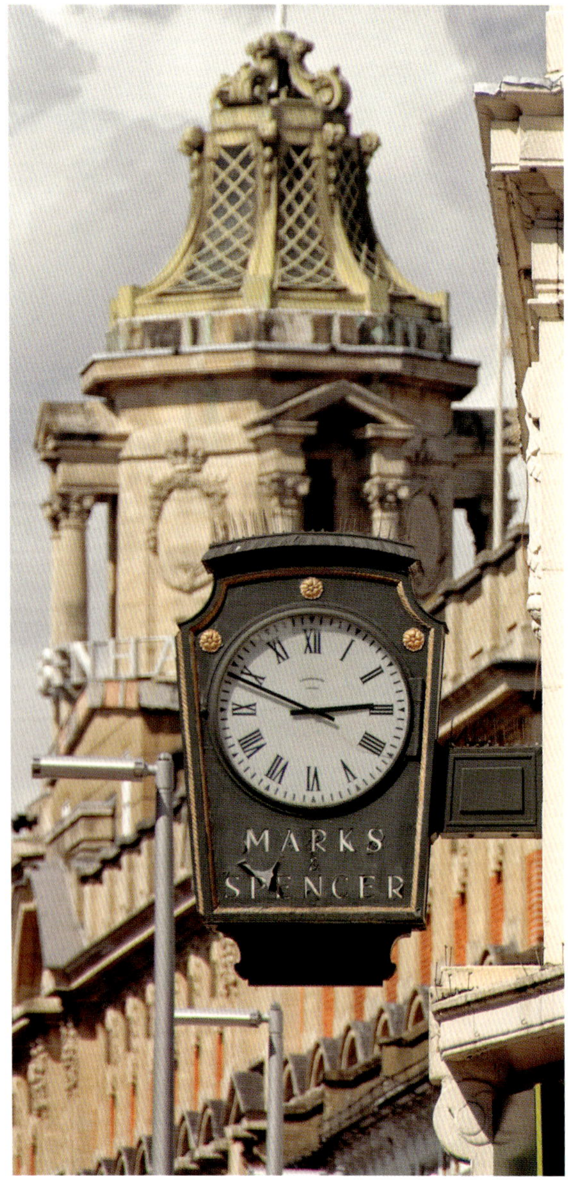

This page: St John's Road connects shoppers from Northcote Road to Lavender Hill.

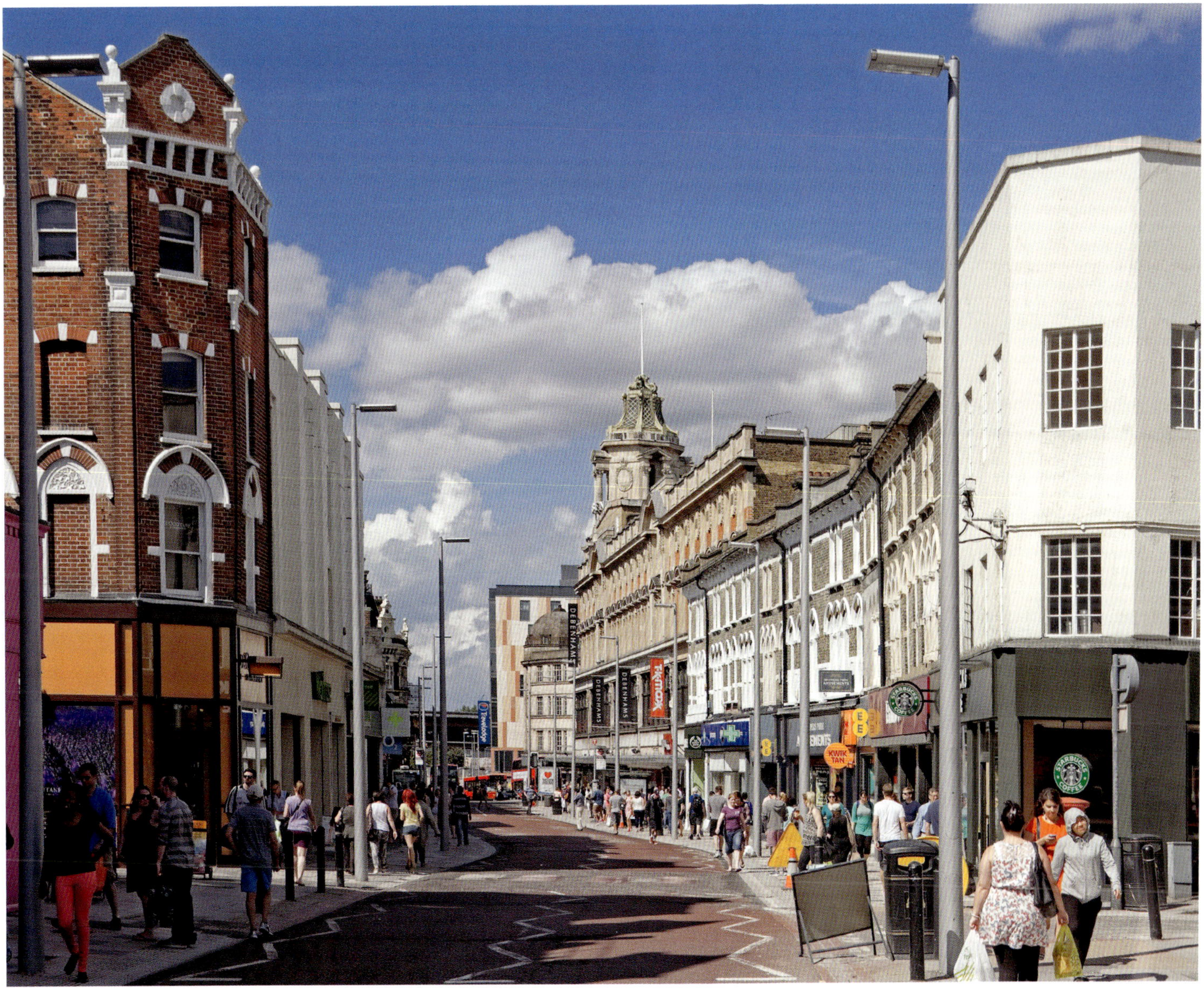

St. John's Hill

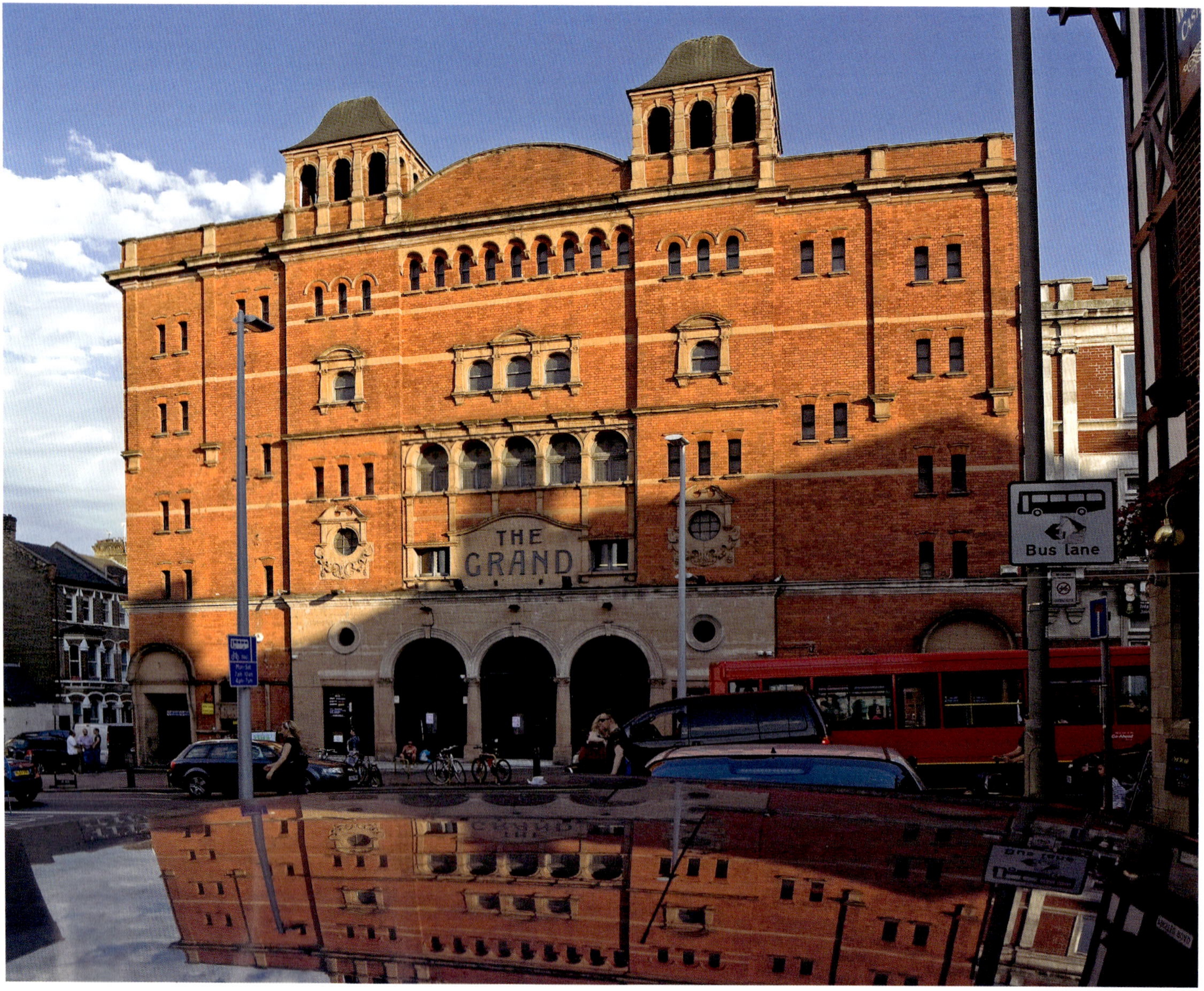

Opposite: The Grand opened in 1900 as a music hall. It has in its time been a cinema, a bingo hall and a nightclub. However, it has just finished a complete refurbishment and has returned to former glories as a live music venue.

Top left: The old Clapham Junction station building.

Bottom left: The large Peabody Estate, which dates from the 1930s and is just off St John's Hill, is undergoing a massive regeneration scheme involving the replacement of many of the old blocks, which are now deemed out of date.

Top right: The street entrance to the station.

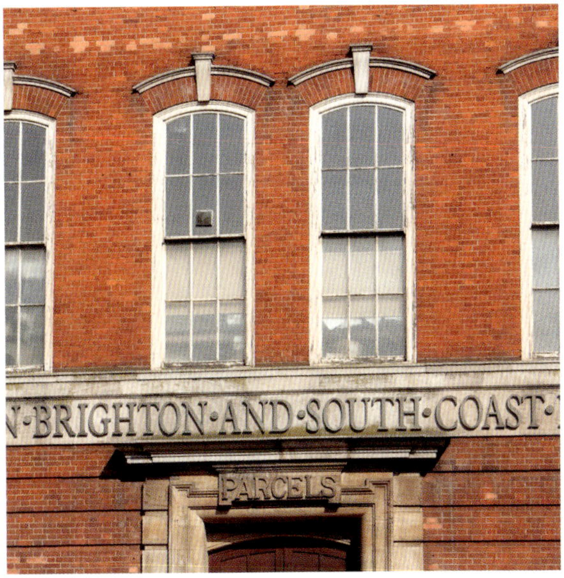

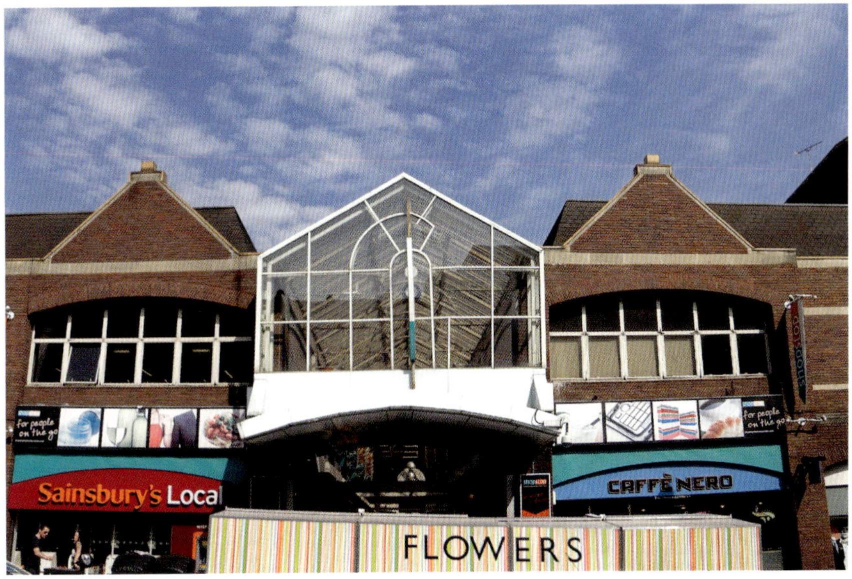

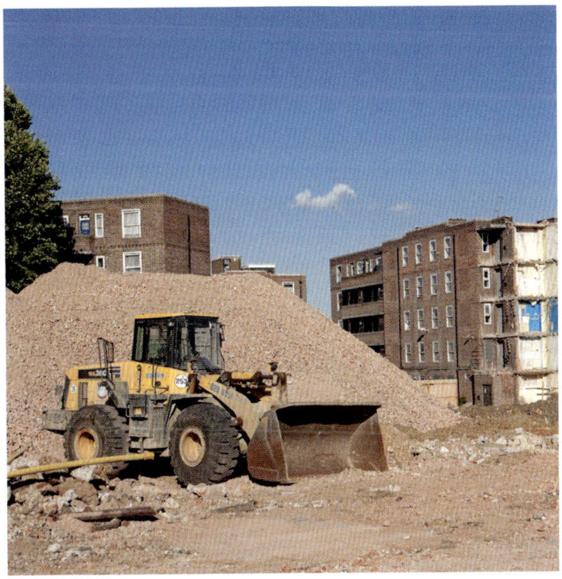

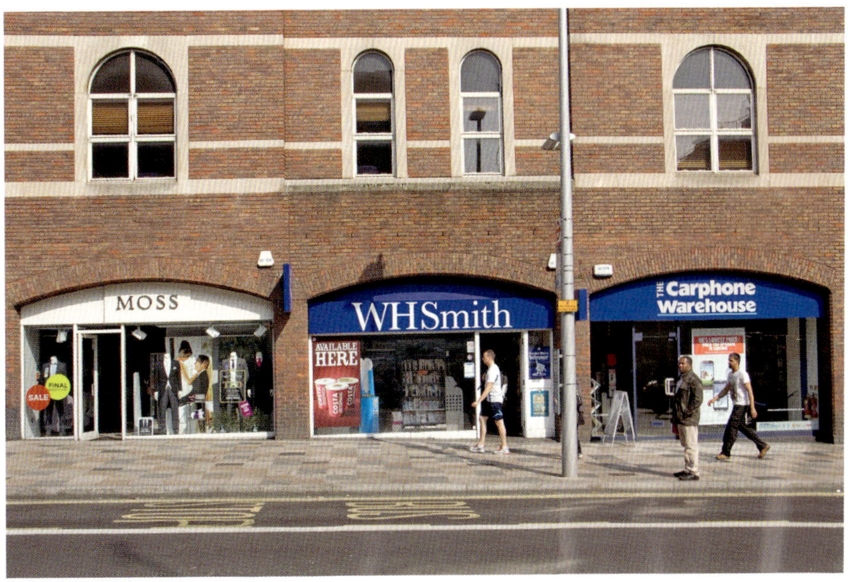

Webb's Road

Running parallel to Northcote Road is the charming little street of Webb's Road, which has probably the most extraordinarily diverse shops and business in Battersea from diving to hi-fi, vets to facials, deli's to dining.

Opposite top right: Webb's Gallery.

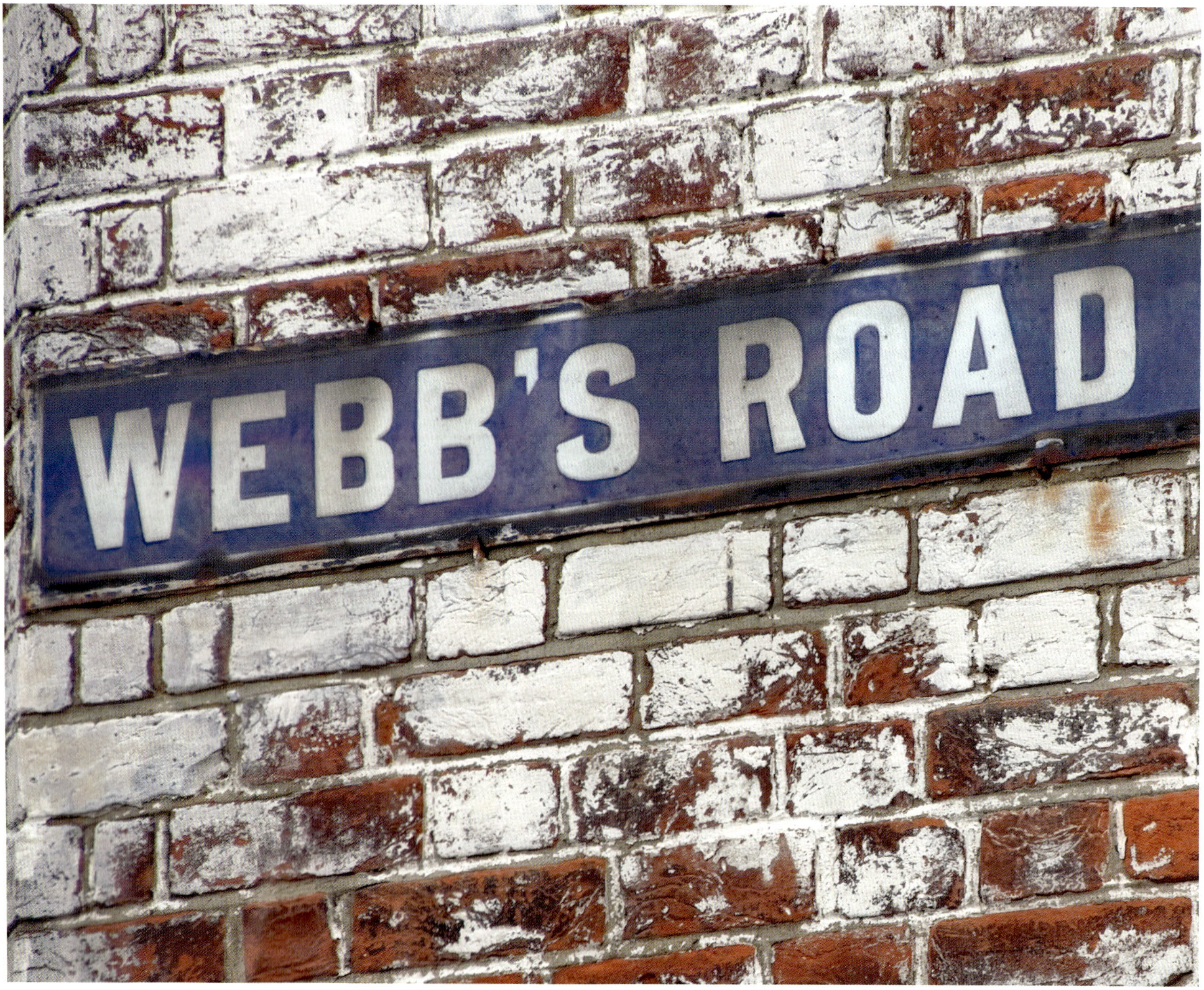

Top left: Philip Beddows and I wondered if this plate found one of the walls near Bennerley Road was an old fire insurance marker. Having checked at the reference library it seems unlikely.

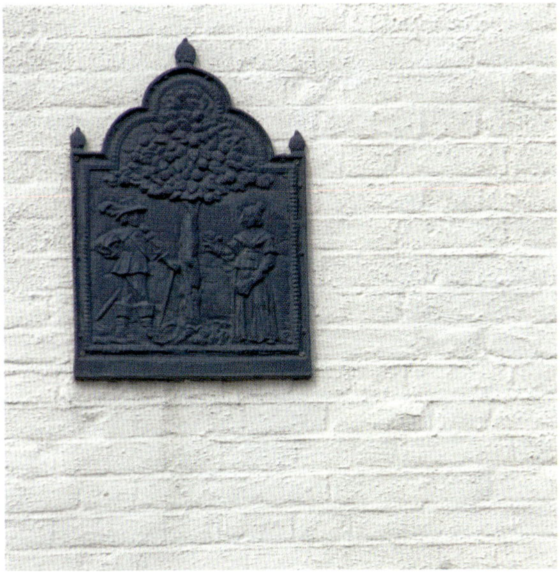

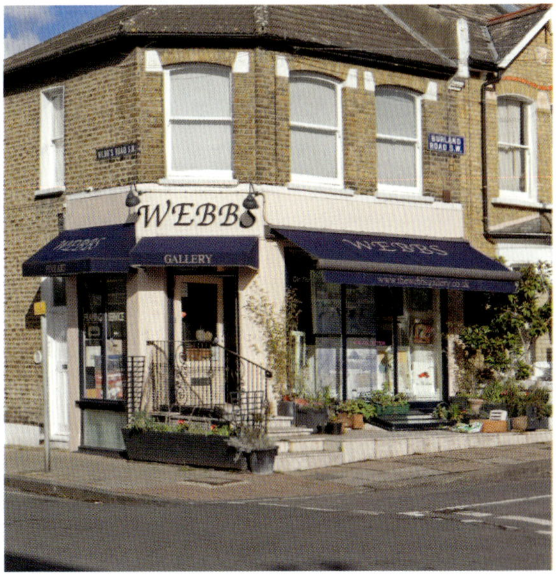

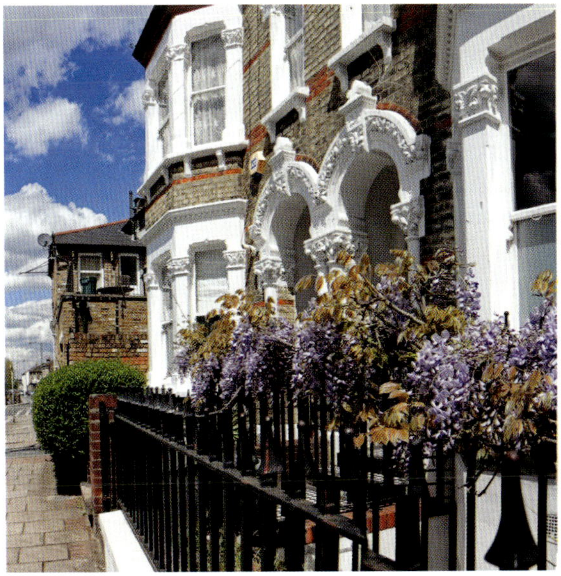

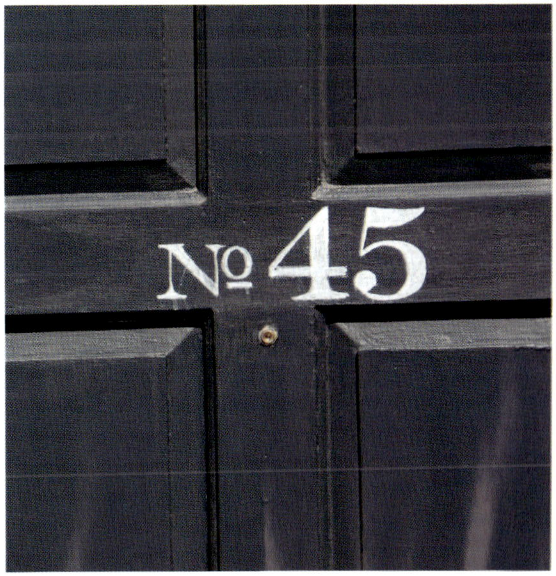

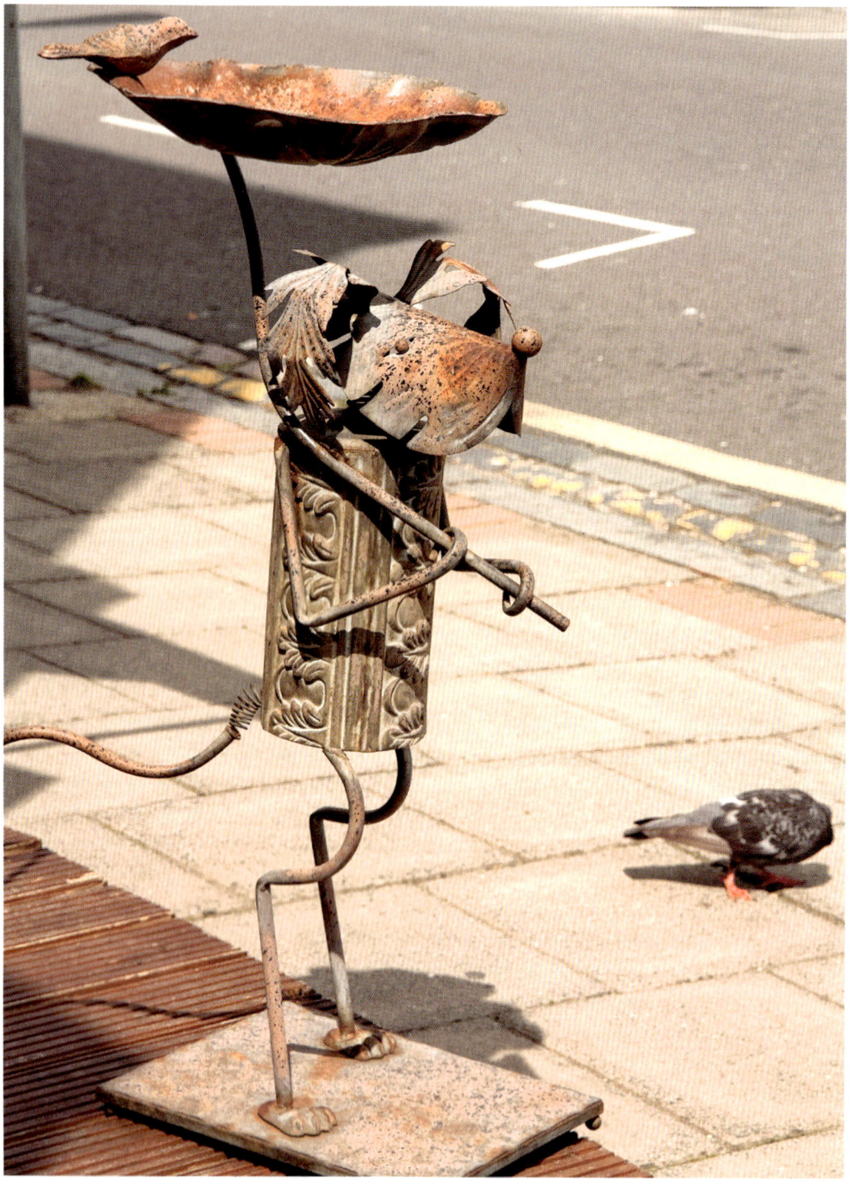

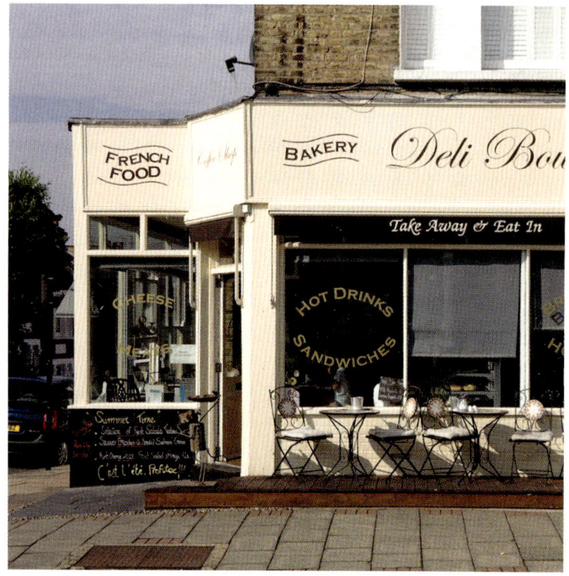

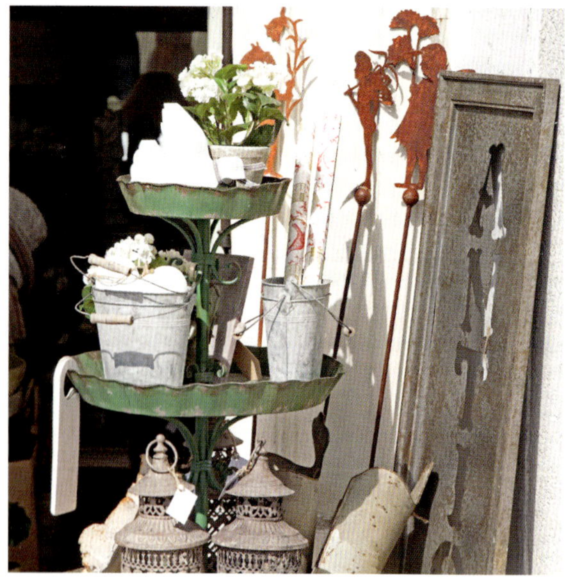

Top right and left: Outside the French food deli they have this rather interesting artifact – ashtray, water bowl? Plus a headless pigeon?

Bottom right: Lizzie's is a treasure trove of a shop with this rather smart display outside.

Opposite: I enjoyed this house's garden, full of pink hydrangeas.

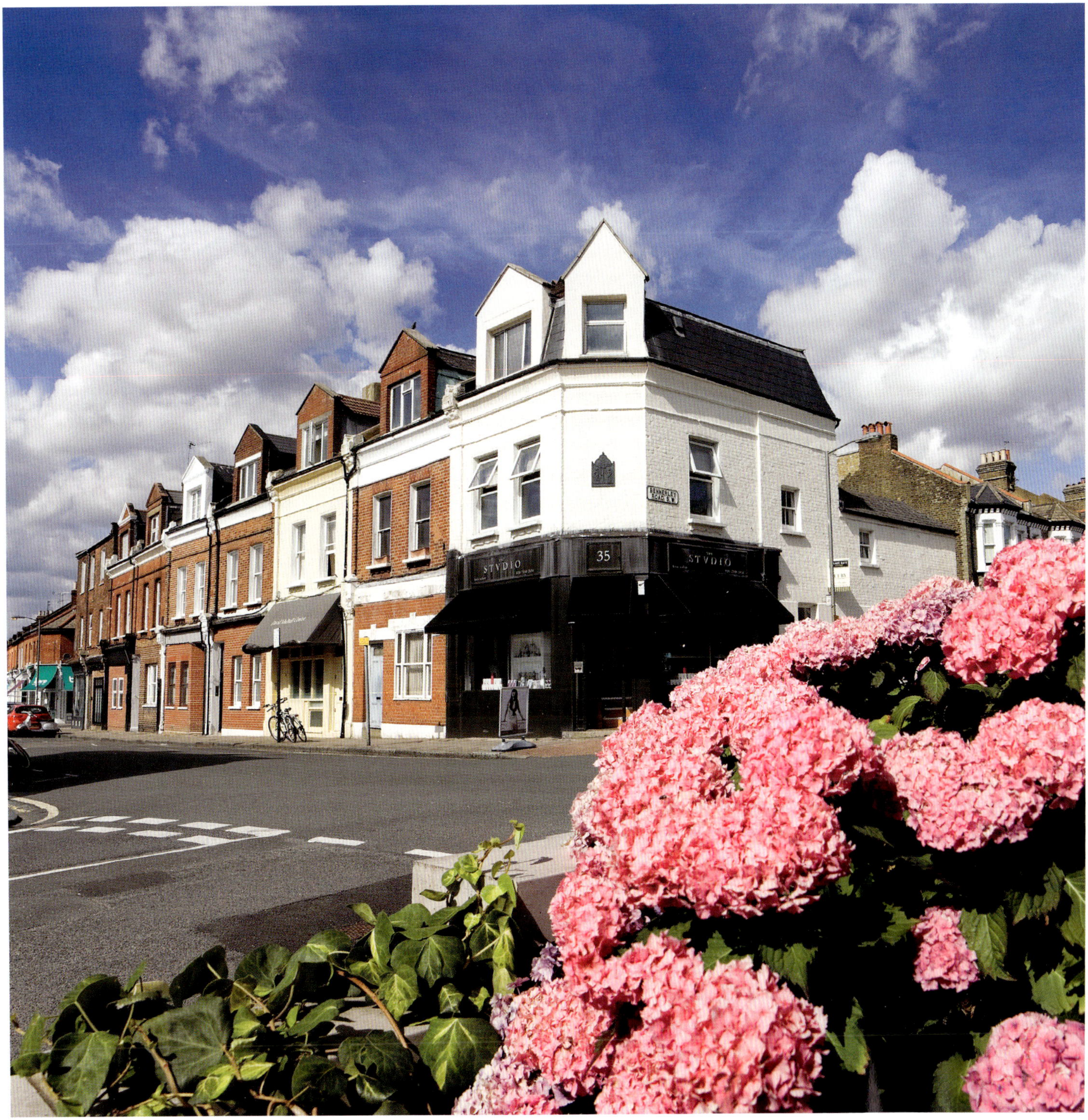
STVDIO
35
BENNERLEY ROAD S.W.
STVDIO

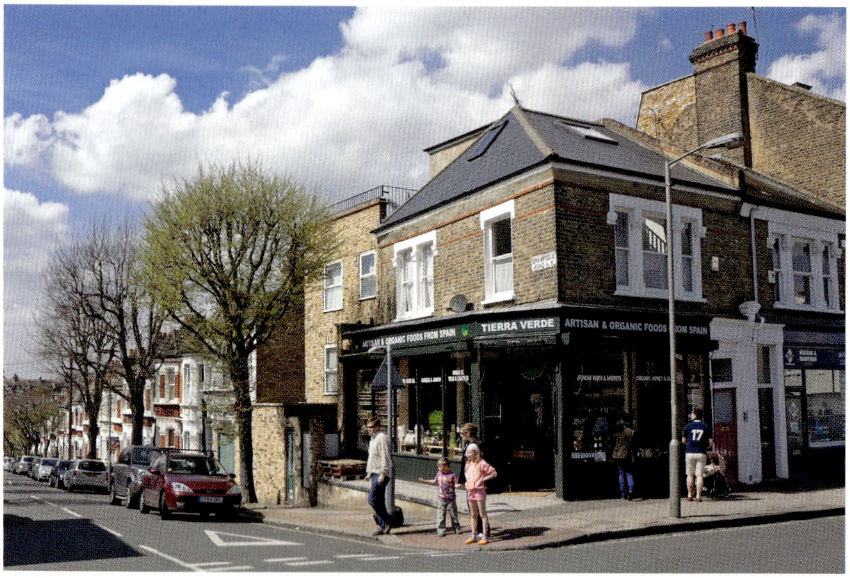

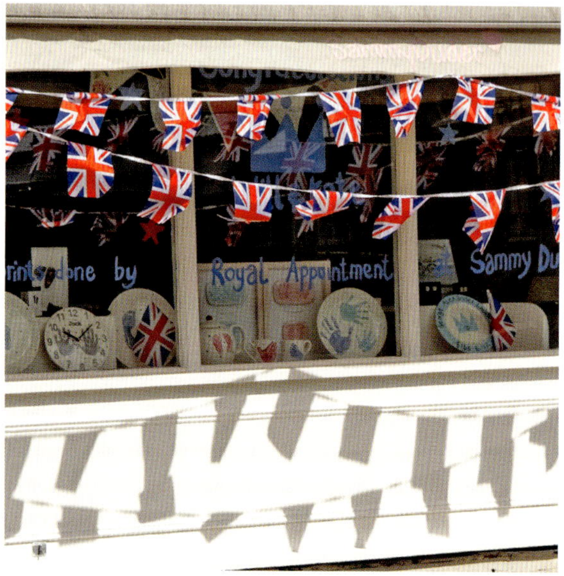

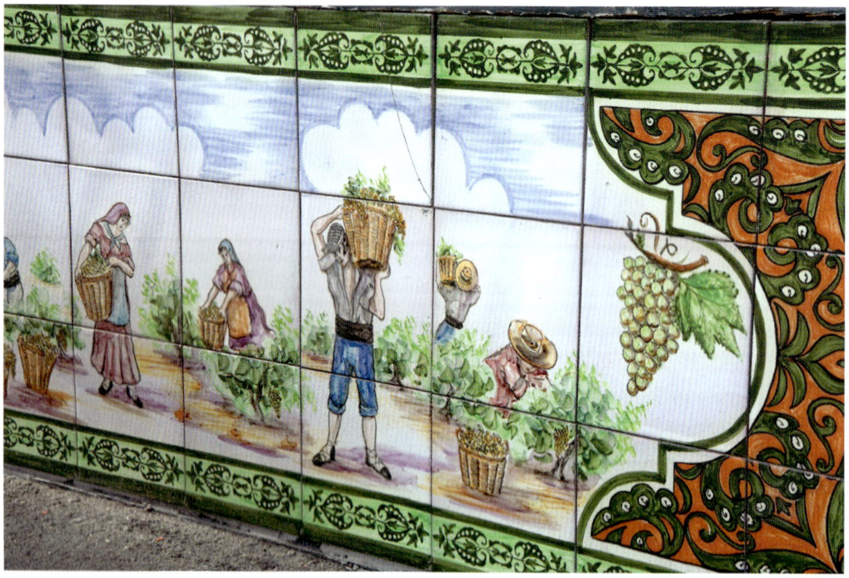

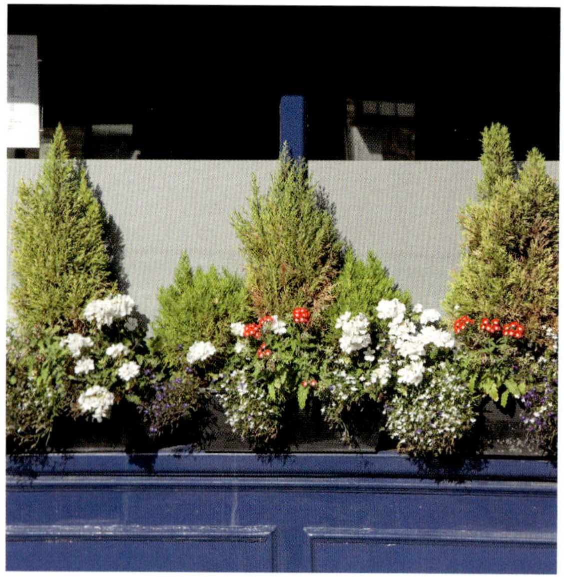

Bottom left: The Artisan Deli has these fabulous tiles on the outside of their building for everyone to admire, as long as you look down that is.

Bottom right: The window box of The Drawing Room.

Opposite: Webb's Road looking south.

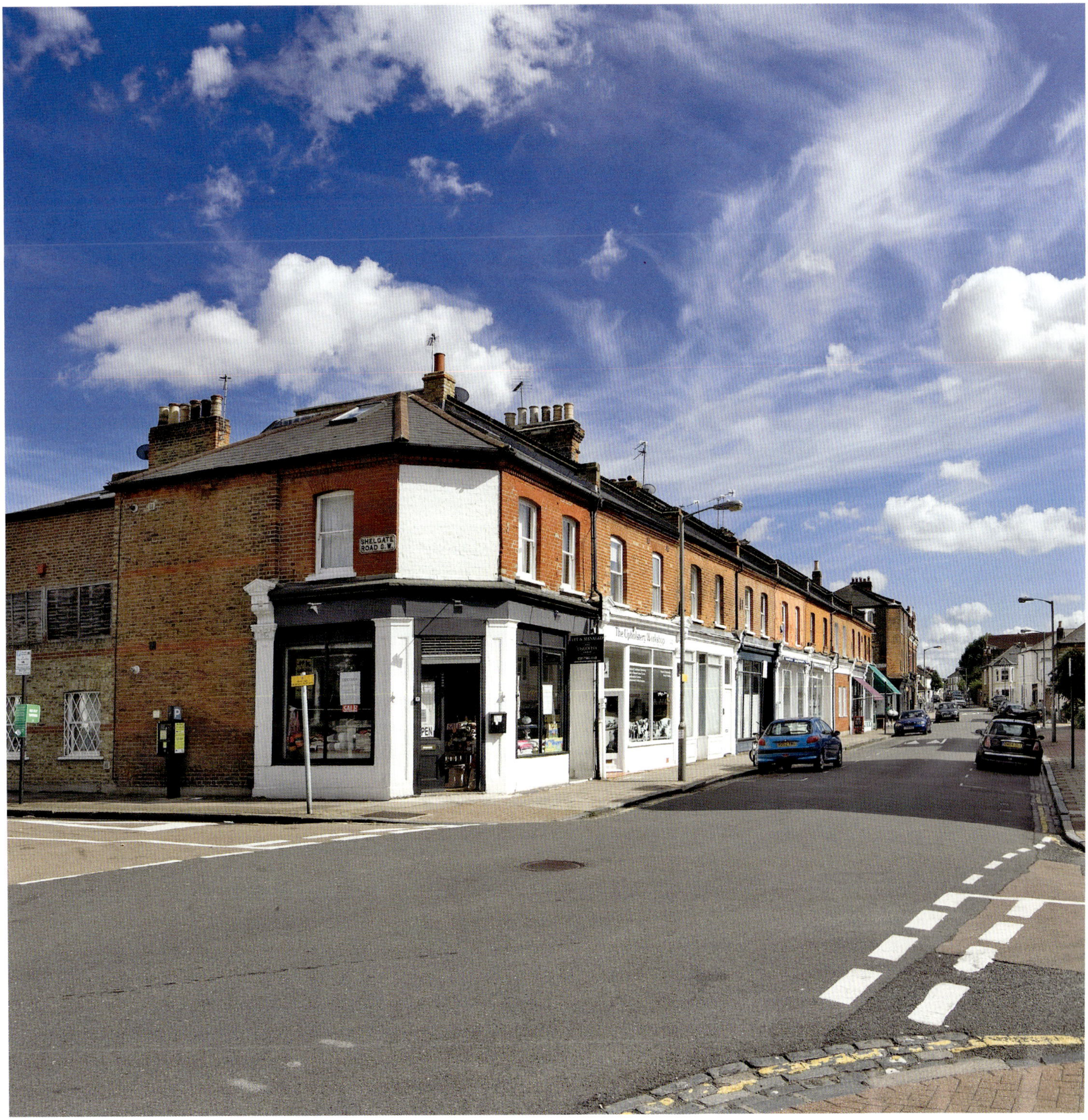
SHELGATE
ROAD S.W.
The Upholstery Workshop
SALE

Schools

Thomas's Clapham in Broomwood Road is a rather confusing name as it is clearly still in Battersea. But then they already have a Thomas's Battersea so I can see their dilemma, but perhaps if they'd added the word 'Common', the geography class would have approved... perhaps they may still do it one day! Formed in 1993, using the building formerly known as Clapham County Girls School, the school educates 570 girls and boys aged four to 13. Thank you to Viki Gillett for showing me around and allowing me to take some pictures, it was a lovely day.

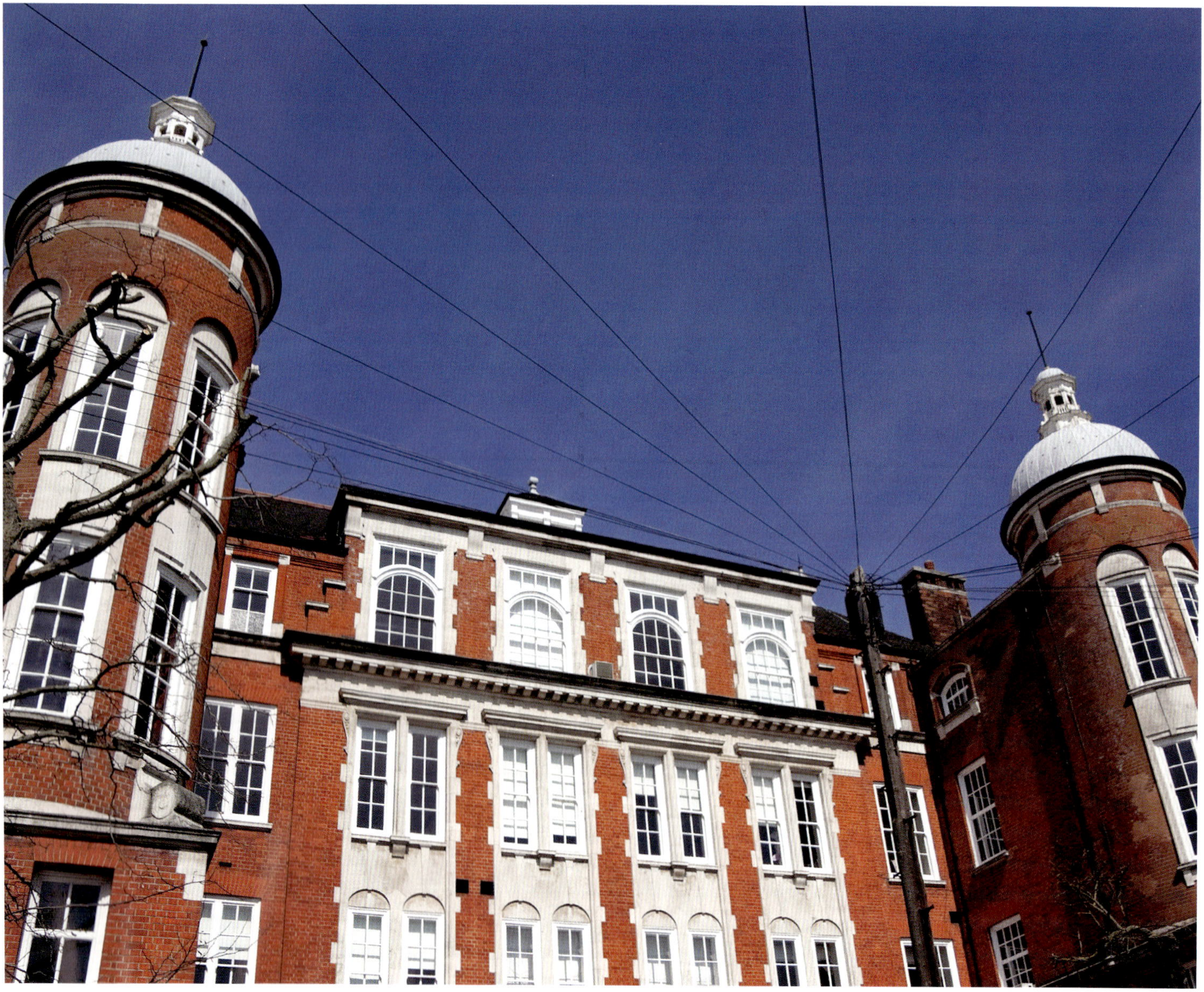

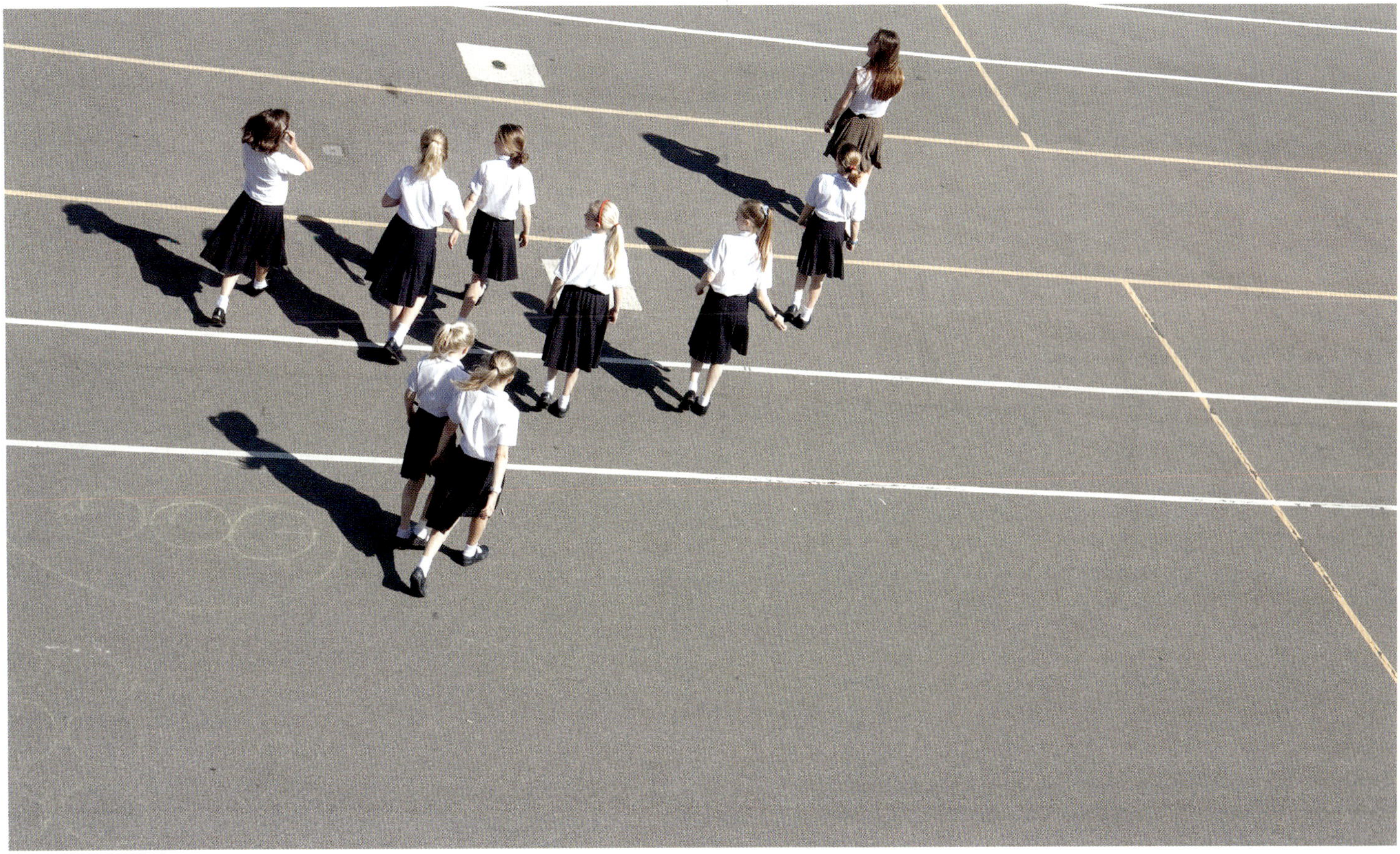

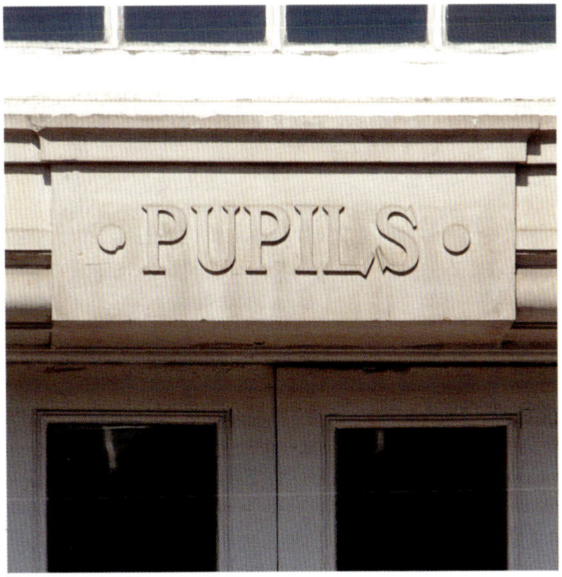
PUPILS

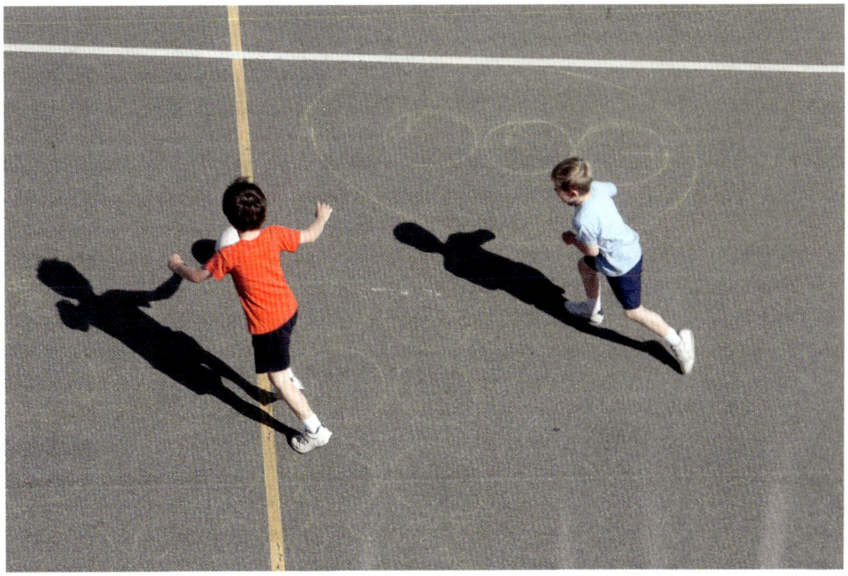

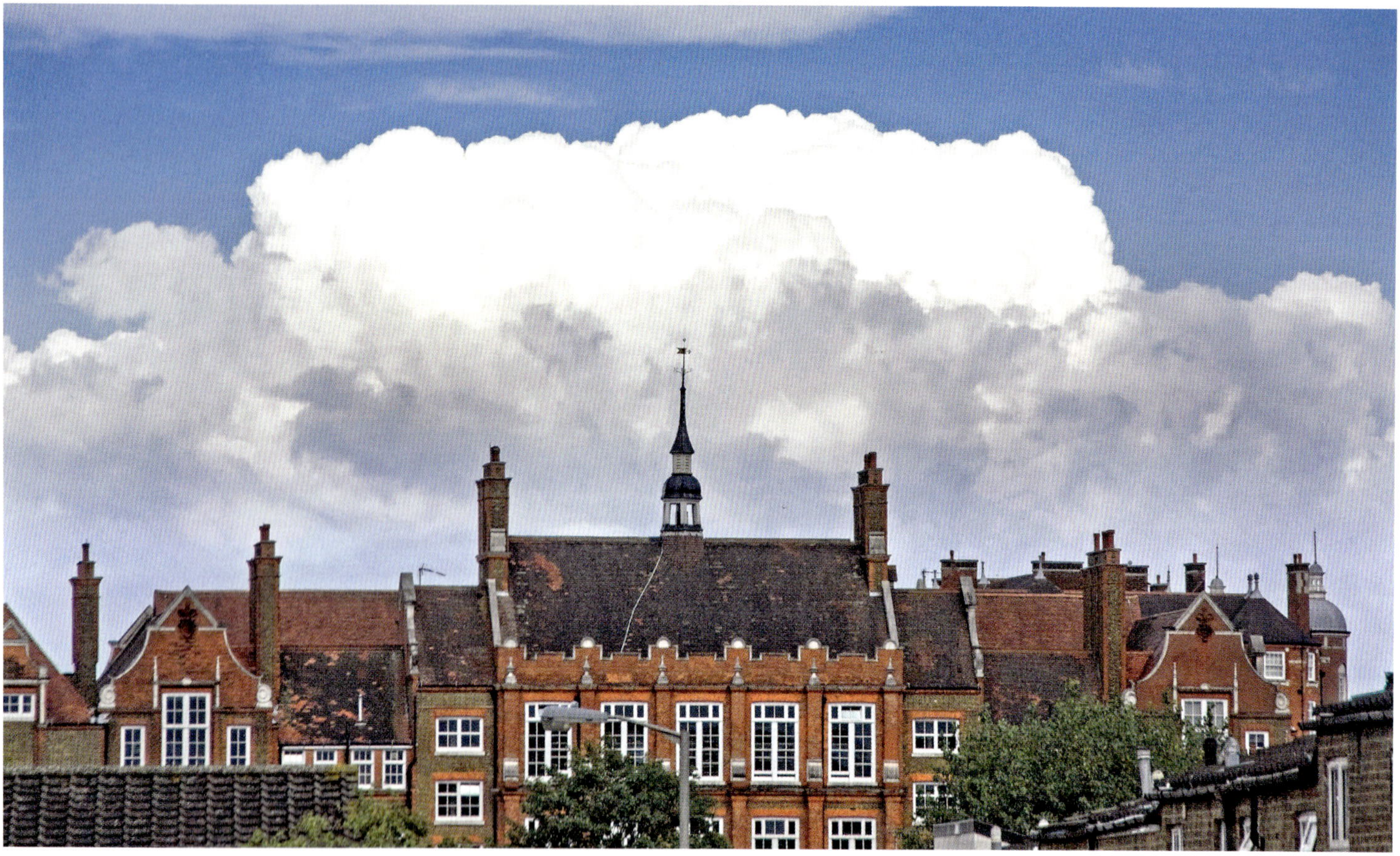

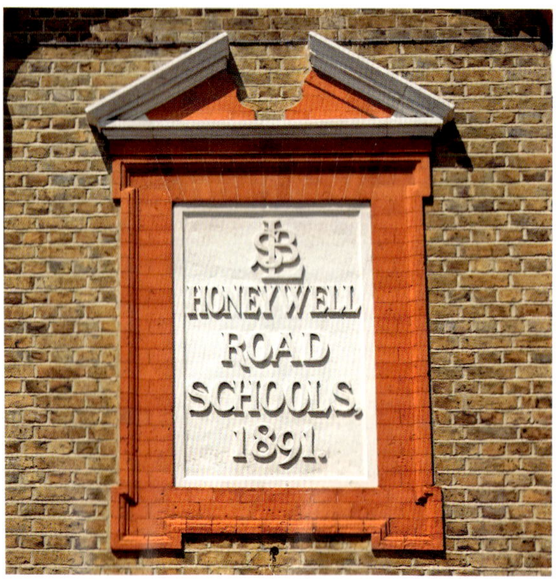

Honeywell Infant and Primary School is an extremely well regarded state school and as the rather elegant stone plaque confirms (left), the school has been in existence a long time. Thank you to the bursar Lynn Hondor Cole for arranging my visit and for showing me around.

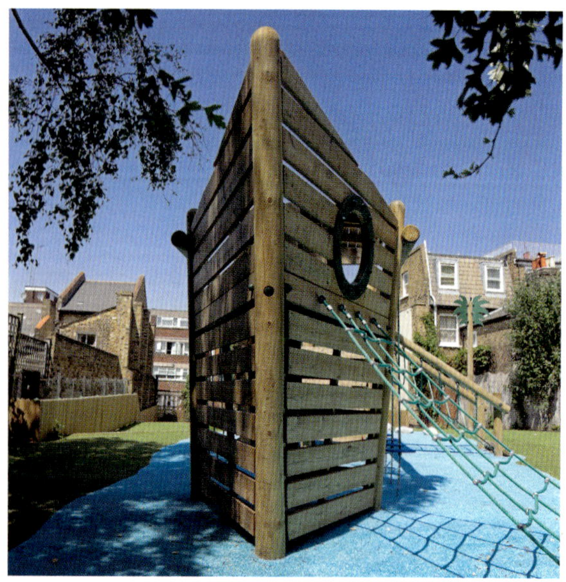

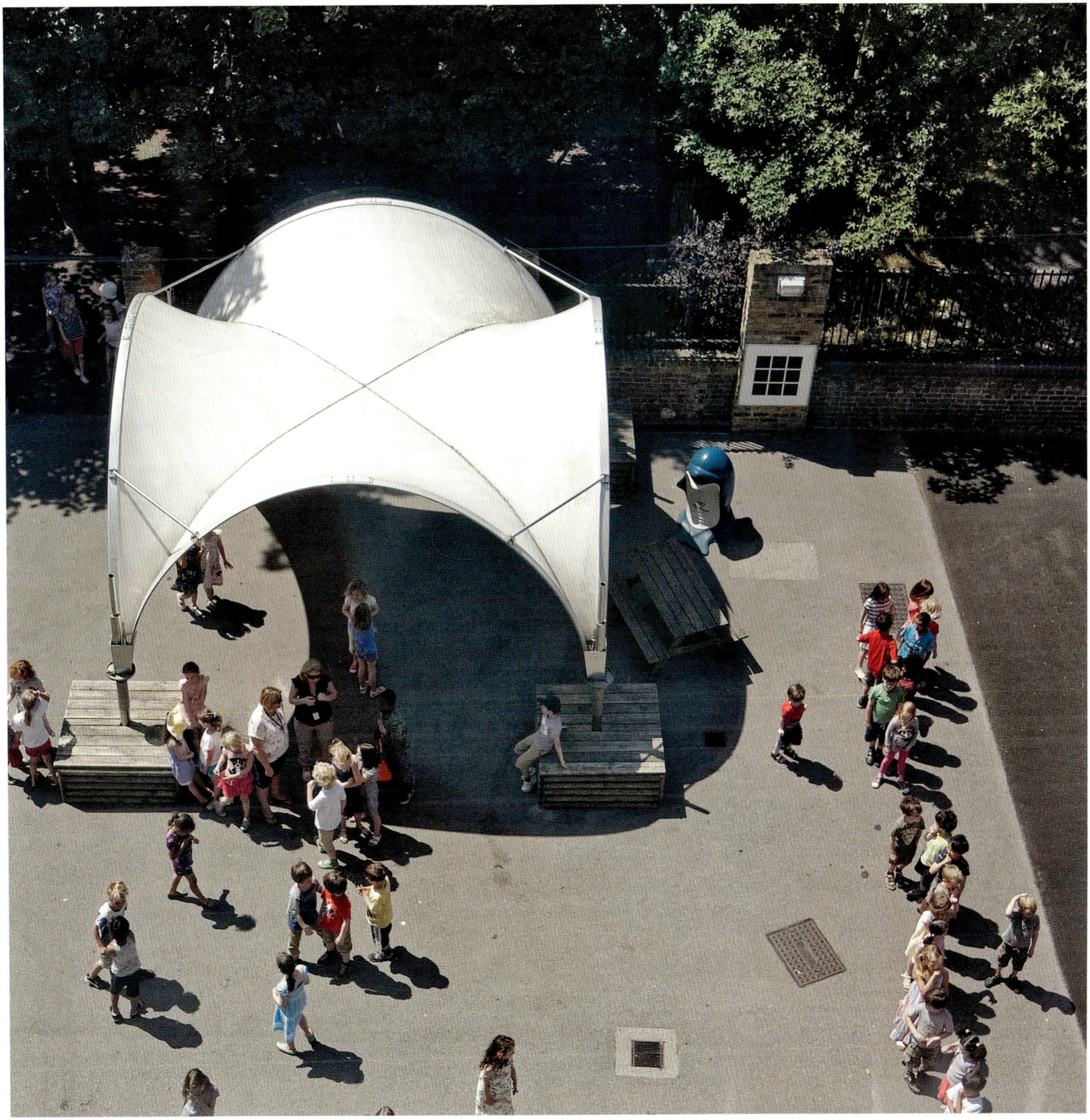

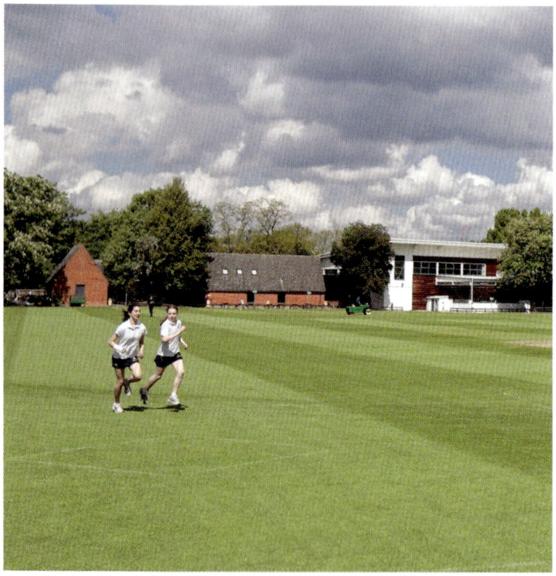

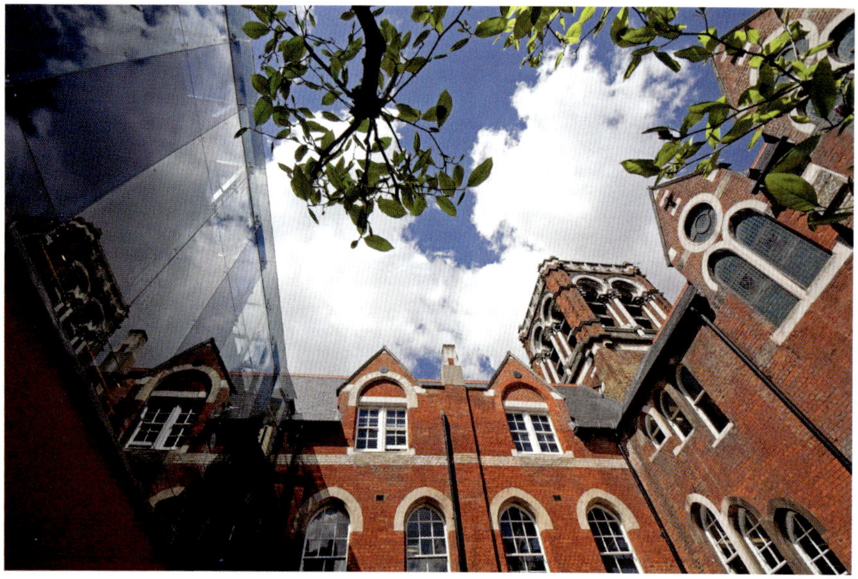

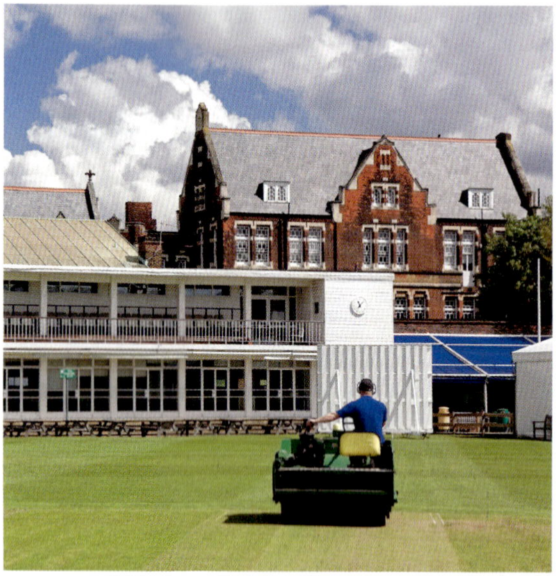

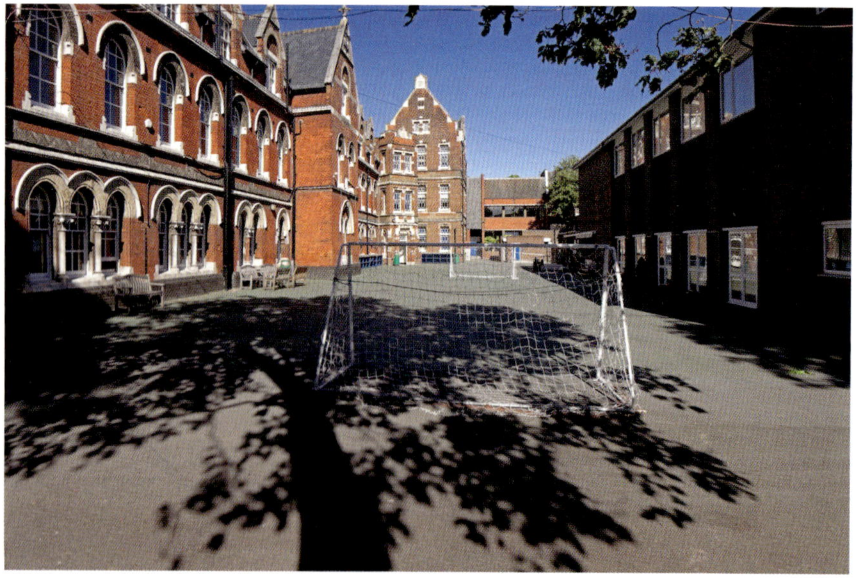

Emanuel School has at its heart a very imposing building. Founded in 1594, I was interested to learn that the school was co-educational from the start, which I'm sure was very unusual back then. Thank you to both John Benn, the deputy head and the head, Mark Hanley-Browne for taking the time to meet with me and show me around.

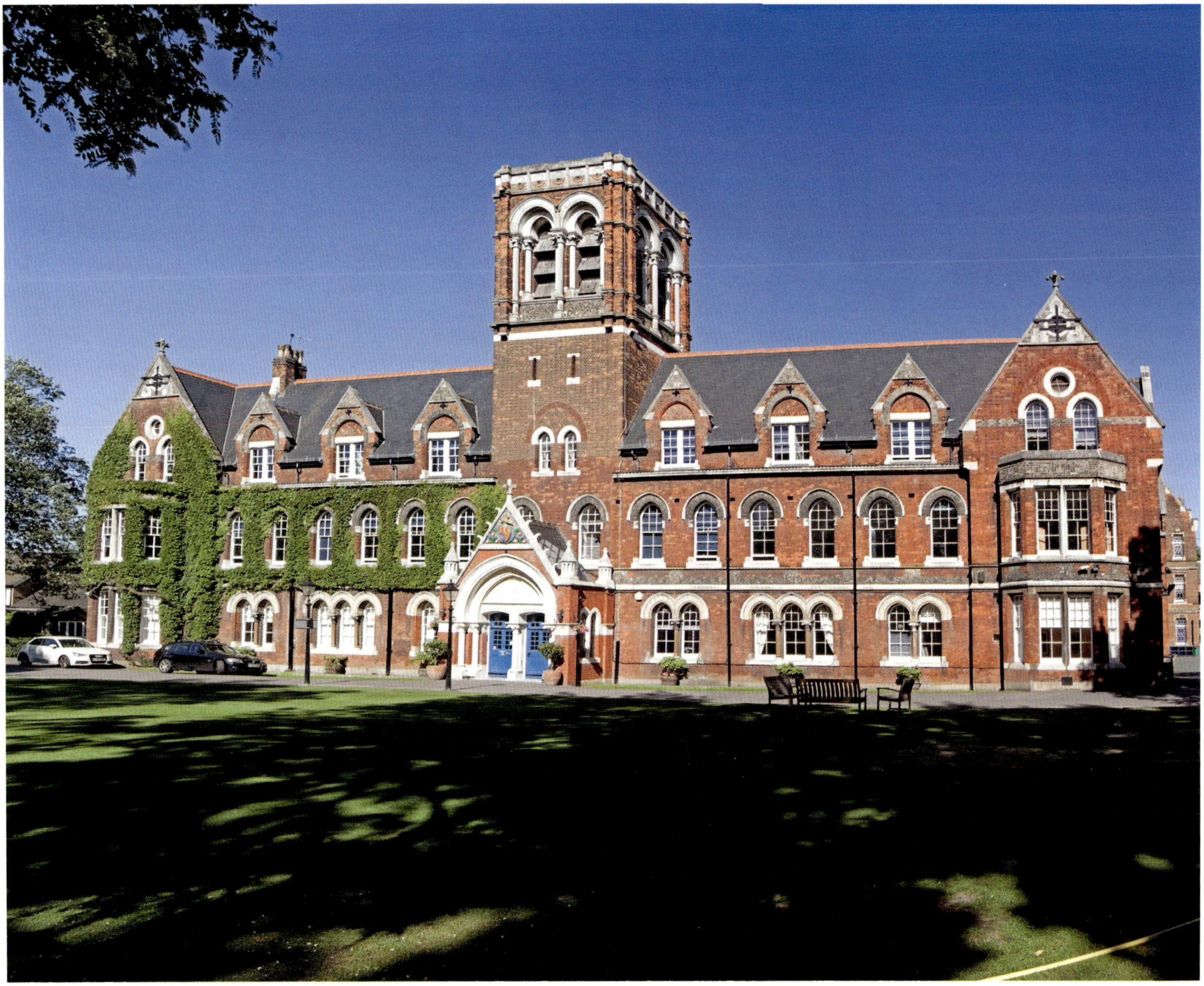

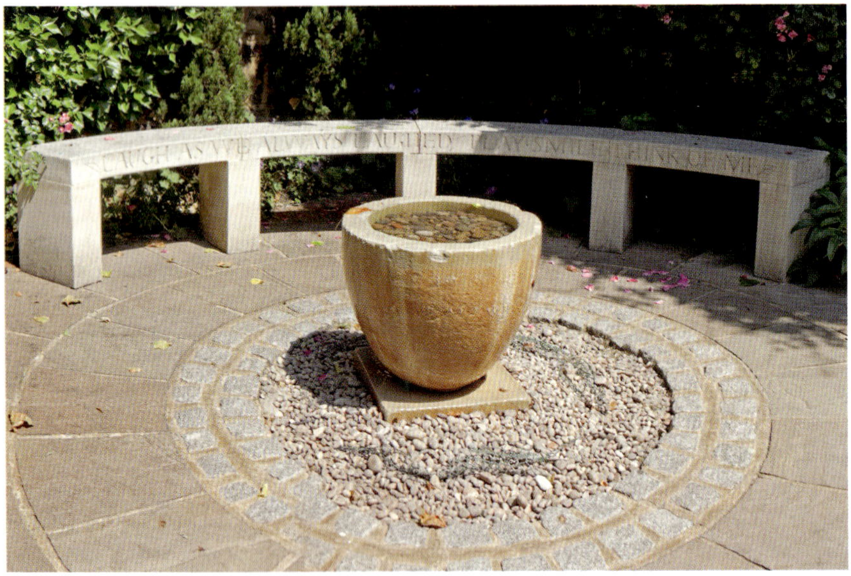

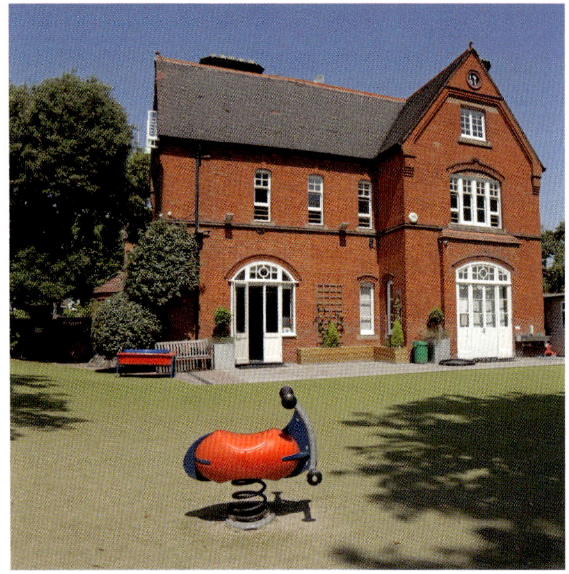

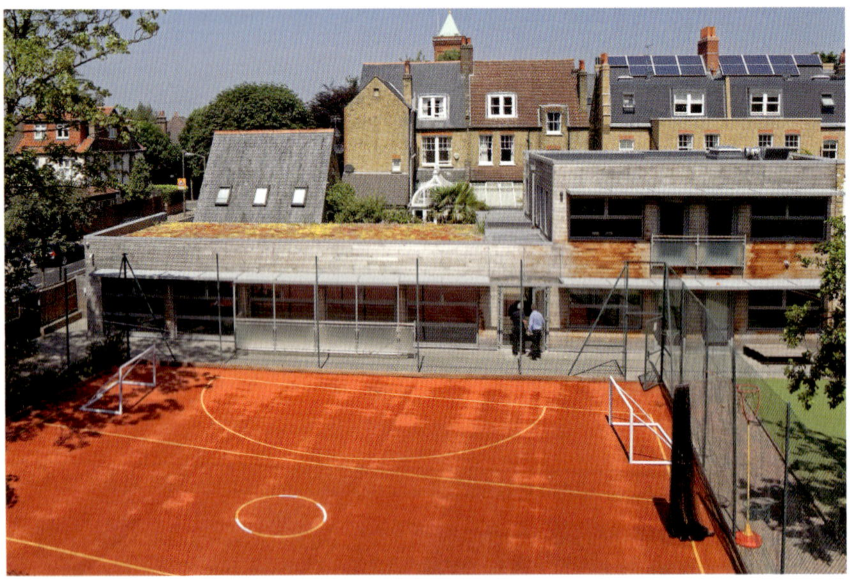

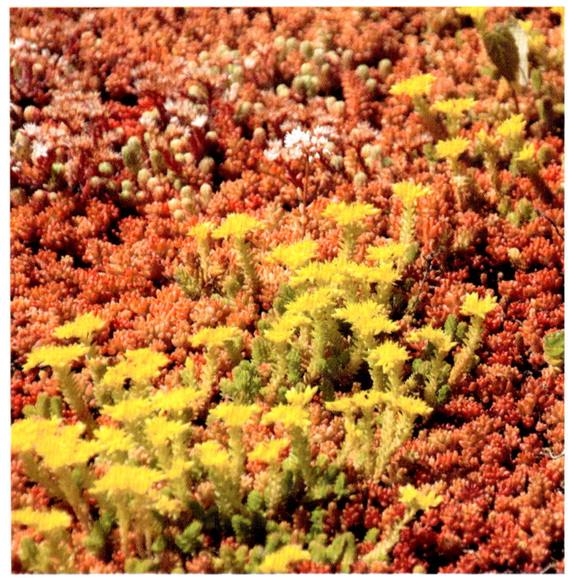

Broomwood Hall Upper and Lower School, top left. Newly painted over the summer of 2013, Broomwood Hall Upper School occupies a lovely building on Nightingale Lane, with an impressive tower, which can be seen far and wide. It was the school holidays when I visited, hence no children. Thank you to Alison Melrose for showing me around on what was an extremely hot day I seem to remember. As part of the group that own the school, they also run Northcote Lodge on Bolingbroke Grove, a prep school for boys.

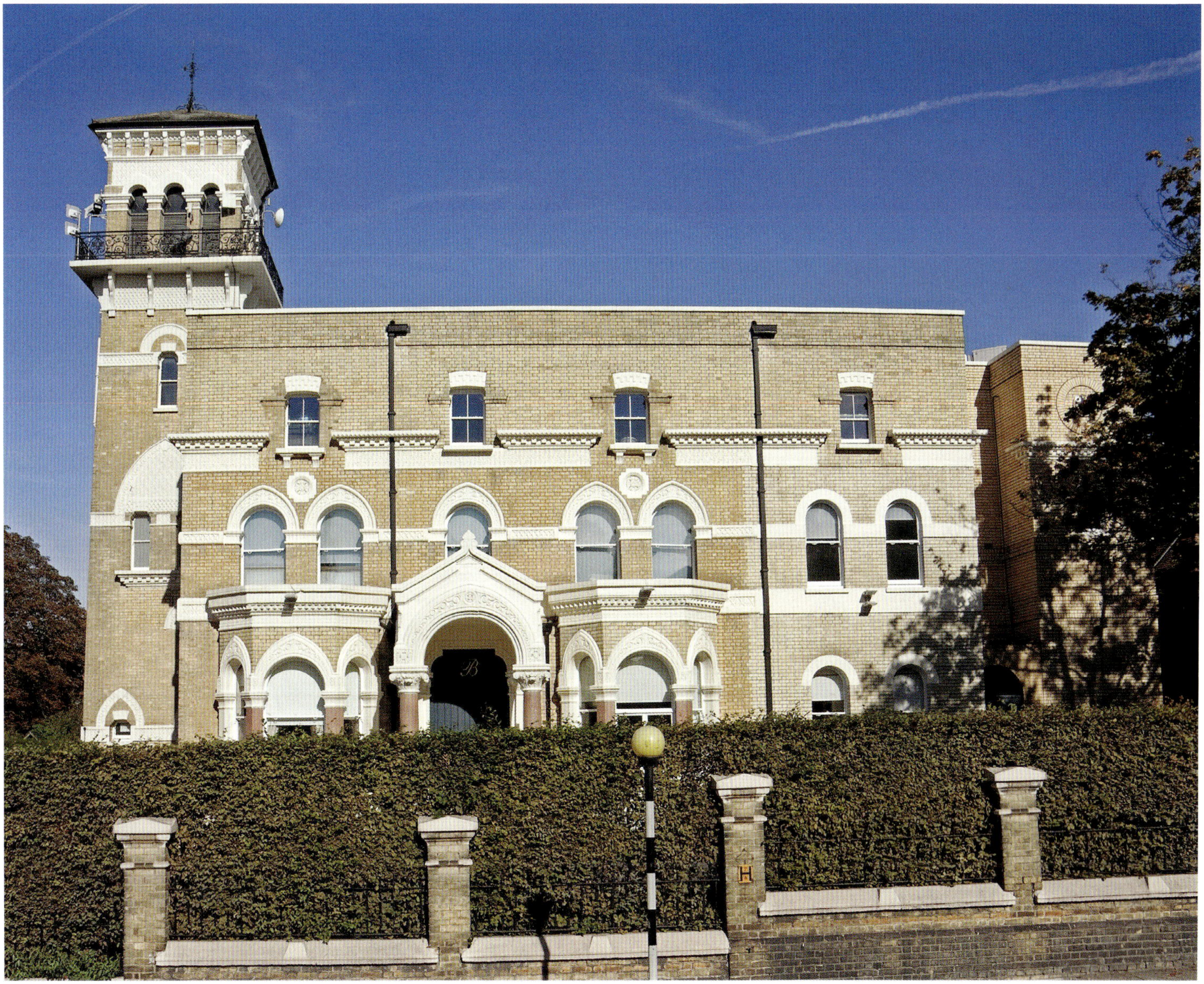

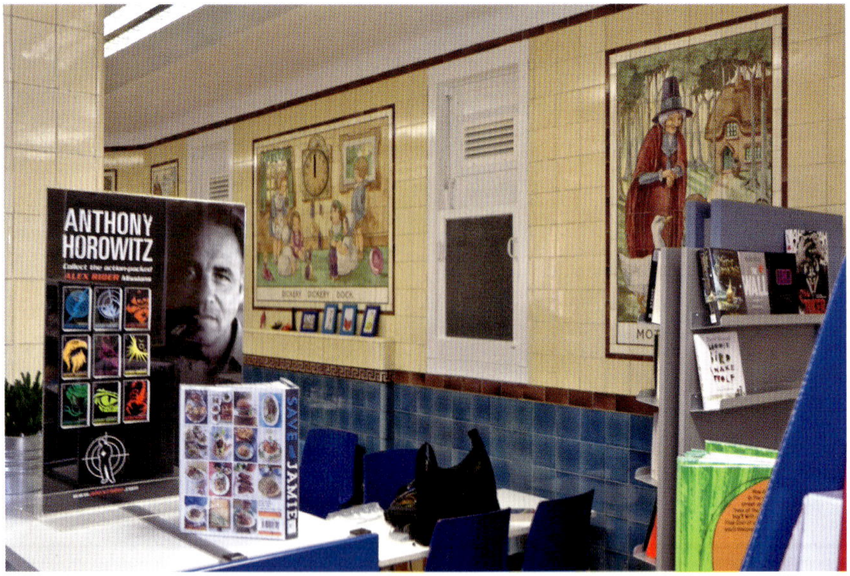
ANTHONY
HOROWITZ

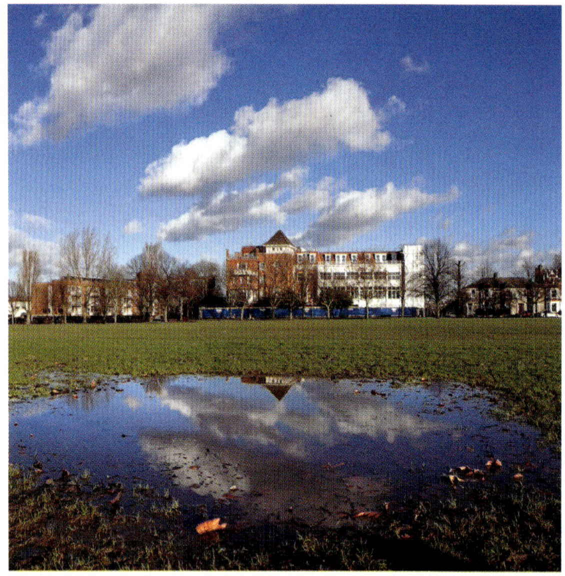

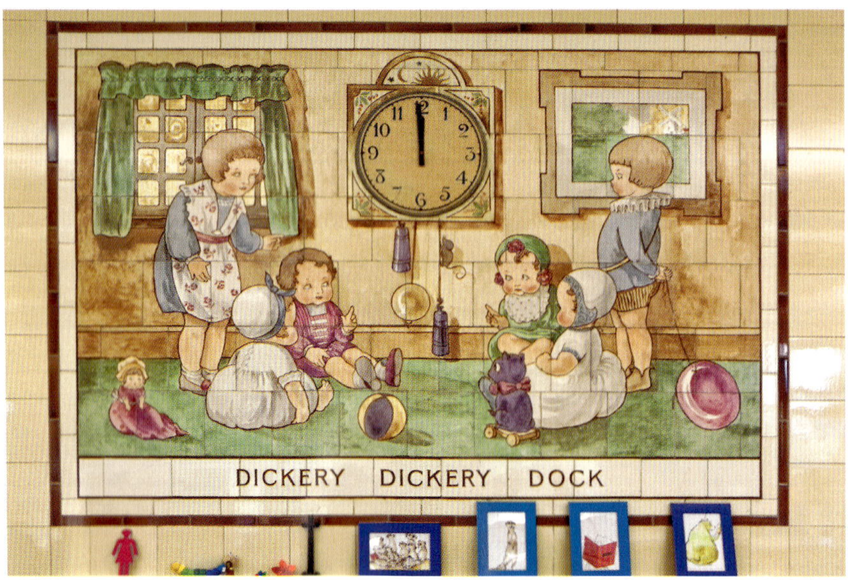
DICKERY DICKERY DOCK

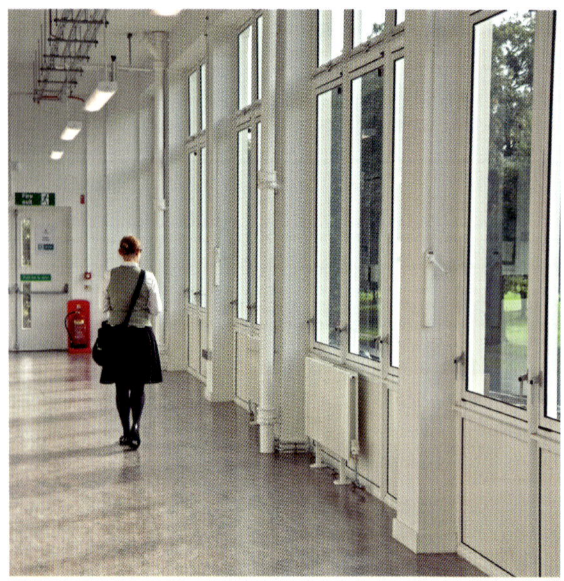

Bolingbroke Academy is a very new school going a year. As I go to press it is still under construction! Familiar to any local person as the old Bolingbroke Hospital; the building was saved from destruction by the amazing tiles that used to be on the wall of children's ward. I don't normally take interior shots, as I just don't have the space, but these tiles depicting nursery rhymes are so impressive that I made an exception. Rather cleverly the school have turned the children's ward into a library. Thank you to Sarah Gilbert for showing me around. They have also kept the marble halls and signs that used to be there; Sarah now has the Assistant Matron's office.

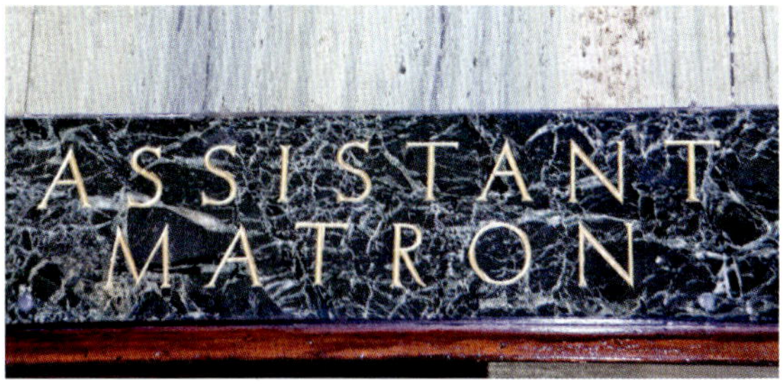

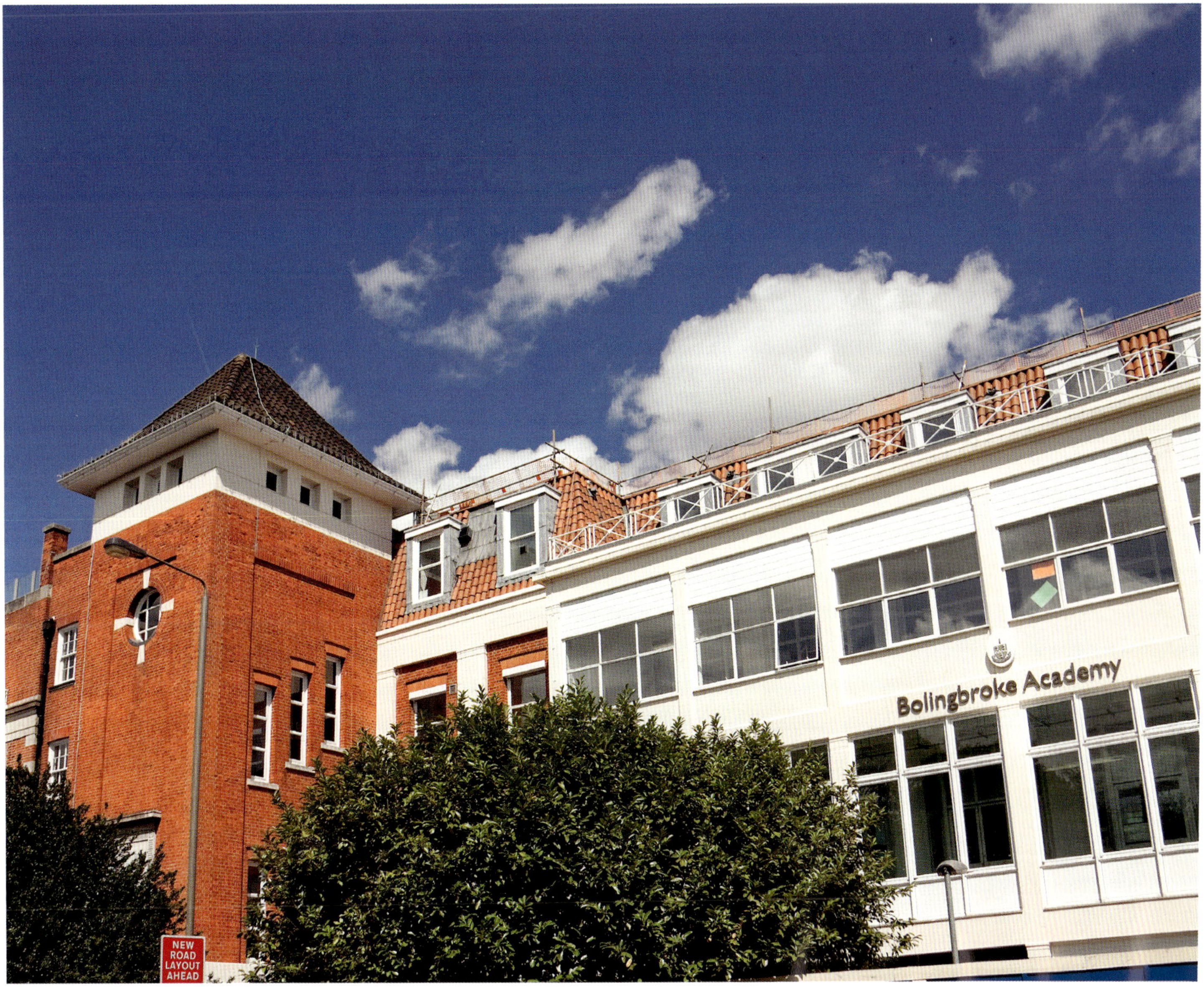

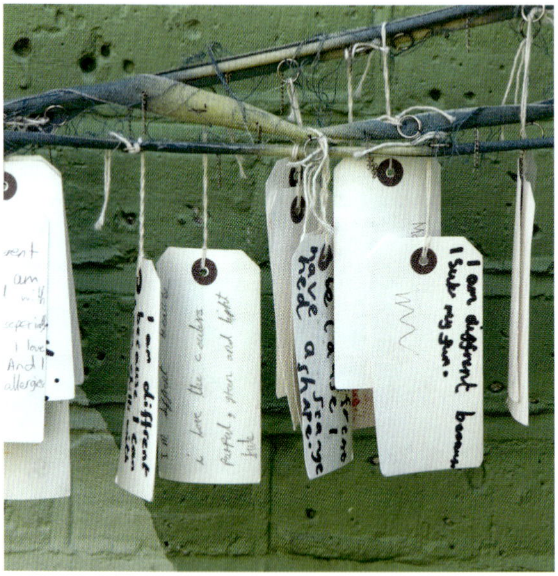

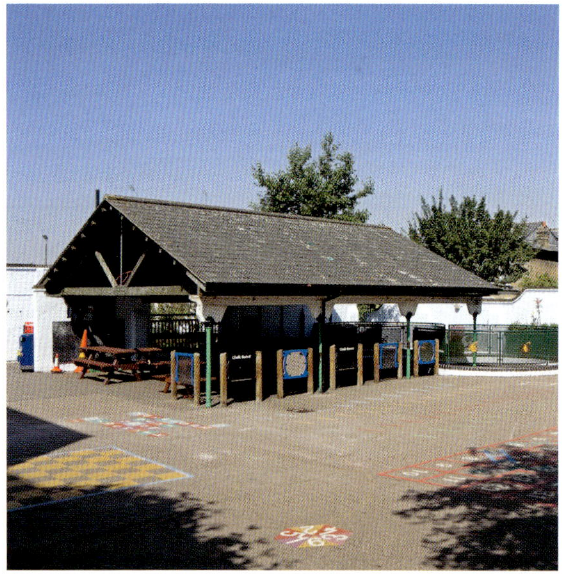

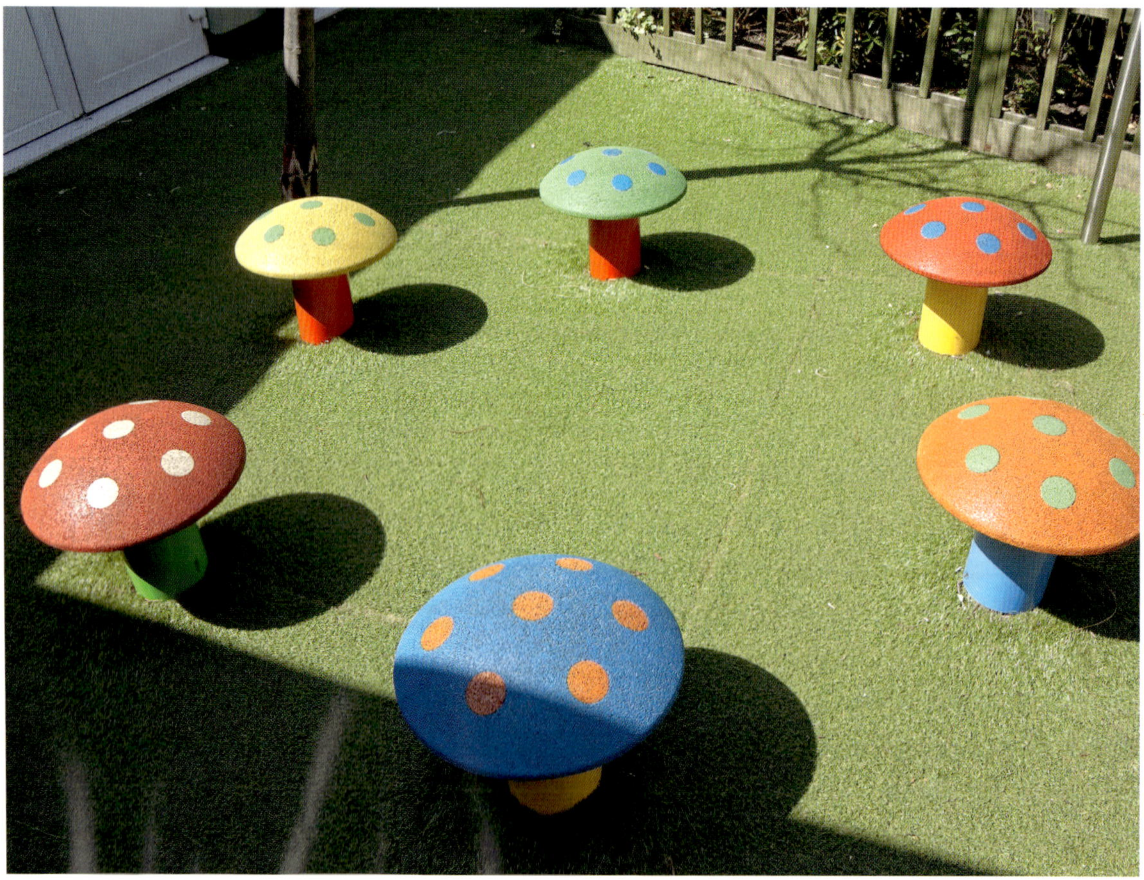

Belleville Primary School is another of the well regarded local state schools and can be found not surprisingly on the corner of Belleville and Webb's Road. The school was given academy status in 2011. The school's emblem is a Bee – an old symbol of Battersea, resulting from the bees that feasted on the Lavender Hill. Thank you to Alexandra Turnbull for meeting with me and showing me around.

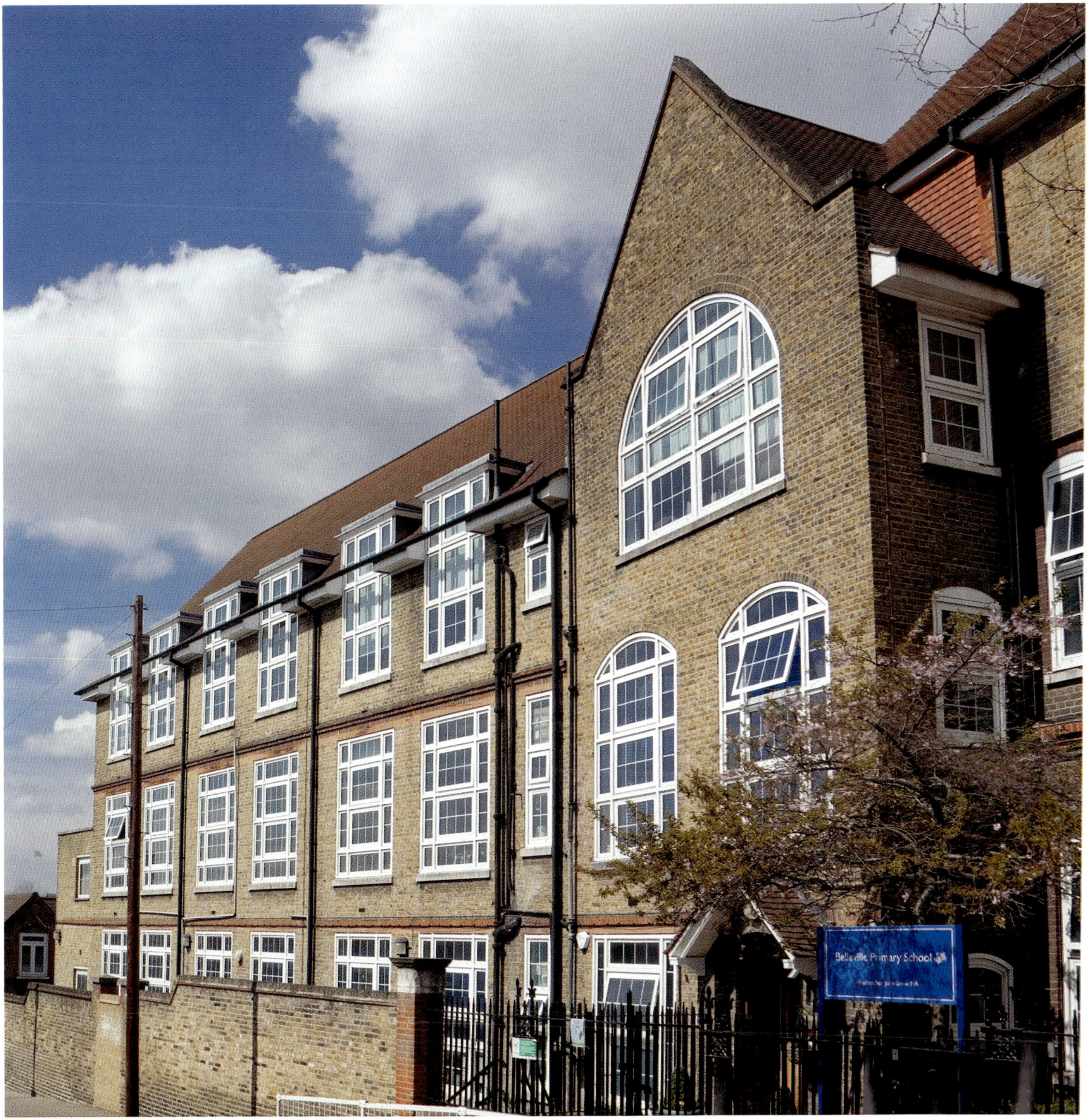
Belleville Primary School

Pubs

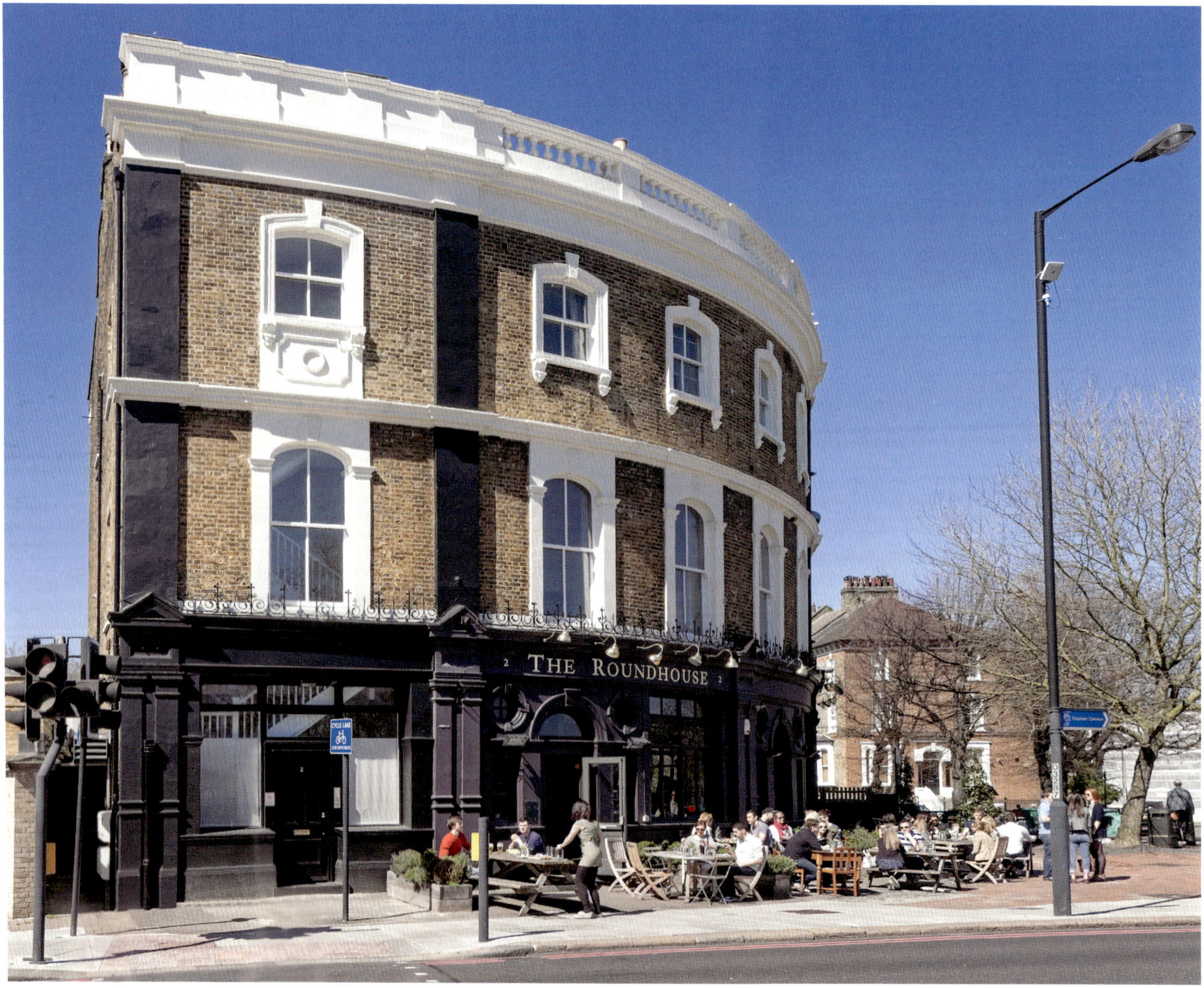

Opposite: The Roundhouse, formerly the Freemasons, on the junction of Battersea Rise and Spencer Park.

This page: The Eagle, Chatham Road, off Northcote Road. Run in the traditional manner, with a wide variety of guest beers on tap, this pub is around 150 years old. It is interesting to note that Chatham Road was the only housing development in South Battersea by 1861 and had three pubs! Given that is was one of the first streets it is rather fitting that the editor of Battersea Matters, published by The Battersea Society (*www.batterseasociety.org.uk*) should live here.

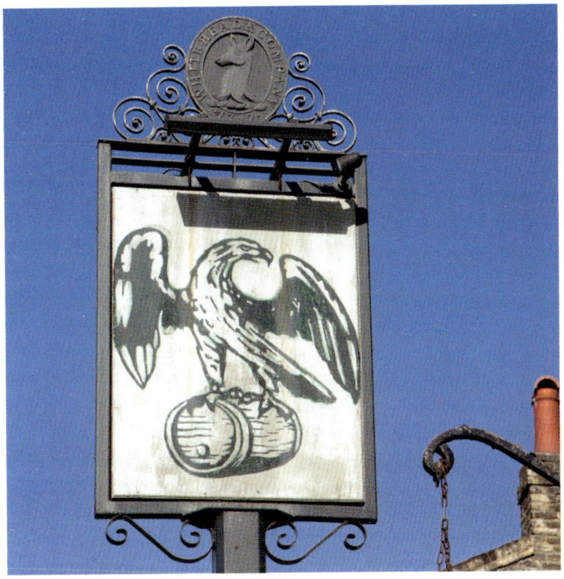

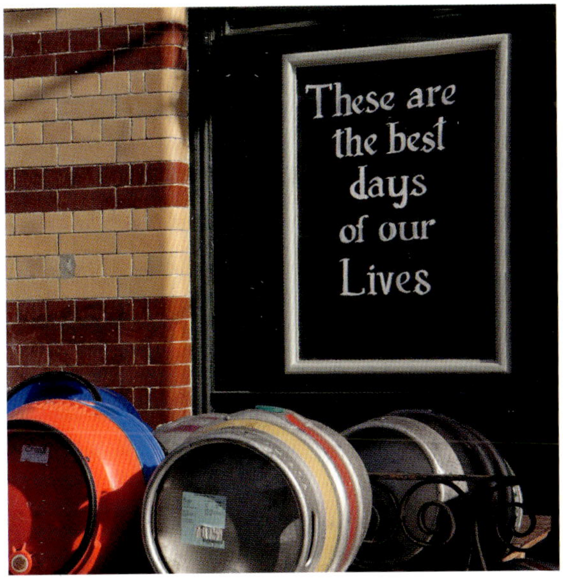

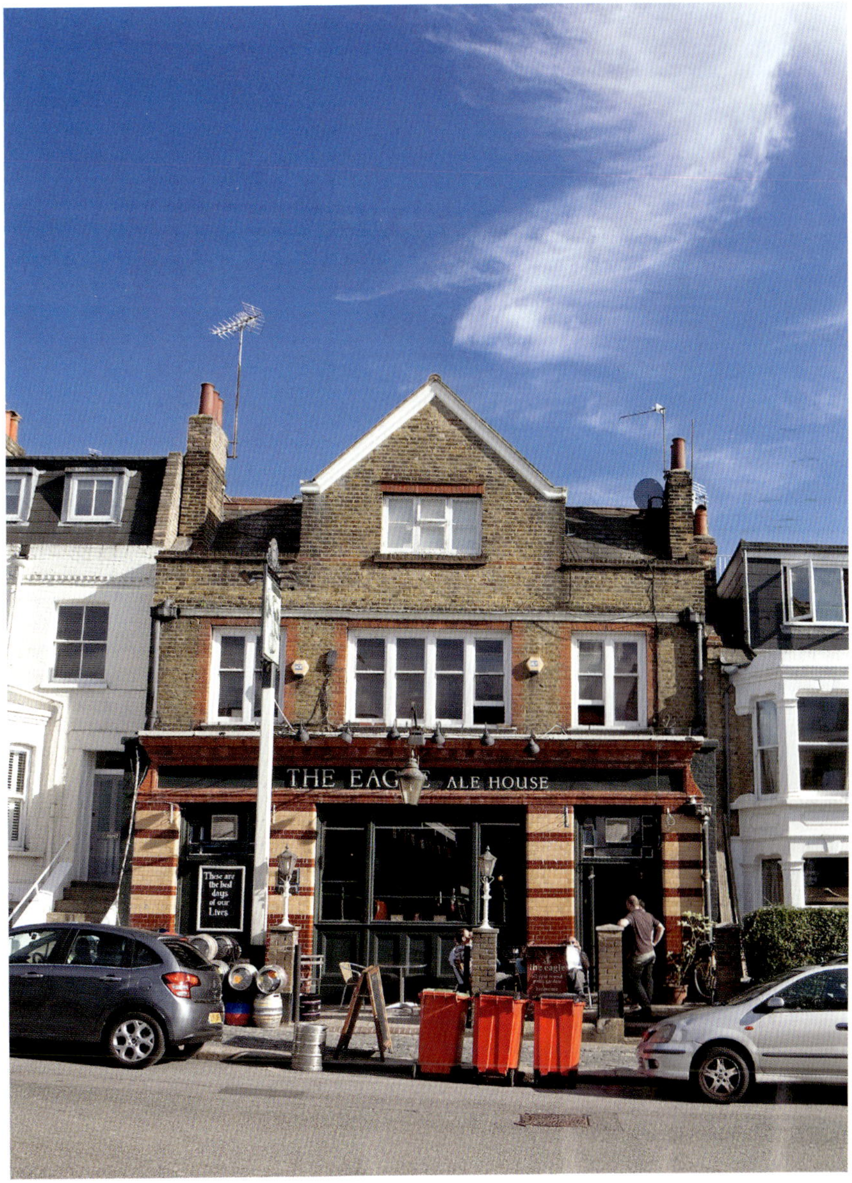

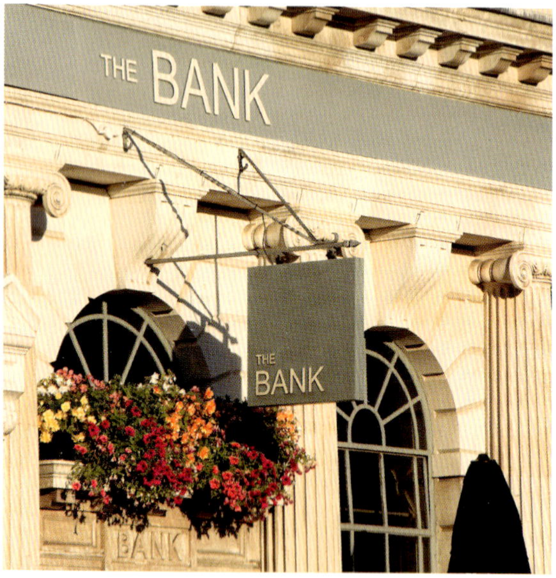

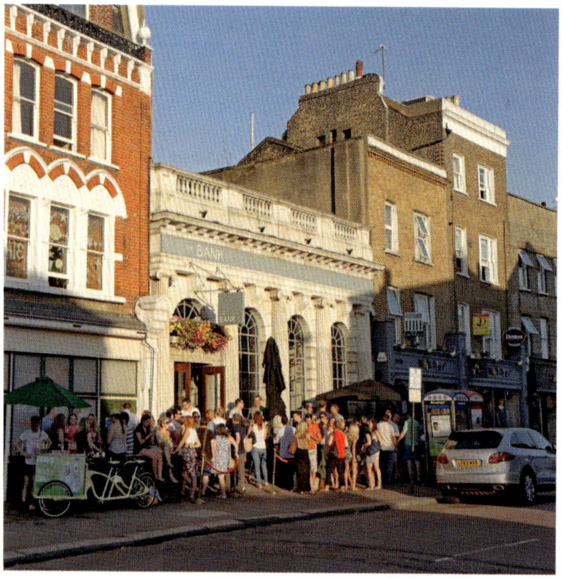

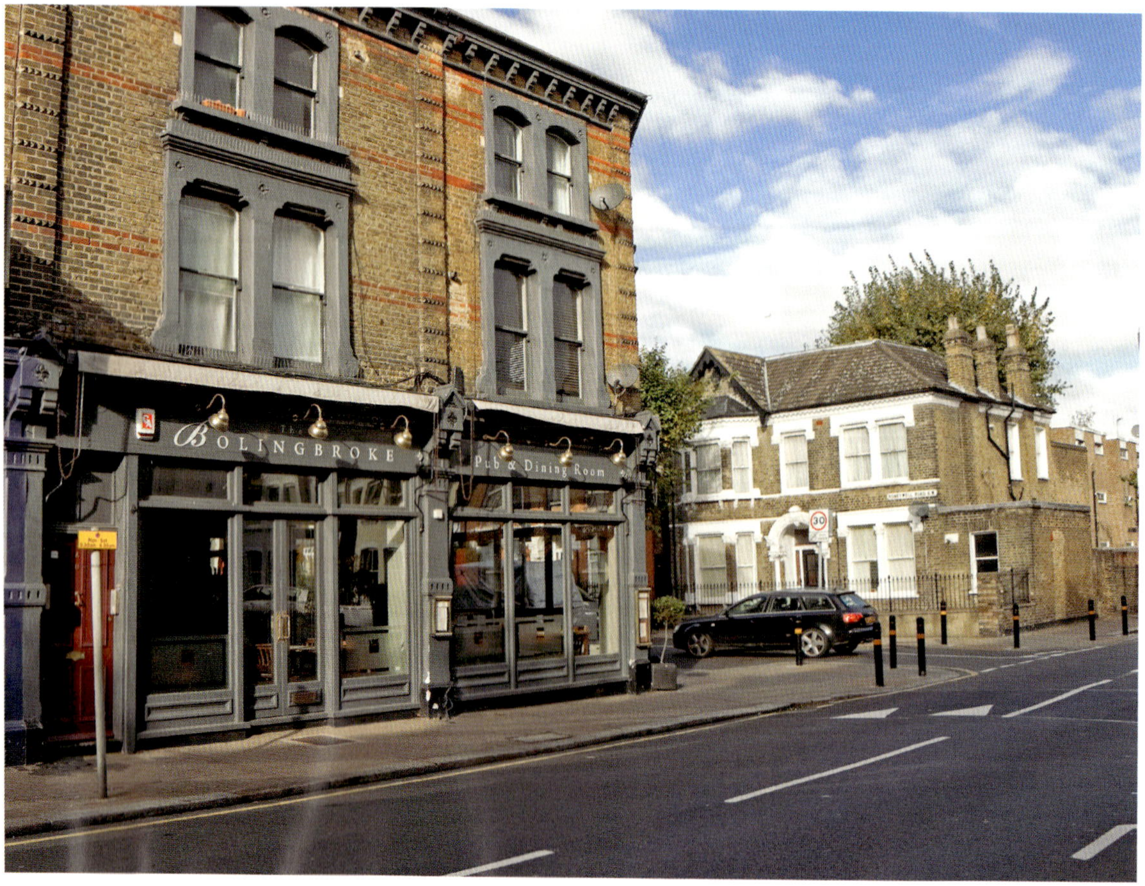

Top: The Bank, Northcote Road.

Bottom: The Bolingbroke Pub and Dining Room, Northcote Road.

Opposite: The Draft House, Northcote Road.

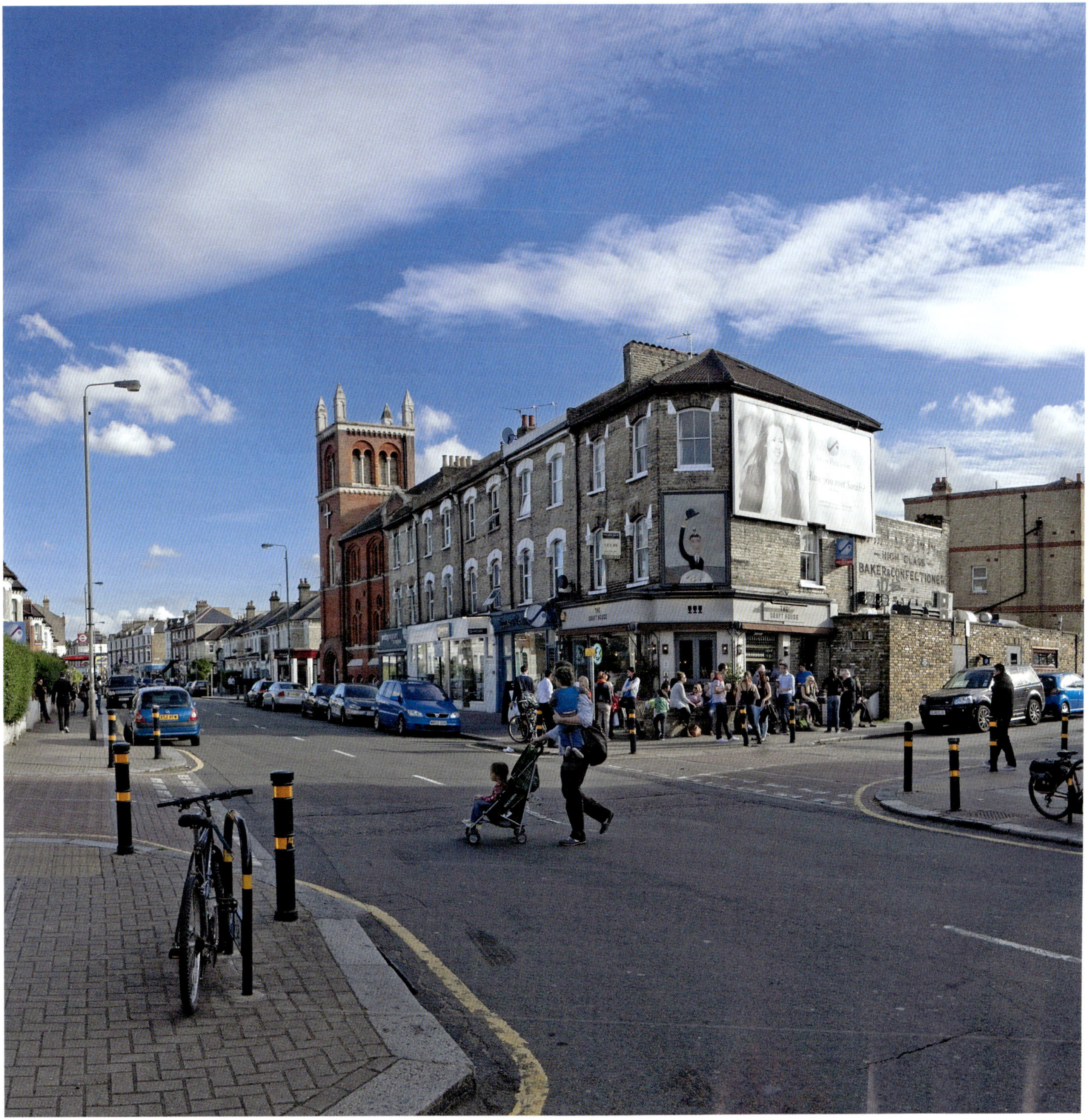
Have you met Sarah?
HIGH CLASS
BAKER & CONFECTIONER
THE DRAFT HOUSE
THE DRAFT HOUSE

Top right and opposite: The Falcon in St John's Hill. Dating from 1887, this pub is Grade II listed and is recognised by CAMRA as a special pub with an outstanding interior.

Top left: The Duck, formerly The Railway Tavern, Battersea Rise.

Bottom left: The Northcote, Northcote Road.

Bottom right: The Windsor Castle, St John's Hill.

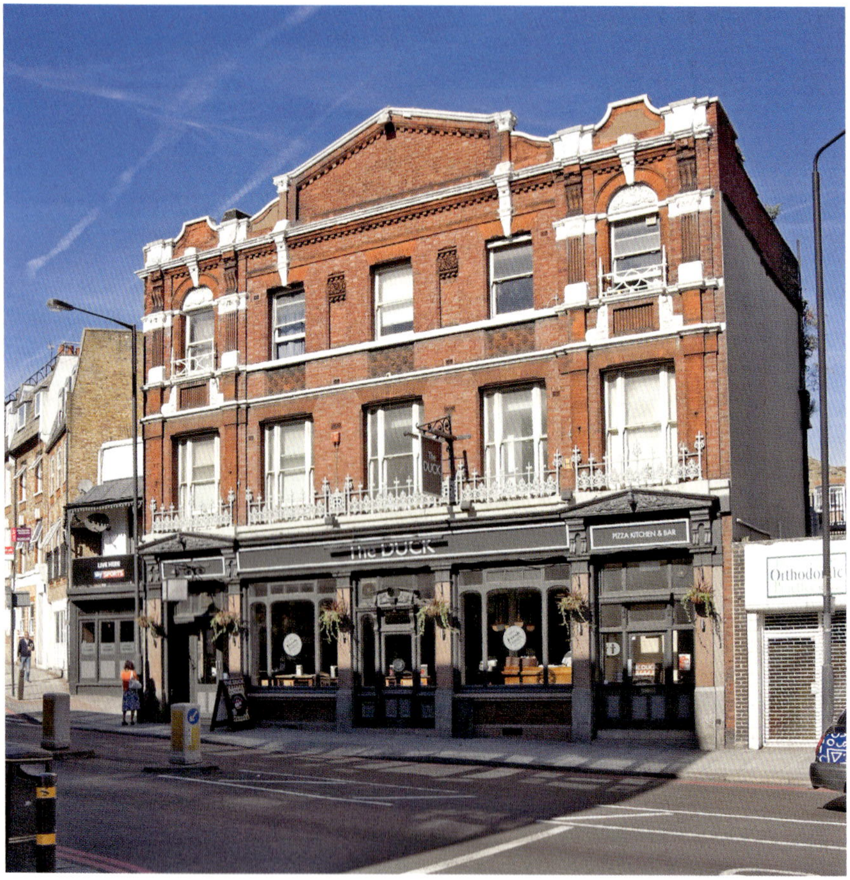

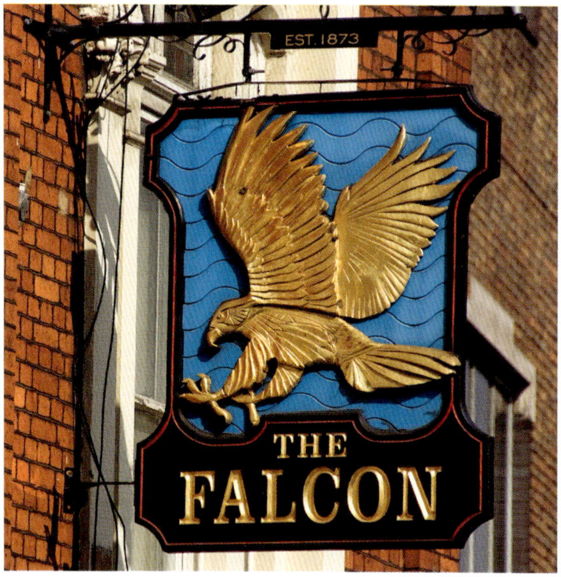

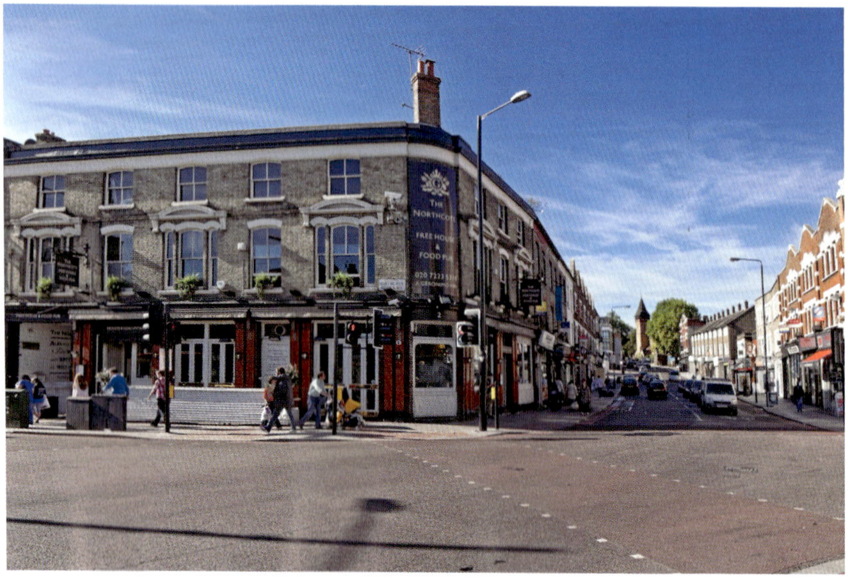

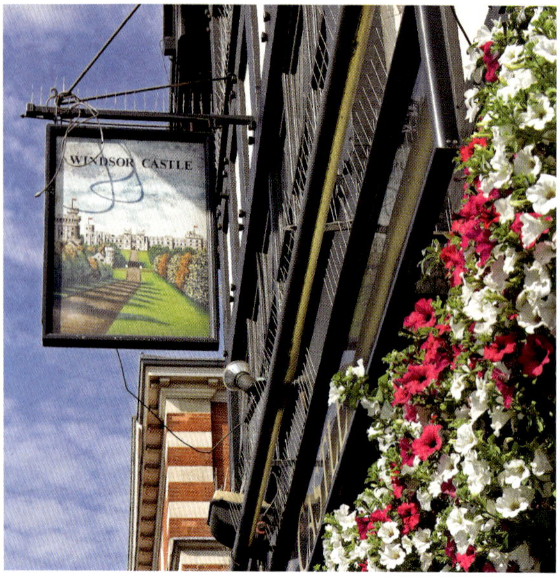

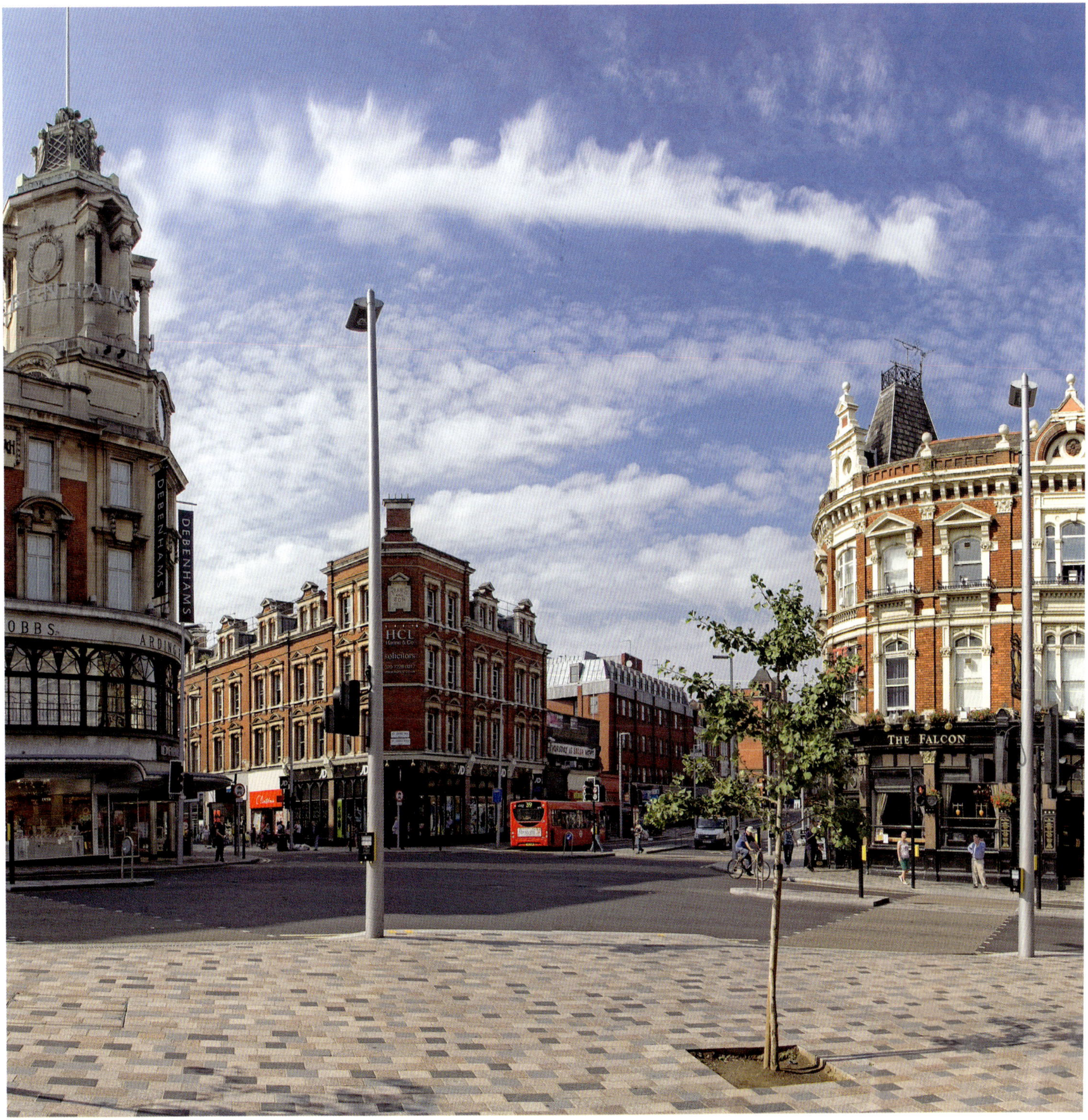
DEBENHAMS
DEBENHAMS
HCL
solicitors
THE FALCON

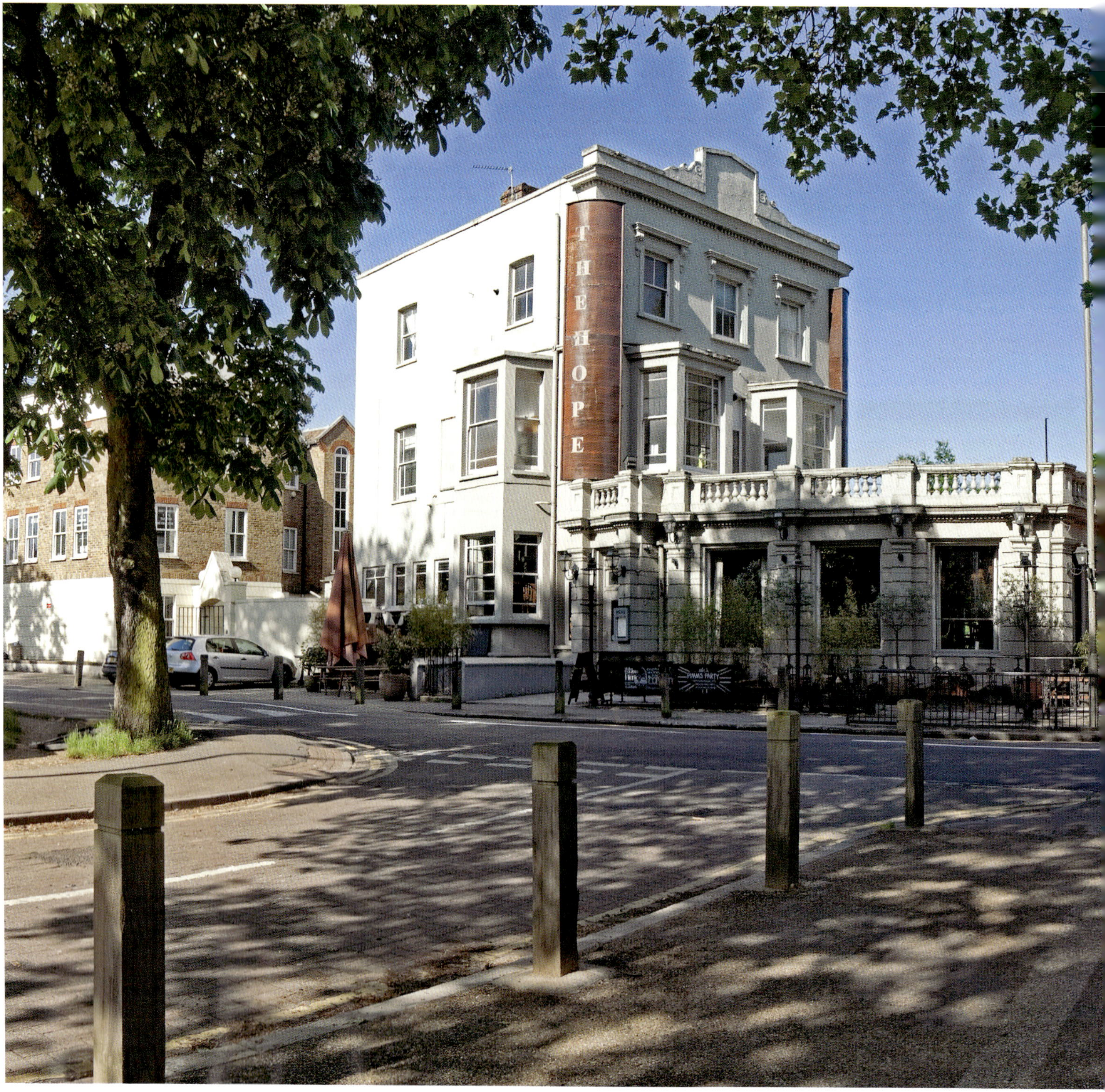
THE HOPE

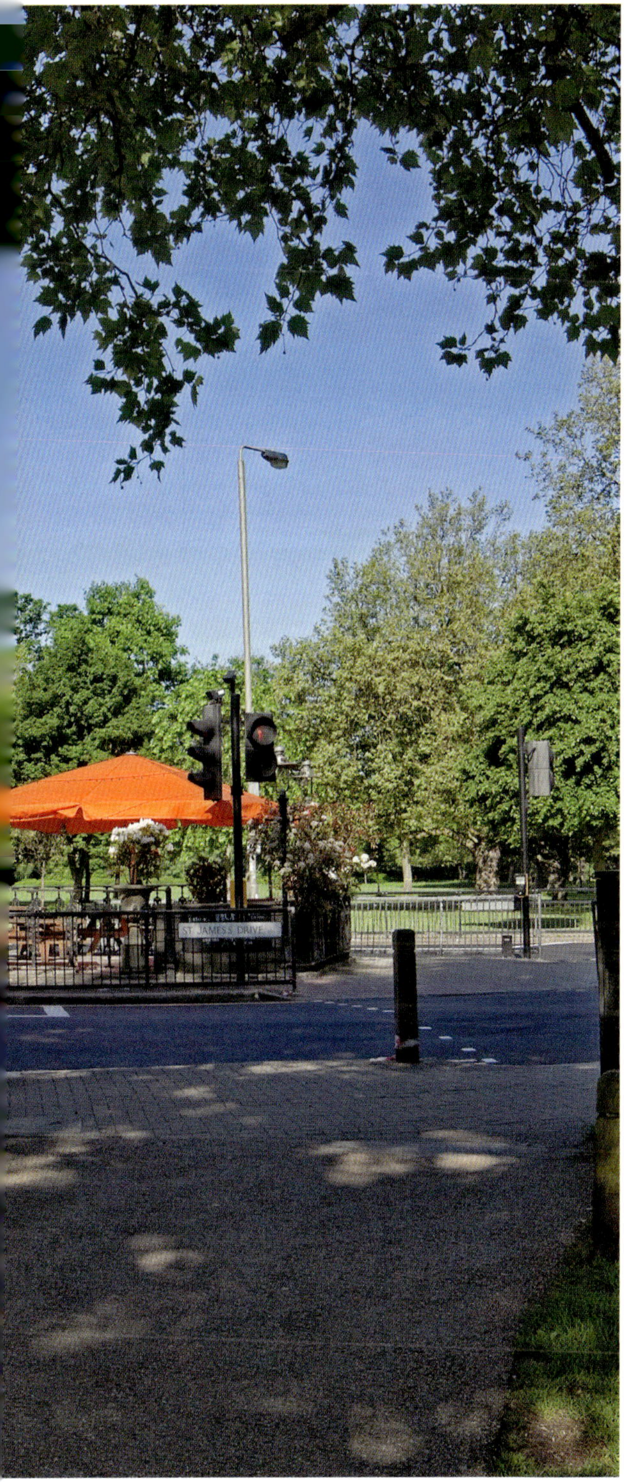

Opposite and bottom: The Hope on Bellevue Road. Handily placed for Wandsworth Common, which they cheekily suggest is an extension of their beer garden.

Right top: The Althorp, Bellevue Road.

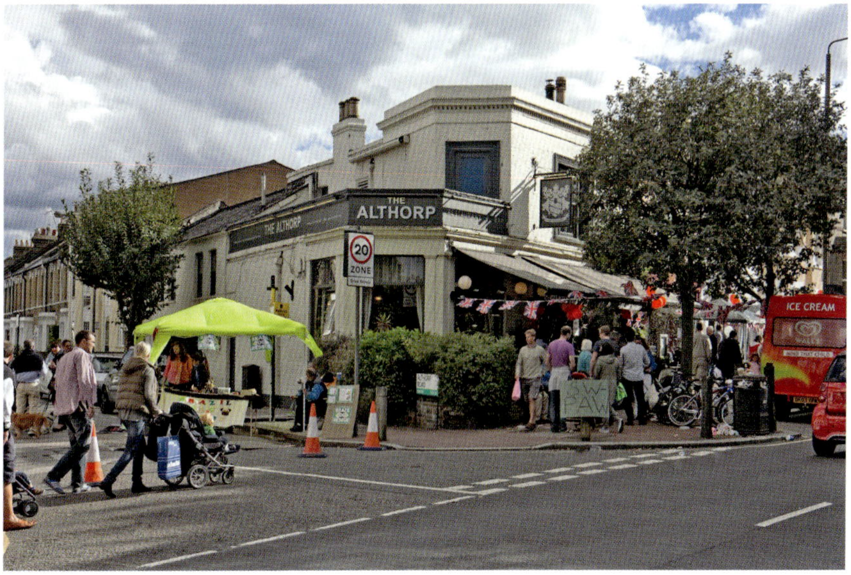

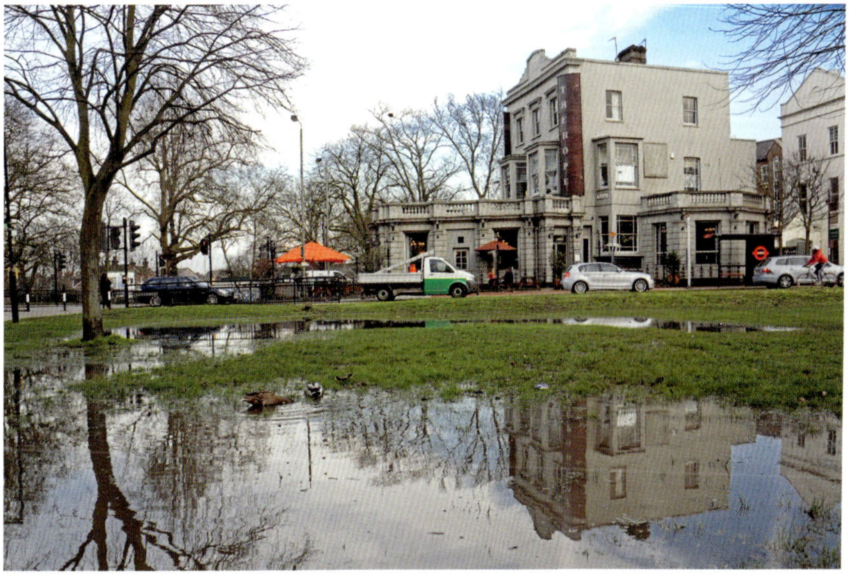

Churches

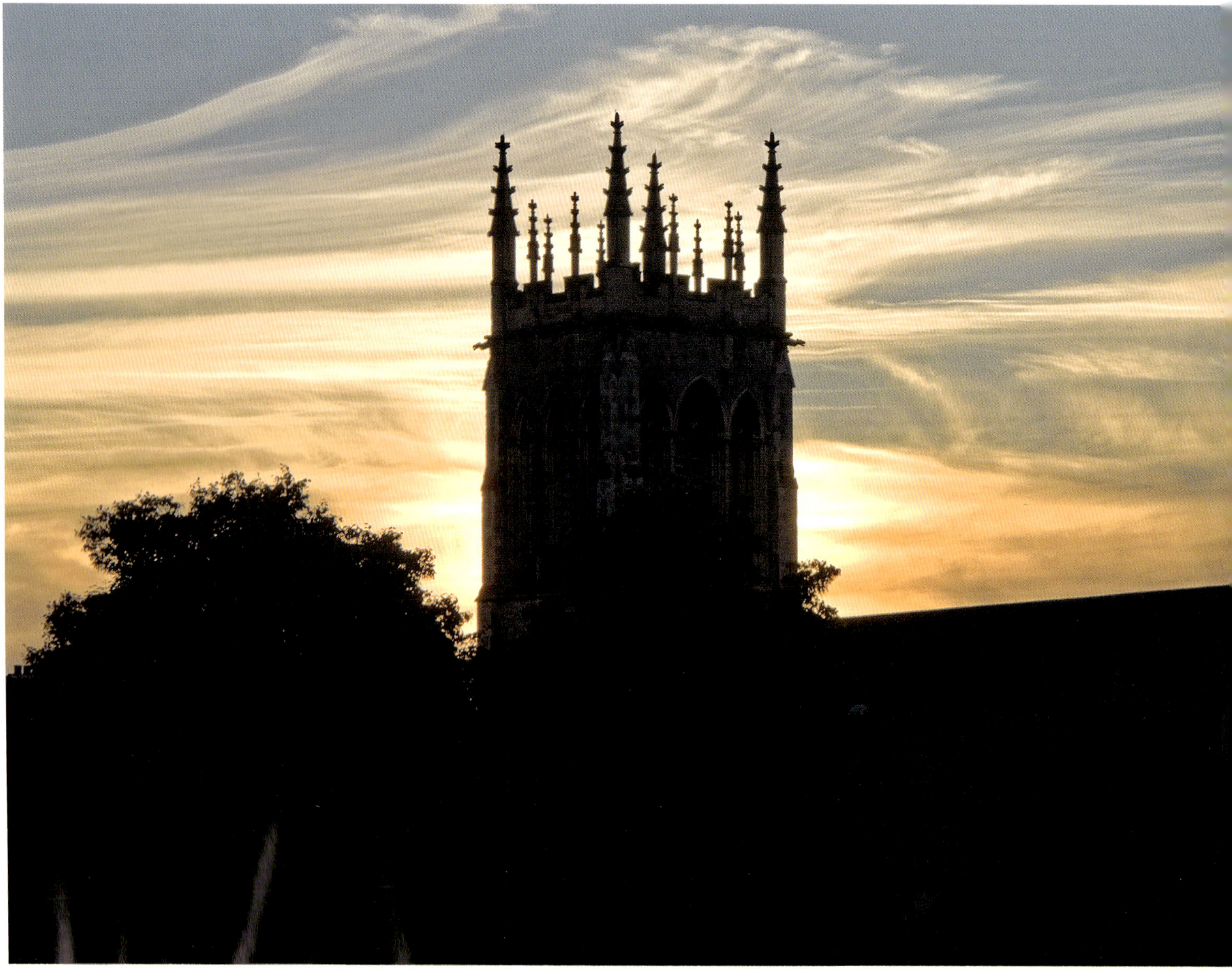

As with other parts of London, most of the churches in Battersea were built in the later part of the 19th century, as the local population grew substantially.

Main picture: St Barnabas on Clapham Common North Side was built in 1898.

Right: St Andrews dates from 1886.

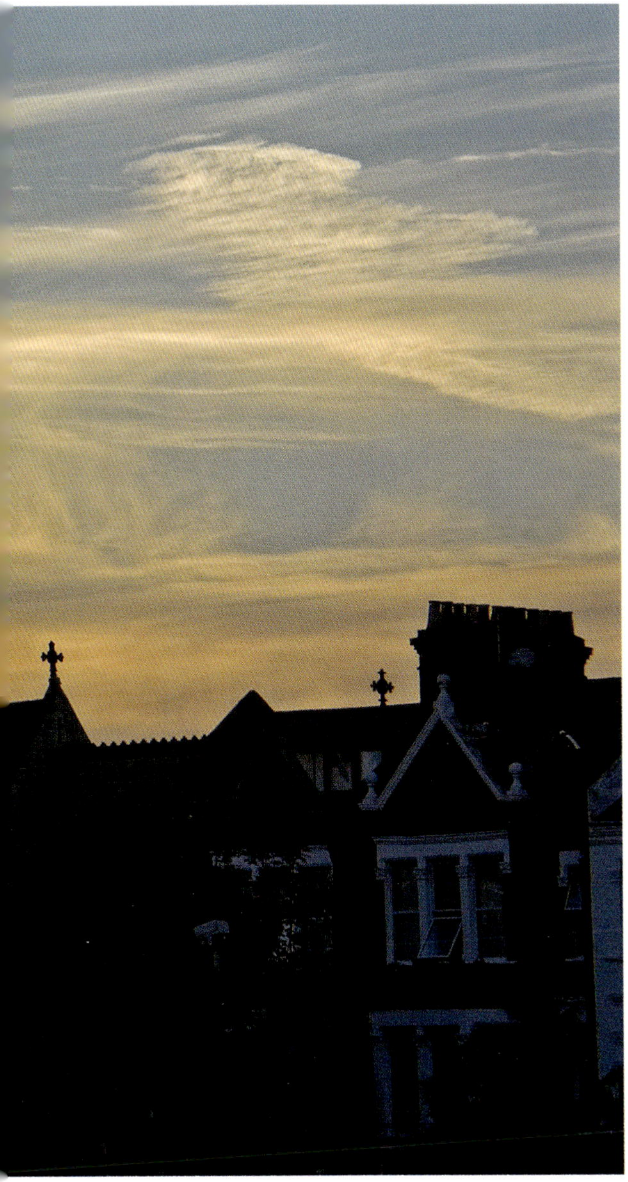

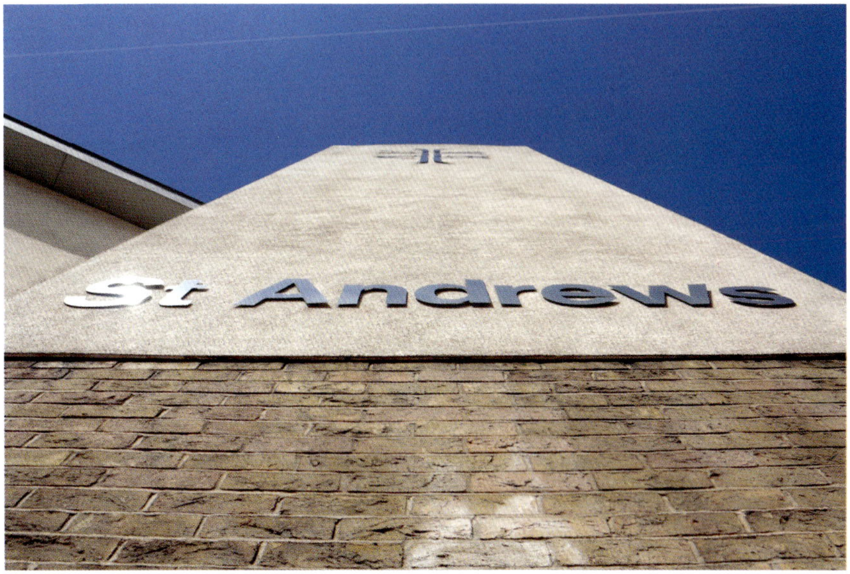

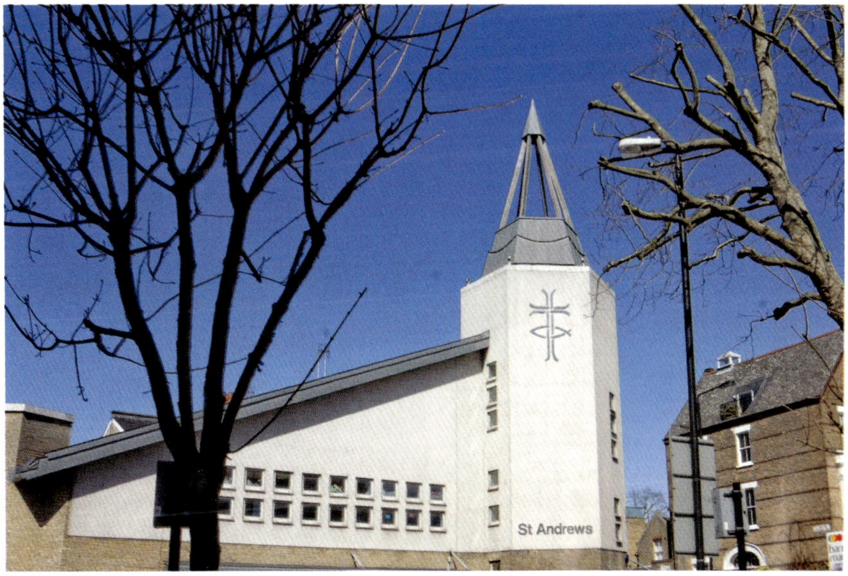

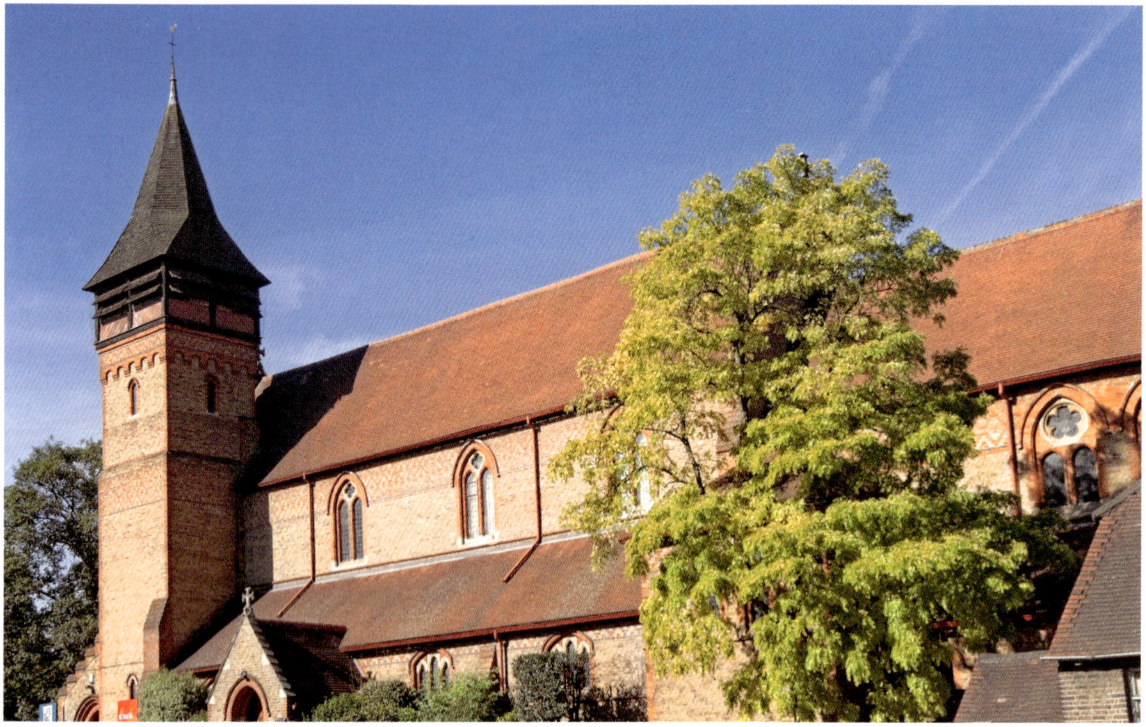

This page and overleaf left: St Mark's on Battersea Rise dates from 1873.

Overleaf right: This is not a church but the notable landmark on the roof of the building that borders Battersea Rise and St John's Road.

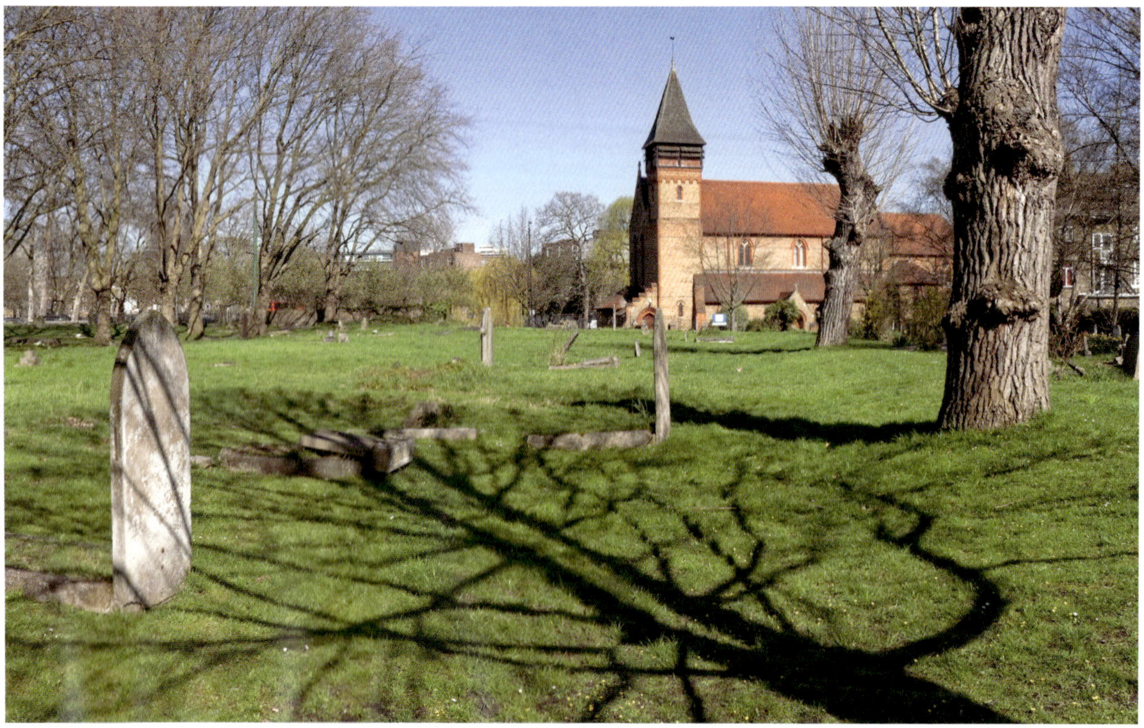

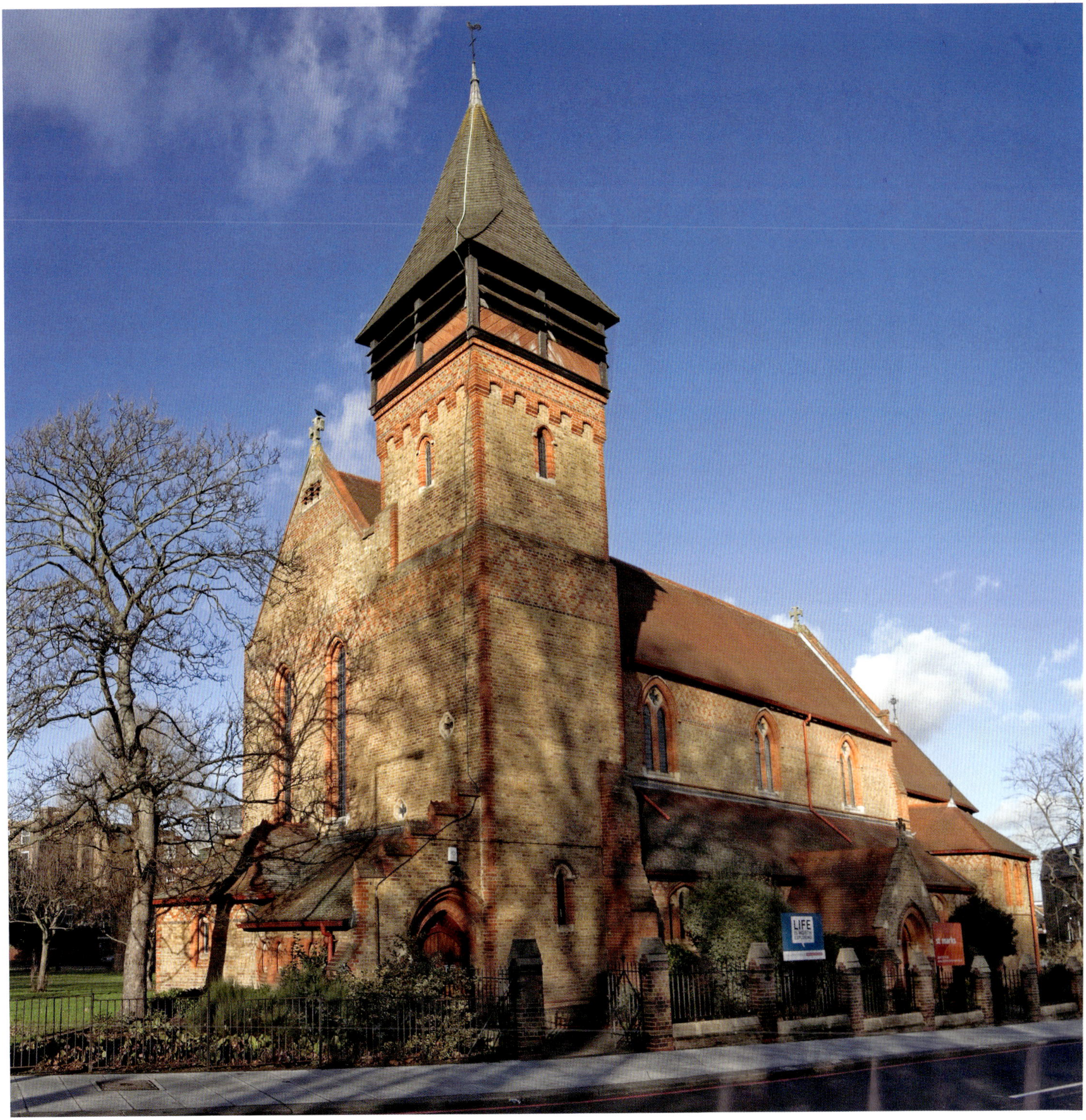
LIFE
st marks

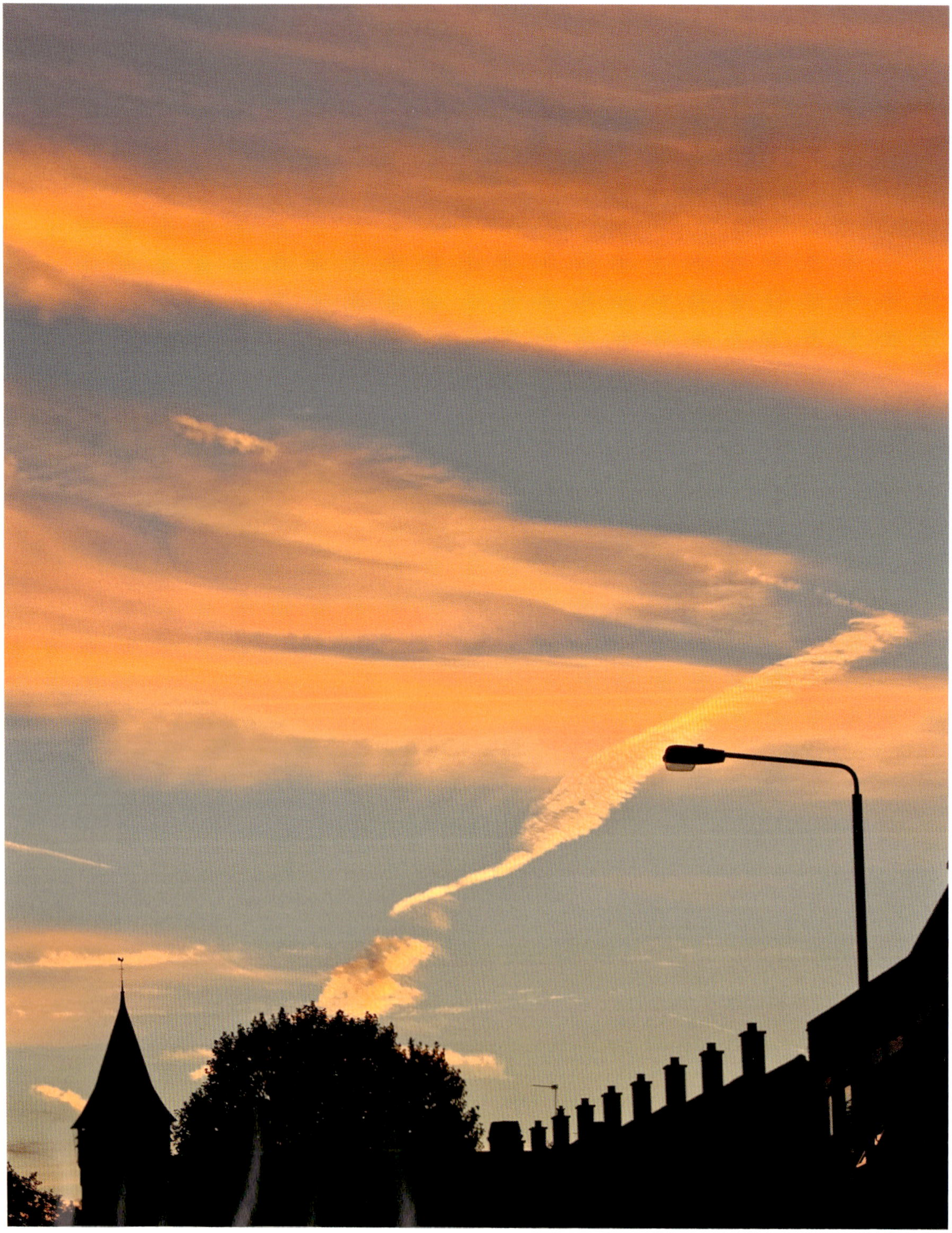

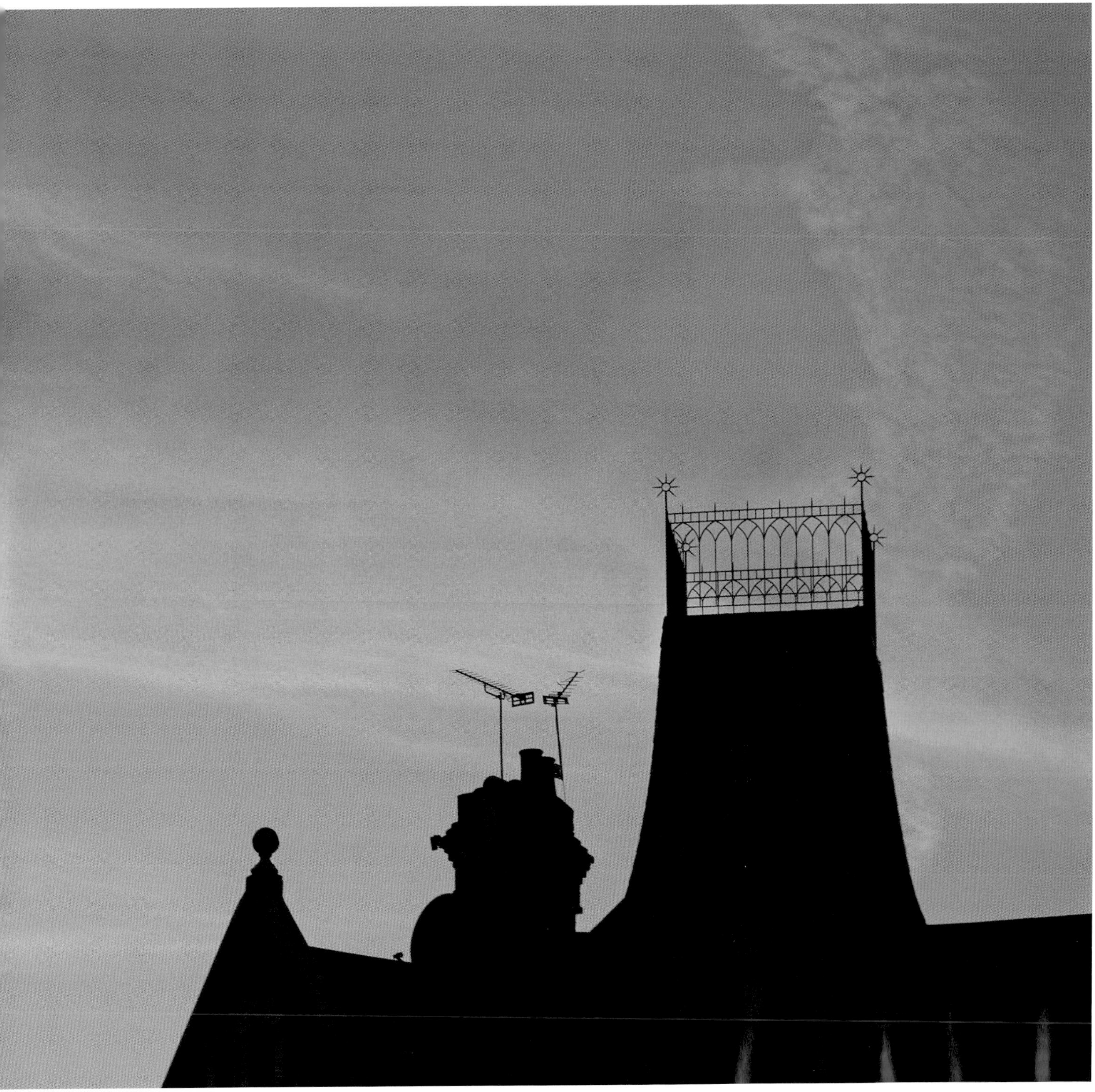

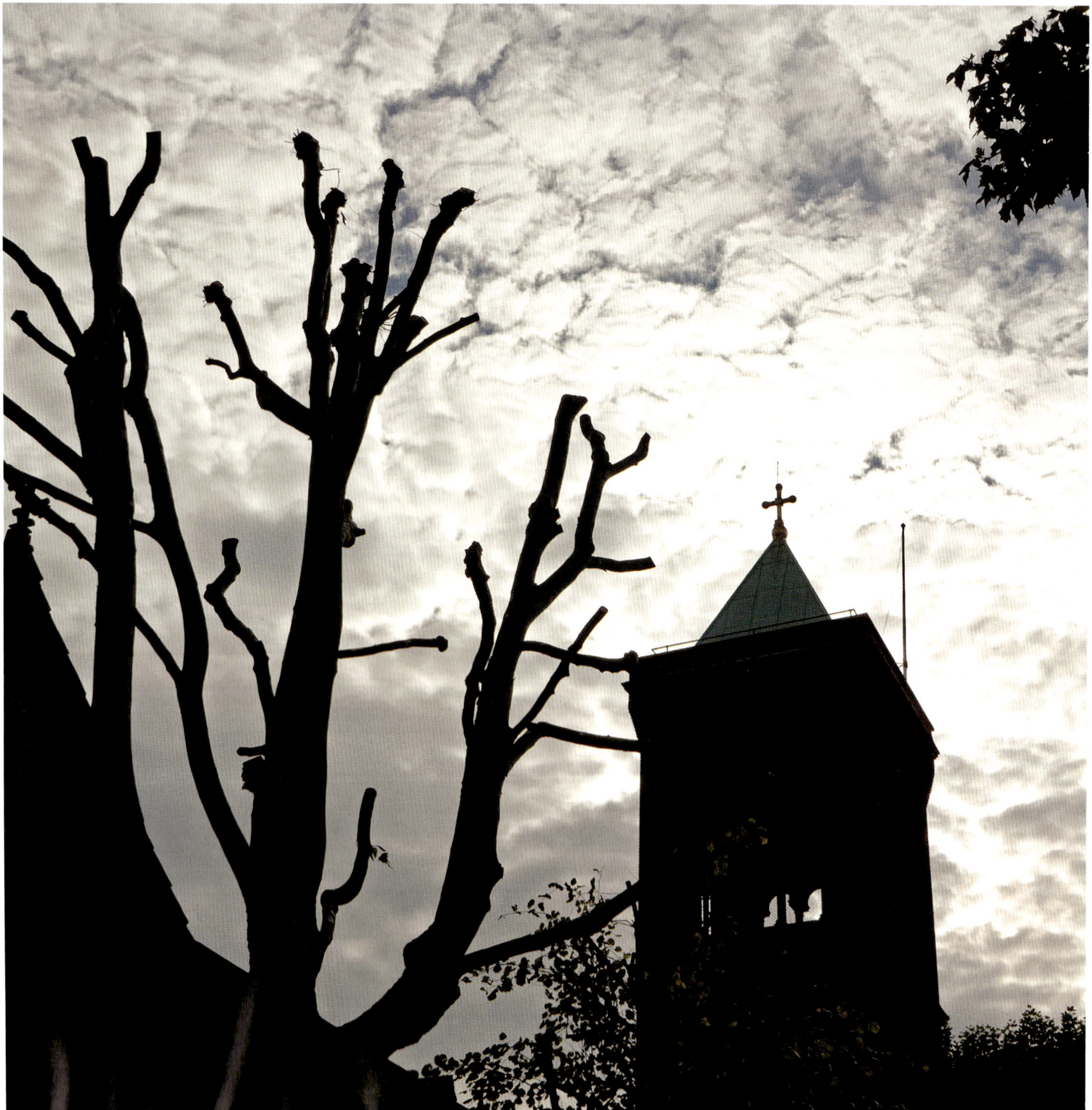

Opposite: St Luke's in Thurleigh Road dates from 1883.

This page: Northcote Road Baptist Church.

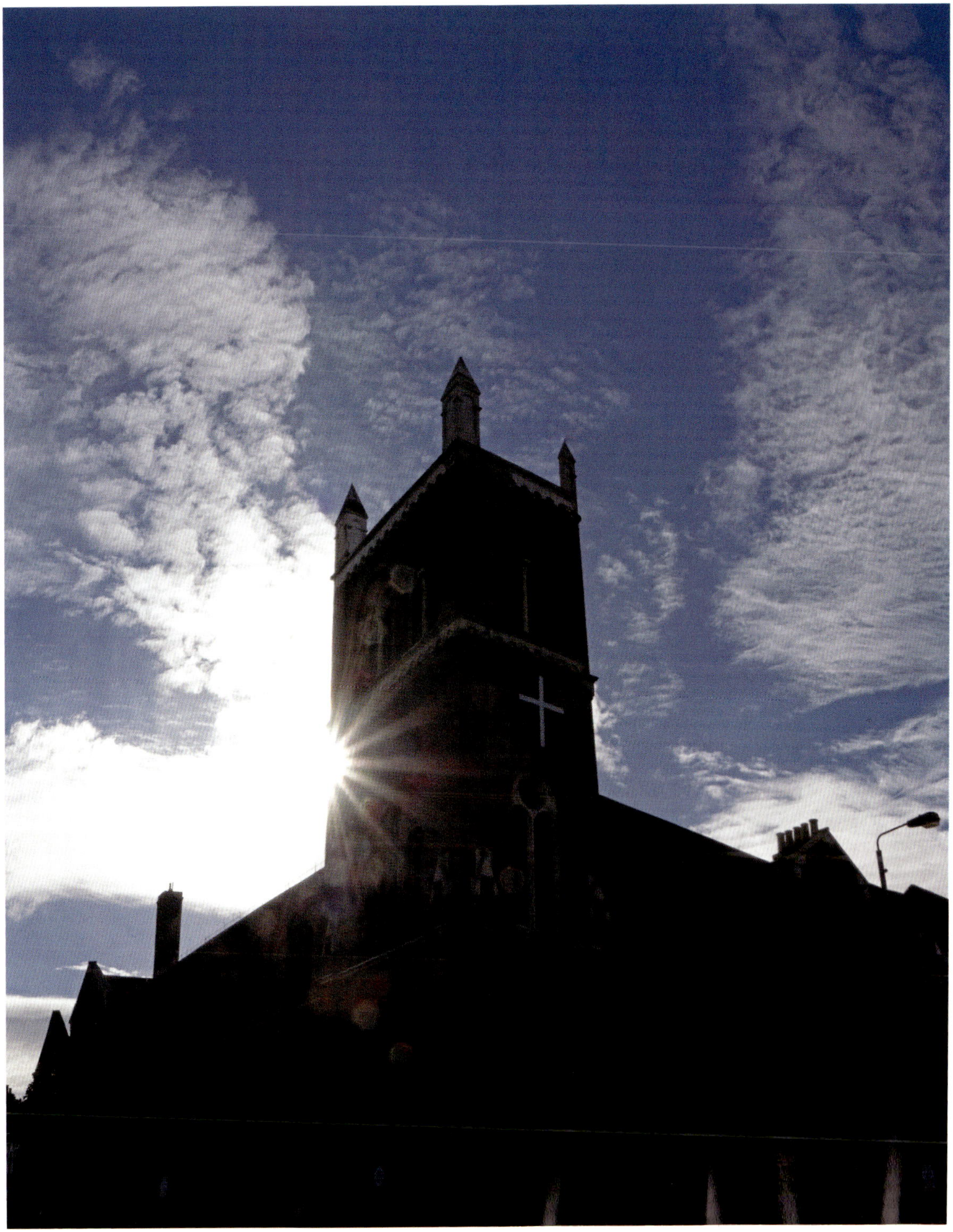

Left: St Luke's.

Top right: Ransom Pentecostal African Methodist Episcopal Zion Church in Mallinson Road.

Bottom right: The Welsh Chapel – one of only two Welsh-speaking chapels in London, built for the Welsh who built the railway and those who brought the milk trade along with it.

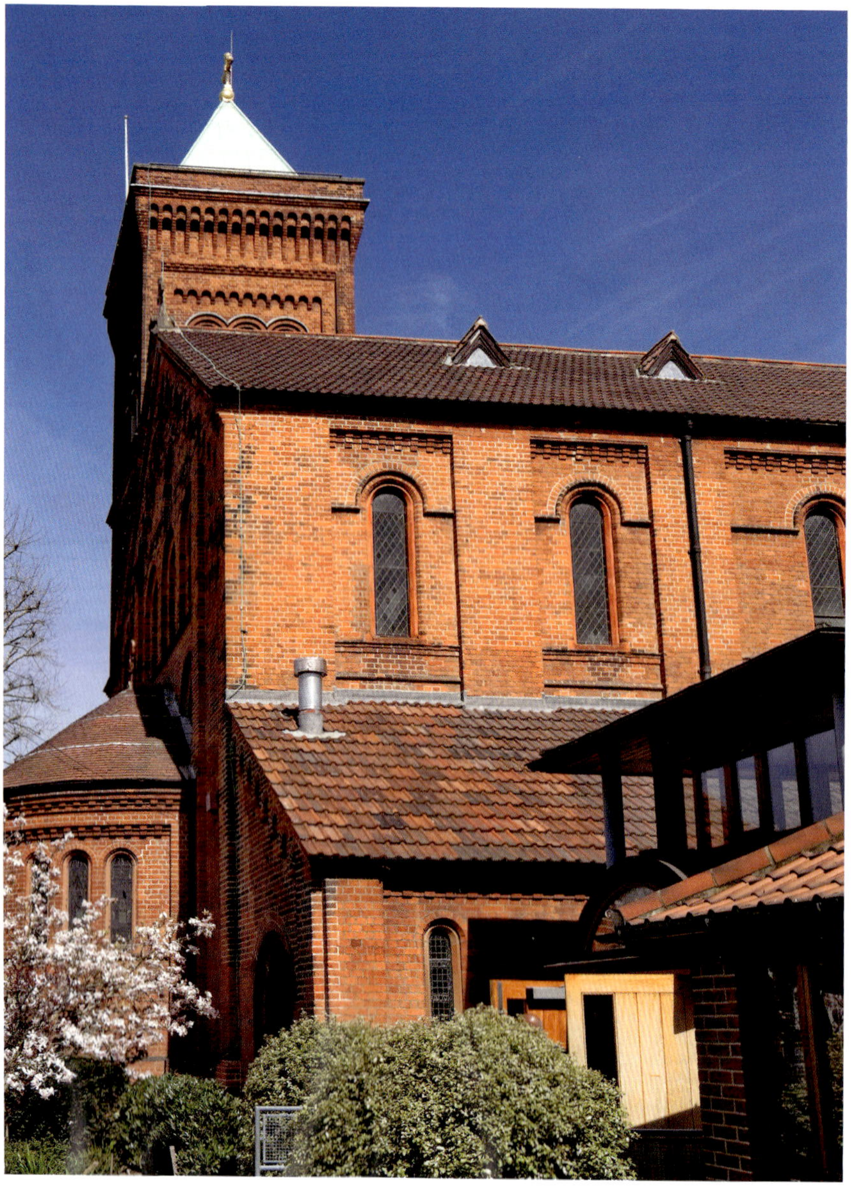

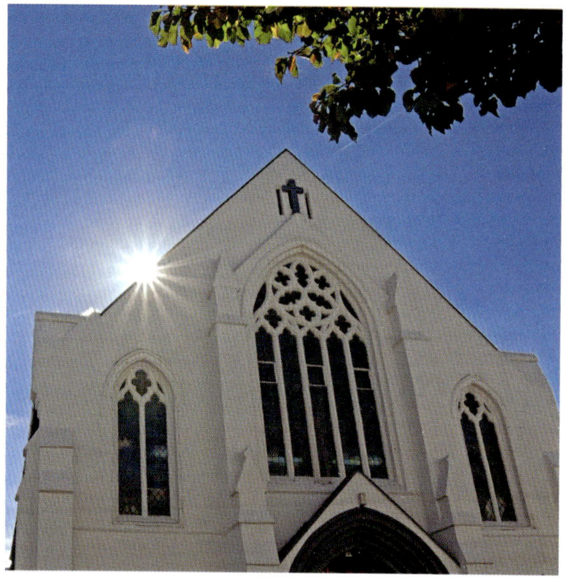

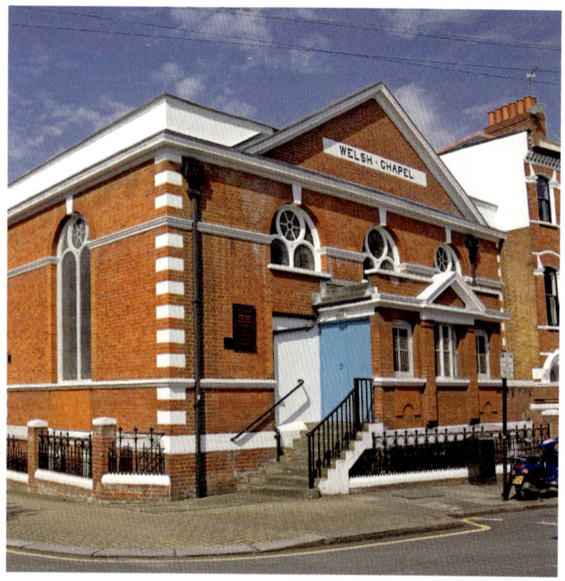

This page: St Michael's, Cobham Close, off Bolingbroke Grove dates from 1880. Originally an iron church, it was completed as it today as a memorial to local benefactor Philip Cazenove and Rev. Henry Boutflower Verdon, who died before he was able to become its first Vicar.

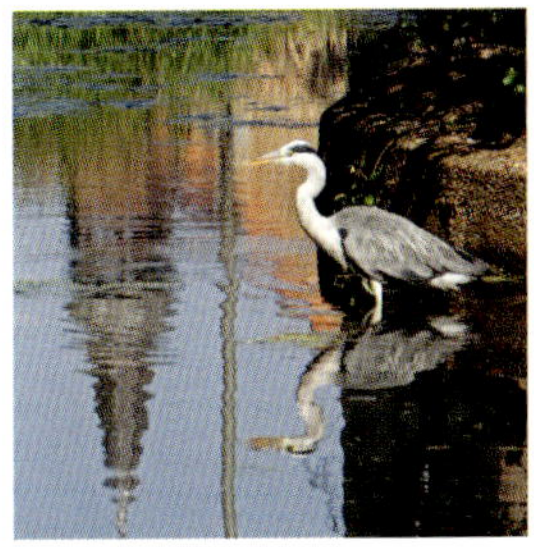

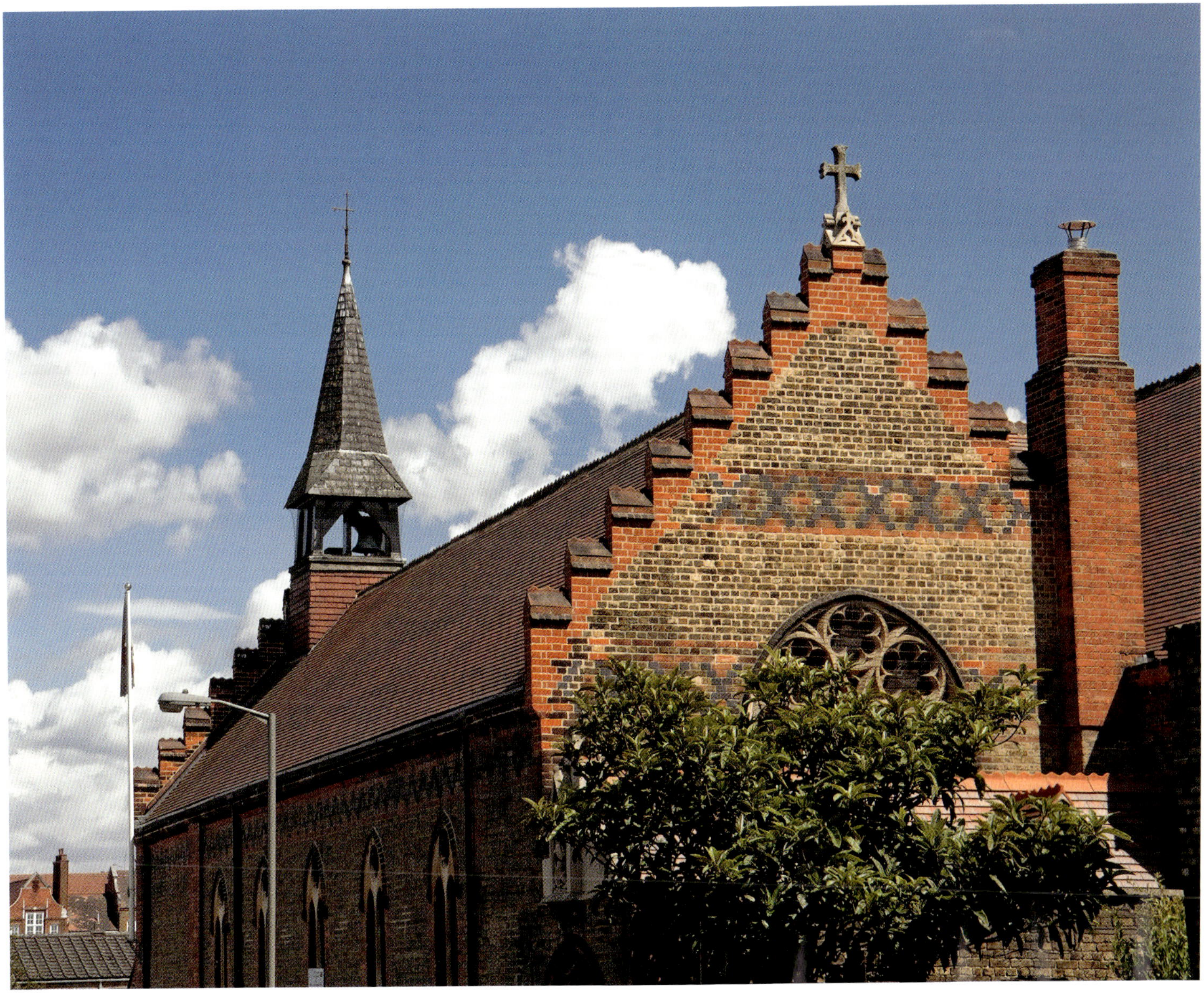

St Mary's Cemetery

St Mary's Cemetery can be found on the corner of Battersea Rise and Bolingbroke Grove and has a spectacular display of cherry blossom in the spring.

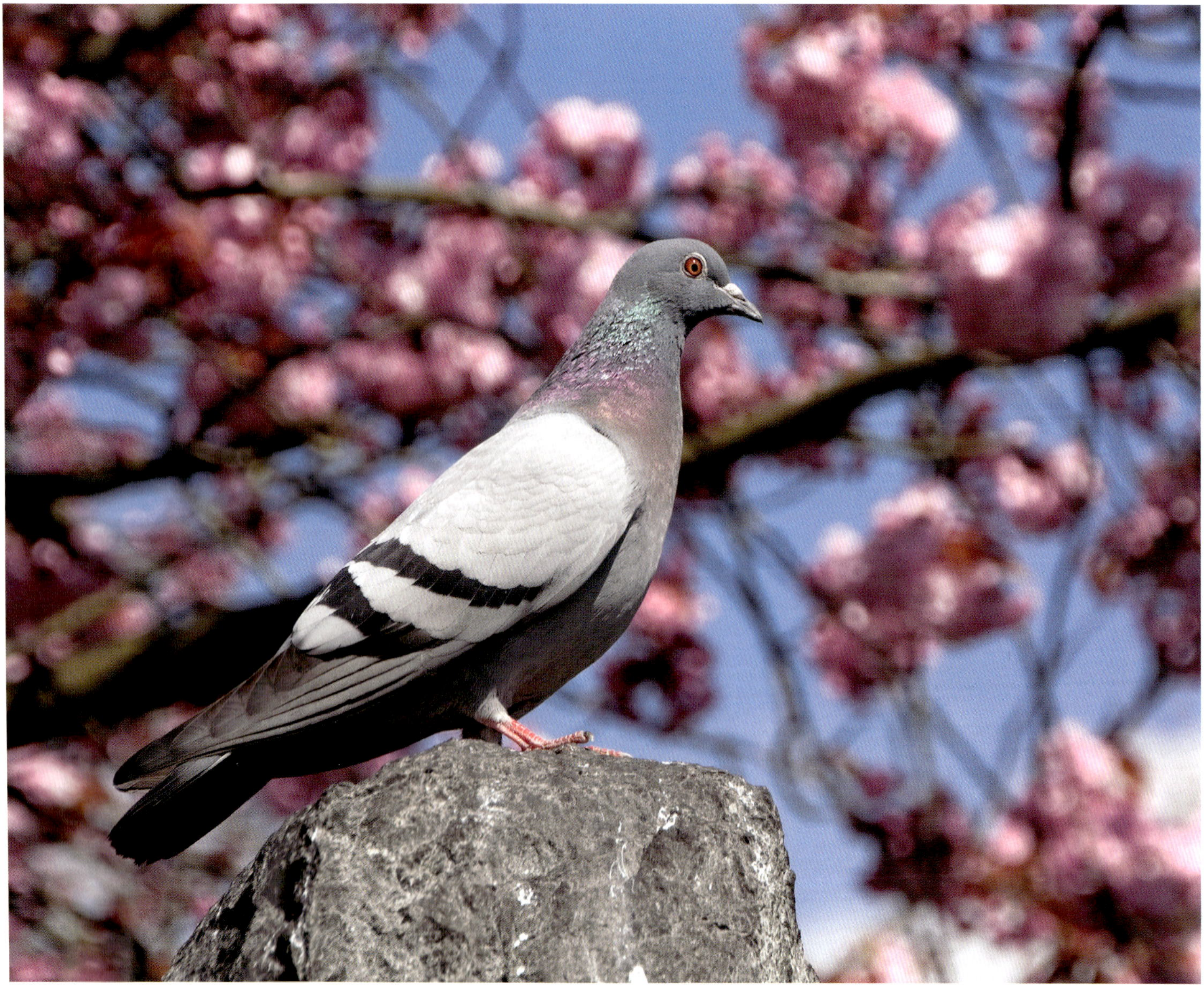

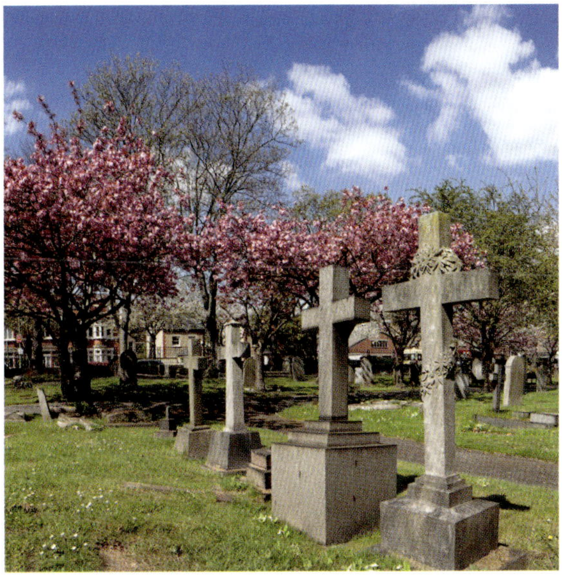

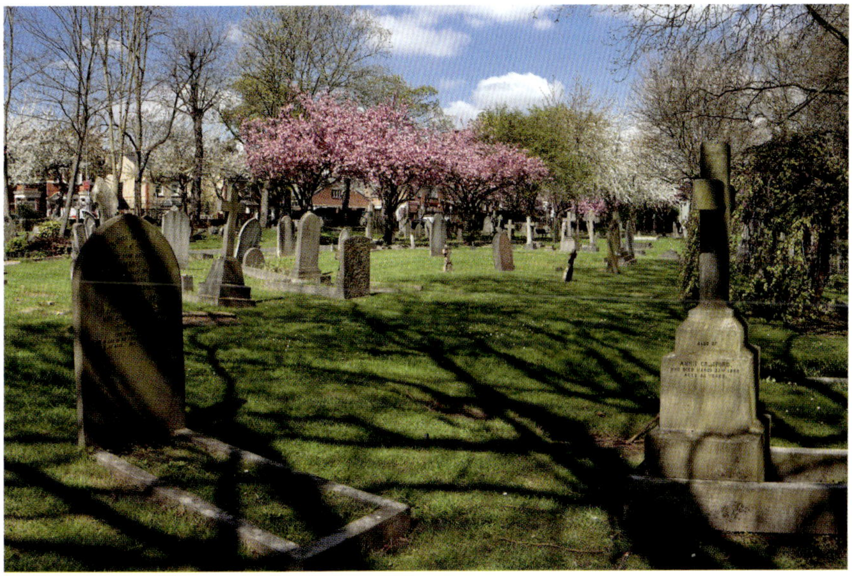

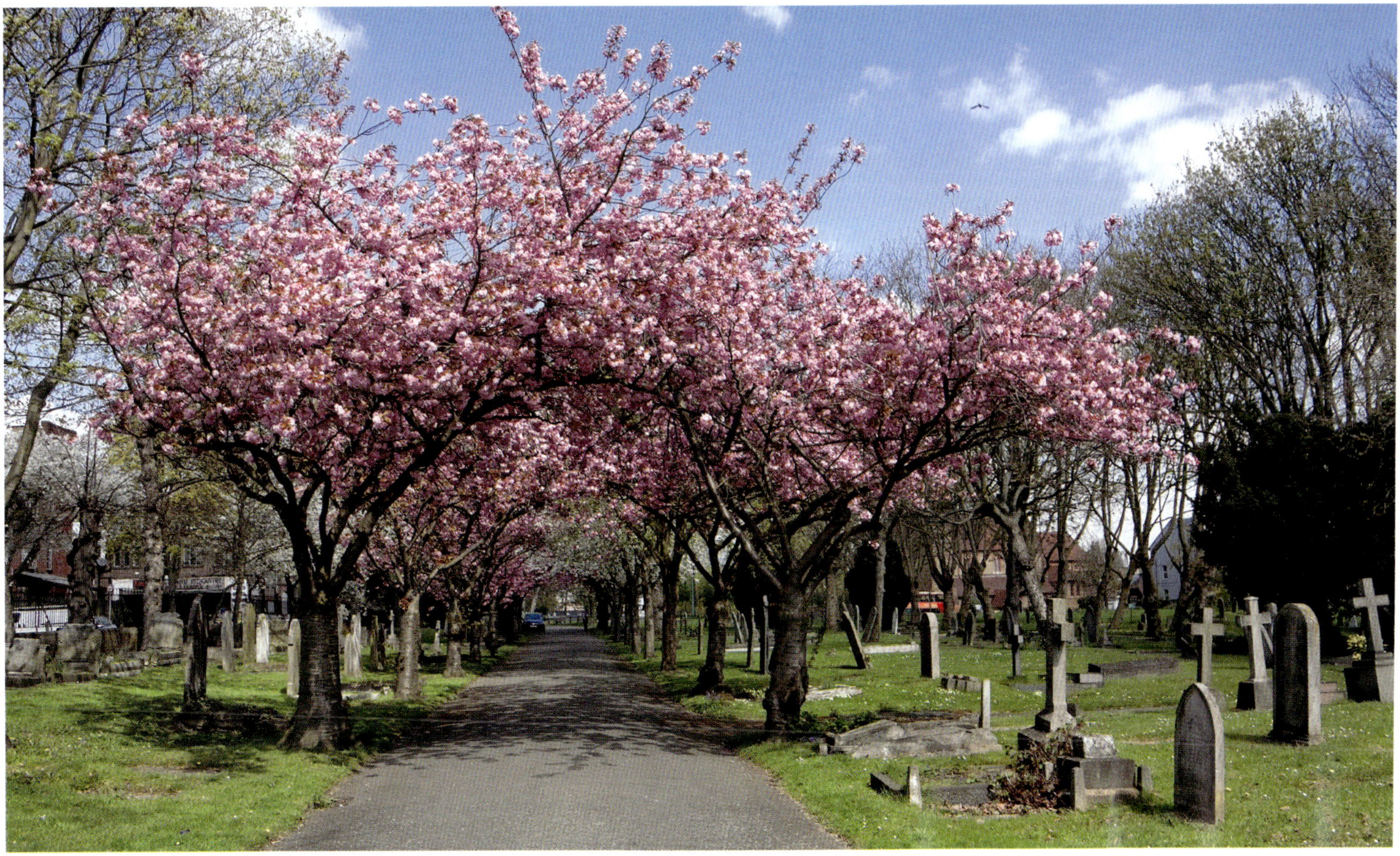

Clapham Common

Clapham Common is split equally between Lambeth and Wandsworth Councils, 110 acres each, although Lambeth maintains it all. Once known as Battersea East Heath, this common land shared for years between the two communities has several outstanding features, most notably the wonderful bandstand, picture right. Thankfully restored in 2005/6 and mainly financed by a grant from The National Lottery Heritage Fund, the bandstand is the biggest in London. A huge magnet for people playing sport, the common also has 3 large ponds, with the two smaller ones used for fishing. Some interesting facts: a public outcry stopped the railway potentially coming right through the common in 1864, and sheep stopped grazing here in 1914. Thank you to the website for The Friends of Clapham Common for the background here – *www.claphamcommon.org*

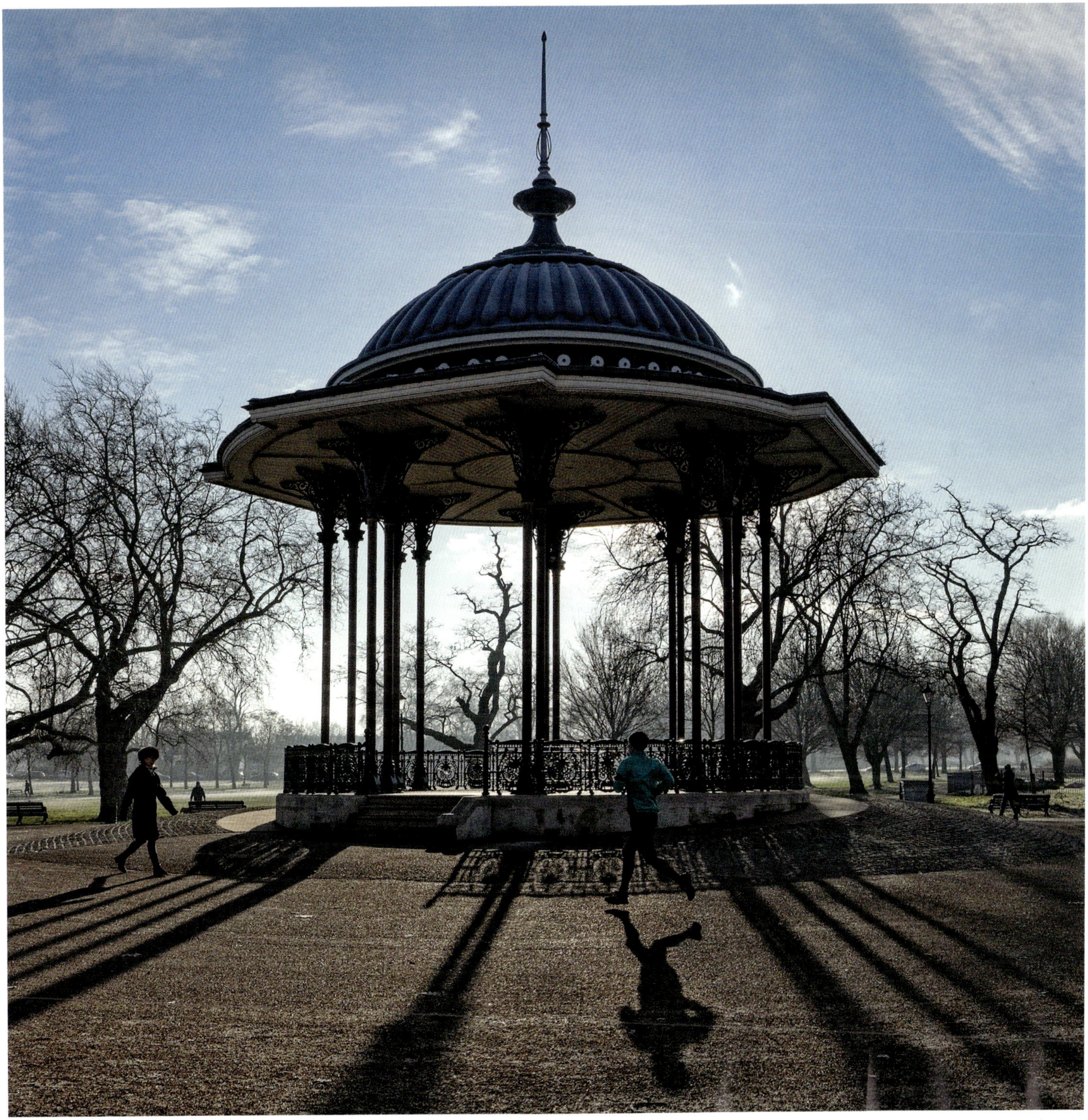

Winter

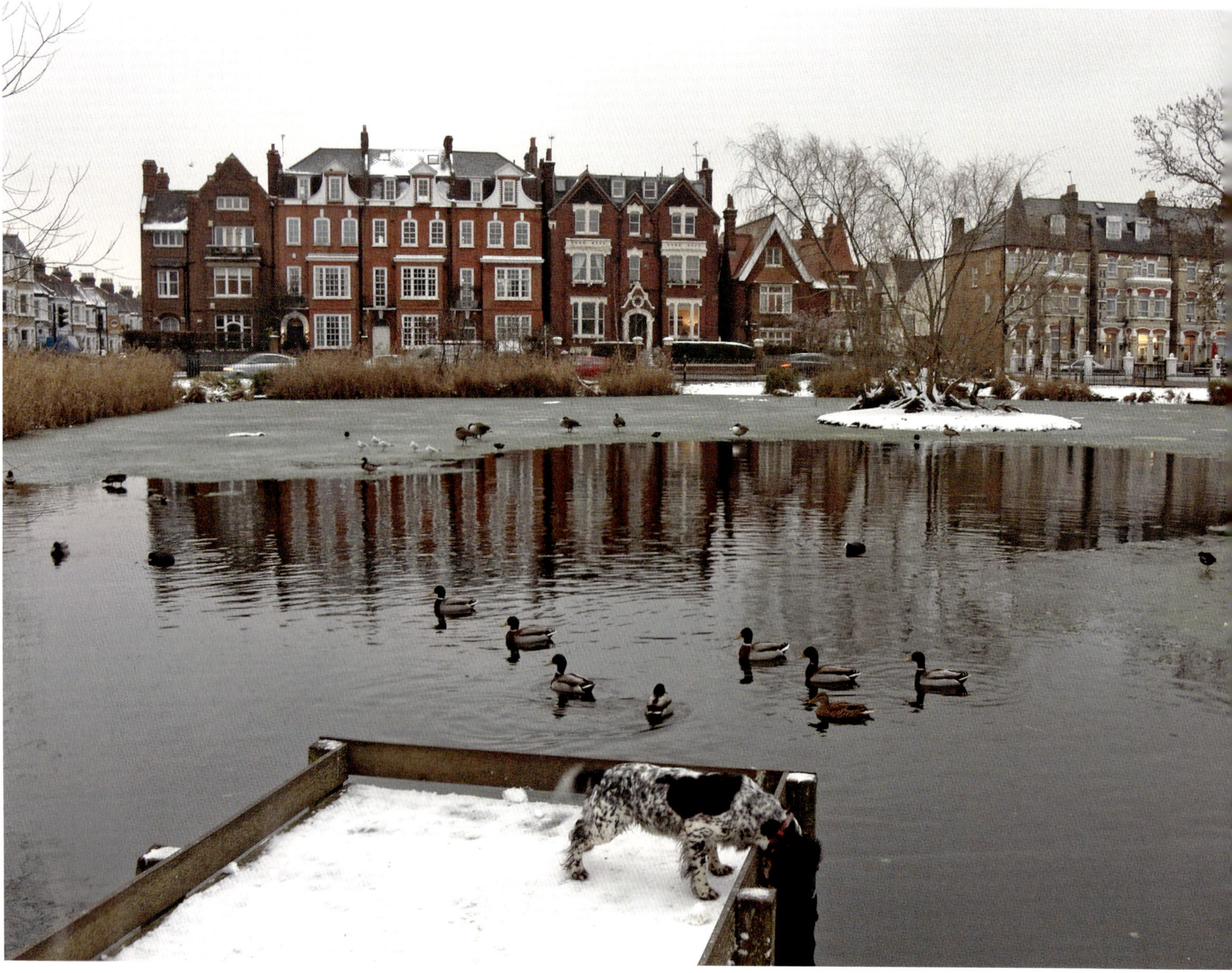

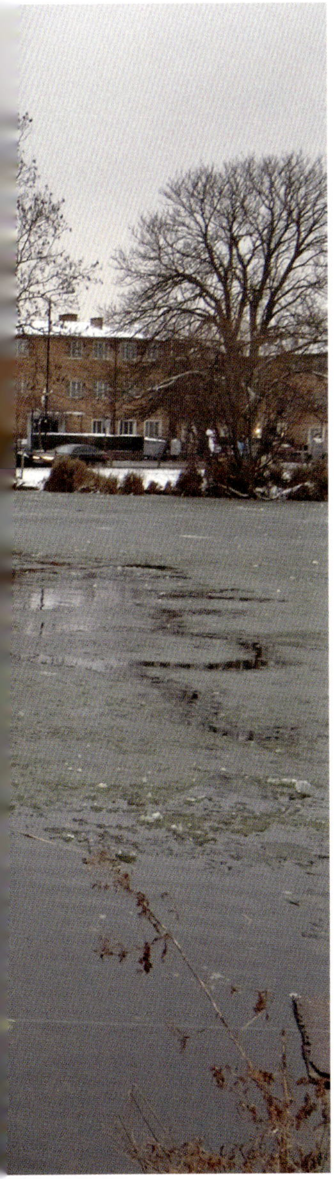

Opposite: Eagle Pond.

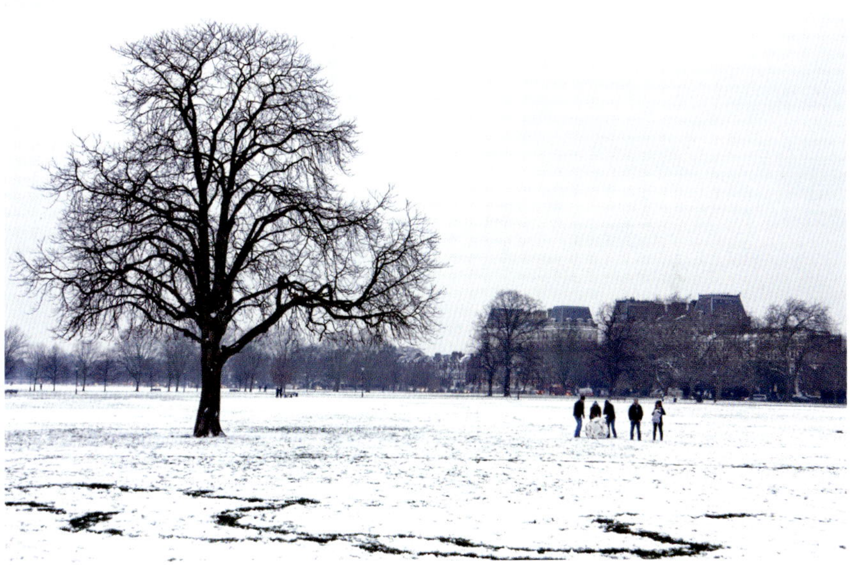

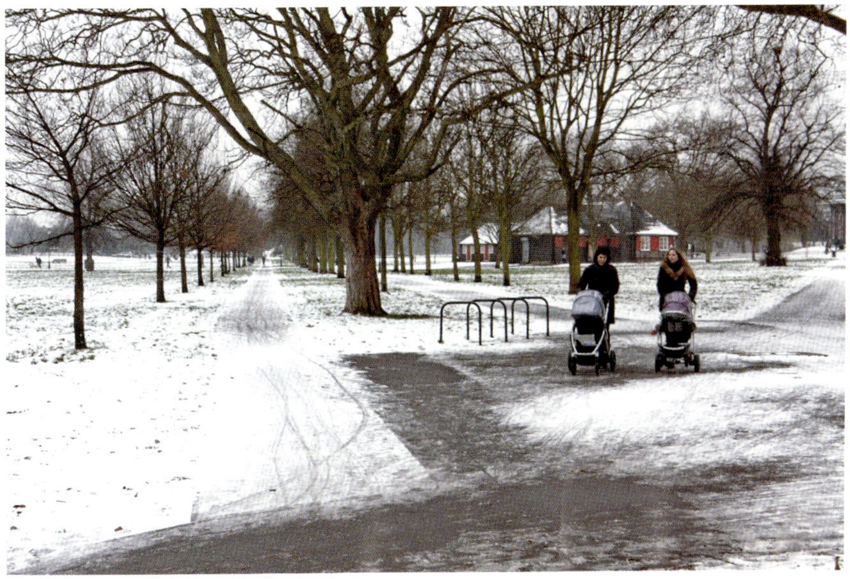

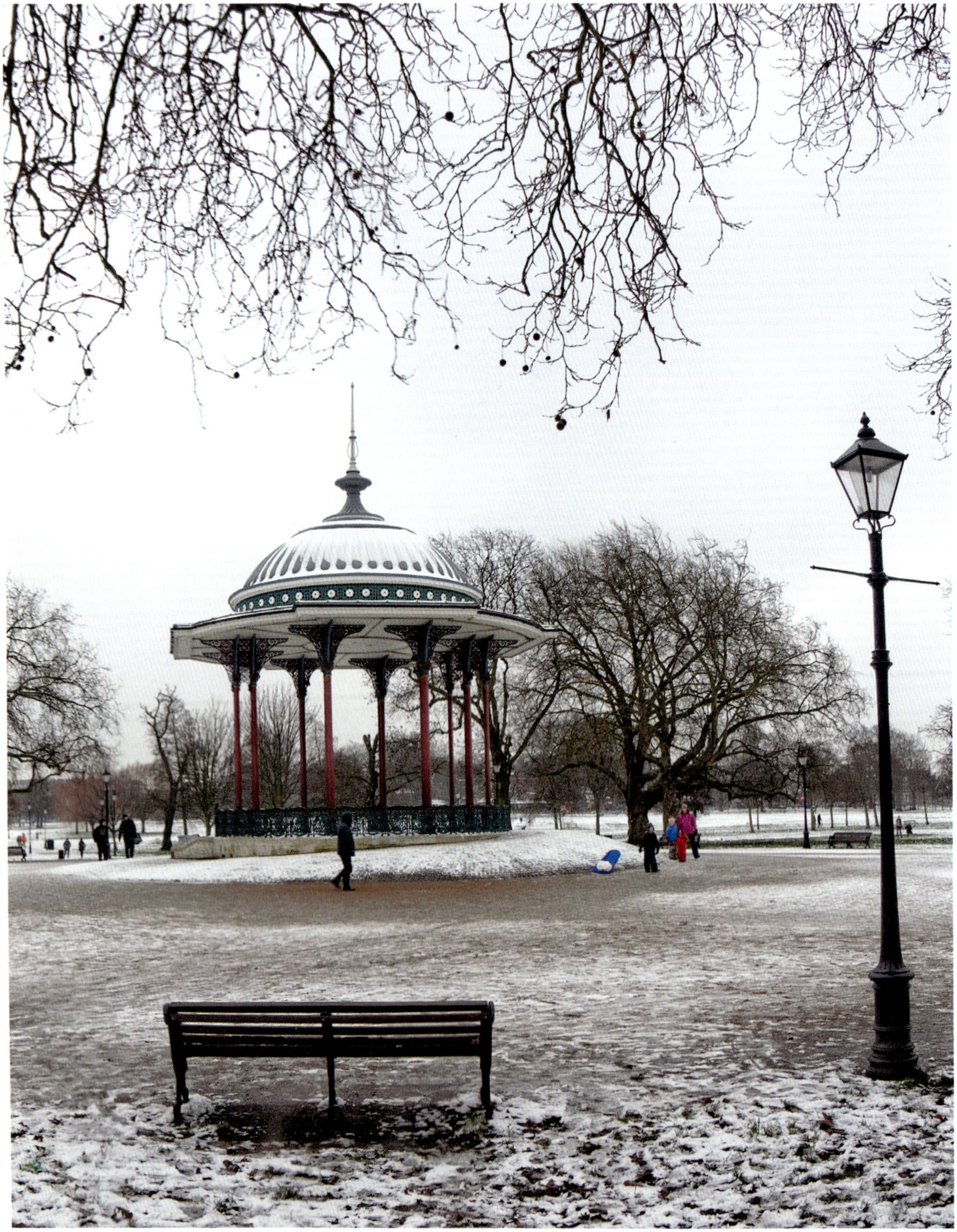

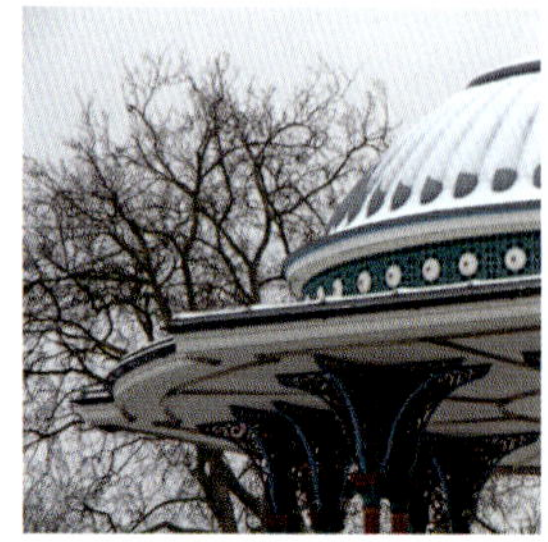

The Bandstand is a Grade II listed building and was erected in 1890. It is the largest bandstand in London and underwent extensive renovation in the mid-noughties. In the summer bands play once again to entertain visitors to the common.

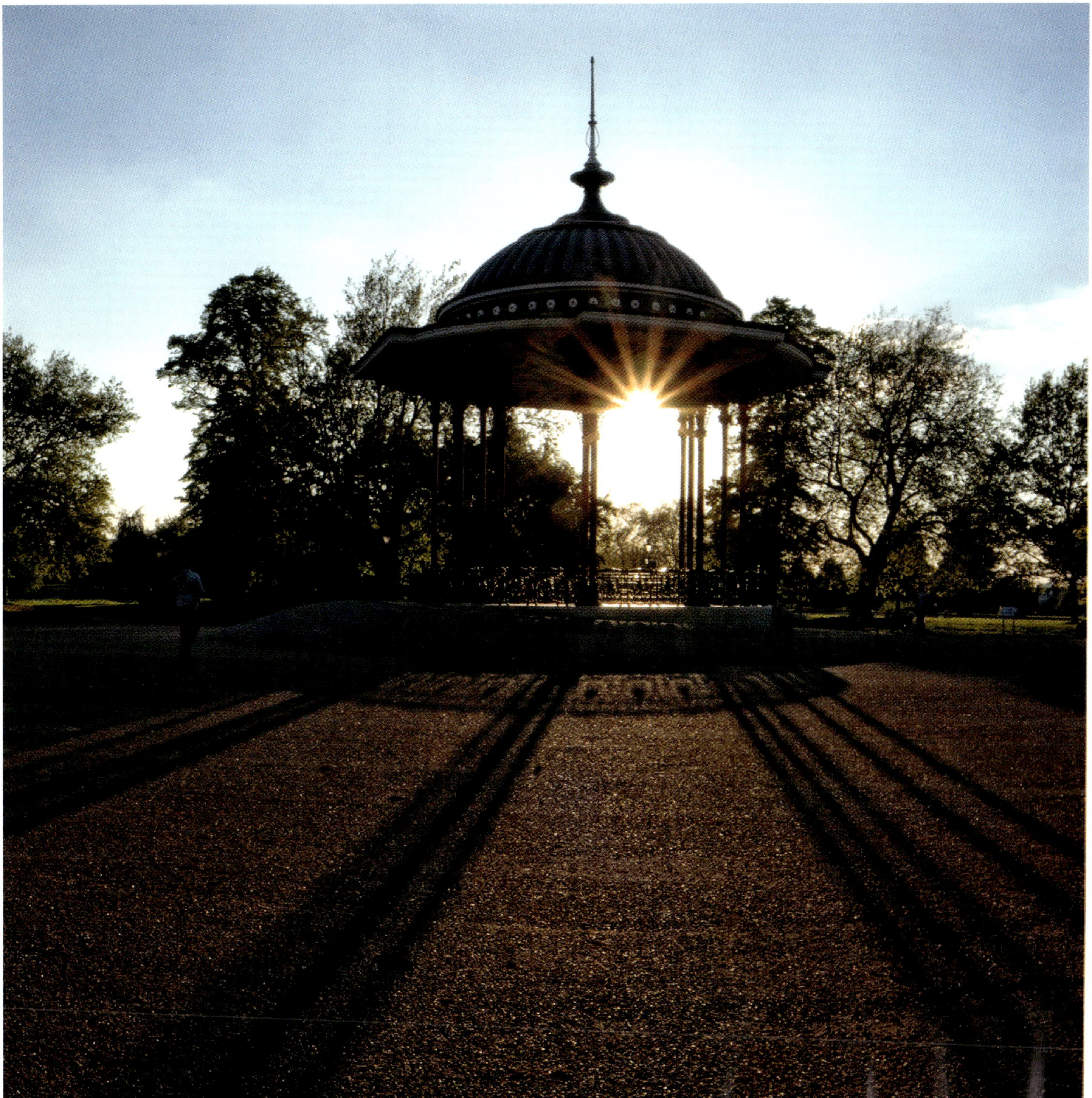

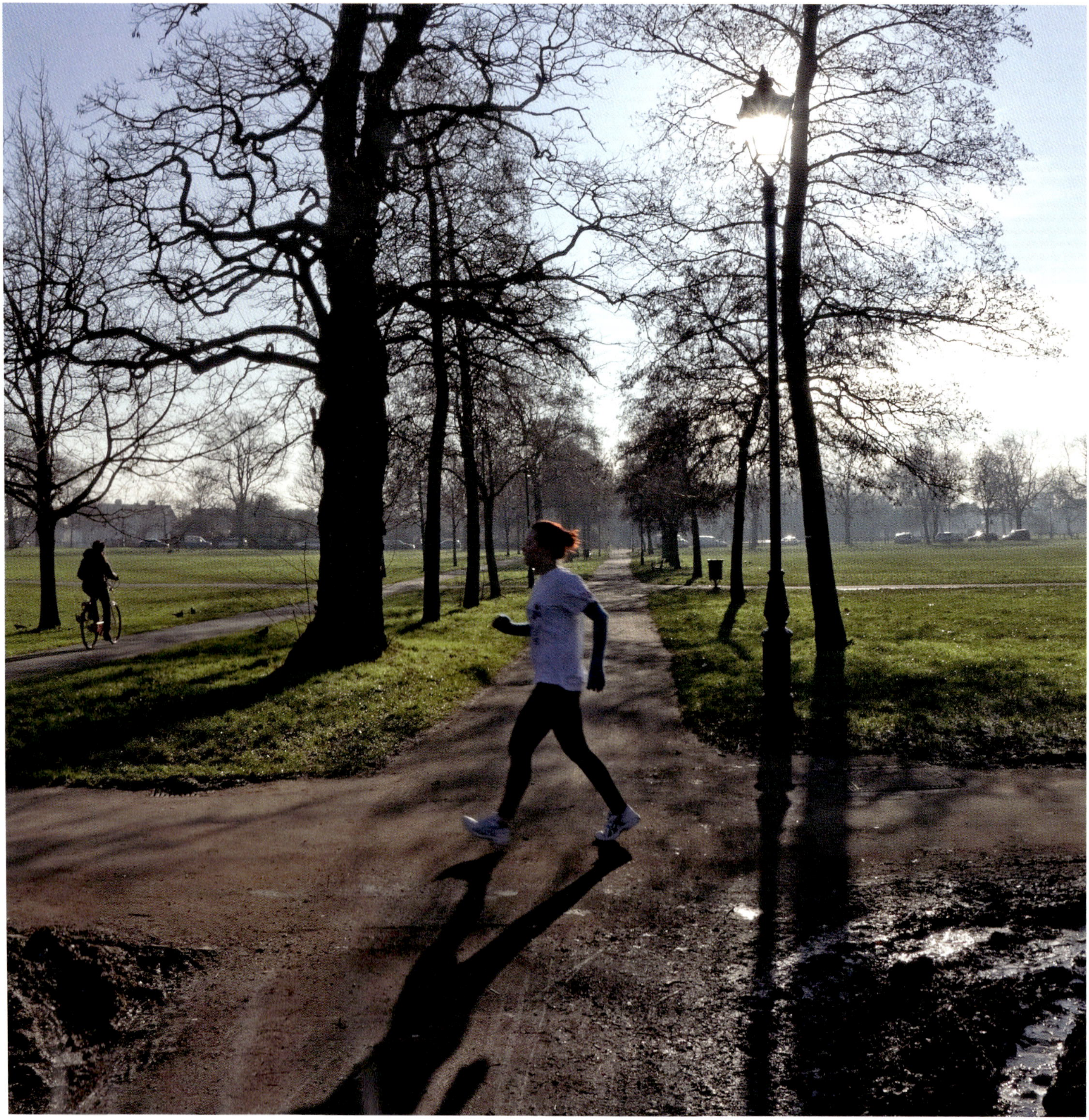

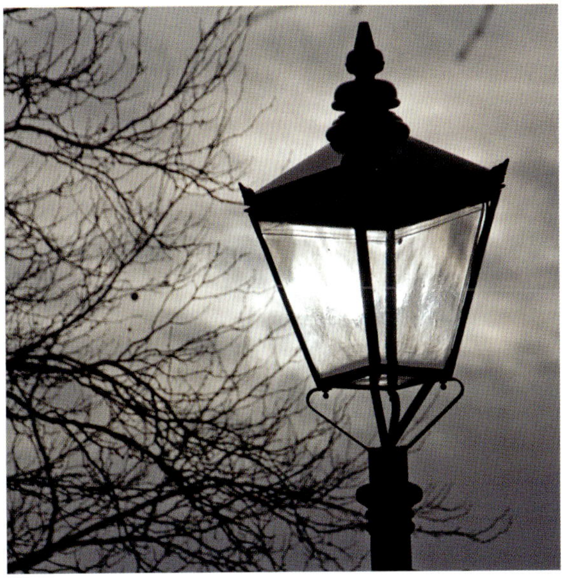

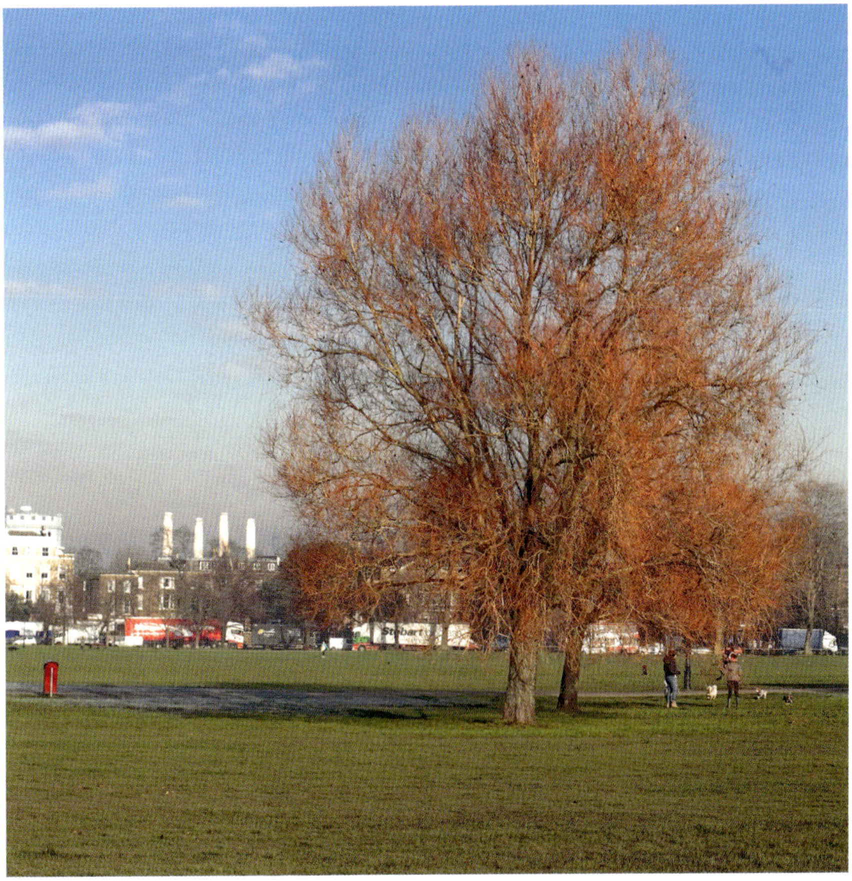

This page and overleaf: Clapham Common in spring.

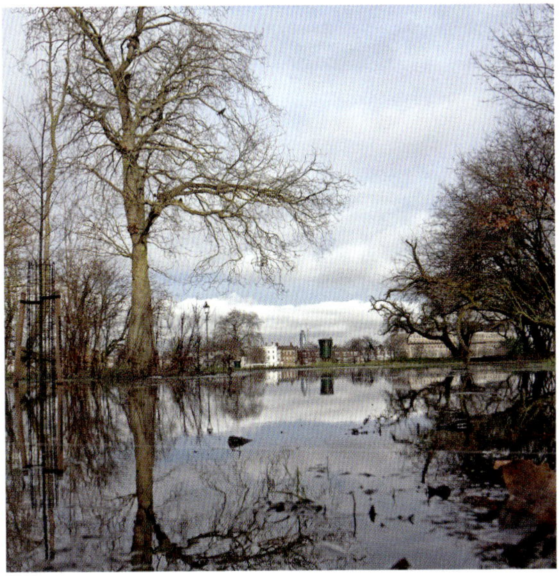

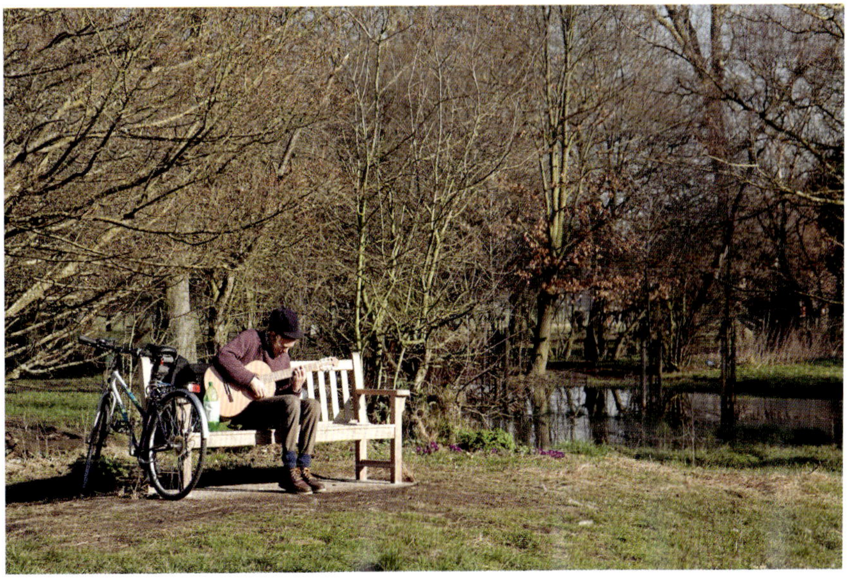

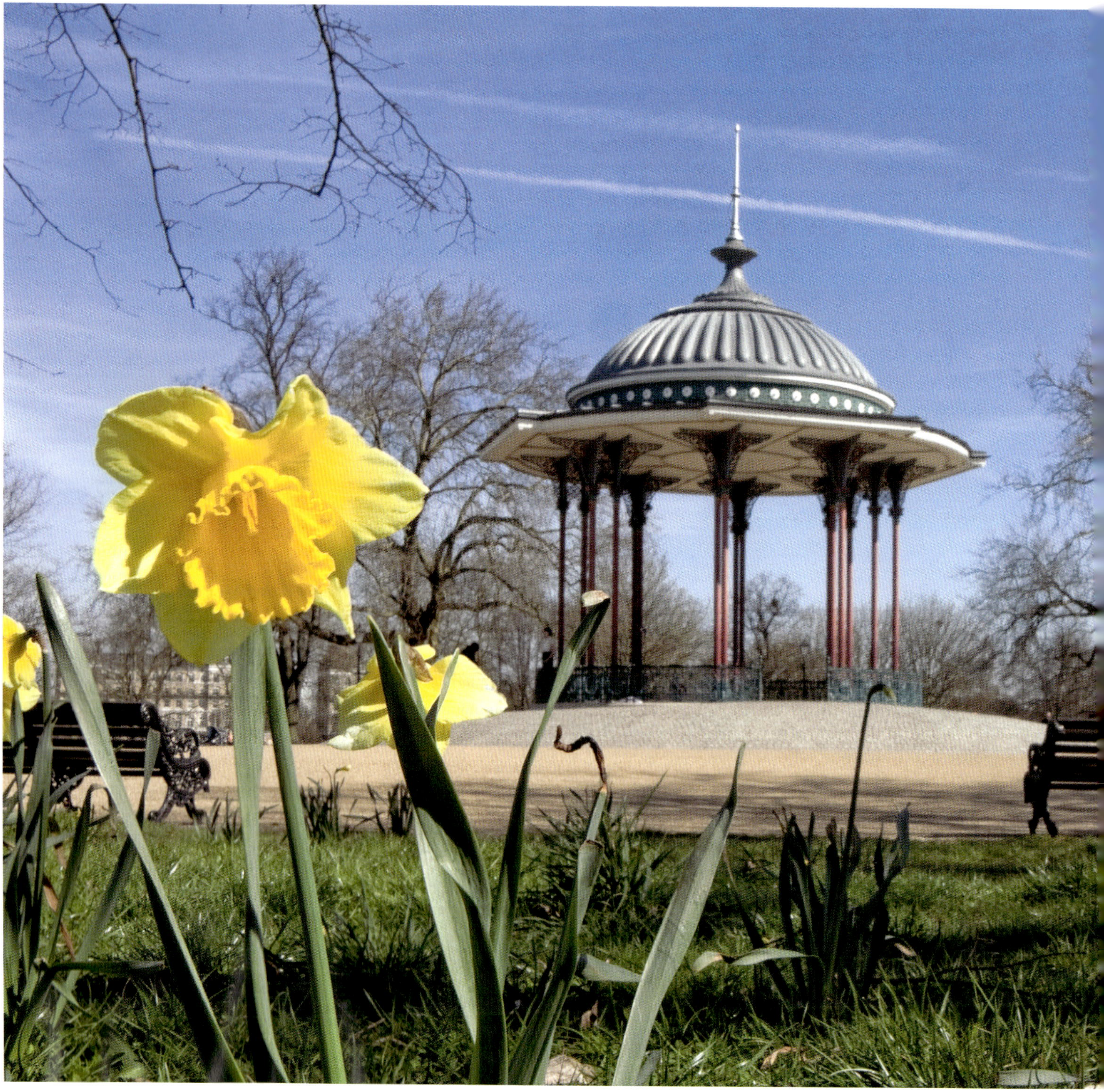

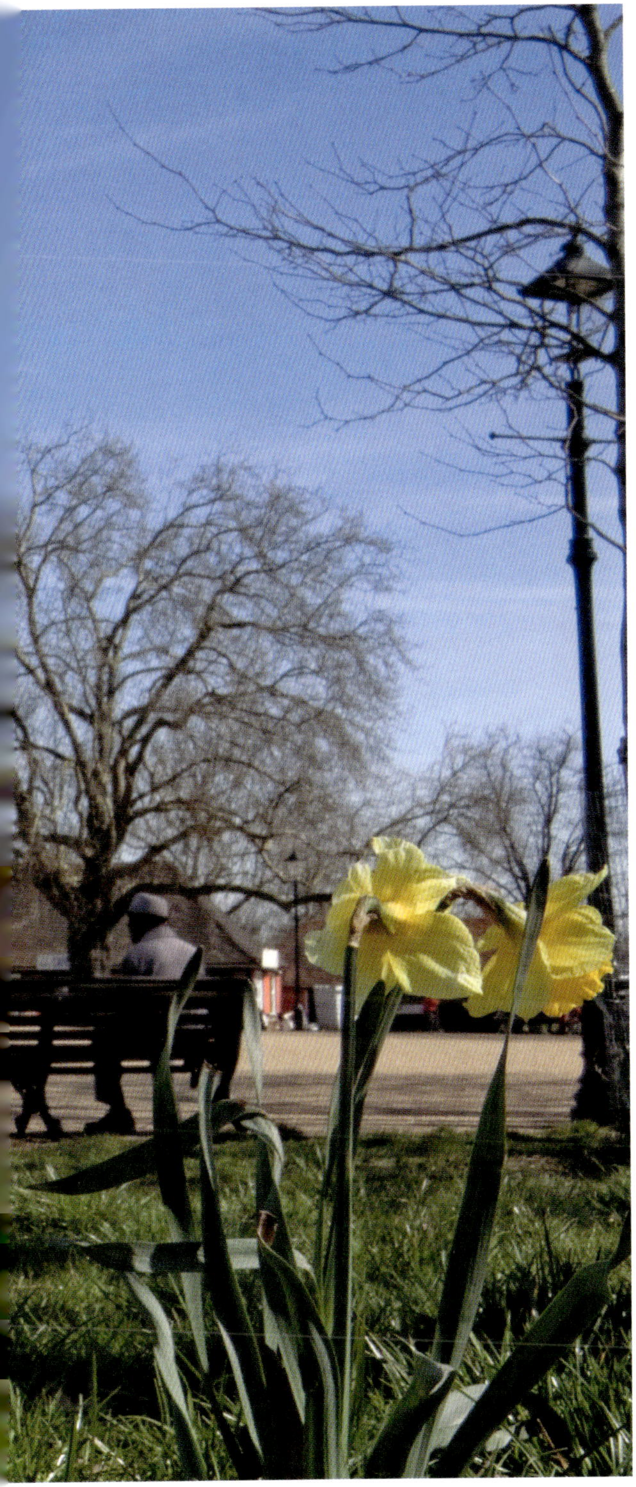

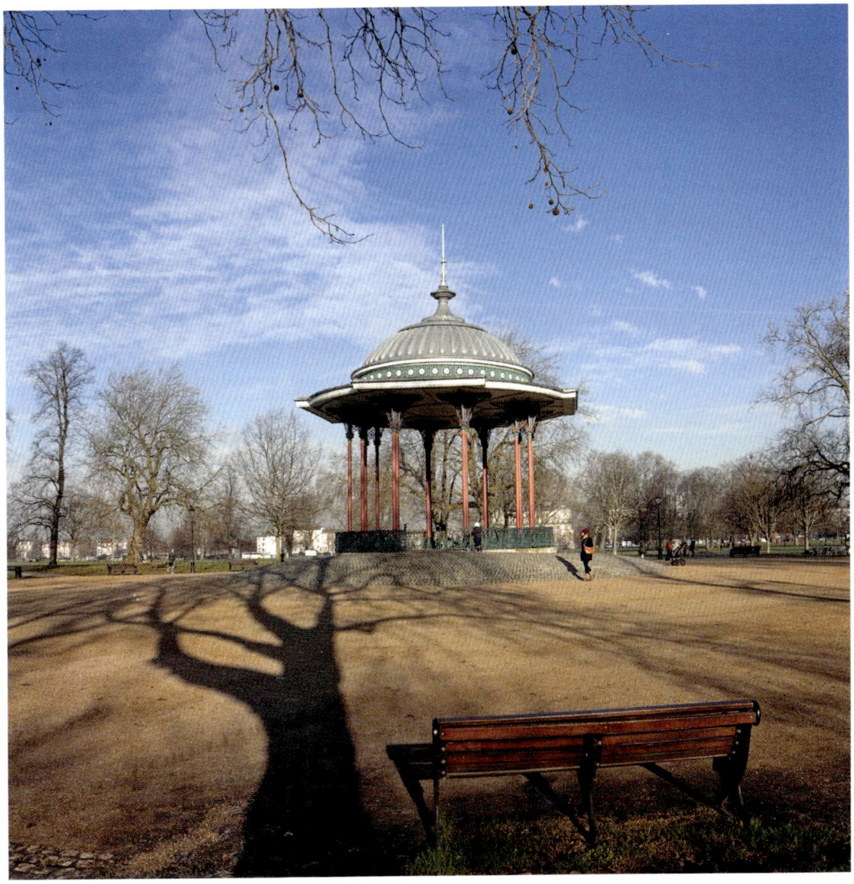

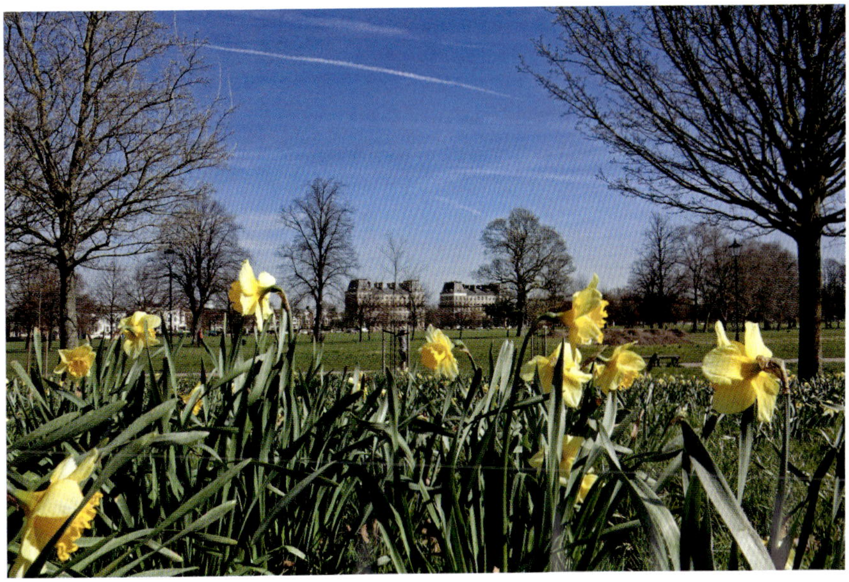

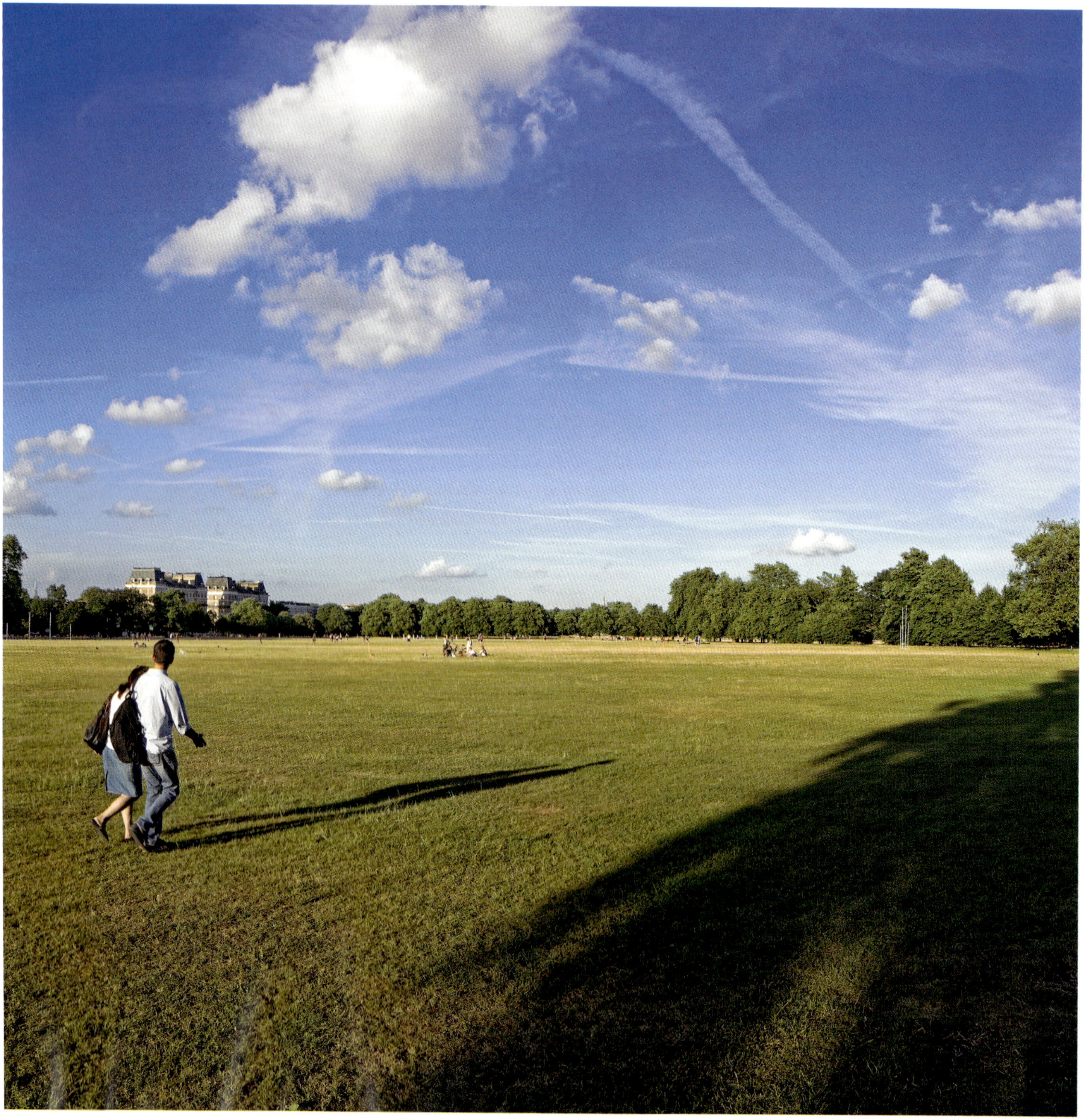

This page: Clapham Common on a fine summer's evening.

Top right: Amongst the many activities that go on throughout the year, one group that caught my eye were the dog walkers, which considering I have one myself is perhaps not that startling.

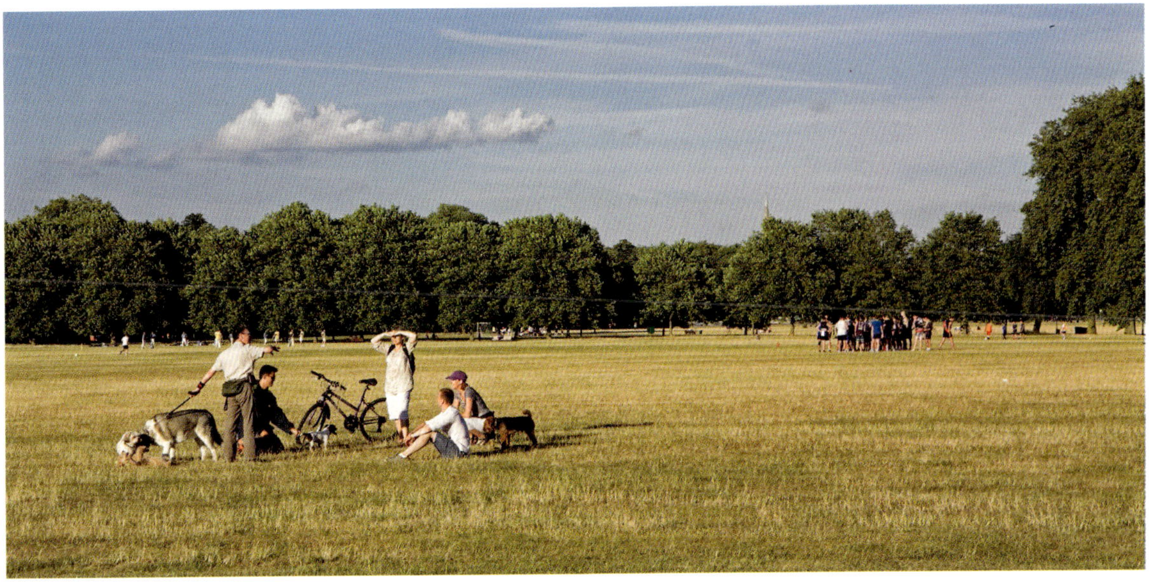

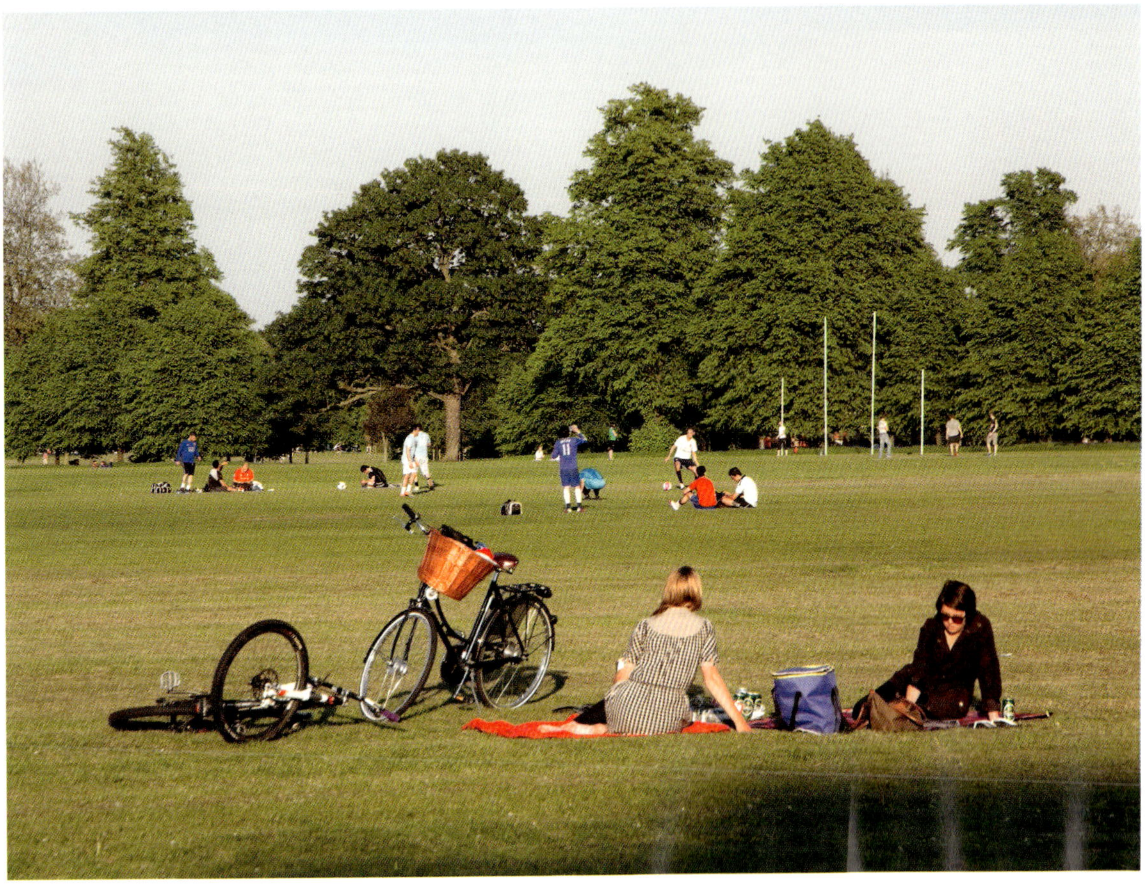

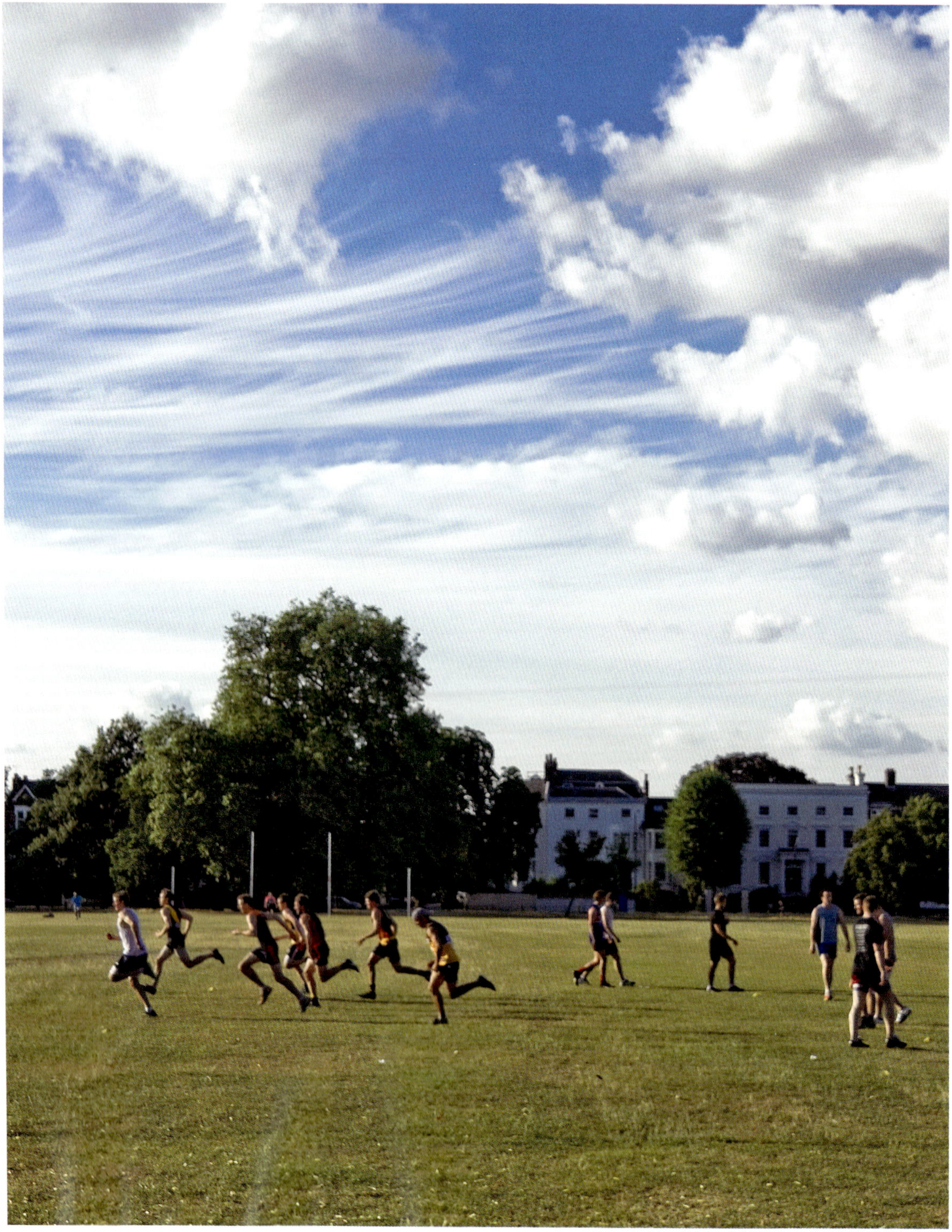

As with all the open spaces in London, sport features heavily on Clapham Common, from the many Get Fit groups, through rugby and Aussie rules (left) and cricket (right).

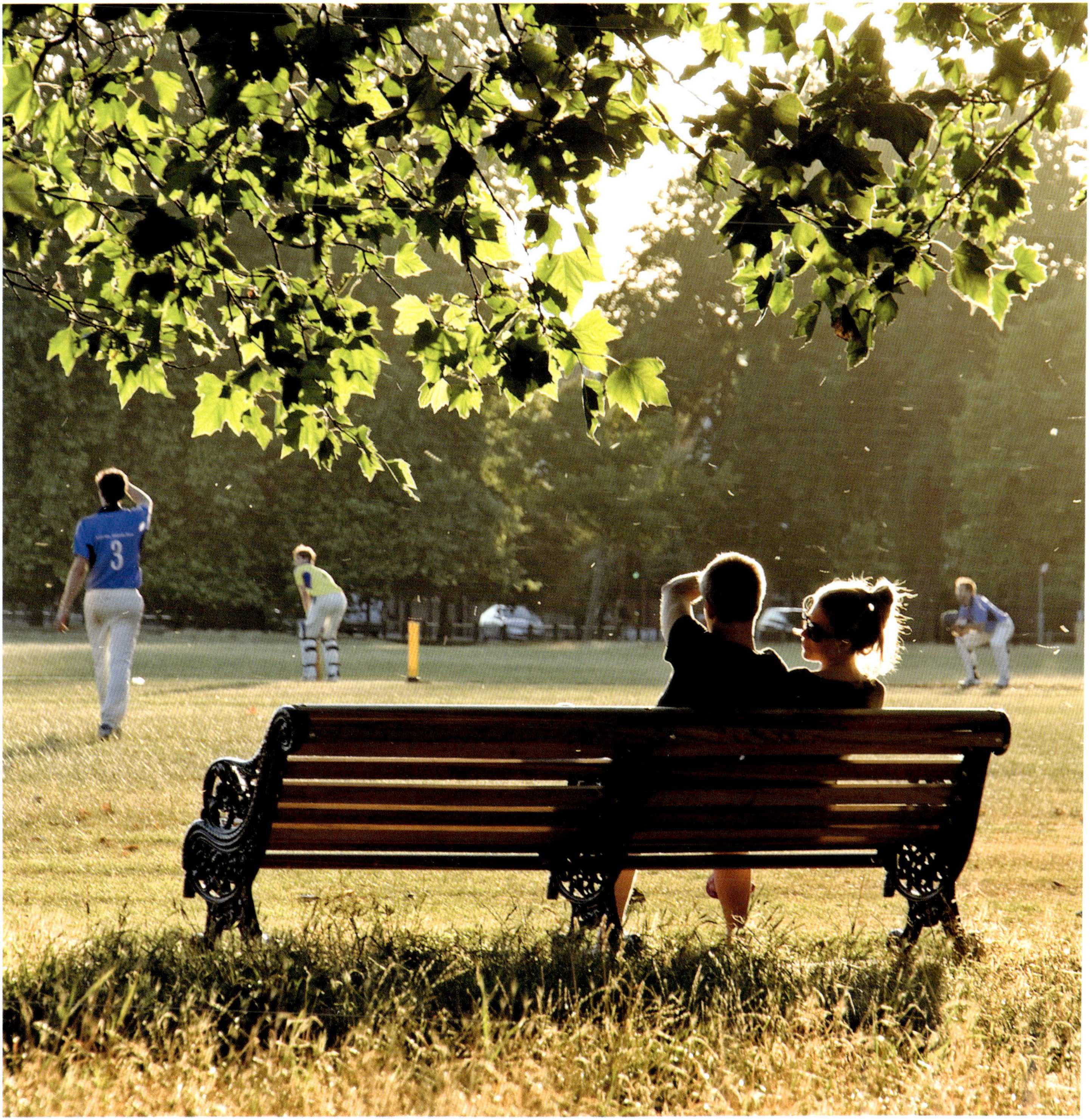
3

The Bandstand in October 2013.

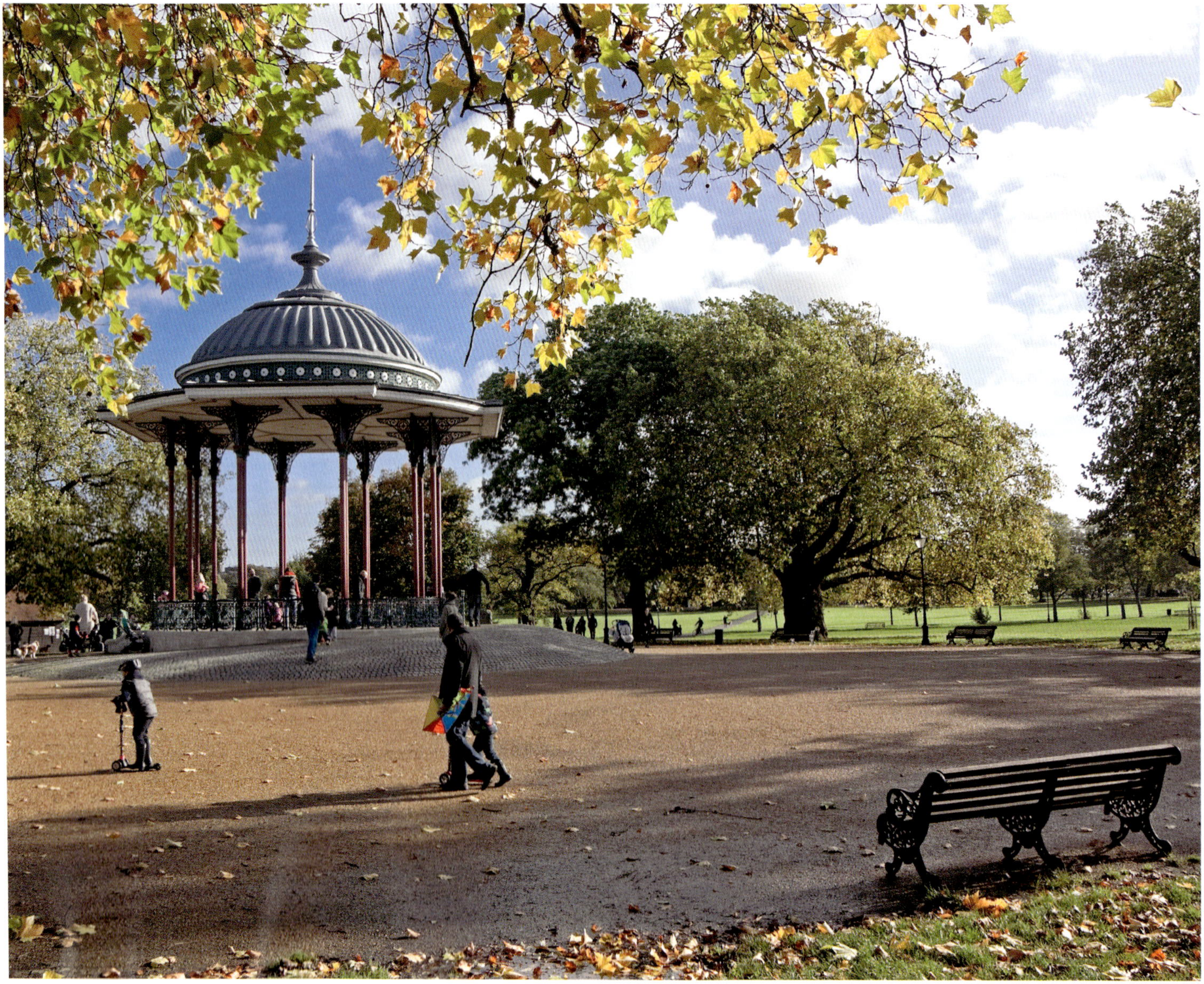

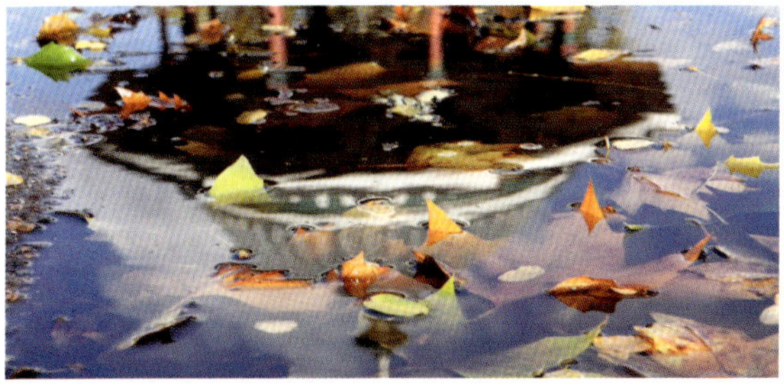

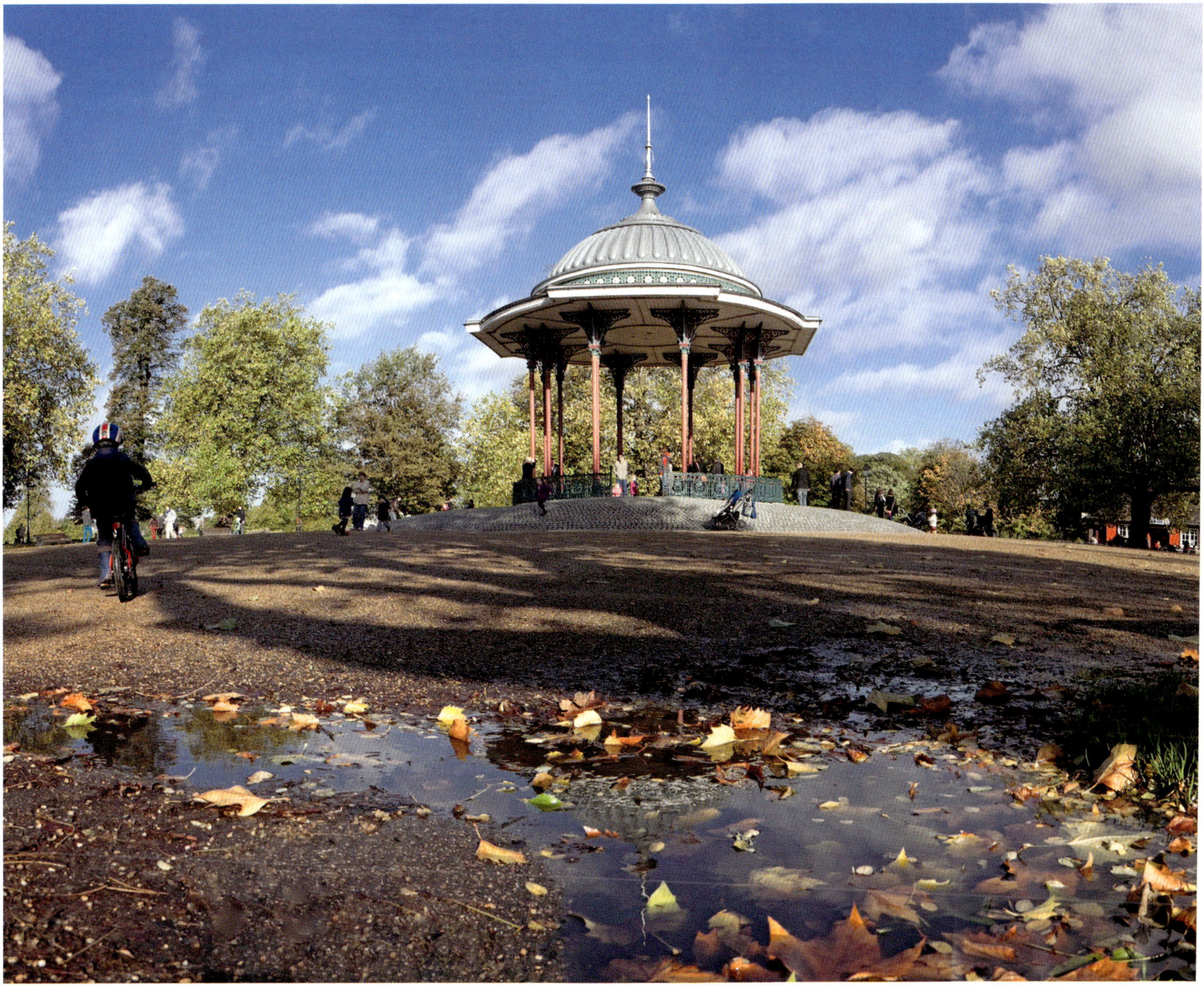

West Side

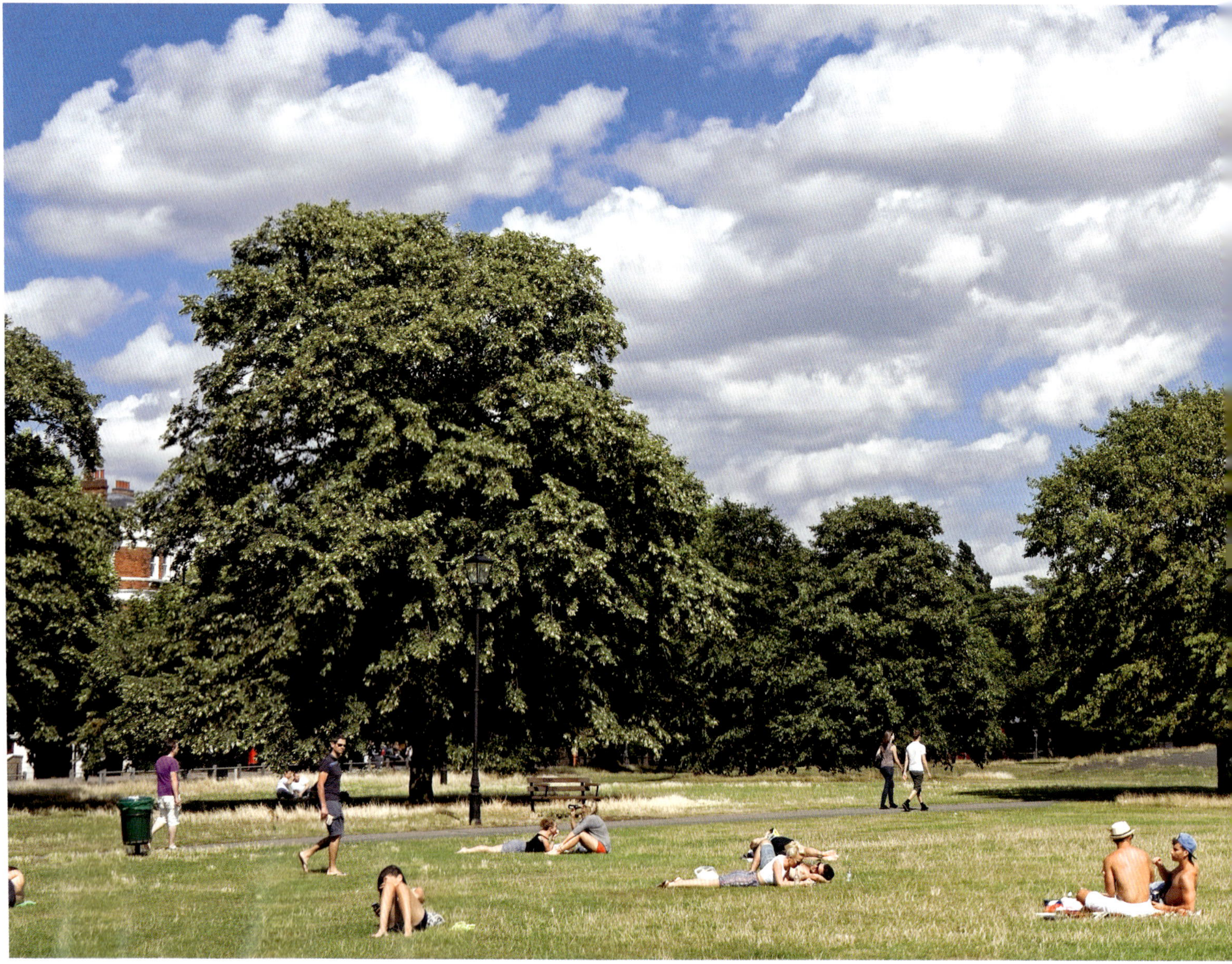

The west side of the Common at the top of Battersea Rise and opposite St Barnabas's Church. The 'humps' now almost entirely covered with grass are the remains of the anti-aircraft bunkers that defended this part of London during the blitz.

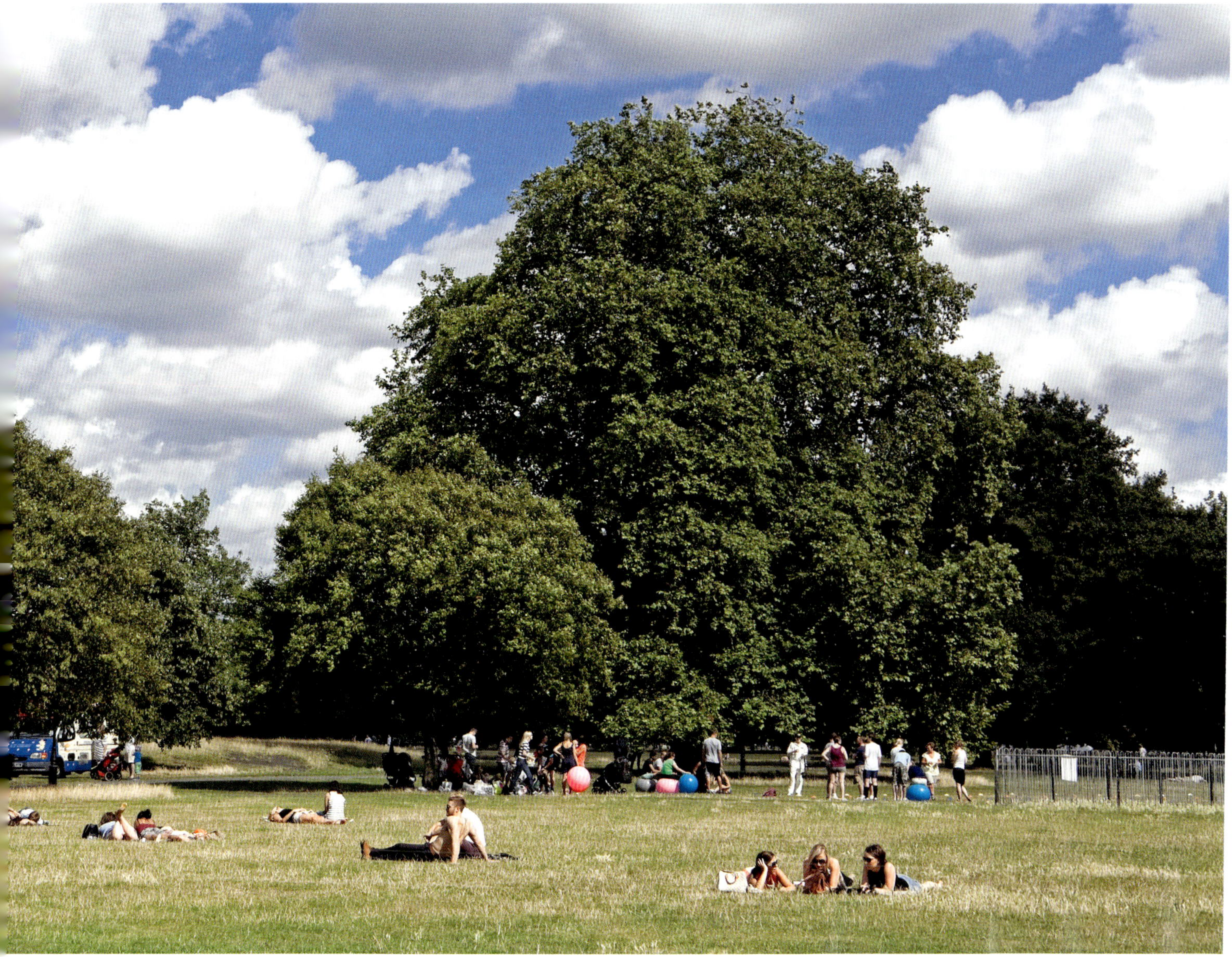

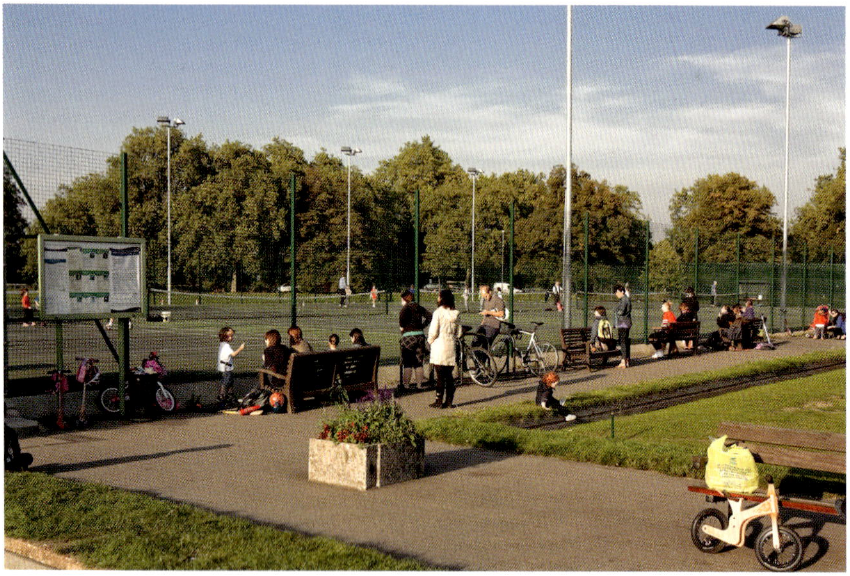
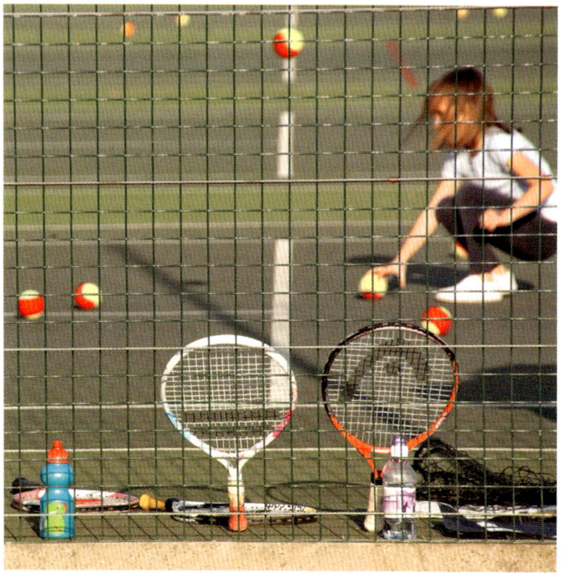
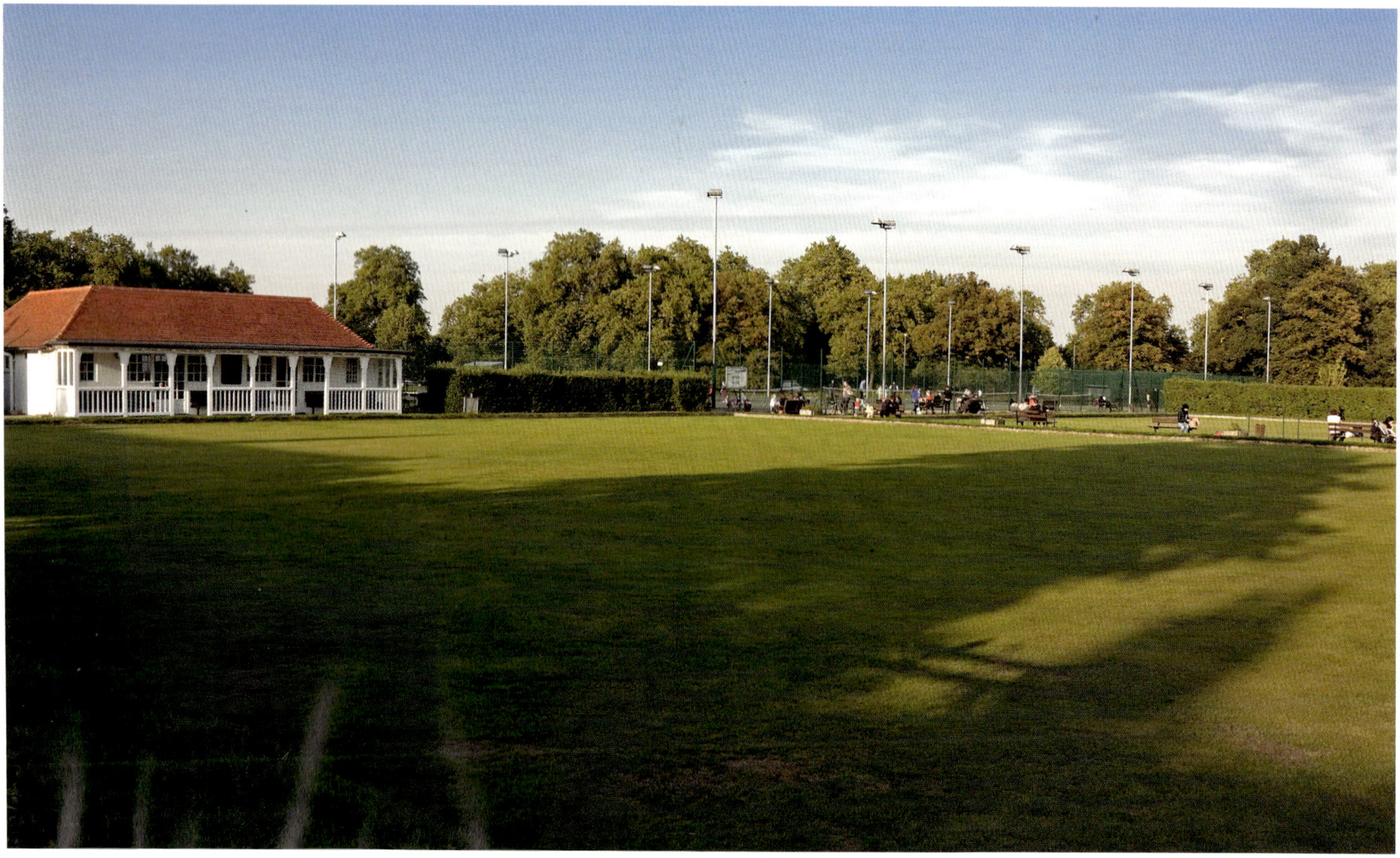

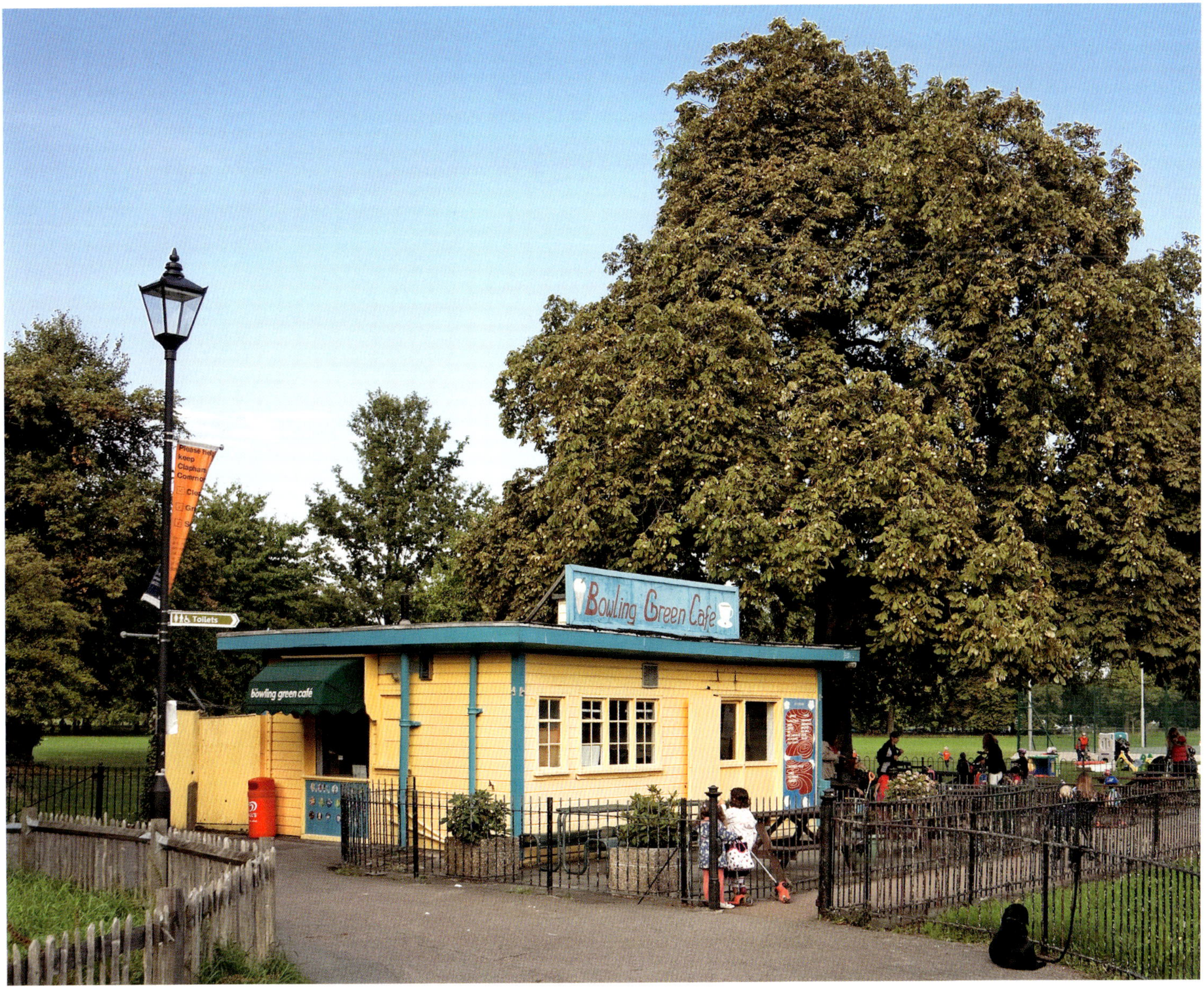

In the south corner of Clapham Common there is a tennis club and bowls green, together with a little cafe.

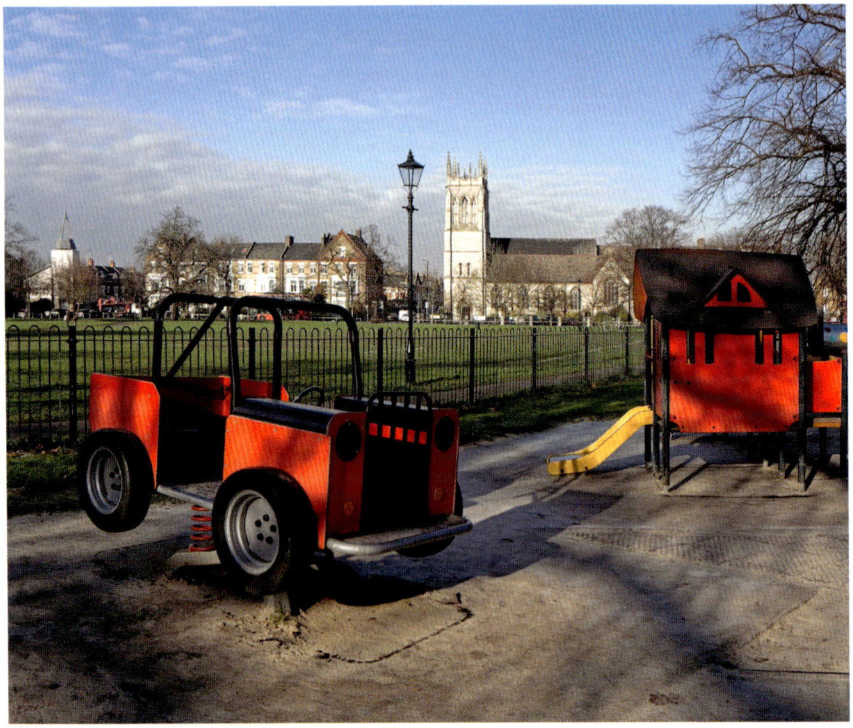

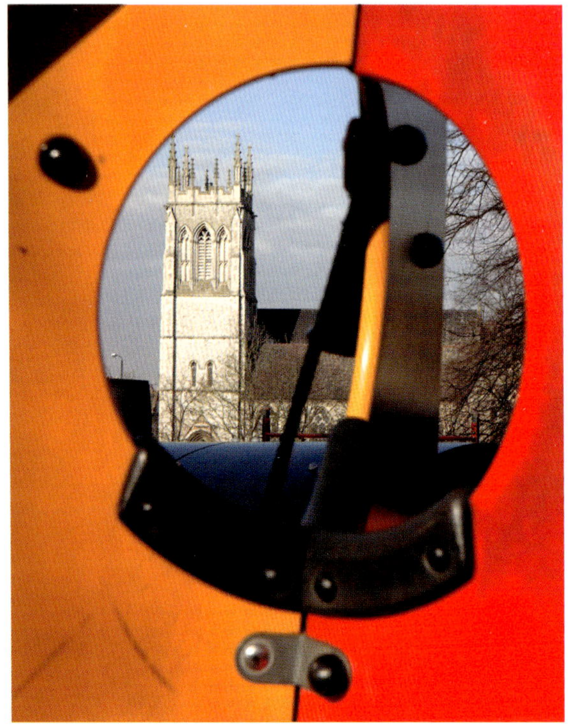

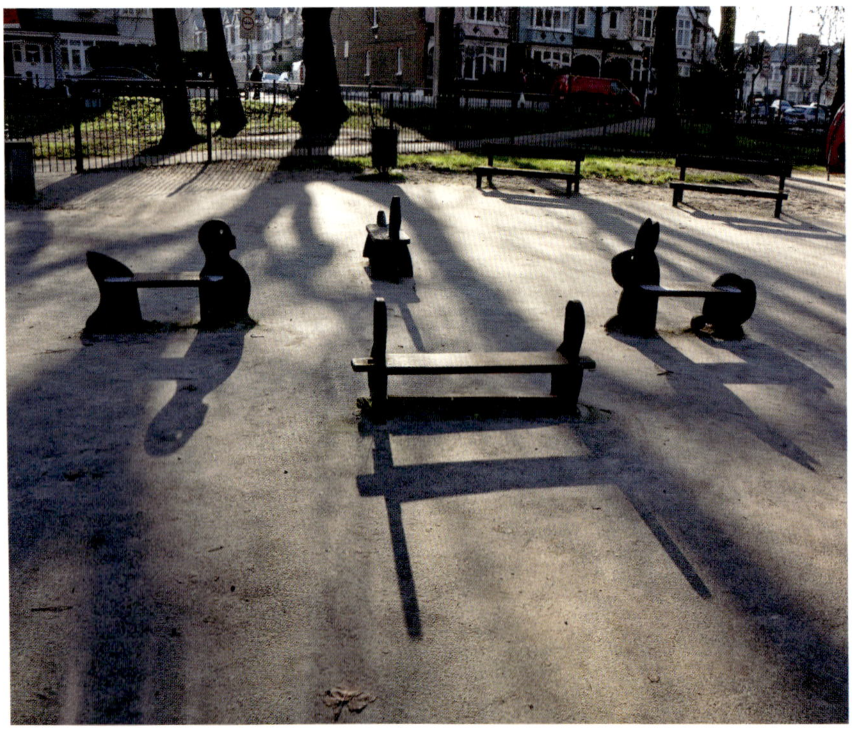

The playground on Clapham Common West Side. This is a particularly fine playground with a huge selection of activities, all in bright red. Best seen in winter before the leaves obscure the light.

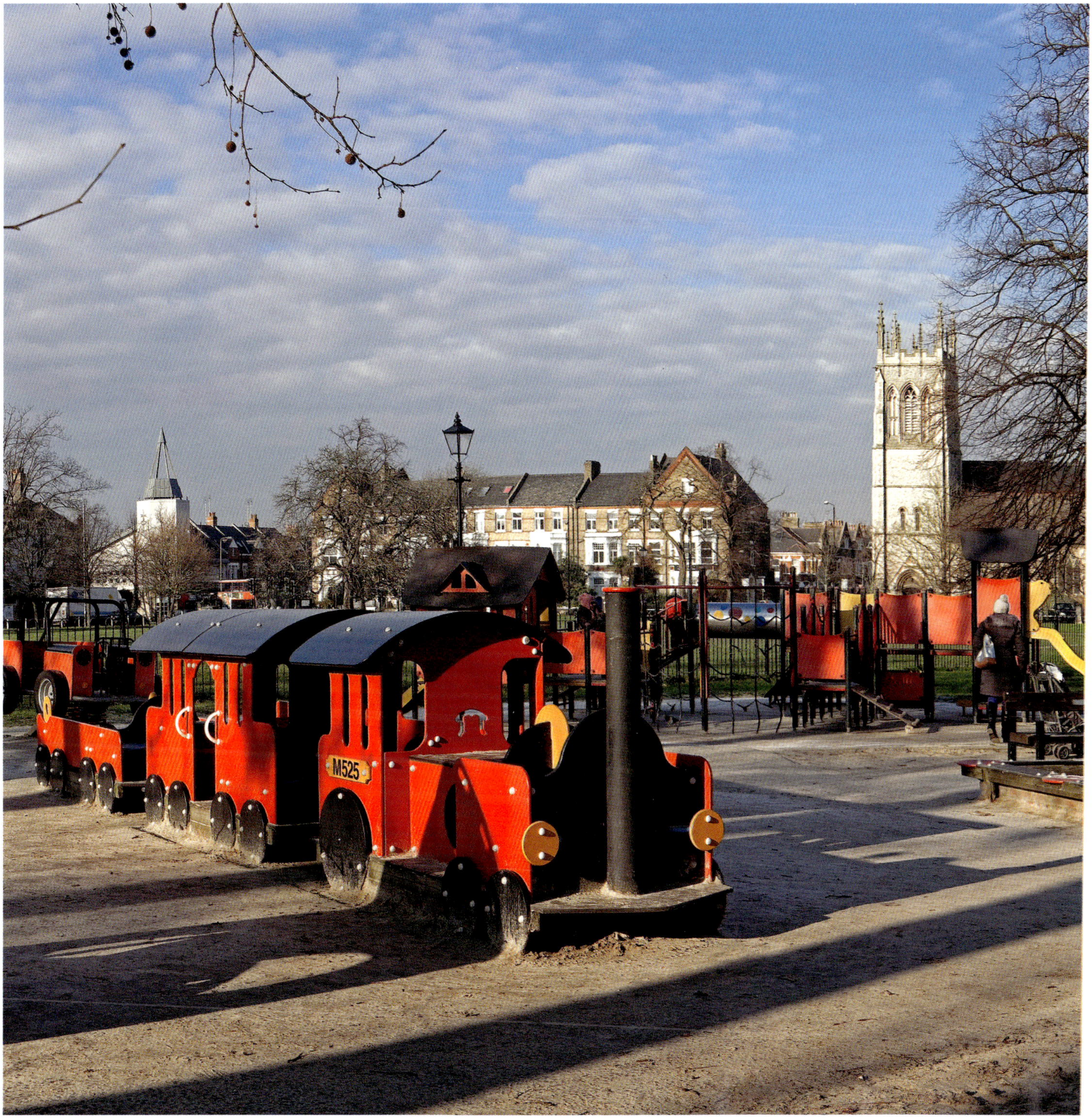
M525

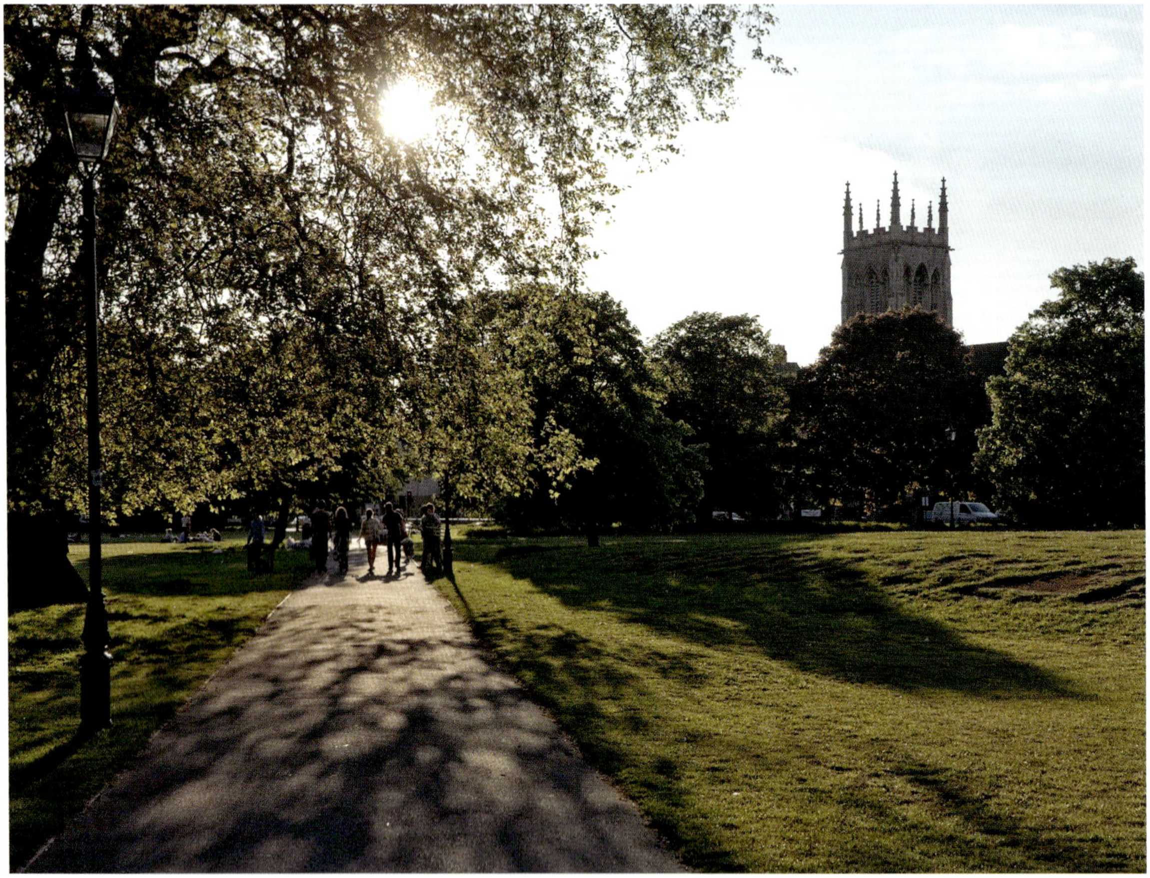

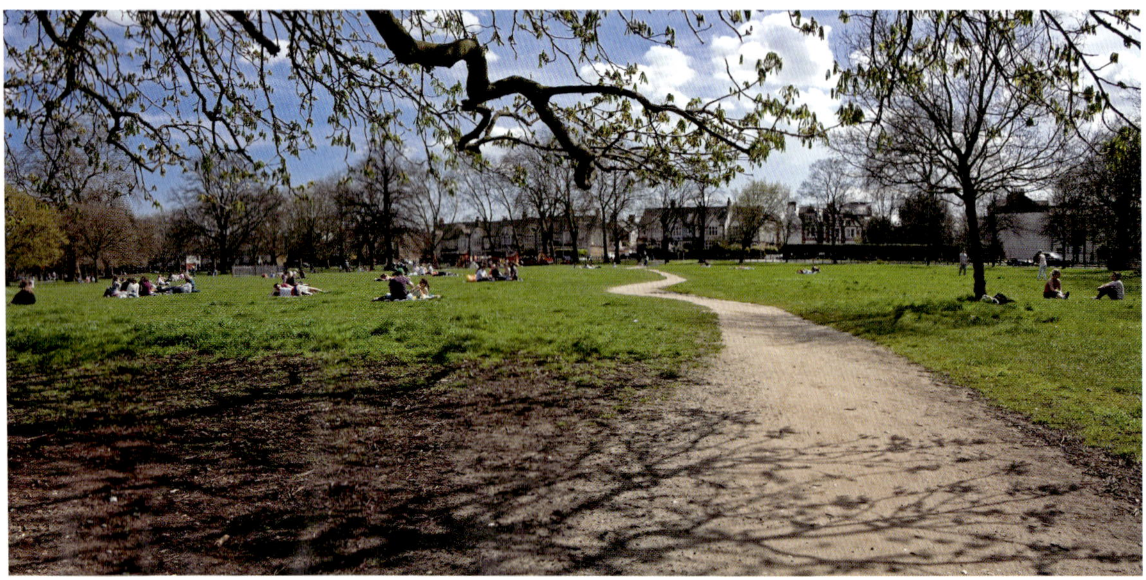

West Side in spring
(bottom left),
summer (top left)
and autumn (opposite).

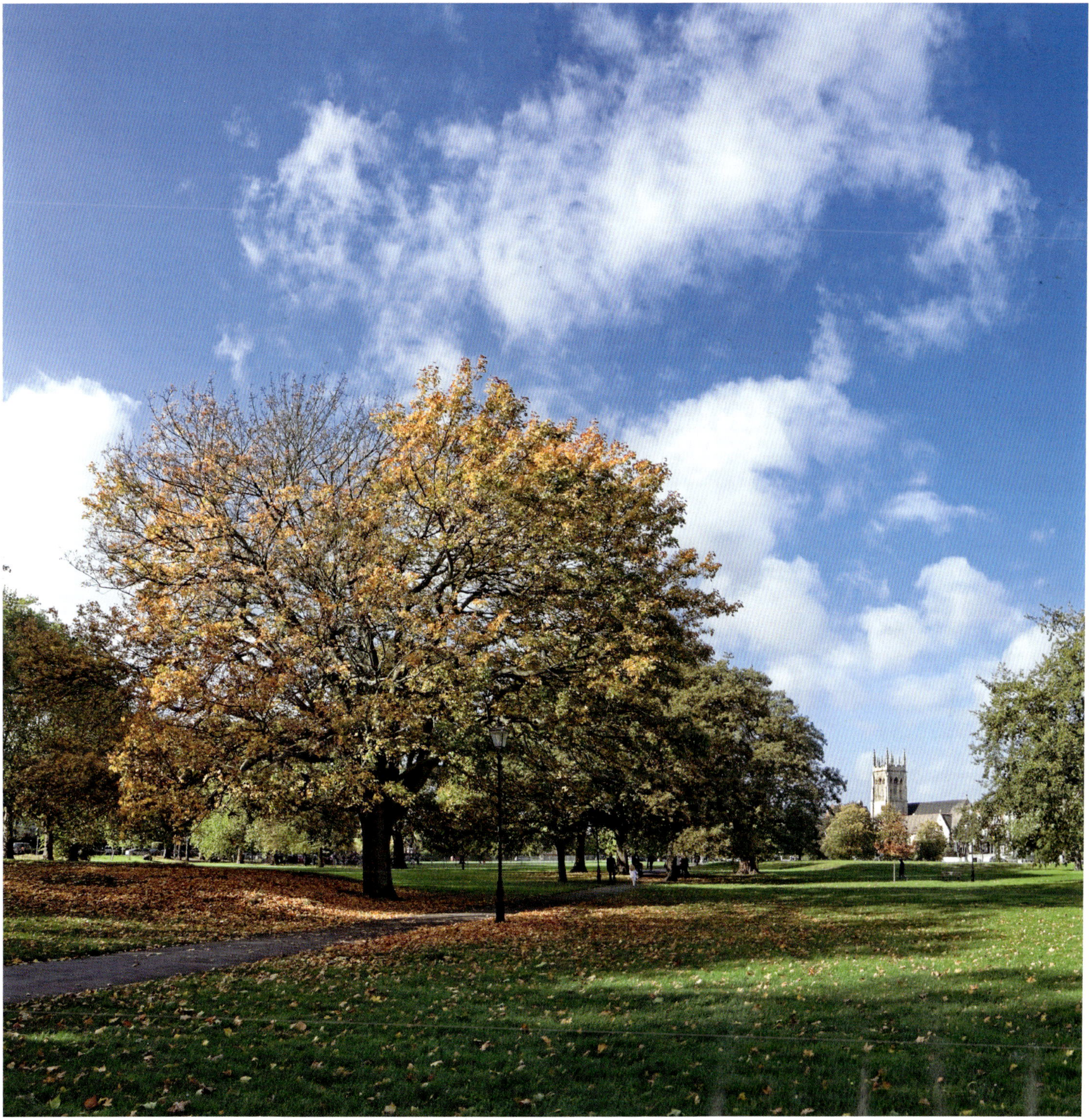

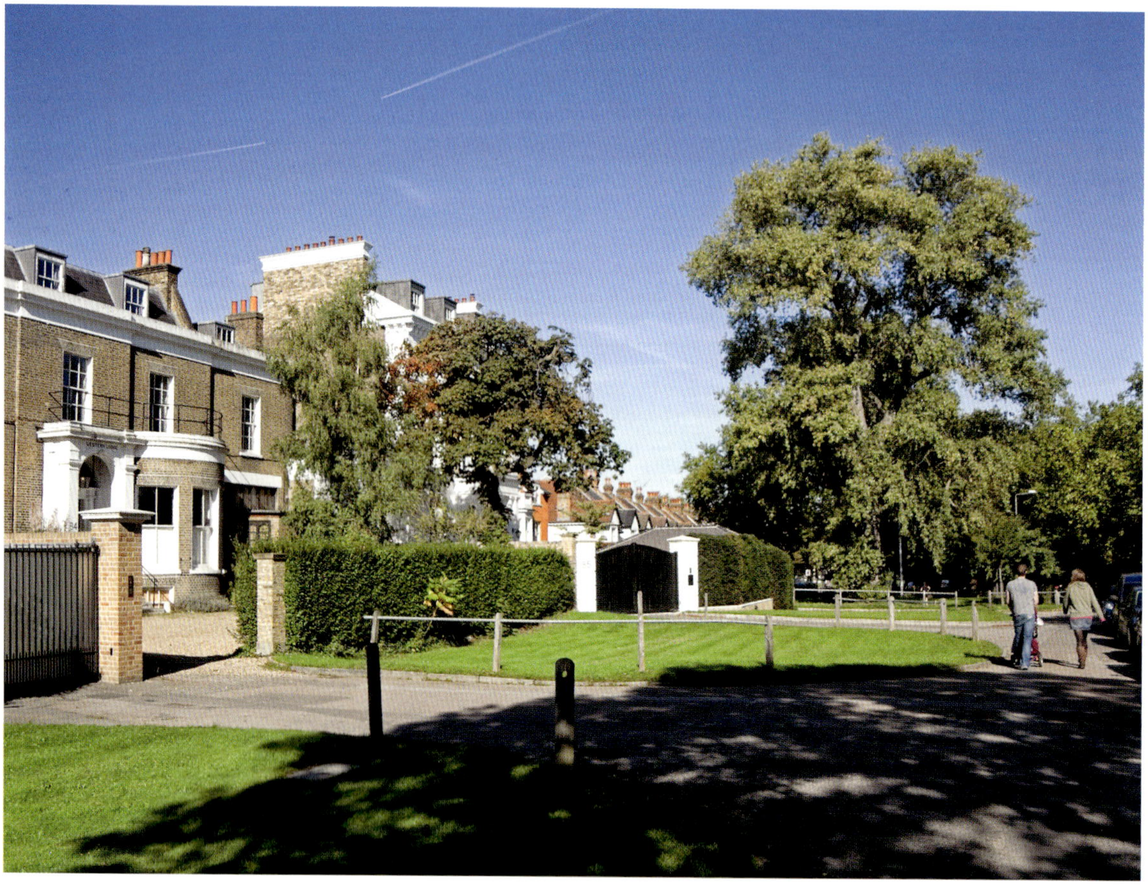

Clapham Common West Side has some magnificent houses and this one caught my eye, with its newly painted boundary marker outside, which marks the boundary of the older County of London and the County of Surrey (which of course used to stretch all the way to the River Thames). Before reverting to a private house, it used to be the home of an extraordinary named society the 'Royal Antediluvian Order of Buffaloes' Club.

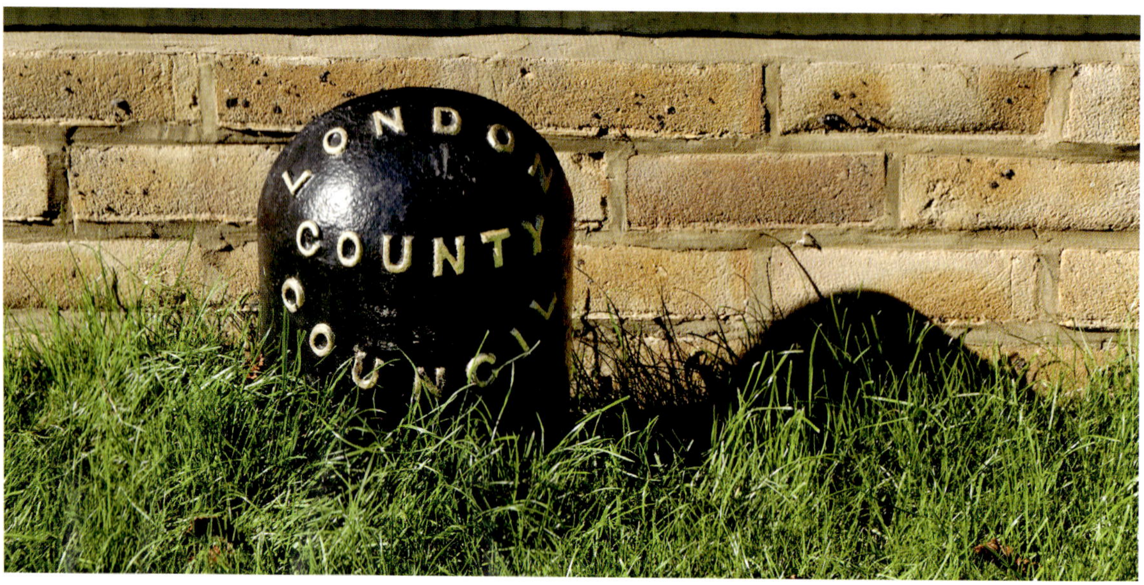

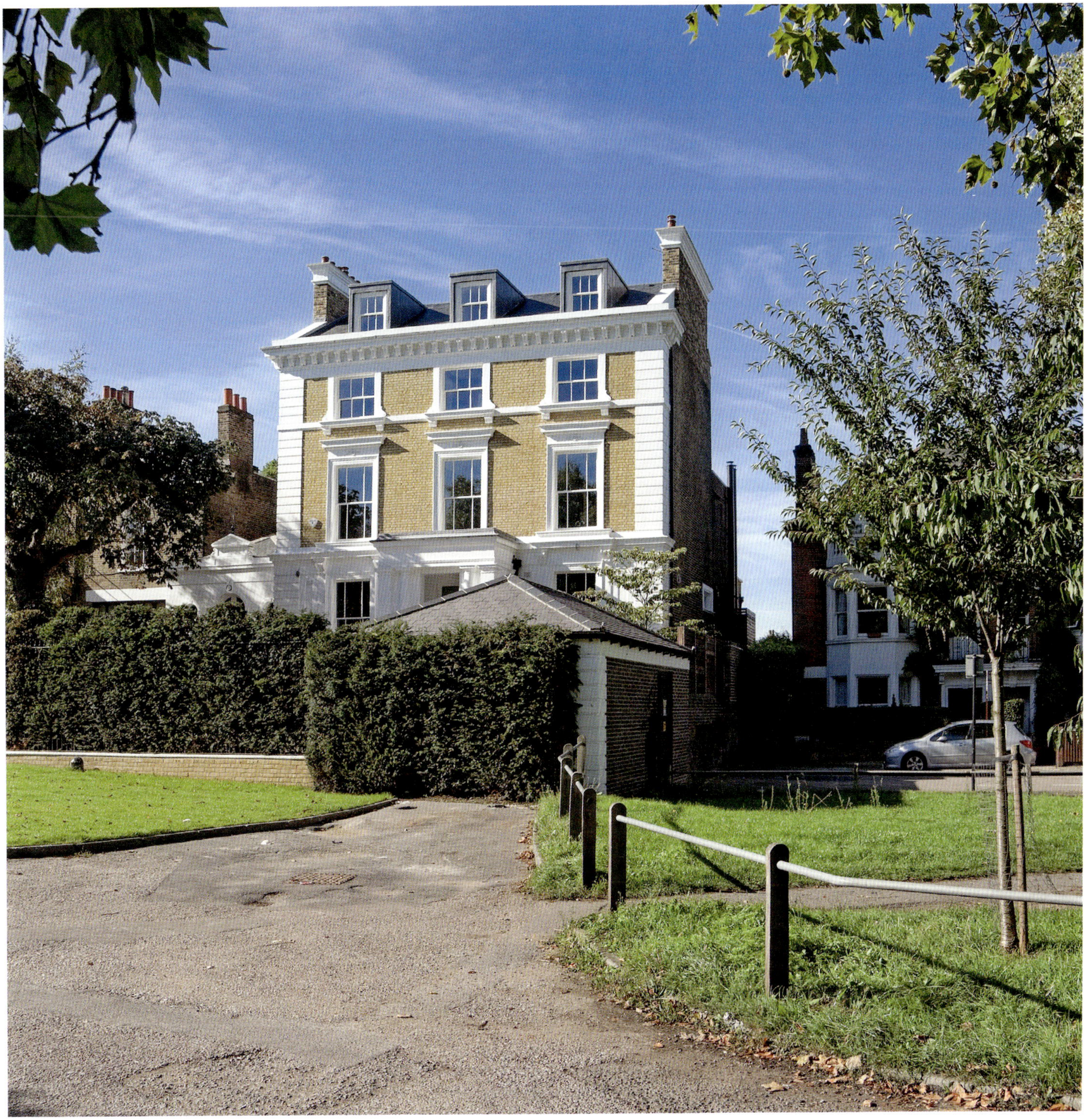

Mount Pond

This is the larger of the two fishing ponds found on the common, the other being The Eagle (see page 158). Found near the Bandstand, it dates from 1746 when it was dug out for gravel that was needed for the Turnpike Road at Tooting (background courtesy of The Friends of Clapham Common – *www.claphamcommon.org*).

Opposite: A Coot wandering across the ice.

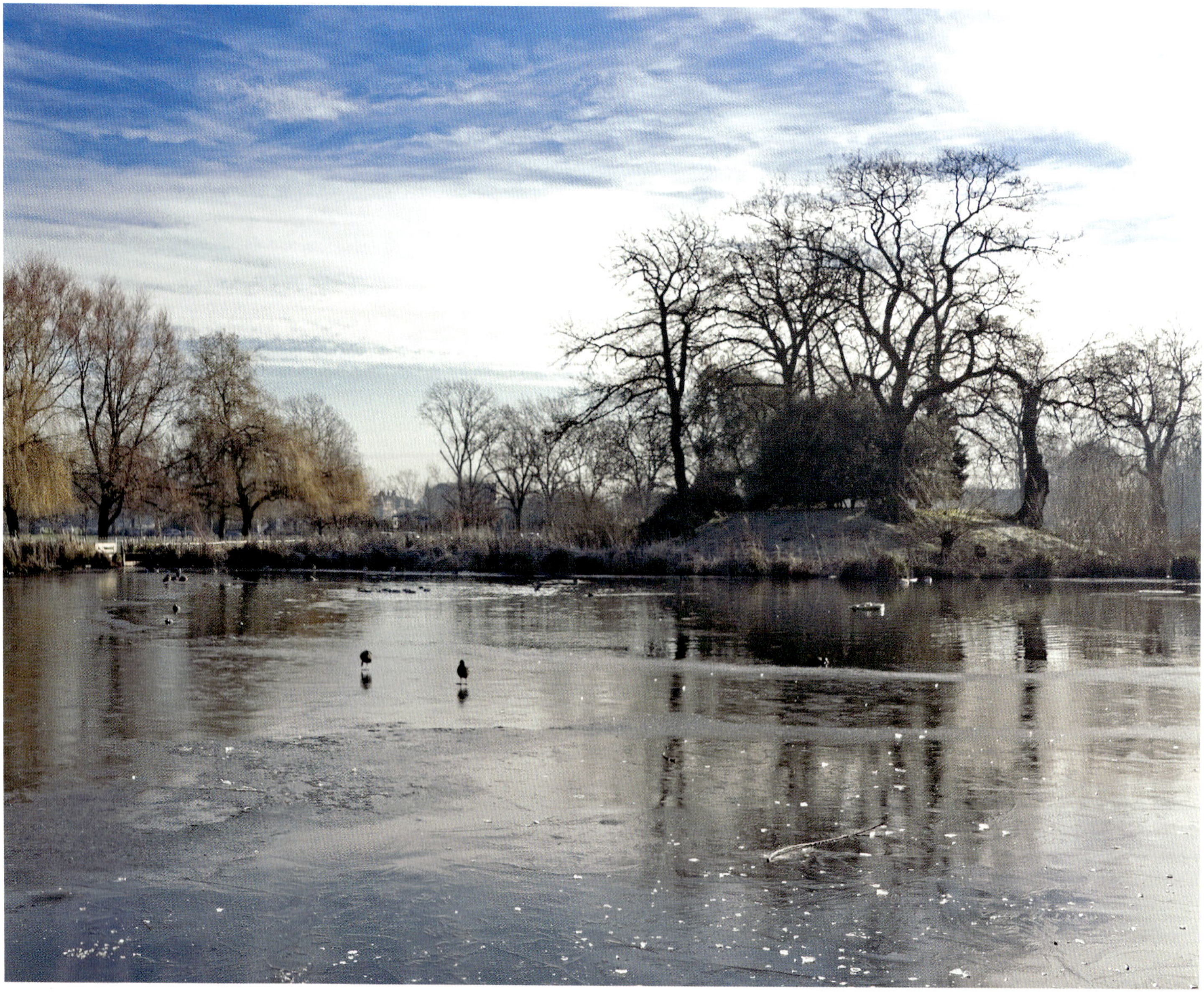

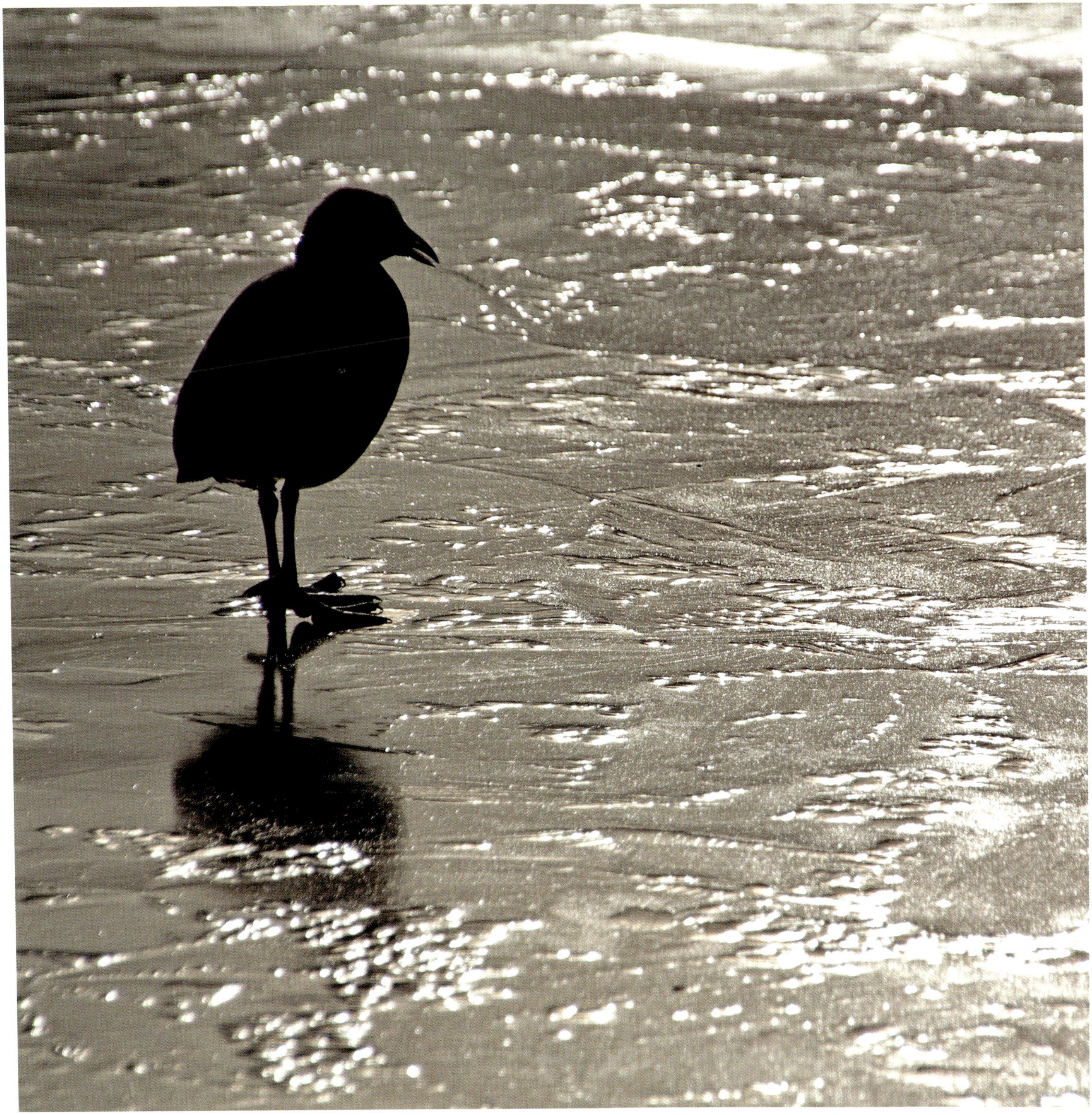

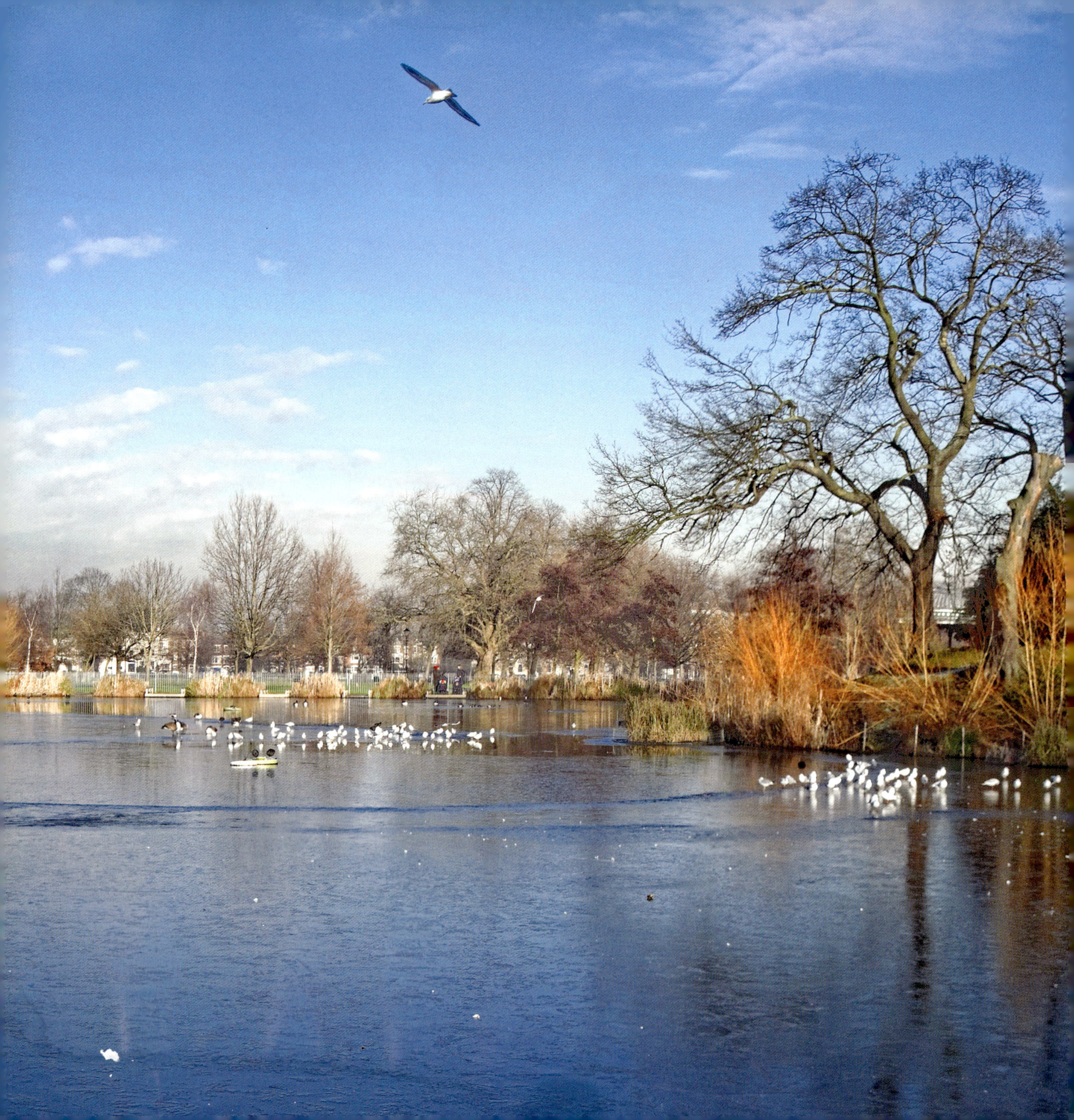

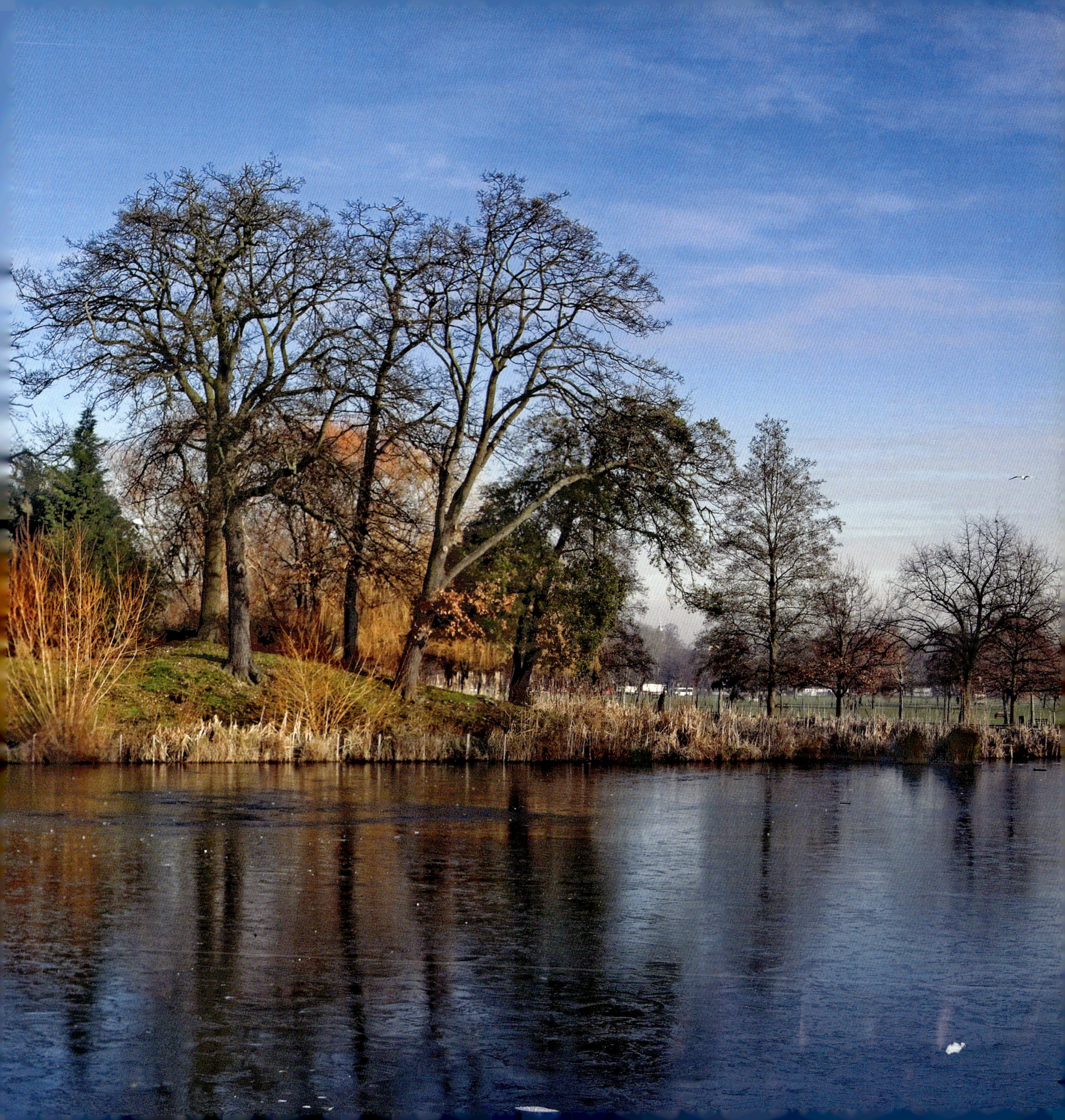

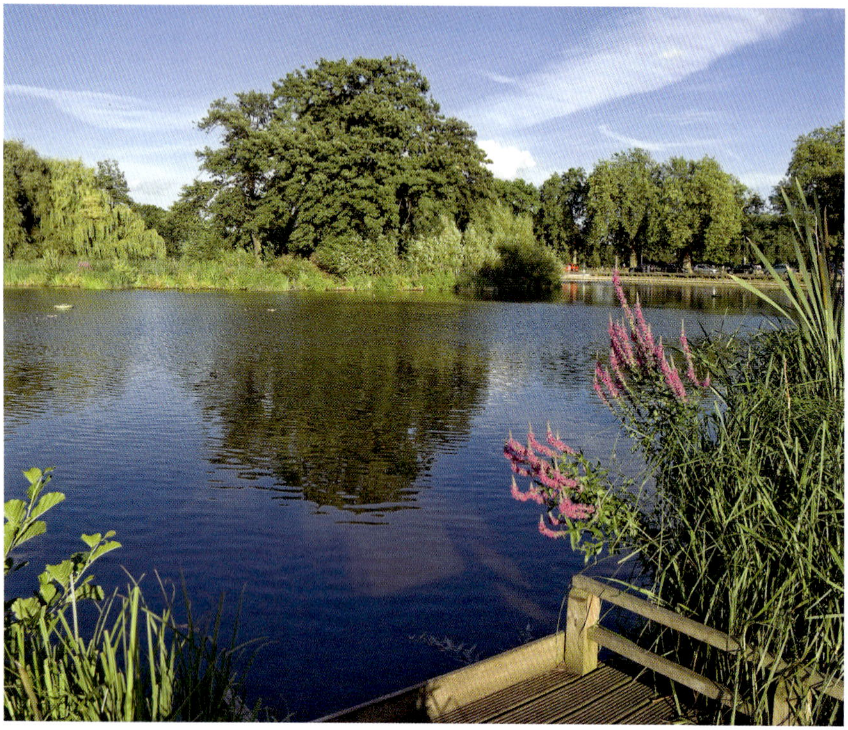

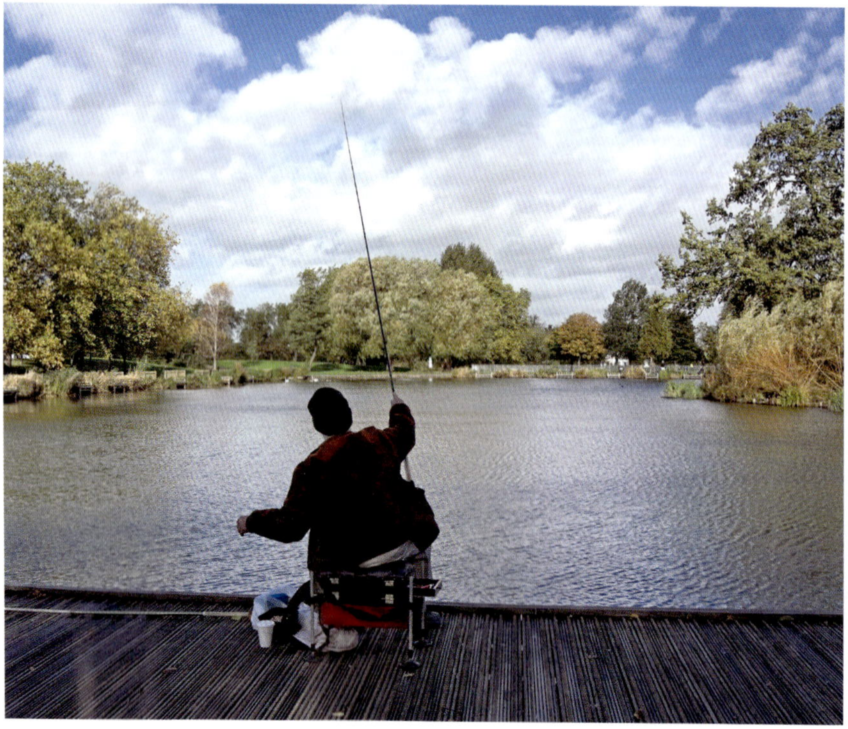

Previous page: The pond in winter.

Top left and opposite: The pond in summer.

Bottom left: The pond in autumn. One of the many fishermen I came across, his name was Len and he had only started coming to the pond this year. Shows how dedicated some of these guys can be, as he'd travelled all the way from Holloway in North London.

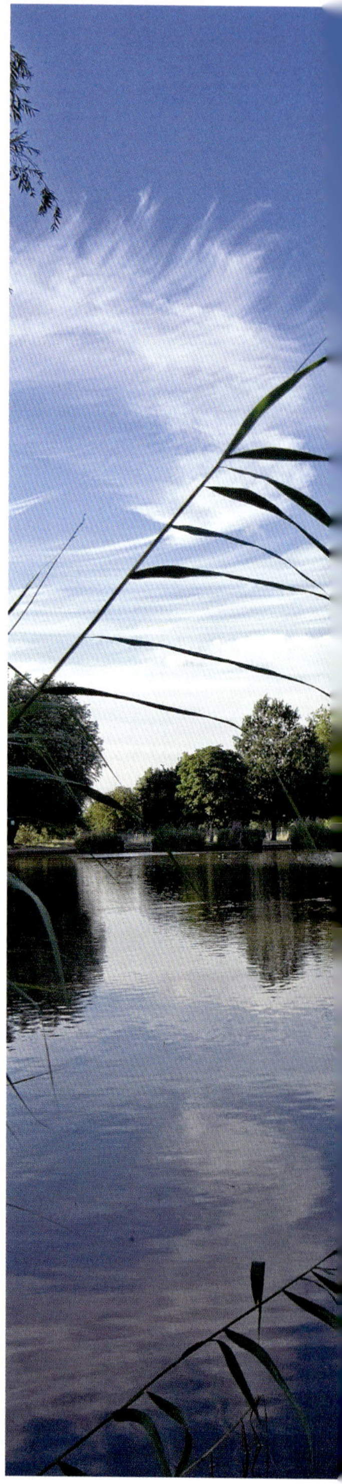

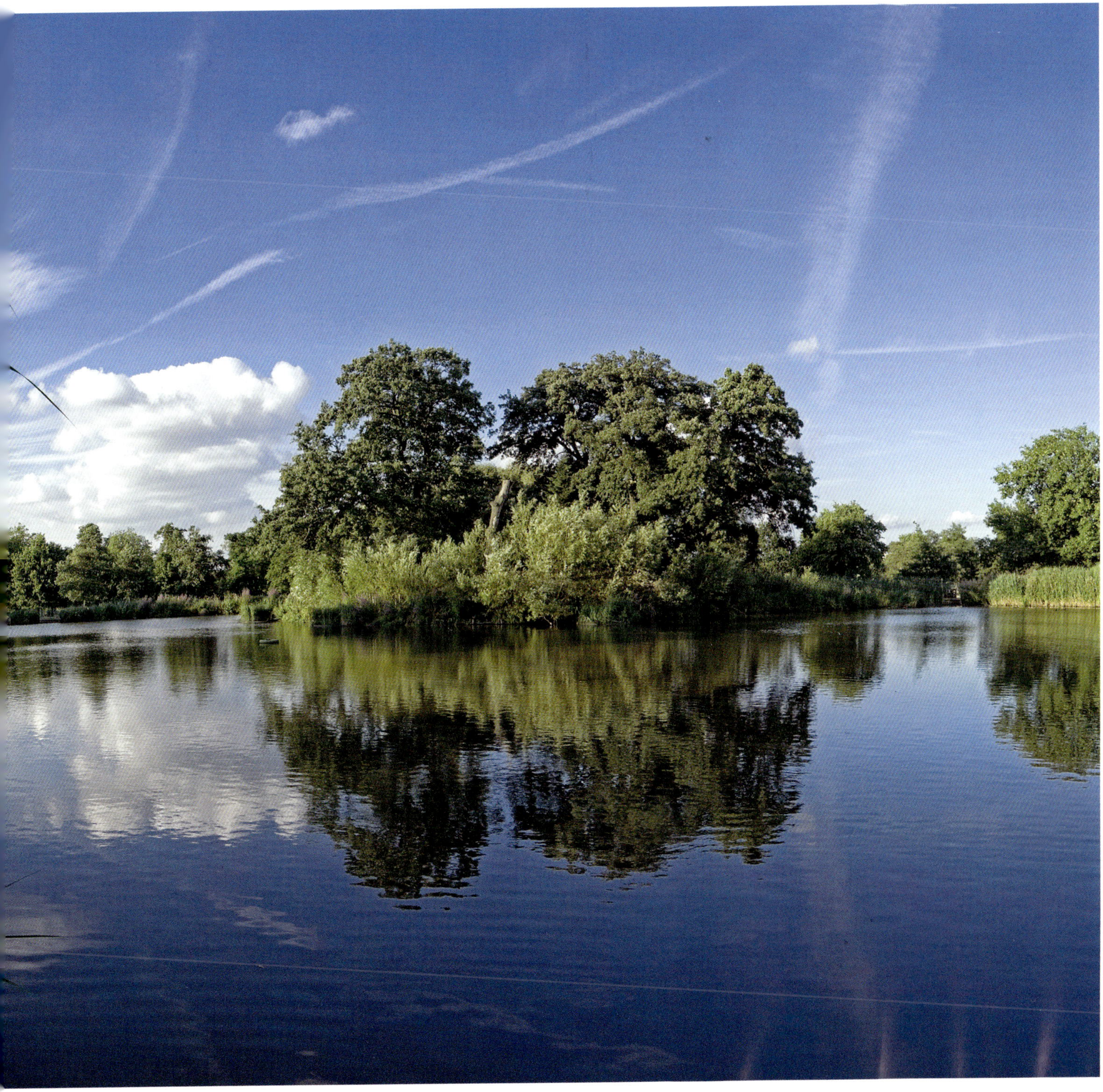

The Long Pond

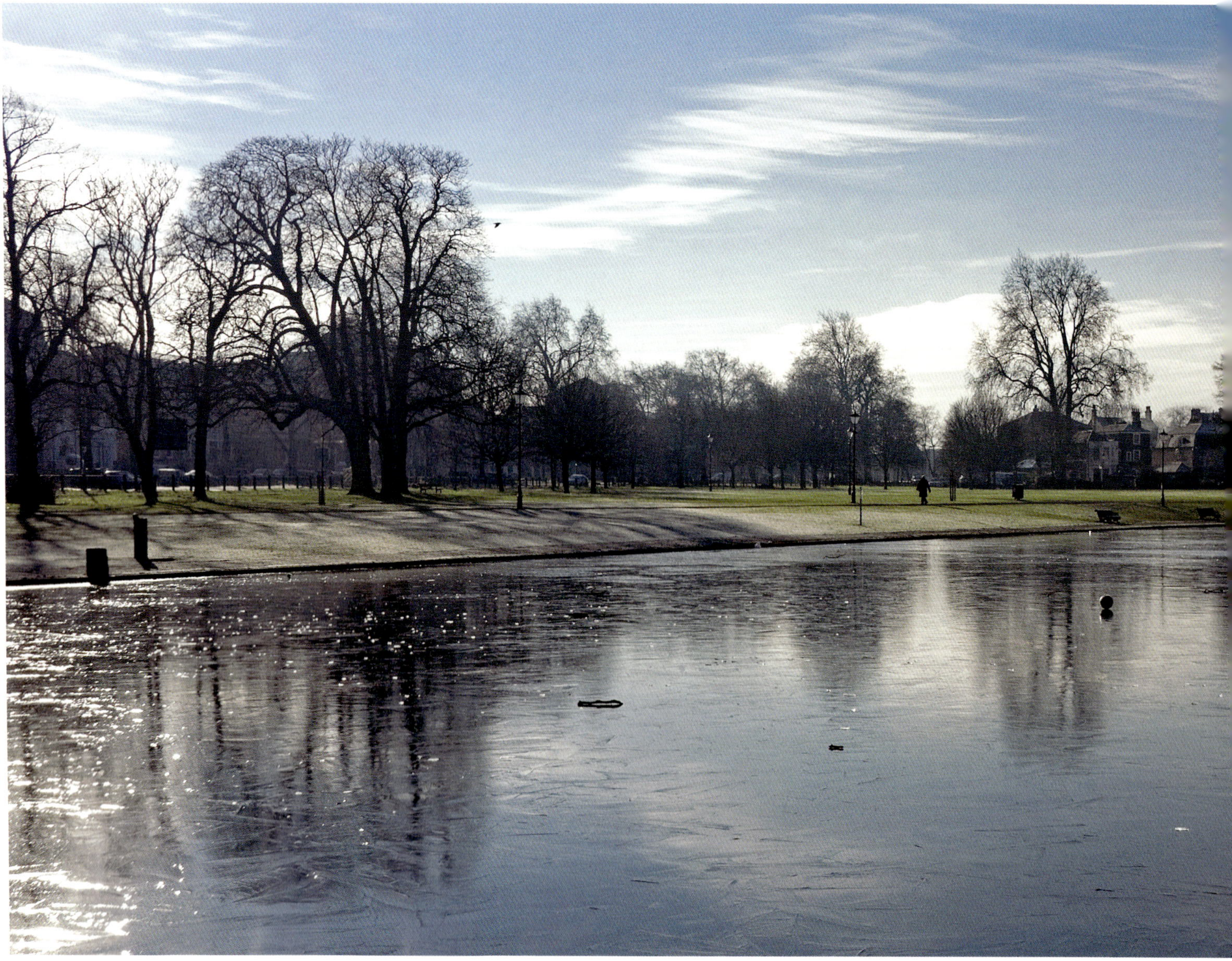

The Long Pond is not in Battersea itself, but on the Clapham side of the common, near Old Town, but is still very photogenic.

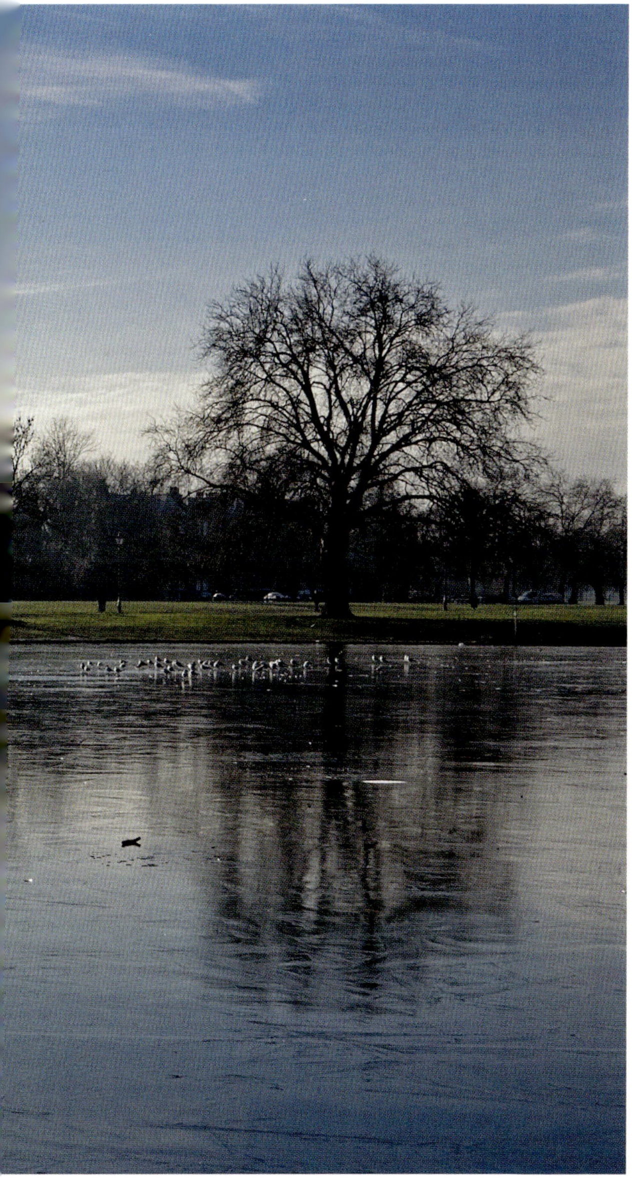

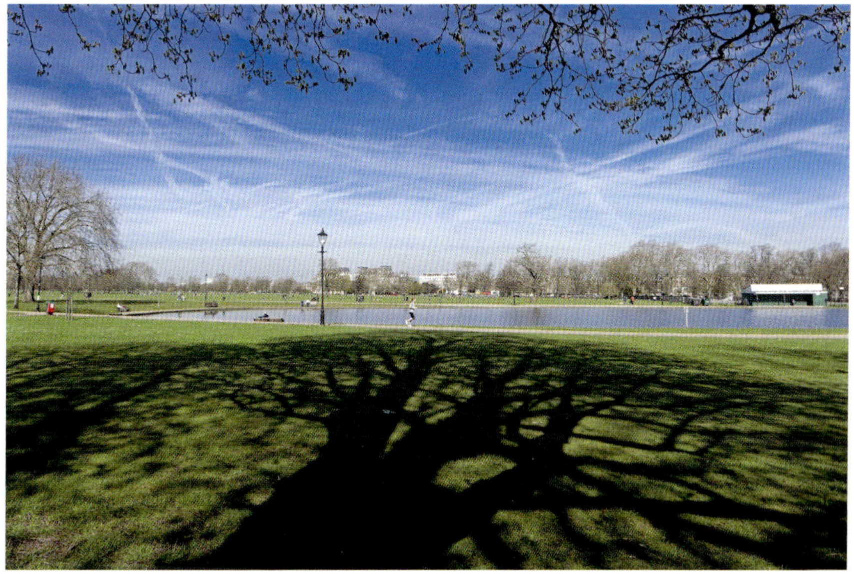

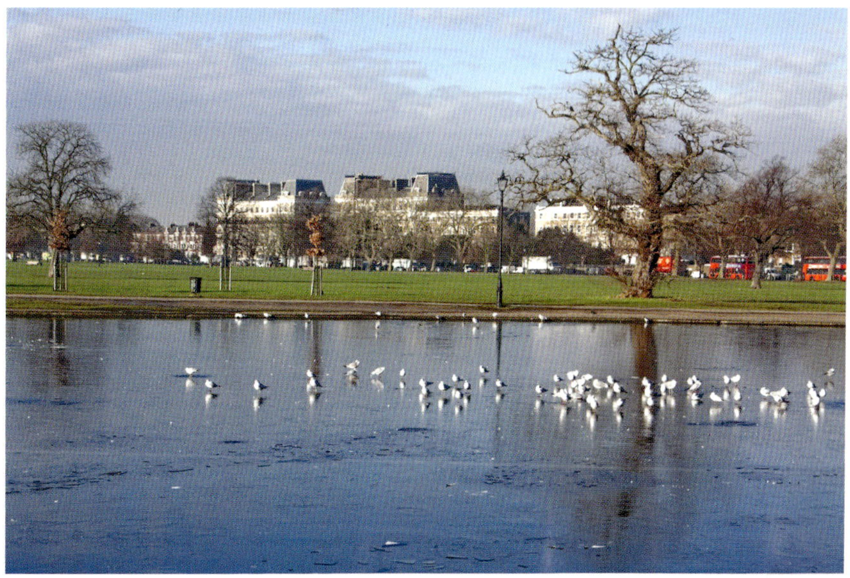

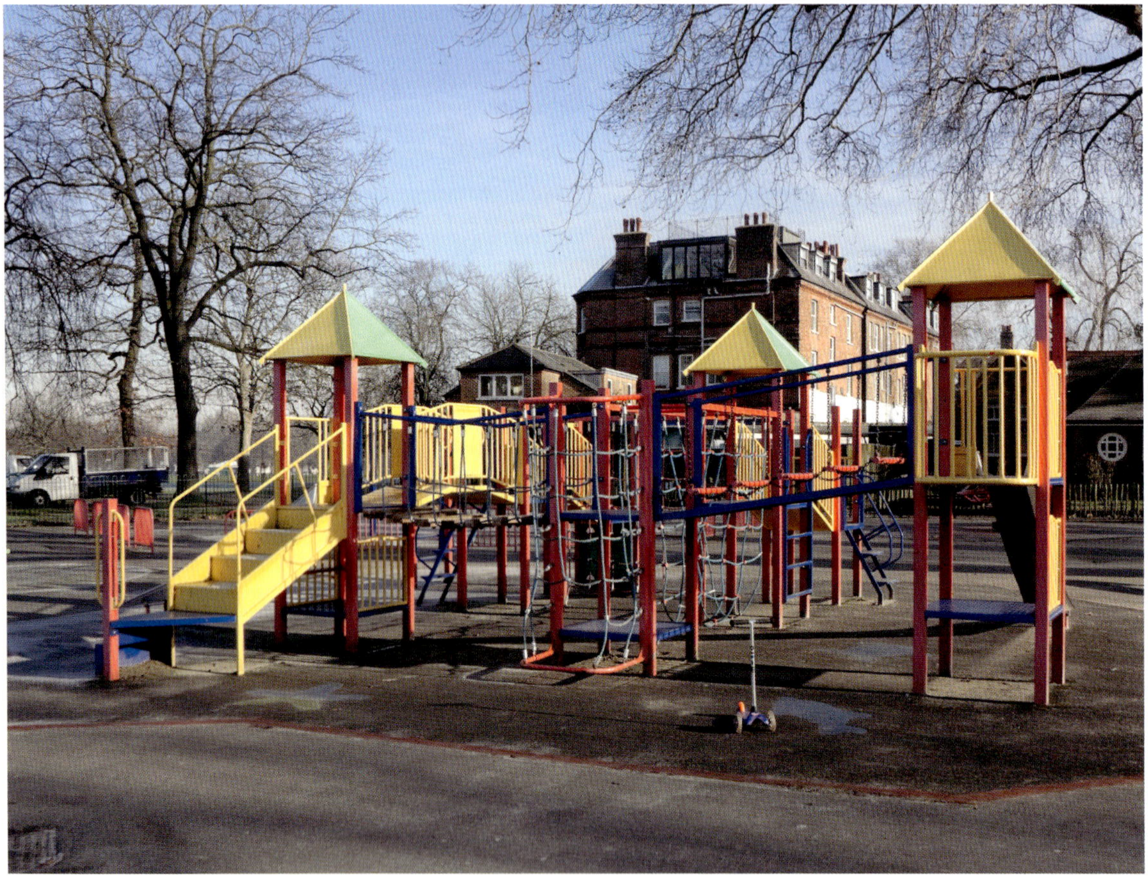

The playground near Windmill Drive.

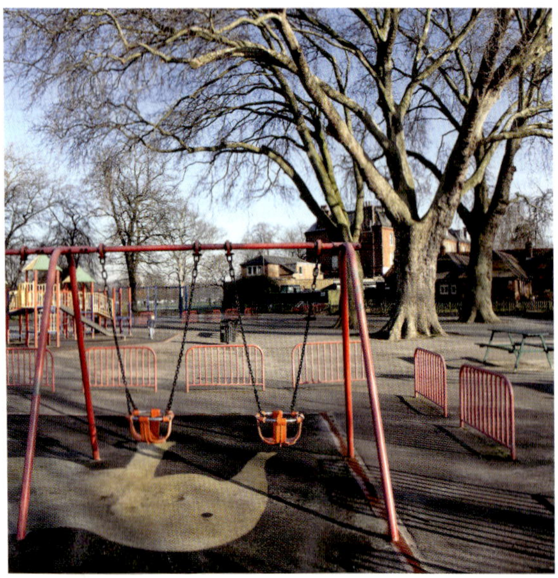

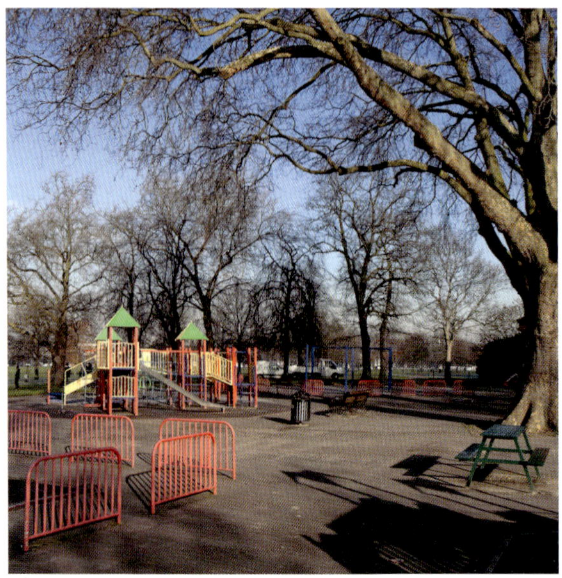

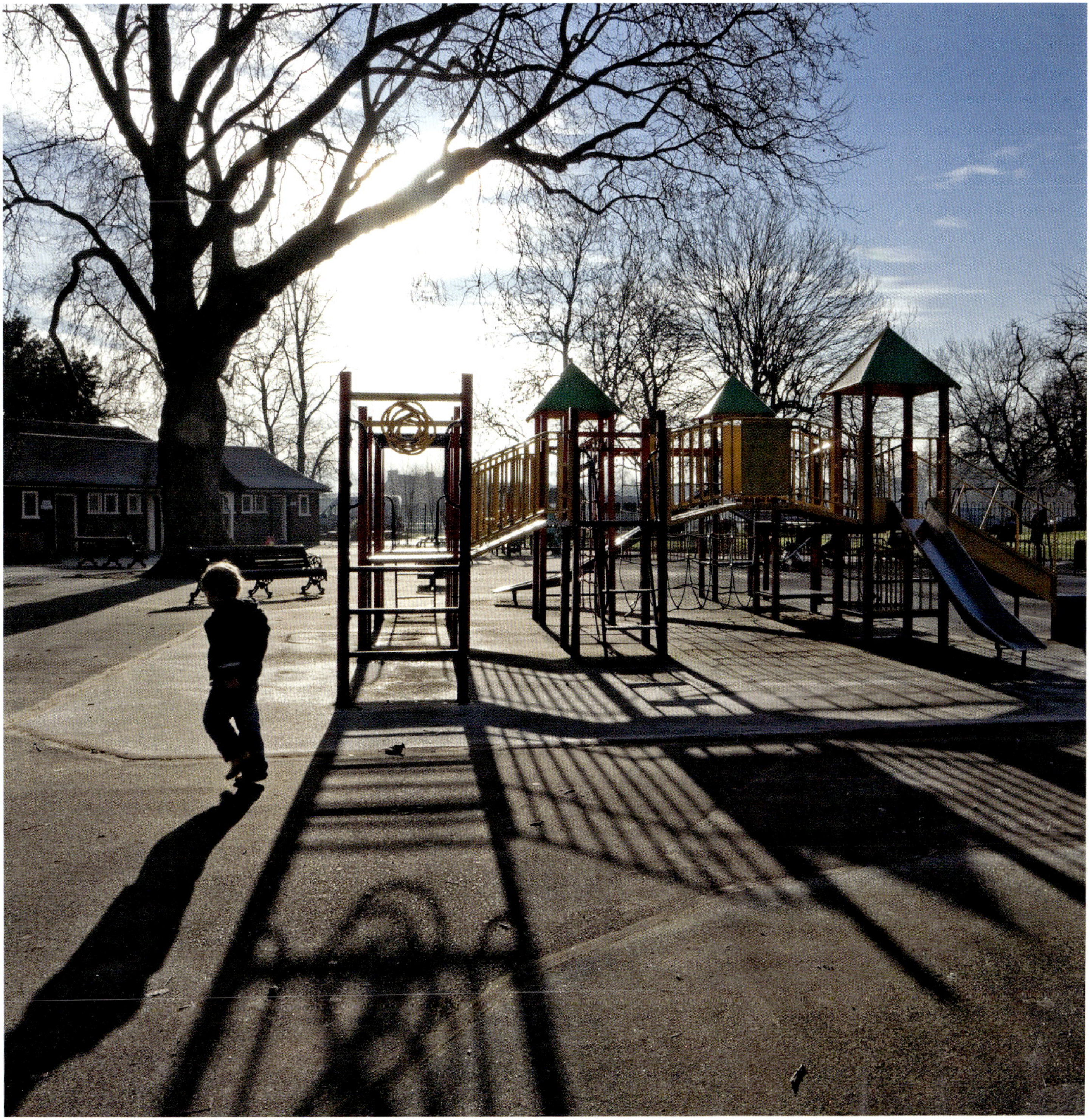

Books by Andrew Wilson from the Wild series

The *Wild* series is available to buy from all good book stores including Barnes, Kew and Sheen bookshops, Wimbledon Books and Music, some branches of WH Smith and all branches of Waterstone's. Also available at Michael Gibbs Bolingbroke Books online and numerous gift shops across town, including branches of Hutton's.

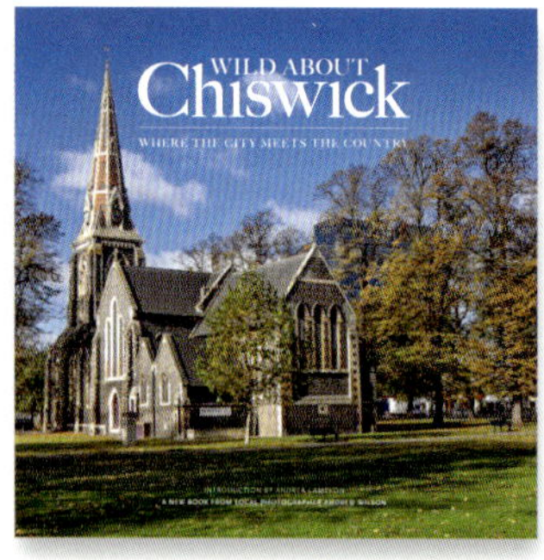

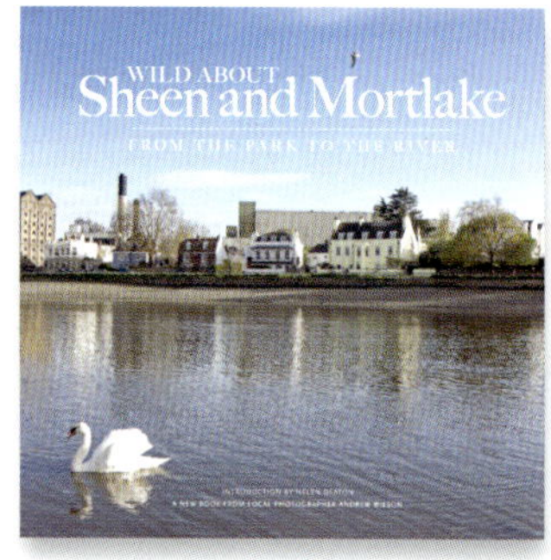

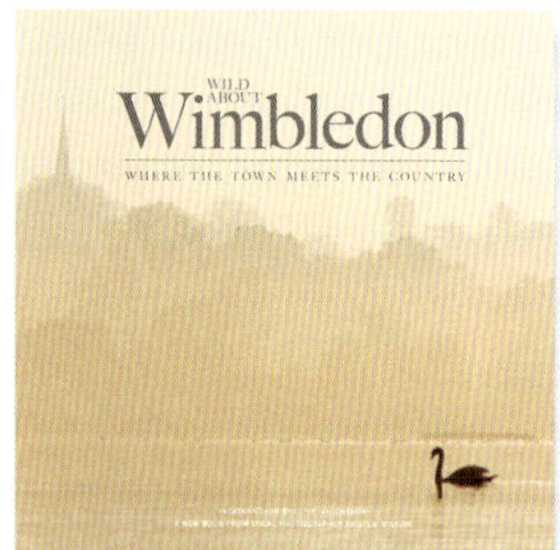

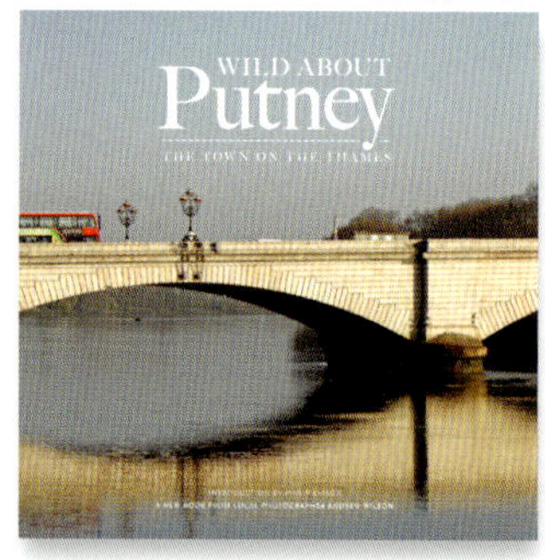

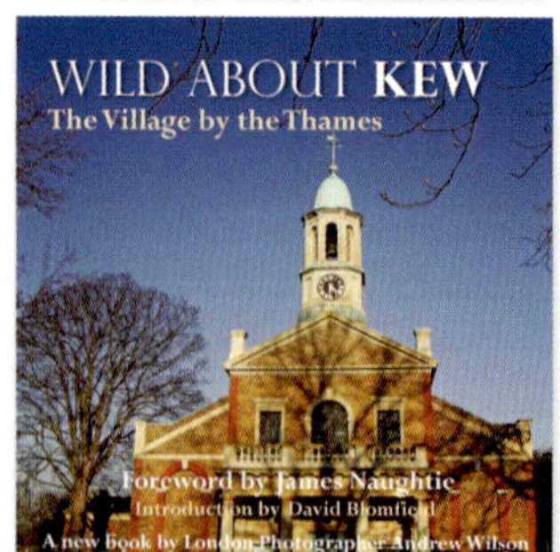

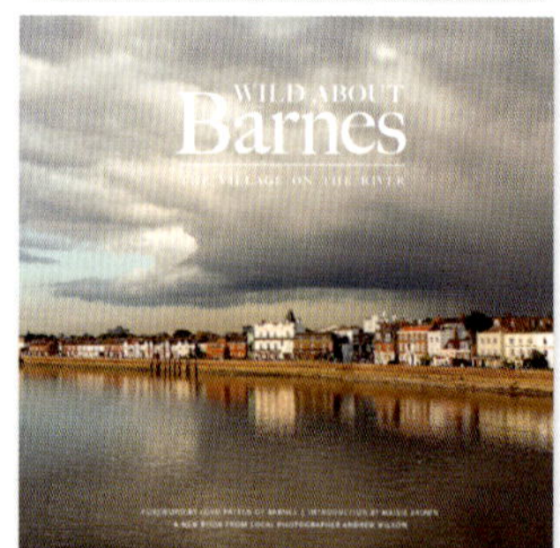

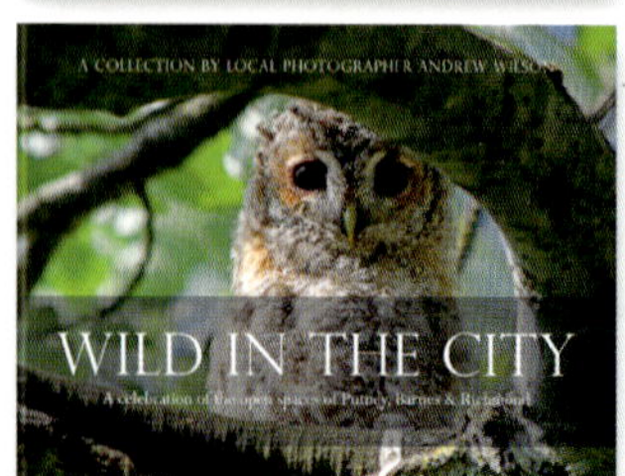

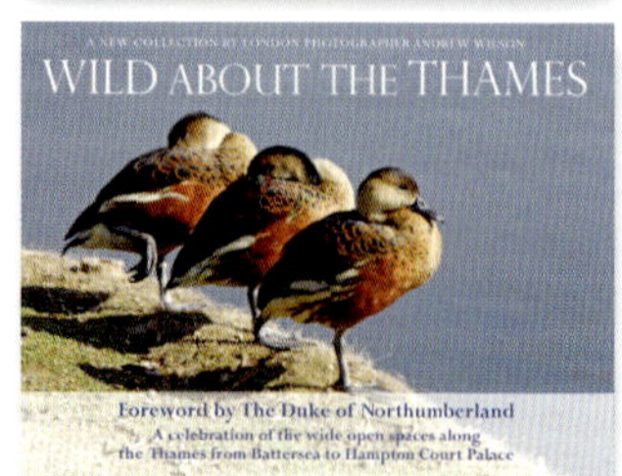

Follow Andrew on Twitter: @andrewpics

Designed by Ball Design Consultancy
www.balldesignconsultancy.com

Proofread by Tom Sears
www.tom-sears.com

Printed by Headley Brothers of Ashford, Kent.
www.headley.co.uk

Paper: Amadeus Gloss 150gsm supplied by Denmaur Independent Paper *www.denmaur.com*

Bound by Green Street Bindery of Oxford
www.maltbysbookbinders.com

Colour Management by Paul Sherfield of The Missing Horse Consultancy.
www.missinghorsecons.co.uk

Published by Unity Print and Publishing Limited,
18 Dungarvan Avenue, London SW15 5QU.
Tel: +44 (0)20 8487 2199
aw@unity-publishing.co.uk
www.unity-publishing.co.uk

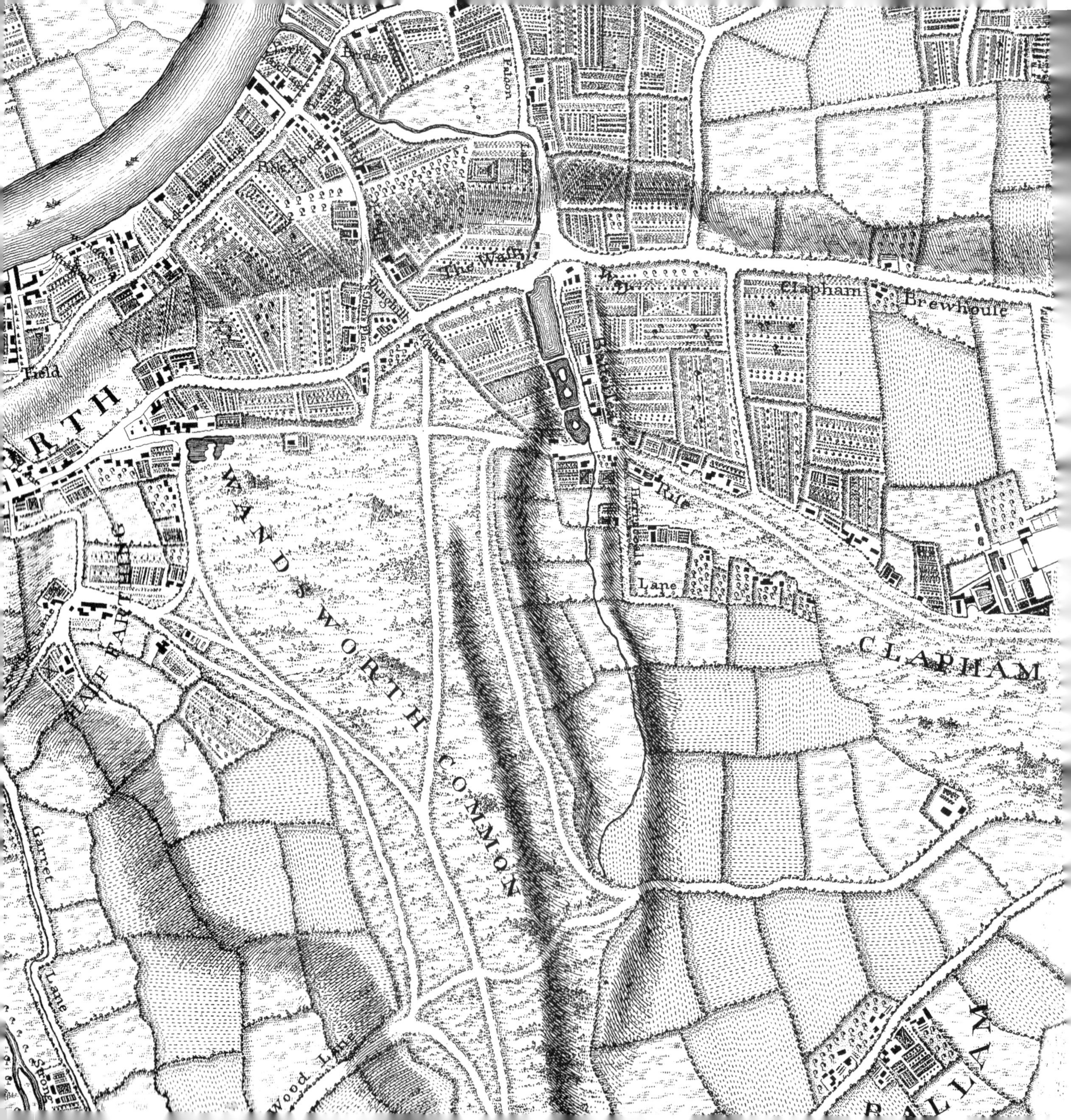

Bridge
Falcon
The Wash
Clapham
Brewhouse
Field
RTH
WANDSWORTH
COMMON
CLAPHAM
Lane
Garret
Lane
Wood Lane